MODERN AMERICAN USAGE

MODERN AMERICAN USAGE

A GUIDE

BY WILSON FOLLETT

REVISED BY

ERIK WENSBERG

HILL AND WANG

A DIVISION OF FARRAR, STRAUS AND GIROUX

NEW YORK

Hill and Wang
A division of Farrar, Straus and Giroux
19 Union Square West, New York 10003

Printed in the United States of America
Designed by Jonathan D. Lippincott
First published in 1966 by Hill and Wang
First revised edition, 1998

Library of Congress Cataloging-in-Publication Data
Follett, Wilson, 1887–1963.
    Modern American usage
        p.   cm.
    ISBN 0-8090-0139-X
    1. English language — United States — Usage.   2. Americanisms —
Dictionaries.   I. Wensberg, Erik, 1931–   .
PE1460.F59   1998
423'.1 — dc21   98-23280

CONTENTS

PREFACE TO THE REVISED EDITION

This book has been revised because language changes and thus adds to our old uncertainties new and bothersome questions. For reasons of politics, commerce, shifting fashions and habits, and excitement over new machines, we are encouraged to learn and use new terms, to call things and people by other names, or to discard old conventions of grammar. Which changes are likely to last, and which others will probably fade? And how should intelligent people with something to say put words together in a manner that is clear, correct, and easy to read?

For more than three decades, tens of thousands of readers from all sorts of occupations have turned to Follett's *Modern American Usage* as an essential guide to writing well. Such a guide, at its best, wears its specialty lightly and sets forth its judgments with reason, good humor, and decent dispatch. You can engage it on a particular word, and its answer will take due account of idiom, etymology, history, and current states of mind and meaning. But rather than say all there is to be said on the subject, the sensible guide tells you only what you need to know in order to say what you mean. A likeness to this ideal companion has sent *Modern American Usage* through fifteen reprintings—justification for bringing it up-to-date in a new and revised edition.

Toward that end I have judged every entry in the original text for its value to the present-day reader, omitting some entries, shortening others, and adding a good many new ones. More specifically, certain words and forms that Follett deplored have slipped out of use, as have some that he hoped to save; I have omitted both kinds. Some that seemed hardy enough thirty years ago have been badly battered in the meantime, and these I have tried to restore to their earlier logic and fitness. Malaprops being as quick to sprout as weeds, I have gathered a new crop to put with the old. I have similarly added three dozen words and phrases to those that Follett judged so mechanical as to have lost all conviction and force. Some general entries also seemed to call for enlargement, such as those on journalese and on popularized technicalities; the latter impart words that lend the tone of science while scanting scientific sense. Lastly, to make the way as straight as possible for the reader in a hurry, I have more than doubled the number of cross-references. Altogether, this edition treats about five hundred words not included in the first. I have gained both space and speed by trimming prolixities in Follett's prose and by making some explanations a bit simpler than he left them.

Wilson Follett was a teacher, a writer, and an editor, and the book he compiled—which readers call simply "Follett"—combines the knowledge and point of view of all three professions. It is a responsive work for the reader with a question and a cautionary one for the professional writer. Above all, it is an authoritative work devised by an editor for his colleagues facing typescript; it serves to anticipate troubles before they creep into print. Ask whether to write *different than* or *different from* and Follett the teacher shows the logic in using *from*—whereupon Follett the editor shows how to sidestep the choice if *from* leads to awkwardness later. The experienced writer in Follett warns against phrases that only obscure your meaning, but the helpful editor offers alternative wording that gets to the point without fuss.

It is in the general entries, with their numbered sections, that the editorial Follett puts to good use a precept learned in working with those who write: troubles often fall into patterns. Look up *rhythm* as a property of style and you will be referred to Sections 2 and 3 of *prose, the sound of*, where rhythm is discussed. But if you read on through Sections 4 and 5, you will learn how word order and leaving words out can also help make your writing easy on the ear. In such general entries, read as much or as little as you like.

Follett modeled the form of his book on a British classic: H. W. Fowler's *Dictionary of Modern English Usage*, first published in 1926. British English differs from the American in idiom, spelling, and pronunciation. But implicit in both these works is the idea that language is our species' greatest invention, and that it rewards our careful use by sharpening our thought and giving it intelligible form.

Wilson Follett died in 1963, before his work on *Modern American Usage* was finished. Jacques Barzun revised and completed the book with the help of six other noted writers and teachers and, thirty years later, suggested that I undertake a second edition. His careful reading of the manuscript saved me from deficiencies of knowledge and, I hope, from errors of tone. He has my deepest gratitude, but should not be assumed to share my opinions.

Nor should others whom I here wish to thank. Lynn Warshow's wise copy editing greatly improved the manuscript, and Mark LaFlaur, who compiled the Inventory of Main Entries, rescued me from some slips. Friends who suggested topics or steered me to helpful articles and books include Rene Buch, Thomas Goodrich, David Herwaldt, Frank G. Jennings, Edwin Krales, Tara McCarthy, Eleanor and Joel Pelcyger, Miriam V. Sarzin, Marcia Schonzeit, the late John Taylor, and Lee Zimmerman.

E.W.

HOW TO USE THIS BOOK

L ook up in the alphabetical Lexicon any word or phrase you feel uncertain about. The entry will explain the point or refer you to a general article in which it is treated in company with similar locutions. Many of these longer articles are divided into numbered sections, each one discussing an aspect of the topic.

For light on broad grammatical subjects, such as ADVERBS, ANTECE-DENTS, NUMBER, SEQUENCE OF TENSES, SUBJUNCTIVE, consult those words in the Lexicon. Note that in all articles the words in SMALL CAPITALS (other than headlines quoted from newspapers) show that there is an entry on the subject in its alphabetical place. Questions of grammar that arise with the use of particular words are answered in the entries for those words; for example, AS; NONE; THAT, WHICH; THIS KIND, THESE KINDS, THOSE KINDS.

For matters of style, consult the entries listed under that heading in the Inventory of Main Entries in the Lexicon; for example, JOURNALESE, METAPHOR, POPULARIZED TECHNICALITIES. If you cannot be sure which style entry will answer your question, consult the Lexicon for the word or phrase that brought the question to mind. Many entries on particular words will refer you to an article, and many articles will end with a reference to one or more word entries. This arrangement may help you investigate stylistic points whether you start with a general difficulty or a troublesome word.

The essay "On Usage, Pedantry, Grammar, and the Orderly Mind" (page 337) gives the reader an idea of the assumptions underlying this guide and may clear up certain questions about the study and care of language. Such matters enter into every judgment in the book, but are not essential to its practical, day-to-day use.

I. DICTION

a, an, the
abbreviations
-ability, -ibility
-able, -ible
about
absent
absolutely
academe, academia, the
   academy
accept
accolade
account for
accuse
acknowledge, admit
acquiesce
address, speak to
adequate
adhere, adherence, adhesion
administer, minister
admission, admittance
advance, -d, -ment
aegis
affinity
agenda
all but
allege
allergic
allude
almost
alter ego
alternate, alternative
although, though

ambiance
ambivalent
ample
and/or
anxious, eager
anymore
appreciate, esteem
approbation, approval
arguable
around
arouse, rouse
as
aside from, apart from
assure, ensure, insure
at about
-athon, -thon
augment, supplement
average
avid
awed, awesome
back formation
balance
based, -based
based on
basically
basis, on the; basis, on a
become, come to be
belie
between
bridegroom
but
careen, career
case

catalogue, catalogued
changing names
character
cohort
colleague
communicate, communication(s)
compare, compared
complicit
compose, comprise
concept, -ion
connive
connotations
consciously
consist (in) (of)
constant(ly)
contact
contemporary, modern, postmodern
content(s)
context
continual, continuous
contrary, on the, to the
controversial
converse, obverse, reverse; opposite,
    contrary, contradictory
convict
convince, persuade
correlate
council, counsel, consul
covering words
cynical, skeptical
dangerous pairs
dare say, daresay
data
defensibles
delineate
develop
diction
different, various
dilemma
discomfit, discomfort
disinterested
divest

doubt, doubtless, no doubt
doubtful, dubious
dysfunctional
echelon
eclectic
education
-ee, -er
endings
enormity, enormousness
euphemisms
every day, everyday
exception
excessively, exceedingly
exciting
execute
expound, expatiate
express
facility, fluency
faculty
fail in
felicitous, fortuitous, fortunate
fewer, less
first of all
fiscal
forbidden words
foreword, introduction, preface
format
Frankenstein
free gift
French words and phrases
gambit
glamor, glamour
graduate
grammatical error
hanged, hung
historic(al)
hopefully
human, noun
humanism, humanist, humanity
icon
identical
identify, identification

if and when
impact
implicit, explicit
imply, infer
in for by, of, etc.
in order to
in terms of
inasmuch, insofar
include for are
inculcate
indicate
insigne, insignia
into, in to
irregardless
-ize
key
lackadaisical
last, latest
Latin and Greek plurals
lay, lie
legend(ary), fabulous
level
libel, slander
like
limited
literally
locate
lost causes
major, minor
majority, minority
malaprops
manner
masterful, masterly
meaningful
means
meld
nature
oblivious of (to)
obviate
okay
ologies
on, upon, up on

one (=I)
ongoing
only
overly
oxymoron
per
permafrost
personal(ly)
plausible
popular
popularized technicalities
practical, impractical; practicable
pragmatic(al), pragmatism
prestigious
prior to
pristine
proselyte
provided, providing
purge
qualification
quote, unquote
rack, wrack
range
re-create, recreate, etc.
reaction
readership
recommend
redolent with
reference
repeat
reportedly
represent
resource person
respective(ly)
same
sanction
sanguinary, sanguine
sex, gender
skill(s)
speaking likeness
spirit of adventure, the
suspect

II. IDIOM

III. STYLE

who(m), who(m)ever
with
without

V. PUNCTUATION

apostrophe, the
colon, the
comma, the

dash, the
ellipsis
hyphen, the
parentheses, brackets
period, the
question marks, exclamation points
quotation marks
semicolon, the
slash, the

LEXICON

A

a, an, the. 1. Unnecessary *a, an*. 2. *A, an* before words beginning with *h*. 3. Misplaced *a, an*. 4. *A, an, the*: definite and indefinite. 5. *The* omitted. 6. *A* with adjective and proper name. 7. *Per* for *a, an*.

1. Unnecessary *a, an*. It is a mistake to think that every noun requires *a, an*, or *the*, called articles, before it. Custom requires omitting the article in certain wordings, especially after a negative which already implies it. Thus it is wrong to say: *Have you no better an excuse?* Here *no* means *not a*; hence *an* is unnecessary. Use *no better excuse*. Similarly, write *no more expeditious way*, not *no more expeditious a way*. Omit the articles in *No braver a deed was ever performed / no more generous a sacrifice / no more useful an invention*. Sometimes using one necessary indefinite article insidiously urges the use of an unnecessary one: *We suggest that a new treasurer be given no larger a salary for doing the same work.* The first *a* is needed; the second is implied by *no* (*no larger* = *not a larger*).

In identifying someone by membership in a broad category, no article precedes the categorical noun. *He offered this concession as owner of the building* implies that he made the offer in his capacity as owner, not in his capacity as lawyer, neighbor, buildings commissioner, or whatever other category he might belong to. The book title *The Playwright as Thinker* offers consideration of playwrights in one respect only, leaving out any treatment of them as poets, as technicians, etc. By contrast, in writing of one playwright's traits, we might say that *R. as a poet is not much* or that *M. lacks skill as an adapter of others' plays*.

One of the articles serves no purpose in *a half an hour* or *a half a glass*. (A pharmaceutical leaflet recommends *a half a glass of water* eleven times in seven inches of print.) The normal wording is *half an hour / a half hour* (no hyphen needed) / *half a glass*. Though correct, *a half glass* sounds odd, and *a half apple* obscurely suggests a fruit that is half apple and half not; cf., *a half-truth*. Omit *a* in *I know how difficult rehearsals must have been, especially at this late a date*; otherwise, the construction would be *this . . . a date*. But note that the alternative *at so late a date* requires *a*, because the construction is *at . . . a date*.

Fail to omit *a* or *an* and you may convert one person into two or more: *She found a carpenter and a stepfather* was meant to refer to one man but instead presented two people; omit the second *a*. Contrariwise, if we say that *a singer, pianist, and songwriter will discuss current music*, we announce one person with several talents. Note also that the sentence *R. is a passionate singer and cook* makes *passionate* modify both nouns equally; *a passionate singer and a cook* leaves the adjective modifying *singer* only and does not say what kind of cook R. is.

The phrase *what kind of cook* rightly omits the indefinite article. It is likewise omitted twice in *know what kind of trouble that breed of dog will get into*. After words like *breed, kind, sort, species, manner, type*, and the like, the object of the following preposition is likely to be a generic word (*trouble, dog*) not a particular one. So in spite of examples to the contrary in the works of great writers, there is no place for *a, an* in *that sort of lie / this brand of oil / what make of car / some sort of trick*. The article is an interloper pretending to clarity or elegance in *the broadest kind of a privilege / This is a terrible kind of a welcome / some kind of a maniac / You must strike some kind of a bargain / She will contrive some sort of an answer*.

The presence or absence of the indefinite article shows whether the conjunction *or* is joining alternatives or synonyms. The phrase *a democracy or a republic* denotes two kinds of political organization; *a democracy or republic* denotes one kind that is being called by two names. If we speak of *a theological or religious objection*, we equate theology with religion, or at least make no effort to differentiate them; *a theological or a religious ques-*tion says that theology is one thing, religion another.

2. A, *an* before words beginning with *h*. In literature we have inherited *an humble and a contrite heart / Whoso breaketh an hedge* and other uses of *an* before words that now begin with a sounded *h*. Such use both Fowler and Follett many years ago declared obsolete and pedantic. It survives today, according to the American Heritage Dictionary, "primarily before the word *historical*." Phrases like *an hereditary trait* the Heritage calls "rare," but it finds *an historic opportunity* a "harmless adornment in formal writing." *An* is in fact preferred before *historical* (but *a* before *history*) in present-day writing and speech. And to dispense with *an* before all other words beginning with the aspirant *h* and accented on the second syllable is to disregard current usage, at least in speech. Speakers neither pedantic nor given to adornment say *an hysterical outburst, an hereditary illness*, and so on according to taste.

3. Misplaced *a, an*. In a few constructions the indefinite article comes between, not before, a modifier and the noun it modifies. This occurs especially after *so, too*, and *how: so heavy a load / too long a fall / how mean a prank*. After *so* the alternative construction is *Your so cleverly arranged departure / a so thoughtful gift*, but such locutions sound unidiomatic now; they served Henry James, but to contemporary ears they sound vaguely French. *An even more desolate occasion* sounds more natural than *even more desolate an occasion*. Awkwardness marks *Let* me put her actions in less bizarre a light (in a less bizarre light). Nothing of substance is lost by keeping to the normal word order, and it can be said in general that the tone of latter-day American English discourages avoidable inversion.

For the omission of a or an before the second of a pair of nouns when the first takes the alternative article, see WHAT IS "UNDERSTOOD"?

4. A, an, the: definite and indefinite. It is particularly likely that writers coming to English from another language will befog the meaning of their words by confusing the definite and the indefinite articles. Sometimes, to be sure, the two can be interchanged without doing damage. No meaning is lost whether we say The proof of the pudding is in the eating (any pudding, any eating) or The proof of a pudding, etc.—though a native speaker will know that the former is traditional. But clarity suffers when a sentence needs the and a or an is used: Several biographers wrote of the actor's coldness and of a mother he had never known (of the mother). So too, when a is needed but the slips in: The agreement is what all parties are trying to achieve (An agreement).

It is unlikely that the actor mentioned in the sentence above had more than one mother he did not know, unlikelier still that the writer of the second sentence envisioned only one possible agreement among several parties. The English language makes a point of distinguishing the particular (that actor's only mother) from the general (any agreement) by means of

definite and indefinite articles. Both kinds of articles assert the existence of the things they point to. In a report of a mystifying assault it was surmised that certain events might have created the animosity. To put it this way was to make an assumption, for there had been no sign of animosity. If the phrase had read might have created animosity, the facts and the supposed animosity would have been differentiated, making the report more accurate.

A and an are indefinite articles, words that point to one thing among other things like it. The is the definite article and isolates something from everything else, similar or not, for our attention. Consider the difference between the Earth as a planet, one among nine, and the Earth as the planet on which—unless we colonize another—we live.

This fundamental distinction must be observed whenever we use a, an, or the. To say Then G. lived for two years with the son she cherished is to state definitively that there was only one such son. Write instead a son she cherished and there remains a possibility that G. had other sons, and that she cared for them as much.

It is difficult to manage a and the with their related nouns if the writer does not keep firmly in mind the definiteness or indefiniteness of the nouns in their context. For example: Given the local critics' taste, an Australian debut of a singer aroused much livelier interest than a new conductor ever could. A debut in a particular country is a single, definite event; so an should be the. Doubtless the writer thought first of a *singer's Australian debut,* and then revised the sentence, adopting the *of* construction. But revising does not change the fact that singers are many, while the debut of any one of them in any one place is unique.

Note further that if the writer spoke of a performance—an event that may occur more than once—the sentence should not read *an Australian performance of a singer;* it should be either *a singer's performance in Australia* or *a performance in Australia by a singer.* The first wording implies something local or native to the country in what the singer did, which is not what was meant. It also compounds the proper indefiniteness of *a singer* with the confusing relation of *performance* to *singer* brought about by *of.* We commonly speak of *the performance of a duty* or *the performance of a play,* but one cannot perform a singer. The sequence *a . . . of a . . .* is in general hopelessly vague. *A daughter of an astronaut was honored last night* is either *the daughter* or *an astronaut's daughter.*

5. *The* omitted. The previous section dealt with singular nouns, whose indefiniteness is expressed by *a* or *an.* To show indefiniteness in a plural noun, we make use of *some* or *any* or else omit the article altogether. *Any* functions in negative statements; *some* in positive: *I will not listen to any objections / You must give him some people to work with.* The negative implication is subtler in *Give me any papers that survived;* what is implied is "any of probably not many." Plural definiteness, like the singular, is expressed with *the: They entered as evidence both the gun* (singular) *and the gloves* (plural) *found in the defendant's room / Bring back the chairs* (all that you borrowed) *after the party.* But plural indefiniteness is signaled by the absence of any article before the noun. *They were met at the Havana airport by the officials of the Cuban government* definitely implies that all such officials were there. If the sentence read *by officials of,* the suggestion would be that only some appeared. *A revolt of the students of Paris touched off the revolution of 1830* implicates all or nearly all the students, *a revolt of students* only some out of the total number. In giving instructions this difference can be important. *I want you to pack the books* obliges the helper to pack every one; *I want you to pack books* leaves the scope of that task indefinite.

Authors and others needing to title a work will consider the effect of putting in or leaving out *The. Pleasures of Music* tells the reader: "These are some of the pleasures; the work is not a comprehensive treatise"; whereas *The Economic Consequences of the Peace* claims to speak of them all without exception. If Charlie Chaplin had titled *The Circus* simply *Circus,* he would have been asking us to see all circus troupes summed up in one. With *The* he suggests a film about one particular company. Conversely, *City Lights* gives us his view of urban life in general.

Caption and headline writers, when they omit articles, work against the awareness of definition elsewhere. Journalists as a group once thought it somehow forceful to strike out the defining *the*, as in *to discuss* [the] *appointment of a new attorney general* or *against* [the] *accumulation of arms.* Perhaps less evident now on front pages, the virus has moved inside. Thus a report on music reads: *Noted English conductor P. will appear on December 15 to 17, leading the orchestra in a program of Berlioz, Beethoven, and Vaughan Williams;* and *Principal percussionist C. is to be the soloist in the first performances of Y's Percussion Concerto.* But if *the soloist*, why not *the principal percussionist?* Writers on business frequently set down statements like this: *Company officials described the new product as a step toward increase in market share.* A sportswriter tells us: *The point of the rule change is to discourage teams from trying for long field goals because of field position lost on misses.* Making *increase* and *market share* and *field position* into indefinite abstractions imparts the tone of science where it has no place. *Increasing* is the idiomatic form for the earlier sentence, just as *their market share* (or *their share of the market*) makes clear who wants what. But *field position* is not after all improved by inserting *the* before it. The phrase is pompous with or without an article; *the ground lost* would do better. (See also SCIENTISM.)

A writer may well object to using a string of *the's: Few are aware of the need for the reorganization of the courts.* But besides the repetition of the definite article, this sentence is afflicted with the NOUN PLAGUE, whose cure is often the gerund (see -ING 1). By substituting the *-ing* form of the

verb for the all too common *-tion* derivative, one can transform *The group is not opposed to the adoption of the plan described in your letter* into *The group is not opposed to adopting.* Similarly, *the need for the reorganization of the courts* becomes *the need for reorganizing.* The static *Nothing is said of the abolition of capital punishment* moves more smartly as *Nothing is said of abolishing.* In such wording as *toward defrayal of the expenses of producing the finest recording*, the normal ear will know that *defraying* is the natural word, displaced by a reliance on a dull abstract noun. Not all sentences, of course, can be thus relieved of both *the* and *-tion*. The refractory will require their logical *the's.*

The lack of forward movement in sentences strung on *the . . . of* (and less frequently *a . . . of*) can be helped a bit when *of* is replaced by another preposition. *He then discussed investment criteria of welfare enterprises* (for) / *the publication of the facts of unsolved cases* (in).

Prose that fails to move will not engage the reader for long. And nothing so arrests its movement as the dead hand of abstraction brought down upon human doings, feelings, and thought. Consider this clump of words in tribute to admirable persons: *In brilliance of insights their careers as neurologists are comparable.* The trouble does not alone rest with the long-delayed mention of those honored. It begins in the first four words, which are unattached to anything at all. What brilliance where? Which or whose insights? The mind finds no direction and no human spoor to follow. Make *brilliance* definite with the defining *the*, which lets us know that concrete things are ahead. And allow those honored to own their achievements: specify *their insights*.

To use abstraction for "scientific" effect robs prose of vividness. Here is someone attempting to describe how people once lived: *Availability of consumer goods wasn't a convenience people outside the big cities had access to.* At first glance the sentence appears to run backwards—not because a preposition ends it, which is all right (see PREPOSITIONS), but because it poses at the very beginning an indefinite entity, something like a physical property (e.g., density, velocity) of *consumer goods.* The writer had no more to say than *People living outside the big cities could not easily buy things* or *had few and small stores to buy from.*

Both idiom and logic determine the use of *the* in certain common phrases. It is idiomatic to say *in view of, in respect of, in pursuance of,* etc., because *view* and the other nouns have lost their literal meaning. Where the definable idea does remain, we continue to say *in the light of* and *with a view to* and *in the face of. In face of destruction* has no force at all, and *in light of ancestral wisdom* no gravity. Present in both should be a feeling of real things: ancestral wisdom gives light and destruction has a face, which makes us want *the* light of the one and *the* face of the other. The parallel with *in view of* does not apply, for *in the view of ancestral wisdom* differs in meaning from *in view of ancestral wisdom.*

Likewise *onstage, on deck, on campus* have different meanings if *the* is inserted. An actor is *onstage* or *offstage*, but a play is put *on the stage.* Similarly, a passenger does not drop his keys *on deck* but *on the deck.* The same professional sense applies to *on campus.* A student may be required to be *on campus* five days a week, but a rare species of elm grows *on the campus.* The supposed puzzle of Handel's *Messiah* (*The Oratorio Society is giving* Messiah) is no puzzle at all. Handel was hardly an accomplished user of English and apparently saw nothing contradictory in the Deliverer not being unique.

Lastly a word must be said about the misdeeds of translators, who too often follow the lead of the foreign original in distributing their *a*'s and *the*'s. Mistakes in this department do more than anything else to impart a flavor of stagy silliness to the Englished utterances of foreign statesmen, novelists, and travelers. To take two examples from literature, it is obvious that Chekhov's short story is entitled "In Court," not "In the Court," which would be appropriate only if the scene were a court*yard.* And Sartre's autobiography, *Les Mots,* appeared in this country as *The Words,* which is devoid of sense. The British translation bears the correct and sense-bearing title *Words.* To sum up, *the* and *a* are excellent vocables, surprisingly difficult to use, and most helpful to lucid communication when rightly used.

6. A with adjective and proper name. Writers of novels and of news stories make excessive use of a locution that was tiresome the moment it was

launched: *It was a reluctant William who turned homeward that night* / *After two rounds, the jaunty C. had no difficulty disposing of a bloody S.* / *. . . an output exceeded only by a later Zane Grey* / *A weary L.C., former governor of . . ., is met by his sister on arrival* / *He fully expected to find a bewildered M., but he was not prepared for an aggressive one.* This last example makes plain what is fundamentally wrong with this formula. It splits the person into as many different doubles of himself as there are adjectives to apply to human character. A *weary* L.C. is in fact the same man as *the weary* L.C. and should remain one and indivisible. This can be done only if he is never *a* [something] L.C. *He expected to find M. bewildered but not aggressive* correctly states the divergent attributes of one person. But when *a passionate Tom kisses a bashful Jane* (otherwise than as a generality personified by the use of names), there is in the report something at once coy and condescending that reinforces the sense that these are not persons but puppets. To the sociologist they may be role-playing, but to the reader a sullen Joe and a blithe one and a startled one and a reassured one do not, however long the enumeration, add up to a convincing whole Joe.

7. *Per* for *a, an.* Such set Latin phrases as *per diem, per annum,* and *per capita* are established in English. By extension the technicians are granted their *mph* (miles per hour) and their rate of acceleration *per second per second.* But for common American usage the following forms

are correct: *$2 a dozen, $9 a yard, fifty miles an hour, three times a day.* The use of *the* in such phrases (*$17.50 the ounce, $3,000 the mile*) is a Francophile affectation that is even less idiomatic than the usually gratuitous *per,* as in *wind from the southwest at thirteen miles per* (an) *hour.* But note that in a few semi-technical contexts *to the* is idiomatic: *three cubic yards to the ton, seventy pulsations to the minute,* etc.

Where the idiomatic *a, an* would lead to an awkward repetition or similar oddity, as in *an allowance of $475 a family a month,* it may sometimes be necessary to resort to *per* for one *a* or the other, or for both. But usually, as in this example, the difficulty is got around by *a monthly allowance of $475 a family*—a reminder that the best solution often lies in avoidance.

a, au. See FRENCH WORDS AND PHRASES.

abbreviations. 1. The modern tendency in both scholarship and popular works is to use English abbreviations in place of Latin ones to indicate examples, other locations of pertinent matter, and the like. For example, *cp.* (= compare) for the Latin *cf.*; *ff.* (= following) for *et seq.*; *above* and *below* (not abbreviations but shortened directions) for *supra* and *infra*; plain *see* for *vide* and *q.v.*; *note* for *N.B.* Two of the Latin particles, *sc.* and *viz.*, which stand for *to wit* and *namely,* have almost disappeared from modern print. Yet some of these marks remain current. The commonest are *c.* or *ca.*, meaning *about* and modifying a date, as in *painted c. 1783; e.g.* and *i.e.,* which will be discussed below; the familiar *etc.;* and the indispensable *ibid.,* which saves time by telling the reader that a quotation comes from the same source as the one just preceding. *Sic* continues to signal that the original word or text is being exactly reproduced, despite a patent mistake or oddity; and *passim,* for *here and there,* informs the reader that the matter spoken of appears at several points throughout the book or chapter.

2. *E.g.* and *i.e.* are often confused. The first means *for example (exempli gratia)* and introduces an instance or a short series of names, words, or other items. The second means *that is (id est)* and introduces a repetition in different words of the thought just expressed.

Etc. and *et al.* are sometimes thought to be equivalent. But *et cetera* (= and the rest), being neuter as Latin, can only refer to things; *et alii* (= and others) can only refer to persons. A list of persons' names should not end with *etc.* and is better with *and others* than with the lawyer's *et al.*

See also INITIALESE.

-ability, -ibility. These suffixes mean *the quality of being* whatever adjective precedes them. *Inscrutability* = the quality of being inscrutable; *readability* = the quality of being readable; *visibility* = the fact, quality, or degree of being visible; etc. Promoters, chiefly advertisers, every so often attempt to disguise the independent noun *ability* as the substantive suffix, coming up

with hippogriffs like *roadability,* which does not mean *roadableness* (nothing does), and *wearability,* which is ambiguous and should not replace the standard word *durability.*

See also -ABLE, -IBLE; SCIENTISM.

abjure, adjure. See DANGEROUS PAIRS.

-able, -ible. 1. Meaning. 2. *-able* with *e* preceding.

1. The root idea in this suffix is the same as in *able* when it stands by itself; the ordinary meaning of *able* is coupled with the passive meaning of a verb. *Manageable* means *able to be managed,* *adorable* means *able to be adored,* *improvable* means *able to be improved.* The sense of the construction is not affected by the spelling *-ible,* which is found in *reversible, deductible, exhaustible,* and other adjectives formed with the intention described. Still, there are in good current usage many words ending in *-able* or *-ible* that require either a mental addition to the verb or some change of its normal object before the compound can be rightly understood. *Reliable* is a prime instance. It does not mean *able to be relied*—no word does—but *able to be relied on. Actionable* means *affording grounds for a court action. Sizable* means *of large size* or *not small.* And *knowledgeable* goes still further afield with the meaning *made able through possessing knowledge.* Only two words in ordinary use have a common stem but meanings that differ depending on whether *-able* or *-ible* is attached: *forceable* means *able to*

be forced open and forcible means achieved by force (forcible entry) and having verbal force (forcible argument).

2. Endings in *-able* that tack onto ordinary words need no intervening *e* unless the preceding letter is *c* or *g*, and then only if the soft sound of these letters has to be preserved. Thus *notice* gives *noticeable*, to prevent the pronunciation *notickable*; and *change* gives *changeable*, the *e* preventing the pronunciation *chang-able*. But *like* gives *likable, cite citable, survive survivability, sale salable*, and so on. To this common-sense rule about the intervening *e* there is an exception: *lineage* (meaning *ancestry*); the *e* is sounded, and the word is pronounced in three syllables, lĭ-nē-ĭj. *Linage*, meaning *number of lines of print*, follows the rule and is written without the *e*.

British English retains a mute middle *e* in more of these compounds than does American. A special case arose in America when Ernest Hemingway asked that Charles Scribner's Sons, his American publisher, use the middle *e* in the title of his memoir *A Moveable Feast*. The standard spelling is *movable*.

See also SPELLING.

about, misuse of preposition. Those who wish what they write to be clear to others, including a reader ten years hence, make a point of avoiding fashionable slang. It dates or disappears or reverses its meaning with astonishing swiftness. They also avoid other fashions that race through the language —

turns of phrase that are up-to-date for a while and are admired by those who do not care what exactly has been said. Fashions subtly intimidate. But repetition soon exposes their glibness and makes them merely annoying.

The fashion that seized on *about* is instructive. One of the several senses of this preposition is *concerning* or *regarding*, as in *Alcott's is a book about a family of daughters / L. talked until two in the morning about the trouble her husband gave her / She seems to have written an entrancing letter about the sojourn in Florence*. The Oxford English Dictionary calls this *about* "the regular preposition employed to define the subject-matter of verbal activity." The American Heritage Dictionary says, "This use has lately been extended to refer to the relation between various non-linguistic entities and the things they make manifest." This sentence would be clearer if it read: "the relation between non-linguistic things and whatever subject the speaker would like to discuss." Examples of the fashion: *Collecting is about being in the presence of beautiful things / Democracy is about increasing debate, not reducing it / I didn't regard the disease as being only, even mainly, about death /* [One sculptor's] *art was about its own provisionality, about what he believed was the impossibility of re-creating in . . . clay what he actually saw / American style is all about making your home or face look as if nothing has been done to it / The play illustrates what its director's own career both is and is not about / What I've done isn't so much about redecorating as creating a different play between light and object / Life is, for better or worse, about expectation / The placement and size of a* [screen] *credit can be the subject of intense warfare that's really all about ego, posturing, vulnerability . . . Which are what Hollywood is all about too / The image calls to mind what Jesus was all about—and what Christianity is supposed to be about: living in communion with a wide range of people, including those who are perceived as riffraff, sinners, and outcasts.*

Nonsensical in the positive, this kind of statement in the negative needs two *abouts* to limp home: *Credit-card companies have realized that their products are no longer about credit but rather about convenient payment for goods and services / Eating is not only about survival but also about sensuality / The life and career of S. are not merely about his artistic achievements. They are also about the manner in which his integrity authenticated his art / Advertising wasn't simply about making sure a company could sell off what it produced. It became about creating new wants.*

A piece of advertising might be said to be *about* a car, a soft drink, or an aspirin: it *concerns* or *describes* such a thing. But *advertising* in general is no more *about* one thing or purpose than it is *about* persuasion, photography, billing, or the office coffee machine. The writer of the last example seems to have meant *wasn't simply attempting to ensure that a company could sell off what it produced. It was creating new wants.* (*Became about* is difficult to recast.)

This use of *about* pretends to reveal the essence of a subject, like a rabbit from a hat, before your astonished eyes. But the trick destroys a primary meaning of *about* and blurs the relation between the parts of a situation. We can guess that the mischief stems from the innocent expression *what such-and-such is* (*all*) *about,* as in *He never understood what college was all about.* This colloquial formula is handy for saying in a vague way what one only understands vaguely or does not care to spell out. The *about* discussed in this entry implies the opposite: uncanny acuteness. It is the twin of IN TERMS OF, which, in ordinary discourse, implies mathematical relations where none exist. *In terms of* began as a fashion and has stayed as a mark of slovenly writing.

See also ICON; VOGUE WORDS.

above, adjective. Perhaps because of its familiar use in *above-mentioned,* which we borrow from legal documents, it seems permissible to use *above* in front of nouns: *For the above reasons Liszt has been neglected for twenty-five years.* But for the demanding ear the commercial tone is still there, just as the legal tone is too strong in the old *the within letter.* Since the other indicators of place are never so used (*the without people, the below remarks* being so far impossible), it seems best in general writing to keep *above* in the same class and say *the reasons above* and *the remarks below.*

A related use of *then* is sometimes ambiguous. *In his younger days he was a member of the then Volunteer Block Watchers.* This sentence probably means *a member of what was then called the Volunteer Block Watchers,* but *then* might equally refer to the superseded voluntary nature of the group. When used of persons and positions (*the then Secretary of State*) the designation of time is better given in more explicit terms: *the Prime Minister of that time / the most popular columnist of the day / the former office of union secretary.*

abrasive. See CONNOTATIONS.

abridge. See MALAPROPS.

absent, quasi-preposition. Those who pilfer legalisms for use in decorating common statements are all too fond of wordings like this: *Absent the right sort of wrench, repair of the wheelchair could take all morning / We cannot leave the car at the border absent any assurance of its safety. Absent* used as a substitute for *without* or *lacking* or *in the absence of* in ordinary writing will always jar, because the reader feels strongly its meaning as an adjective. Worse, the literary reader will also know its older use as a verb, as in Hamlet's "Absent thee from felicity awhile." Lawyers may insist on the need of the word as a quasi-preposition in law. It is only pompous elsewhere.

absolute words. Some words defy comparison or degree; they denote what is superlative or complete, and they must be handled accordingly. The most familiar example is *unique*: something can be *almost unique* (near but not the real thing) but not *very unique* or *even more unique.* Nor can

an explanation or a theory be *too simplistic* or *very simplistic*; the word by itself means *too simple.*

Other such words are less commonly recognized, judging by their frequent misuse. *Discomfit*, for example, means to wholly undo, to defeat. It is foolish to say either *a little discomfited* or *thoroughly discomfited*, especially if, in either case, one means *discomforted.* (See DANGEROUS PAIRS.) Similarly, and by definition, *unqualified* and *incomparable* become empty salesmanship in phrases like *a more unqualified triumph* or *an even more incomparable performance.*

Degree is excluded by a similar logic. No man should be said to be *every bit the equal of Martin Luther King, Jr.*: he is the equal or he is not; *every bit* weakens the force of *equal*, an absolute. If a theory *does not hold much water*, the argument against it is lost; the theory has some value because it holds some water. Another sort of fiddling with absolutes produces glaring tautology, as in *general consensus, universal panacea, fully completed.*

There remains *perfect*, which looks like the absolute word par excellence. Yet the Constitution speaks in its preamble of *creating a more perfect union.* Usage has in fact authorized *more perfect* and *less perfect*—on the understanding, perhaps, that nothing on earth achieves perfection and that the degrees of approximation to it deserve to be named.

absolutely. American English seems always to need a VOGUE WORD to express emphasis or assent. In the first edition, this book said of *definitely*: "It is used both in and out of print to replace with a standardized noise . . . *decidedly, emphatically, clearly, indisputably, certainly, absolutely, assuredly, far and away, hands down, yes indeed, beyond argument."* As the century ends, *absolutely* has overthrown *definitely* to assume the selfsame function. Advertising boasts of *absolutely lowest prices,* and a review of a movie states that *this is absolutely the wrong film with which to begin the holiday season.* Few conversations endure a mere *yes* or *I agree* when *absolutely* can lend its affirmative jolt. Not downright objectionable, the word cannot avoid being tiresome. And as it becomes mere noise, its meaning of *without condition or limitation* must be conveyed by other words.

absorb. See PRONUNCIATION 1.

absurd. See PRONUNCIATION 1.

academe, academia, the academy. Midway in the twentieth century the impressive terms *academe* (from Greek) and *academia* (from Latin) came into frequent use to denote institutions of higher learning as a collectivity or abstraction. *Academe, medicine, finance, and law drew many members of his class, and most have had successful careers* / *While Europe has continued to pay him homage over the years . . . only academia and a few regional theaters have offered him respect and a refuge in the United States.* Much earlier, Shakespeare, Tennyson, and James Russell Lowell misunderstood *Academe,* which is the alternative

spelling of *Academos,* the name of a Greek hero. Plato taught in a grove near Athens associated with Academos, and Platonic philosophy came to be called the Academy (with a capital A). To call universities collectively *academe* is equivalent to calling them *John Harvard.*

Academia is the Latin place-name that Cicero gave to his two houses in remembrance of Plato. For the modern generic usage, *academia* is preferred. Still, the question arises: must we choose between two affectations? No one thinks we need *familia* to refer to families in general, or *biblioteca* to denote the collectivity of libraries. As simple English, *the academy* (with a small *a*) has served for many years, and should continue to do so in contexts where it cannot be confused with a particular academy of science or letters, a private school, or a professional organization.

accept. This verb should not be saddled with either of two constructions: the infinitive and the *that* clause. Both outrage idiom. The infinitive: *But American public opinion will not accept to be bullied* (will not accept bullying, being bullied) / *We accepted as our purpose to give a clear account of how the scientist works* (accepted . . . the giving of a clear account, accepted it as our purpose to give). The *that* clause: *I accept that your intentions were good but mourn the terrible outcome* (replace *accept* with *recognize* or some similar verb that tolerates *that*).

In short, *accept* takes as its object a

gerund (a verb made into a noun and ending -ING), as in *will not accept bullying*; it will of course also take a noun or pronoun. Among pronouns, *accept* will take *it*, which may in turn lead to an infinitive, as in *accepted it as our purpose to give*. Some writers stitch on a clause by means of *the fact that* (*I accept the fact that your intentions were good . . .*). But the locution is lumbering, and they had better consider whether "the fact" is a fact.

acceptance, acceptation. See DANGEROUS PAIRS.

access, noun and verb. See SCIENTISM 1.

accolade. Reporters who make frequent use of *accolade* to signify praise, approval, and similar signs of recognition will on other occasions report that, after conferring a medal or prize, a European dignitary, acting according to custom, kissed the recipient—soldier, scientist, or diplomat. The fact is that no reporter ever saw such a kiss but saw instead an *accolade*, which consists in touching the recipient's cheeks alternately with one's own. The word is from the French root *col*, meaning *neck*. By extension the term is often used to denote the tap on the shoulders with the flat blade of a sword which is part of the ritual of knighting. Since real *accolades* are still conferred, the figurative word for *praise* is misleading.

according. See DANGLERS, BENIGN.

account for. As a synonym of *explain*, this verb phrase would be difficult to mishandle; but it has an unfortunate currency as a synonym of *consist of*, and in this guise it has the same disabilities as REPRESENT. *Ninety-seven percent of the nation's exports are accounted for by* (consists of) *fish and fish products* / *Over half his library is accounted for by* (consists of) *musicology*. Sometimes the two ideas of *consist of* and *explain* are fused: *X points out that most of the congestion is accounted for by tourist traffic*. In such places *account for* is legitimate.

accrue. See TRANSITIVE, INTRANSITIVE.

accuse. It seems obvious that an accused person must stand accused of some crime, offense, or dereliction; if no charge has been named, the word is misapplied. It follows that this sentence is foolish: *In announcing Mr. M.'s suspension, the* [newspaper] *management pointed out that "Mr. M. had neither been accused nor convicted of any charge."* Most likely M. had not been accused or convicted *on* any charge; but as it stands, the sentence states that he is not accused of any accusation. The juxtaposition of *charge* with *accused* makes the sentence go in a circle and come out meaningless.

See also CONVICT.

acknowledge, admit. We acknowledge a fault or acknowledge being at fault. We also admit a fault or being at fault. It was formerly common to admit *to* being at fault, though this idiom is on its way out. But what of *acknowledge to? The handsome, gray-haired Jesuit readily acknowledges to being the conqueror of a ten-and-a-half-pound bonefish that graced his outer office* (omit *to*). The extra *to* is probably an unconscious borrowing from *confess to,* an idiom not only alive but overused for ironic apology. Like *confess, admit* most often implies reluctance; *acknowledge* acquires that connotation only from context and is otherwise neutral.

Admit takes *of* when it has an impersonal subject and means permit: *This impasse will not admit of half measures or stalling. Permit* itself once commonly took *of,* but no longer needs it.

Again, *admit* implies some sort of challenge. It should not be used as a synonym for *stated* or *remarked,* as in *The new ambassador admitted that he enjoyed living abroad.* Nobody, presumably, had charged him with denying this preference and forced him to *admit* it.

acknowledging. See DANGLERS, BENIGN.

acquiesce. For at least a century and a half, *acquiesce* has required the preposition *in: If you acquiesce in our way of life, you will find contentment.* Writers who want to use *to* for *in* forget that *acquiesce* differs from *agree* and *assent* (which take *to*) in implying silent or quiet compliance.

See also PREPOSITIONS.

acronyms. See INITIALESE.

acting out. See SCIENTISM 2.

additives. See LINKING 3.

address, speak to. These verbs need no explaining in their age-old concrete senses: *T. addressed the absent losers with more love than he evinced for the howling winners / Whatever I blurted out at that moment was not addressed to her / When X at last addressed his wife, the tone of the letter abruptly changed / She should speak to her husband about his habit of humming along with the singer / If you speak to Y on the weekend, remind her that we're meeting on Tuesday.* The words become LEGALISMS when the concrete act of speaking or writing is both figurative and abstract: *Your suggestion does not address the complaints of the loggers whose market has already shrunk / We must address the accelerating disappearance of factory jobs / Will your program speak to the needs of fifth-graders? / Your attitude does not speak to his pain.* In everyday life, suggestions do not address, and some person answers complaints. Similarly, school programs do not speak; those who draft or compose them do, and have real fifth-graders in mind. In politics such impersonal usage may practice deception in plain sight: the candidate who vows to *address* a shortage of jobs or the plight of refugees makes no promise to accomplish anything at all.

See also FORBIDDEN WORDS 2; VOGUE WORDS.

adequate. From the Latin for *make equal to, adequate* takes *to* when it takes anything at all. *The preparations* *were adequate* is a sufficient statement. *The preparations were adequate to an occasion of solemn significance* shows the *to* followed by what usage demands: a noun or a noun form. If the object is an action, it must be put as a verb in the gerund, the noun form ending in -ING: *She did not feel adequate to subduing* (not *subdue*) *a soprano bent on vengeance*. In this construction *adequate* is parallel with *equal*; we say *equal to subduing*, not *equal to subdue*.

Adequate with nothing following it still implies a complementary phrase. *His income is adequate* means an income equal to all his ordinary demands on it. And by context the word can be given a belittling or even pejorative slant not inherent in it; for example, the critic's patronizing phrase *adequate performance* denotes performing equal to moderate or low expectations.

Only a sleepy writer will attempt to compare adequacies, as in *sufficiently adequate* or *adequate enough*. Both phrases merely say *sufficiently sufficient*. To write that *the merchant fleet must carry a more adequate share of international trade* is to misconstrue the trouble on board, which is not lack of adequacy of cargo but no adequacy; the fleet *must carry an adequate share*. *Adequate* is as resistant to comparison as any other absolute word. See ABSOLUTE WORDS.

adhere, adherence, adhesion. As an intransitive verb *adhere* seems safe from misuse. Objects are made to adhere with glue; people adhere to a cause, a party, or one another.

Webster lists *adhere* as a transitive too, with the definition *to cause to adhere,* but the usage is rare in American English.

Of the two nouns *adherence* and *adhesion*, the first is generally for figurative use, the second for literal. One *adheres* to the principles of a party, and this constitutes one's *adherence* to it; the surgical tape *adheres* to the skin, but its firm *adhesion* holds the bandage in place. Similarly, the surgical term to denote the postoperative sticking together of tissues that should remain separate is always *adhesion*.

Because in French the idiomatic use is the reverse of the English, and French books tend to be translated at sight, *adhésion* has begun to make its way into English and American writings on politics as *adhesion* (to the Republicans, to principle, to one's pledged word). Given the established medical sense, this is not a desirable innovation.

adjudge, adjudicate. See DANGEROUS PAIRS.

administer, minister. Oaths of office, first aid, and sacraments are *administered*. The person so served is *ministered to*, not *administered to*. Being a transitive verb, *administer* works with other nouns as it does with the oath, the physical aid, the ceremony; thus one *administers* a business. Being intransitive, *minister* acts *to* or toward the persons who receive the benefit. When X *administers* artificial respiration, he *ministers to* Y, who receives X's *ministration*.

See also DANGEROUS PAIRS.

admission, admittance. Regrettably, dictionaries have blurred the once-sharp distinction that usage makes between *admittance,* the act or fact of entering, and *admission,* the right to enter. A magazine approved this sentence: [*J. College*] *practically guarantees admittance to the A group.* But the academic practice is to speak of *admission to college, admission blanks, officers, interviews*—never *admittance.* And on business premises the mysterious little door around the corner bears the sign NO ADMITTANCE, never NO ADMISSION. On invitations the phrase is *Admission Free.*

See also ACKNOWLEDGE, ADMIT; DANGEROUS PAIRS.

admit. See ACKNOWLEDGE, ADMIT.

admitting. See DANGLERS, BENIGN.

advance, -d, -ment. The difference between *advance* and *advanced* as adjectives is the difference between being this side of a point regarded as usual (*advance notice, advance guard, advance copy*) and being far along on the other side (*advanced mathematics, advanced age, advanced standing, advanced ideas*). Thus one requests *advance warning* (no *an*) or an *advance payment* as being ahead of a usual or accustomed time. *Advanced mathematics* and *advanced ideas* presumably leave most people trailing.

The nouns *advance* and *advancement* are not hard to distinguish. The first refers to any progress, literal or figurative; the second is restricted to individual progress in a career, bu-

reaucracy, or hierarchy. A candidate may or may not achieve a great *advance* in popularity, while making little *advance* in wisdom (idiom gives an indefinite article to the first, no article to the second). A waiter may win *advancement* to the job of captain or of cashier. We seek *advancement* deliberately but can only hope to have made an *advance* once the effort is over. As for *making advances,* these are attempts to secure surrender, love, or friendship; the phrase can carry an edge of disapproval.

adverbs, vexatious. 1. It is widely and wrongly believed that adverbs all end in *-ly;* follow this misapprehension and adverbs will remain a mystery. *Fast* and *slow, right* and *wrong, good* and *bad:* these words and many others appear to be adjectives and sometimes are; but they are often adverbs. We go *straight to the point,* not *straightly;* we drive *fast,* not *fastly,* and by the same token drive *slow.* On formal occasions we try not to *dress wrong* and we hope that the food will *taste good.* Only uninformed gentility makes us wonder whether we should *dress rightly.*

A bare adverb that can take *-ly* may take a different meaning in doing so. *I expect to hear from him direct* means I count on him to communicate with me without anyone's intervention; *I expect to hear from him directly* means I count on hearing from him right away. If we *eat right,* we are consuming a proper diet; but if we *rightly eat,* it is proper that we eat instead of fasting. When we say that we *drive carefully,* we describe the way we drive; when we *drive slow* or *fast,* we describe (with an apparent adjective) the motion of the car.

Advertisers muddy the waters, as usual. Believing that the adjective *fresh* is magic, they will use it any way at all to keep it in that form: *What do you want in a deodorant? Most people want fresh! Fresh-baked bread* as descriptive of a way of baking is silly, for it implies its opposite, stale-baked bread.

The uncertainty over adding *-ly* arises from the failure to ascertain the function of the word: is it working in the sentence as an adverb or as an adjective? Consider: *What comes easy is rarely accorded its proper value.* Should one say *easily,* an unmistakable adverb modifying *comes?* One might, but in the sentence *comes* is very close to *is* in meaning, and in *what is easy, easy* is an adjective modifying *what.* There is no correct choice here; some writers will choose by the rhythm they want, others by a belief that adverbs ending in *-ly* are weaker than their cognate without *-ly.* The choice is easier with *Two men stood silently, struck by the grandeur of the view.* Let the silence refer to the standers, not the standing: *Two men stood silent.*

2. Sooner or later much debate over adverbs comes down to whether we should *feel bad* or *feel badly.* American usage chooses *feel bad* (adverb) for both feeling ill and feeling regretful; British English retains *feel badly* for being indisposed.

3. It may be a desire to imitate British UNDERSTATEMENT that leads some writers to modify adjectives with adverbs that weaken their force: *We find*

this a moderately terrifying prospect. The emphatic *terrifying* is here toned down almost to extinction. Occasionally this device will produce a striking OXYMORON. But most often it is used as a trick that readily becomes a bad habit. A writer should guard against stylistic trademarks; the reader will first notice, then collect examples—and soon prefer the game to the meaning of the prose. Avoid the likes of *rather exhaustive / a little repulsive / pretty meaningless / somewhat forbidding / rather abominable.*

4. Short and long words alike act as adverbs while looking like adjectives. Among the long ones are *relative, preparatory, preliminary,* and *irrespective.* Like the short ones, these must be so used as to forestall uncertainty about what they are doing. In this statement *irrespective* is clearly an adverb modifying *are: They are on the refugees' side irrespective of the immigration officials.* Less clear is this statement: *He made exquisite calculations preparatory to opening the bidding.* Does *preparatory* refer to the calculations or to his making of them? If it refers to the former: *preparatory* (adjective) *calculations before opening.* If it refers to the latter: *Preparatory to opening . . . he made—* or, more simply, recast: *Before opening the bidding, he made exquisite calculations.* Above all, avoid the accepted but hopelessly awkward *preparatorily. In preparation for* and *to prepare for* are always available.

Consider another two-faced example: *The grants will enable three international agencies to broaden their study of radiation effects independent of the policies of governments.* Are the effects to be thought of as independent or is the broadening? If the former: *effects that are independent of.* If the latter: *broaden . . . independently.* (See also OVERLY.)

5. Where to put the adverb in the sentence is a question that in contemporary writing receives more diverse and worse answers than all the preceding questions put together. It is a new question: until a few decades ago instinct about the rhythms of the mother tongue served instead of principles. Now explicit tips are needed to fill the place of instinct. The chief ones are these: (a) An adverb intended to be emphatic goes before the subject (*Unfortunately he could not foresee this consequence*). (b) An adverb not required for emphasis comes after the subject of a simple verb (*The Smiths generally dine with us once a week*). (c) With a compound verb—that is, one made with an auxiliary and a main verb—the adverb comes between auxiliary and main verb (*He will probably telephone before starting* / *I have often had that thought myself* / *The clock is consistently losing five minutes a day*). (d) If the verb is compounded with two or more auxiliaries the adverb comes after the first auxiliary when its force is to apply to the whole compound (*They have certainly been forewarned* / *He will undoubtedly have had some news by this time*). (e) If the adverb modifies the participle alone, it comes immediately before the participle (*It has been confidently asserted* / *It will have become firmly established*). (f) An adverbial element that runs to several

words is put outside a compound verb—ordinarily after it (*He has been asked over and over again* / *We have been hearing this particular argument off and on for several years*).

These principles were practiced for many generations without anyone's having to think about them. Then strange things began to happen. Some influential source promulgated the doctrine that the compound verb is an indivisible unit, and that to wedge an adverb into it is a crime akin to the splitting of an infinitive. The results are uniformly bad: *It long had been known* / *It officially was announced the other day* / *They unfailingly have been led by a brilliant passer* / *This session of Congress doubtless will see a lot of potshots fired in M.'s direction* / *This quiet man steadily was gaining the respect of his players* / *The strike that otherwise inevitably will be in effect at midnight* / *The people upstairs always are pounding* / *whether a 450-room skyscraper accurately can be termed a motel.* Most of these examples transgress either (c) or (d) above; the last one transgresses (e); *unfailingly have been led by* might come under (d) or (e), according to what it means. For rhetorical effects, especially in spoken discourse, one may put the adverb in a place where it will enforce a pause and heighten a feeling, but then the adverb must be set off by commas: *The Communists, presumably, are making headway with their propaganda.*

It is clear from this list that the position of the adverb can affect meaning. The word *also,* notably, varies in meaning according to its position. The obituary of an industrialist names the companies of which he had been president and continues: *He also had served as a director of* [six companies]. This means—or should mean—that he had served with some others on the board: the intended meaning, that he had filled other posts, calls for *had also served*. In *The next Pope also will have to decide*, we ask, Who before him had to decide what? The intention was to refer to previously named matters awaiting the Pope's decision. Other adverbs will similarly betray when misplaced. *Few of them were doubtless aware that they played on what was once Millionaires' Street* probably tried to say that no doubt few of them were aware, but managed to say instead that few were aware with unquestioning certainty.

A last principle about adverbs should encourage writers to place them before the simple verb, instead of between it and its object. That is the principle of elegance. In English the adverb should precede the verb whenever possible. Consider *Usually I understand entirely his motives*. Quite apart from the repetition of *-ly* and the awkwardness of having two modifiers of unequal power and scope struggling over the verb they flank, the putting of *entirely* between *understand* and *motives* is felt as the erecting of a wall. *I entirely understand* is the natural order. *The youngest must take part if they are to advance effectively their beliefs* (are effectively to advance; or even, are to effectively advance—see SPLIT INFINITIVE) / *I want you to imagine a state of affairs in which people would have for-*

gotten mysteriously their past (would have mysteriously forgotten).

aegis. We borrowed this *shield* from Greek, in which it was the impregnable defense with which a god might favor a mortal. By extension the earthbound meaning now includes many sorts of protection: *Such dangerous research could only continue under the aegis of a government laboratory* / *Now that I worked under Jacob's aegis, I could explore the town without fear.* In casual borrowing the word often stands for mere formal sponsorship or workaday commercial backing: *Classes in lifesaving will begin at the lake under the aegis of the Red Cross* / *The series opened in the fall under the NBC aegis and was dropped in November.* In such uses no hint survives of lofty protection, and the noun becomes merely ornate. Careful writers prefer common words for ordinary uses. Note that *aegis* hardly bears modifiers: *He sailed through all difficulties thanks to the eager aegis of his teacher.* Nor is there such a thing as a *reluctant aegis*, even though *reluctant protection* is readily imagined.

affect, effect. See IMPACT 4.

affinity. This standard word for relationship by marriage has, by legitimate extension, the meaning of strong mutual attraction, as between those who fall in love at sight. An affinity is *between* two such persons; each has an affinity *with* or *to* the other. In keeping with its use in early chemistry to denote the force combining elements into compounds, *affinity* expresses a mutual relationship, not someone's attraction to a passive or insentient object—and it does not denote a propensity for doing or being something. *He has some affinity for mathematical studies* is a misuse: it could hardly be said that mathematical studies have an affinity for him. *Aptitude* is doubtless the word sought. *C. is practically devoid of affinity for pursuing such a career.* Again *aptitude* might serve, or *qualification*, or *capacity*. *The six-time winner of the American League batting championship has an affinity for making news when* (1) *he does something*, (2) *he does nothing*. Has a gift? A talent? An instinct? A knack? (But *knack* requires *of*, as in *get the knack of*, not *for*.)

African American, Afro-American. See CHANGING NAMES.

against. See PREPOSITIONS.

-age. See -ABLE, -IBLE 2.

agenda. Now useful as a singular, this Latin plural once denoted tasks to be done. Over time these tasks have combined to mean a program of collective action or a list of subjects to be discussed at a meeting. Taken up by politicians, *agenda* has had its meaning beaten out of it. Too often it vaguely refers to anything on anyone's mind.

See also LATIN AND GREEK PLURALS; VOGUE WORDS.

aggravate. See DEFENSIBLES.

ago, before. Both adverbs refer to time past, and both relate it to another time as a point of reference. Normally the point of reference is *now* when we say *ago*, and *then* when we say *before*. *Ago* covers the range from indefinitely far back to now; *before* covers the shorter range from indefinitely far back to a fixed point already past. *I knew it long ago* is from a point of view in the present. *He had known it long before* is from a point of view in the past. *Ago* = earlier than now; *before* = earlier than then. (There is an apparent idiomatic exception in *I knew it before / This has happened before*, etc., which imply a present point of view, but this *before* means nothing but *previously*; it does not call attention to the stretch between one point in time and another.)

The distinction is worth a moment's notice, because popular fiction is much given to the false *ago*. *She married in college, then worked in a travel bureau. Ten years later she moved to Chicago: she had been divorced six months ago.* This *ago* looks back from the author's position in the present, not the character's; it should be *before* or *earlier*, from the character's position within the past tense of the narrative. Similarly, someone at the present time looks back over the *past year*; someone in the past recalls the *previous year*.

The commonplace words *ago* and *before*, idiomatically used, have an obvious correspondence with the rather bookish word *hitherto* and the much more bookish word *theretofore*, respectively; and *hitherto* (= up to now) is often used by those given to this sort of vocabulary when they should use *theretofore*—exactly as *ago* is used for *before*.

When *ago* is combined with *since*—e.g., *it is two months ago since I have heard from him*—it says the same thing in two ways at once: (1) It was two months ago that I heard from him; (2) It has been two months since I heard from him.

See also SEQUENCE OF TENSES; SINCE, YET 1.

agree. See PREPOSITIONS.

ague. See PRONUNCIATION 1.

aim, verb. See PREPOSITIONS.

air strike. See EUPHEMISMS.

all, adjective. 1. When *all* is elbowed out of its natural position and at the same time converted into a pronoun, it stands out unpleasantly and may mislead. Its natural position is before what it modifies: *All heads turned at the shriek / All the Brothers Were Valiant / All things come round to him who will but wait.* Here it is in the unnatural position: *Is this all leading toward a permanent reduction in employment?* The inversion makes the subject of the sentence stylistically indistinguishable from the *we-all* and *you-all* of Southern dialect—pleasing expressions in their setting but outside the patterns of normal prose.

All we like sheep have gone astray, from Isaiah, is unidiomatic in modern prose, but the cure is not simply *We all.* In everyday unpoetic writing the sentence becomes *We have all, like sheep, gone astray,* or *All of us . . .* Where *all* modifies a pronoun subject of a compound verb, *all* properly follows the auxiliary: not *They all would be calling each other at all hours of the day and night,* but *They would all . . .*

2. A modern ellipsis with *all* should be kept for colloquial speech only: *He has his facts wrong is all* [that's the matter with him] / *I forgot to wind my watch is all* [that kept me from getting here on time].

3. *All . . . not.* For sentences such as *All liars are not thieves,* see NEGATIVES, TROUBLE WITH.

See also UNNECESSARY WORDS 4.

all, singular or plural. See NUMBER, TROUBLE WITH 2.

all but. As meaning *virtually, nearly, almost,* or *little short of,* the phrase *all but* is one of those crystallized idioms that accept no tampering.

See also SET PHRASES.

all that, intensive. See UNNECESSARY WORDS 4.

allege. In the passive voice (*He is alleged to be an opportunist*) *allege* is followed by an infinitive. In the active voice it is followed by a noun or by a *that* clause: *We allege his full cooperation in the swindle / We allege that he fully cooperated in the swindle.* Moreover, *allege* should always carry an implication of complaint; it is a word colored with accusation and criminality. Thus it cannot be the word wanted in *the number of performers alleged to* *have played in Carnegie Hall.* Substitute *thought, said, believed.* The verb *claim* is a slippery cousin of *allege* and likewise bears watching. In *She claimed to be descended from Toussaint L'Ouverture,* the verb *claim* implies that the descent is contested. For cases where no dispute or doubt is implied, use *said* (that she was), *asserted* (that she was), *professed* (descent from), etc.

allergic. The victim of an allergy is abnormally and pathologically sensitive to pollen, dust, feathers, shellfish, or some other substance that has no adverse effect on people in general. Such a person is said to be *allergic* to that substance. The adjective is not, then, an everyday synonym for *averse, hostile, unreceptive, cool*; nor is it interchangeable with verb phrases like *repelled by, disgusted by, left cold by.* Adopted first as a witty exaggeration for strong dislikes, the word soon came to cover even that which everyone dislikes, e.g., earthquakes, pain. As funny now as most other jokes that are fifty years old, *allergic* should be suppressed not alone for its inexactitude but also for its displacing of more apt and expressive terms.

See also VOGUE WORDS.

allowing. See DANGLERS, BENIGN.

all right, alright. See SPELLING.

allude. An allusion is the kind of glancing mention that does not name its object but gives the reader a means of making the identification if he has the knowledge or the wit to do so. The competing word, needed nine times out of ten where *allusion* is a misfit, is *reference.* A reference *is* an identification, whether a precise one (e.g., a footnote naming the source and location of something quoted or used in the text) or an approximate one (e.g., *Seward's Folly* for Alaska or for the purchase of Alaska). The borderline between approximate reference and mere allusion is hard to draw; we might put it that one man's reference is another man's allusion. When an editorial writer calls the conflict with Spain in 1898 *Mr. Hearst's war* he is making a reference, but one that may be taken as an obscure allusion by an uninformed reader. If, on the other hand, he represents someone as *sighing for more worlds to conquer* he is alluding (not referring) to Alexander the Great. Allusion and reference are clearly enough differentiated at their extremes but may overlap midway.

Sometimes *allude* is carelessly used where there is neither allusion nor reference. An example: *The common phrase "the irony of fate" alludes to an apparent mockery of destiny.* This sentence is clearly a definition, and for *alludes to* should substitute *means.*

Allude in its authentic meaning has no synonym. It is therefore one of those words whose meaning will be destroyed by repeated misuse, leaving the language with no single word to express a useful idea.

allure, lure. See CONNOTATIONS.

almost. One might suppose that the use of *most* for *almost* was a patent illiteracy in a class with *we ain't* or *he don't*. Fiction writers reproducing the colloquial or dialectal *most* (adverb) commonly give it an apostrophe: *'most always, 'most any schoolboy*, etc. Nevertheless this scrap of dialect does keep turning up in formal print: *An increasing number of college women are found on the basketball courts most every pleasant Sunday*. And an eminent sports reporter for one of the great newspapers comes out with *Then came a play that would have unsettled most any pitcher equipped with less fortitude than the lanky . . . right-hander*. There are, then, those who can use a reminder that there is no short form for *almost*.

alone. Following a noun, as it commonly does, *alone* is often ambiguous in grammar and therefore in sense. *Stupidity alone accounts for his having been caught*. Does this mean that stupidity unassisted by other causes was enough, or does it mean that stupidity was the only possible explanation? One cannot tell. The second meaning had better be rendered by *Only stupidity accounts for*; the first by *Stupidity by itself accounts for*. In *R. alone was competent to handle the situation*, read, for one meaning, *R. was the only one competent*; for the other, *R. unaided was competent*.

along with. See AS 11.

also. See AND; TOO 1.

alter ego means *other self*, or *duplicate self*, not counterpart, partner, or frequent companion. It follows that an *alter ego*—like a TRIUMVIRATE, another classical borrowing—is rarely encountered in ordinary life. It is certainly not encountered in the newspaper report of an overbearing thirteen-year-old and his younger partner in crime: *In the strange, perilous crucible of boyhood friendships, the two appear to have been alter egos, leader and follower—*which is to say notably unlike.

See also JOURNALESE.

alternate, alternative. The difficulties that accompany these words come under two headings: 1. Making clear which of two meanings you assign to the noun *alternative*; 2. The tendency to confuse the adjectival and adverbial uses of *alternate(ly)* and *alternative(ly)*.

1. Some readers remember that *alternative* can be either (a) a statement of choice between two possibilities or (b) one of the possibilities to be chosen. The first meaning is rarely used now, but is present in *The alternative is to remain and starve or to move on to God knows what manner of survival*. *To be, or not to be* makes, in this meaning, one *alternative*, the choice between being and not being. *That is the question* means: that is the alternative. Most writers now use *choice* for such a statement, lest they be misunderstood.

The second meaning of the noun *alternative* is: one of the two possibilities offered; in this meaning *to be* is one alternative, *not to be* the other. By loose extension *alternative* has also come to mean any one of three or several possibilities. *Of these alternatives the least unpleasant is the fourth* (or nth) is frowned on by the purist, but it passes most readers without notice, even those who would not write it themselves.

2. One standard meaning of the adjective *alternate* is related to *alternation*: *Mom visits us on alternate Sundays / The alternate angles are equal.* But in the United States *alternate* long ago acquired currency as a noun meaning *substitute, second choice, one designated to act in the place of another*; this meaning is established and inescapable. We appoint delegates to conventions and also *alternates*, who, if need be, can serve in their stead. This use is easily transferred from persons to things. For example, a book club chooses a book every month and, for those who do not want it, proposes an *alternate*. By this route *alternate* has arrived at a function widely confused with that of *alternative*.

Thus a spokesman for the United States Army writes to a correspondent: *Requests to use alternate* (i.e., alternative) *test dates are also received from other groups and individuals for various reasons.* Newspapers use the two words interchangeably: *Guests can drift from the formal living room to the . . . family room. Alternately* (Alternatively), *the family room can be used as extra space for food preparation / Scores of flights were ordered to alternate* (alternative) *landing fields from Pennsylvania to New England.* One can even find a perverted *alternate* and an orthodox *alternative* in the same context: *Another problem which will have to be met if Africa's wildlife is not to go the way of the dinosaur is that of finding an alternate way of life for the tribes which do most of the poaching.* And a few lines farther: *because he has no alternative means of supporting himself and his family.*

The adjectival meaning of *alternate* is *occurring by turns.* Consider then: *The alternate modes of travel are by snowmobile and plane.* Common sense tells us that no one will be boarding a snowmobile and a plane by turns, and that *alternative modes* was meant. *He asked that the experiment be continued eight months, during which the buses would have tried alternate routes.* This sentence suggests an experimental shifting back and forth between routes, but the context shows that the point is to try out a number of *alternative* routes. A last caution: note that the sentence above in which *flights were ordered to alternate . . . fields* suggests, by bad linking, the verb *to alternate.*

although, though, concessive conjunctions. The useful questions about these conjunctions are these: 1. What is the difference between them? 2. Does the sentence contain a real concession? 3. If it does, have I put the conjunction with the right clause? 4. Is the conjunction masking a dangling participle?

1. A concessive word or phrase or clause limits what is stated in an adjoining word or phrase or clause; hence what connects the two members is called a concessive conjunction, even if it begins the sentence. *Although Senator P.'s audience was larger, both speakers drew large crowds;*

here the conjunction *although* begins the clause that limits the statement following. In beginning a sentence some writers prefer the weight of *although*; but most agree that in this position *although* and *though* are interchangeable: *Though it seemed to her that he never stopped talking, he heard all that she said / Although nothing succeeds like success, her election doomed their affair.* In these examples the two conjunctions could be interchanged.

There are three respects in which *though* and *although* differ in usage. (a) In an inverted order that shifts the conjunction from its natural leading position, *though* is idiomatic: *Desperate though the situation was / Modest though his expectations were.* (b) *Though* is also idiomatic (because short) in joining two adjectives: *E. was happy though famished / We have been desperately busy even though ill.* (c) In the foregoing sentence, note that the intensive *even* can modify *though* but would sound affected preceding *although*.

2. Before one uses either of the concessive conjunctions one must ask whether it belongs. A concessive word, phrase, or clause states something despite which the main statement is true. Where this opposition or shading is not founded in logic, or where it occurs only between the apparent concession and something unsaid, a concessive conjunction is out of place. *Temperatures may rise to 98 degrees Fahrenheit, though the ideal temperature is 75 degrees.* Between stating the possible extreme and the temperature preferred there is no contradiction at all; the two statements are separate and logically unrelated. Omit *though* and use a period or semicolon after *Fahrenheit.* Quite as unrelated are the two statements in each of these sentences: *The climate is gradually changing, although there is little agreement about the causes / I was lucky enough to get through the winter without a cold, though I had an infected tooth.* To be sure, the writer in each case feels some opposition between the two statements made; but in fact in both sentences the concessive clauses refer to thoughts left unsaid. In the second sentence the unexpressed opposition seems to be *I was lucky enough to get through . . . without a cold, though unlucky enough to have an infected tooth.* As written, the sentence requires the reader to fill a blank.

3. Too often a concessive relationship is carelessly stood on its head: one clause is made concessive when it is the other clause that should be. *He habitually exceeded the speed limit, though he had never had an accident.* Read: *Though he habitually exceeded the speed limit, he had never had an accident.* Similarly in *She had ransacked the office, though no trace of an intruder was found,* the sense is clearer when *though* is moved: *Though she had ransacked the office, no trace of an intruder was found.* In such sentences the concessive clause may well have been an afterthought; the writer misassigned the conjunction by failing to distinguish the broader statement from the concessive one.

4. When *though* or *although* begins an elliptical clause (a statement from

which one or more words are omitted but assumed), there may be a hidden clash between the key word of that clause—usually an -ing participle—and the word that would fill out the clause to completeness. Where we detect such a clash the sentence is weak or off balance. *He is an extremely learned man, though wearing his erudition lightly.* Wearing seems to float in the air, belonging to nothing and no one. Expand the elliptical clause by putting in *he* to make a full clause. It should read not *he is wearing* but *he wears*—the obvious improvement. *I think this action the right one, though hating* (I hate) *the arguments heard in its favor.* On the other hand, no participial change is needed in *Though overworking already, he could hardly refuse this demand on his time;* the ellipsis is clear as it stands.

It should be noted that *though* (not *although*) can be used as a terminal adverb with a meaning akin to the adverbial (and ponderous) *however: Our April temperatures run twenty degrees lower than yours; we have a comfortable absence of humidity, though / The flight takes just under four hours; it takes almost an hour to get to the airport, though.* In this idiomatic use, *though* performs the simplest concessive function. Some of the unsound examples above could be fixed by changing the conjunction to the terminal adverb: *He habitually exceeded the speed limit; he had never had an accident, though.*

See also WHILE.

ambiance. To Webster's Third New International Dictionary, this word from the French, once used with exactness in the criticism of painting, now means "surrounding or pervading atmosphere." To the American Heritage Dictionary, third edition, it means "the special atmosphere or mood created by a particular environment"—something either in the air or within the mind. Small wonder that the term as now used is often so indefinite as to be meaningless. *Luscious fabrics emphasized the ambiance of luxury and warmth that ran all through the collection.* An atmosphere cannot run through anything or be emphasized. What is meant here is *general effect, impression,* or *suggestion.*

ambiguity. Those who come fresh to questions of usage often wonder: When does ambiguity matter? They notice that many words sound alike (homonyms) and can thereby provoke doubt or contradiction. *Toast,* a solid, is eaten in the morning and *a toast,* liquid, is drunk at night. Such similarities of sound rarely cause confusion. Why then fuss about other ambiguities when a little thought about context will show what the speaker or writer meant? *A woman with a snub nose appeared to conduct him to the door marked Private.* It takes little time to decide that she did conduct him and did not merely appear to do so. Is rewriting needed?

The answer is yes. The momentary halt, the bringing to awareness of two or more meanings, the look at the context or at the probabilities of the case are unwarranted demands on a reader's patience. And a writer who is habitually blind to the chances of even slight misreading will sooner or later produce a sentence in which the doubt cannot be resolved. *Those who venture to the canyon rim must be ready to check their pets / In the entire entering class there was not a single man to be found.* Likelihood may suggest that the sentence from the guidebook means that pets should be restrained; but *check* could also mean looking to their condition or surrendering them temporarily as one might a coat. As for the second sentence, it is anyone's guess whether no individual man or no unmarried man had enrolled. In short, many a common word loses its straightforward character when the company it keeps brings out some hidden weakness.

ambivalent. This pet word of amateur psychologists is already threatened with corruption and decay. A literary biographer discusses a writer's *early ambivalence between poetry and prose,* and this misuse is encountered frequently enough to prove that the term does not fill but usurps a place in our thoughts. *Ambivalence* does not mean indecision between different objects or desires; it means a state of simultaneous attraction and repulsion. An ambivalent lover is not one torn between rival affections but one teetering between love and hatred of the same person. *I can neither live with her nor live without her* is the characteristic declaration of ambivalence. A punctilious use of the noun occurs in the following: *Such is the ambivalence of educational researchers that very often their recommendations (for discontinuing homework, for example) run counter to their experimental findings.* The noun *ambivalence* is also misused when the intention is to say AMBIGUITY: *B. is ambivalent* (= undecided); *there is ambivalence* (= ambiguity) *in everything he does.* The words in parentheses here are not only the ones wanted; they are stronger and clearer than the pseudoscientific *ambivalent, ambivalence.*

among. See BETWEEN 1.

ample. Unmodified, *ample* means *large enough* or *roomy enough*—sometimes *more than enough*. The author who writes *a niche in Mount Washington's hall of fame ample enough for his sturdy frame* is committing not only the misdemeanor of unwanted rhyme but also the sin of redundancy. *Ample enough* is just as bad as *adequate enough* (see ADEQUATE).

Because it suggests absolute size and amount in the abstract rather than the concrete, *ample* should not be used to suggest a particular quantity. One says *a man of ample means* and *the provisions were ample* but not *spaghetti ample for twelve.*

analogy, analogous. See PREPOSITIONS.

and. A prejudice lingers from a bygone time that sentences should not begin with *and*. The supposed rule is without foundation in grammar, logic, or art. *And* can join separate sentences and their meanings just as *but* can both join sentences and disjoin meanings.

Also, on the other hand, is not a linking word and should not be used as if it were. *Also* is an adverb that suggests similarity of form or manner. (Hence the combination *and also* is not, as some think, redundant.) *Also* can therefore begin a sentence only if it qualifies some word or phrase in that sentence: *Also present were* / *He found the living-room lights still on. Also noting a faint odor of gas, he paused.* But not: *He graduated with high honors the following June. Also he married immediately, to everybody's surprise.* The last sentence should begin *And he* or *And he also.*

See also BUT.

and/or. Only a lawyer can prove beyond a reasonable doubt that legal documents need this expression; anyone else is entitled to the view that it has no place in ordinary prose. One such intrusion may stand for all: *A majority of the tourists come here with camping and/or fishing on their minds.* Suppose this is written *with camping or fishing on their minds.* Any sensible reader will presume that some camp without fishing, some fish without camping, and some do both, nothing being said or implied to prevent the three equal possibilities. Note, besides, that these possibilities would be the same if *and* alone had been used.

We see in this example one of the usual effects of borrowing language from the professions: it obscures the sense of the plain words fit for the case. In this case *and* is fit to suggest *or*, and *or* will generally include *and*. The weatherman's *snow or sleet tomorrow* is no guarantee that we shall have only the one or the other. The phrase EI-

THER . . . OR was invented for situations in which it is important to exclude one of a pair.

Indeed, if the users of *and/or* were as logical as they pretend to be when they insist on the legalism, they would have to say *and or or*, since their assumption is that the two cannot coexist. The writer who thinks readers have been so corrupted by the abuse of *and/or* as to misunderstand a simple *or* should courageously repudiate the hybrid and write—using our first example—*tourists come here to camp or fish or both.* Let us remember that, lawyers excepted, English speakers and writers have managed to express this simple relationship without *and/or* for six centuries.

See also SLASH, THE.

-ant, suffix. See RESOURCE PERSON.

antecedents. 1. An antecedent almost invariably comes ahead of the pronoun that represents it; *ante* means *before*, affirming that the antecedent comes first. And it must be unrivaled, unmistakable, the only substantive that its appointed pronoun could refer to; not merely "the one that makes sense," not "the one I meant," but the only one.

Neither precept is observed in this example: *I did not see it that way as a student, but the basis for the success I've achieved in life was my education.* This says that the speaker when young did not know what produced his or her success thirty years later. To find out the writer's meaning, we must find the antecedent of *it*. Clearly, the pronoun

I, although it comes first, is not what *it* stands for. Looking at the six nouns that follow, we cannot imagine that *it* stands for *way* or *student* or *life* or even for *basis*; no one can see the base of what has not yet taken shape. Likewise, one cannot see *success* that has not been achieved yet. We deduce that *education* is the antecedent of *it*, and what the writer meant was: *As a student I did not see the importance of my education, but it has been the basis of the success I've achieved in life.* This is not a splendid sentence, but no one could fail to understand it.

A pronoun that points to some person or thing not yet named is a puzzling distraction. But a pronoun that tries to represent a verb or an adjective flouts both grammar and logic. In this example *it* tries to claim the verb *browbeat* as an antecedent: *They thought they could browbeat the lawyer, but she refused to take it seriously* (refused to take their bullying seriously). A railroad station in Texas used to display the warning *Don't spit on the floor,* to which some wag had added: *Spit on the wall and watch it run down.* Graffiti may need no analysis, but notice that *spit* is used here as a verb, and *it,* once again, tries to treat a verb as a noun. Likewise, a pronoun may try to represent a noun that is working, for the moment, as an adjective, as *shark* is here: *In the old days no shark fishing took place, and they were caught only occasionally* (and sharks were caught only occasionally). Again: *Washington State is the largest per capita small-boat market in the nation. Many of these are built in Anacortes* (Many

small craft are built). The remedy when a pronoun lacks a competent antecedent: drop the pronoun and supply the noun you need.

2. It is not only pronouns that try to assume a relation to false antecedents. Observe an attempt by the adverb *there* to treat the adjective *Oregon* as a noun: *An Oregon draft bill to limit the use of a pesticide there has drawn opposition from farmers.* For *there* to represent a specified place, the sentence must say *In Oregon a draft bill,* etc. (Or one could simply drop *there* and leave the sentence as it is.) In like manner, the demonstrative adjective *that* too often tries to link its adjoining noun to a spurious antecedent, here the adjective *Scottish: She has loved everything Scottish since her childhood friendship with a man of that practical, plainspoken people* (of the practical, plainspoken Scottish people).

3. Perhaps the possessive noun is the part of speech most often mistaken for an antecedent. *On the Vice President's arrival at Kennedy Airport, he explained to reporters that . . .* The pronoun *he* could represent *the Vice President* (no 's), because both are in the nominative case. But the possessive *Vice President's* is no *he*; it serves as an adjective. Rewrite: *The Vice President, on his arrival . . . explained.* To be sure, a possessive noun can be the antecedent of a possessive pronoun, since *both* act as adjectives: *The Vice President's explanation was made on his arrival.*

4. An antecedent noun used in a general sense will not link itself to a pronoun used in the particular: *The*

town has known little crime since 1995, and so this one is all the more shocking. Here the noun *crime* means the general condition of crime, whereas *one* refers to a particular crime earlier mentioned. The statement is best rewritten so that noun and pronoun are both particular: *has known few crimes . . . and so this one,* etc. Again: *Students of science who are not already concentrating on one* (concentrating on a particular science).

5. A pronoun that tries in one sentence to stand for two antecedents will end up representing neither. *The usual reviewers heaped the film with praise; it helped sell tickets in the first weekend but wasn't enough to keep it from failing thereafter.* The first *it* refers to *praise,* but the second one means *the film.* A similar switch of allegiance occurs in a memoir: *The crowd disrupted the proceedings three times, its* (the crowd's) *conviction of injustice outweighing any hope that it* (the injustice) *might be corrected.* A writer who avoids repetition wherever possible might use *its grievance* instead of reiterating *injustice.*

6. Negative forms derail an antecedent as readily as they do other parts of a sentence. (See NEGATIVES, TROUBLE WITH.) The preface to an admirable biography claims: *There is nothing in the book which has not already been published in some form, but some of it is, I believe, very little known.* What can *some of it* be except some of the nothing which has not already been published? Much simpler to begin with an affirmation—*Everything in the book has already been published, but some of it,* etc.

At times an antecedent, though duly put ahead of its pronoun, lands in an obscure position. *A full year of law school came before his first solo concert, during which he saw what his lifework should be.* Did the subject glimpse his lifework during law school or during his first solo concert? The pronoun *which* is drawn to the subject of the main clause: *year.* But all pronouns are likewise attracted to the nearest substantive—which is *concert.* Reading on, we find that it was during the concert that the subject foresaw his future. Conclusion: *concert* occupies a murky place in the sentence at hand and must be moved to a place where its pronoun can readily claim it: *After a full year of law school, he played his first solo concert, during which he saw what his lifework should be.* The tie between *which* and *year* is broken as soon as *year* becomes what *concert* had been: the object of a preposition. *Which* bonds at once and alone with *concert.* A principle emerges: antecedents are firm and unmistakable when they are the subjects or objects of a preceding verb; they are feeble and dim when they are the objects of prepositions.

A last example of misplacement shows an antecedent shrouded twice over: *Meanwhile, in letters to his sister and brother, he trimmed his account of recent events to suit the stories he had woven for them over the years.* The two commas signal that the phrase they enclose is of little importance—even though it contains the antecedent of *them,* which is *sister and brother.* That antecedent is obscured again by being made the object of the preposition *to.*

To put important words where they cannot be missed, rewrite: *Meanwhile, in letters he told his sister and brother of recent events, trimming his account to suit the stories . . . for them over the years.*

7. "Make a pronoun agree in number and gender with its antecedent." All college grammar books carry versions of this rule, with two refinements. (a) When antecedents are collective nouns, naming a group—*audience, crowd, family, mob, band, team,* etc.— they are most often thought of as singular and take singular pronouns: *The band was at the top of its form, and the audience responded with its own high spirits;* but when members of the group are acting as individuals, the antecedent is treated as a plural: *The family discussed their differences all the time and wherever they went / One by one the jury wrote their votes on slips of paper.* (b) Antecedents like *no one, anyone, everybody, who, any, nobody, someone, one, each, either, neither, kind, sort, person* look singular and are; each calls for a singular pronoun: *Which one was it that you wanted? / Judged among other inaugural addresses, neither was thought to have flown from the chamber and into the hearts of its hearers / Each had its custom-made frame and its proud position on the wall / The kind we want is short-haired and low to the ground, its disposition thoughtful.*

Some dictionaries and books on usage note excellent writers who once in a great while gave plural pronouns to singular antecedents. A sampling: *But God send everyone their heart's desire!* (Shakespeare); *Everyone in the house were in their beds* (Henry Fielding); *. . . it is too hideous for anyone in their senses to buy* (W. H. Auden). This pairing of singular and plural goes on all the time in colloquial speech. But no esteemed writer of English, early or late, has been cited as using this oddity page after page, in work after work. Rather, some grammarians point to it as one of the dodges by which to avoid an age-old convention now widely opposed: the linking of a figurative *he, his, him,* and *himself* to antecedent pronouns like *everybody, anyone, any,* etc., and to antecedent nouns: *Anyone driving tonight had better keep his eyes on the road / No former resident of Atlanta would think himself in the city he had known / In our own society the artist is an exceptional person, and has to . . . keep his soul his own / A visitor unwilling to follow the route as prescribed had better know what he's after.* For centuries readers have assumed that the forms of the pronoun *he* in such statements referred to both males and females. And writers have assumed that the figurative pronouns were unimportant parts of the statement.

The writers of the following almost certainly shared these assumptions: *To throw off this straitjacket is the recurrent dream of the modern novelist, after the age . . . of thirty or thirty-five; before that, his dream was the opposite: to come to New York (or Paris or London) to meet other writers / . . . No one who saw them do "The Continental" or watched the great, tense, seductive dance they perform to Cole Porter's "Night and Day" has ever quite forgotten* The Gay Divorcée—*even if he thinks he has.* Statements like these by the novelist Mary McCarthy and the film critic Pauline Kael are thought by some feminists to "exclude" women novelists and women moviegoers. Some theorists see—or tell us that readers see—the figurative *he* as referring only to men, although such literal reading would be new in the history of English. Some college textbooks on grammar instruct the student to ban the figurative masculine pronouns in every context. These books advise: (a) change antecedents and pronouns from singular to plural (*Anyone driving tonight had better keep his eyes on the road* would become *Persons driving tonight had better keep their eyes on the road*); (b) rewrite the sentence to omit the pronoun (*had better steadily watch the road*); (c) change the masculine pronoun to paired masculine and feminine (*keep his or her eyes on the road*). But having suggested pairing, these textbooks then warn that its frequent use will prove "annoying" or "stylistically awkward." *The Random House Handbook* adds the recommendation that a student writing an essay substitute *she* for the figurative *he* throughout; the reader "will become quickly adjusted to the change," the authors assert. The *Harbrace College Handbook* adds that the writer avoiding the figurative *he* can change a sentence from the active to the passive voice; but the authors immediately warn that statements in the passive tend to be wordy and weak. As it happens, that particular change does worse than to weaken our test sentence: *Eyes had better be kept on the road by anyone driving tonight.* And the use of paired

pronouns would ill serve Kael with *even if he or she thinks he or she has.*

The assumption behind all this confusing advice is that cultivated writers and speakers have agreed to shun an age-old convention. The evidence suggests instead that many practicing writers choose their pronouns for reasons of economy and sense, not in obedience to prohibitions. The writers of the following samples from recent print (five of the nine are by women) assume the reader's knowledge that restaurant patrons, parents, cooks, readers, and the generalizing *no one, everybody, who,* etc., all include women, though the writers use forms of the figurative *he*: *No one is ever going to leave the XYZ Grill saying that he has just eaten the greatest meal of his life / A cynical reader might reflect that at a certain point every parent in the world discovers with dismay that his children are foreigners to him / The cook may have spent years relying on recipes, thereby losing—or perhaps never developing—an instinct for using salt and pepper. Or the cook may be impervious to his own taste buds / Anyone who wanted to sponsor a parent or grown child as an immigrant would have to have an income of at least twice the poverty level for his family . . . / The man A. married (and separated from after many unhappy years) was—the reader who doesn't already know this will fall out of his chair—B.G. / Having worked his way through D.'s treatise, the reader is led to ask . . . why the Anglo-American academic world has bought into the "lie" so enthusiastically / Who isn't fat and depressed—or at* least doesn't think he is fat and depressed—in New York? / Usually the [electric] charge is strong enough to bring the captive to his knees / If anyone needs further proof that the House of Representatives is behaving recklessly when it undermines the nations' . . . pollution laws, he will find it in the federal report.

In these statements he is everyone — nonspecific—and so attracts no attention. Compare this passage: The [World Wide] Web . . . bestows a curious mixture of personal power and humbling populism upon its users. For $20 a month, the cost of an America Online account, anyone can become her own broadcast network. Yet she does so knowing that she's only one of thousands upon thousands of people spouting off. Many readers automatically imagine a particular yet indistinct female, not the cipher that the figurative he has for centuries been. Trying to convey the experience of undifferentiated thousands, the writer instead distracts by carefully designating a female. The reader duly notes that the writer bears women in mind; but that unremarkable fact has nothing to do with use of the World Wide Web. Likewise distracting is a writer who tells us how to be courteous to the blind: Speak when you enter a blind person's room . . . Only take her hand if she offers it to you. Let her know if you are leaving . . . When showing a blind person to a chair, place his hand on the back. He will seat himself . . . When changing a blind person's money, let her know what each bill is. We need no heavy hints to remember

that blindness afflicts both sexes. Laboring what everyone knows, the writer sees to it that his useful tips on courtesy are forgotten.

Much contradictory advice and awkward contriving could be saved if English had a common-gender pronoun in the third person singular, like they in the plural. Inventions to achieve this symmetry have included co, E, et, heesh, he'er, heris, hir, hizer, ho, im, iro, ne, nis, ons, s'he, (s)he, thon, and many more. The public wants none of them. The British feminist Brigid Brophy points out (quoting the linguist Mario Pei) that Hungarian has just such a word to mean he, she, and it but adds that "Hungary is not a discernible jot more sex-egalitarian than Britain or the USA." Still, those who believe that by changing an English idiom they change women's lot will go on asserting that the figurative he is no longer figurative and is not to be used. Those who think that changing English idiom is a long way around to a good social end will use common sense and give words in a sentence due weight as before. (For more on excessive literalness, see also WHAT IS "UNDERSTOOD"?)

8. Just as they is unfit to represent a singular antecedent, so first- or second-person pronouns will mismatch with third-person antecedents: Whenever a father asked for leave to take care of his child, they showed you (him) no consideration / How could the neighbors know that she needed help when we (they) never got so much as a greeting? / Who could play the ardent suitor when some dolt on your (his) left was

fulminating into a cell phone? Note that *who,* by itself a third-person pronoun, obligingly takes on the person of its antecedent: *to me, who am* (not *is*) *a skeptic in these matters / They insist on talking to you, who believe* (not *believes*) *in him.*

When the pronoun *one* stands for everyone or all persons in a known category, it should not act as the antecedent to another pronoun: *Back then, one embarked upon pregnancy for general "fulfillment" but found herself* (*oneself*) *in the end with a very particular baby / The complaints seem extravagantly sweeping, but one senses also that he* (*one*) *must not dismiss them entirely.* The British are severe in denouncing the American habit of *one . . . he*—and no less steadfast in braving the repetitions that *one* often sets in motion: *One is entitled to do as one likes as long as one does not trample on one's obligations to one's fellows.* Such a sequence can sound labored and fussy to Americans, making them jump to some other pronoun after the first *one.* The misgiving is apt, the solution not, since a doubt can arise whether *one* and *he* are the same person: *One can't make one's point with this anecdote if he offers too many embellishments.* Is *he* a bystander or the speaker? Where following through with *one* would entail too much repetition, forgo it in the first place; use instead *we, you, no one,* etc., and proceed accordingly.

One works differently when it is not indefinite but about to be identified clearly, as in *one who* or *one from among others: One who thought so*

should have his head examined / one who frequently lost his temper / Of the two, one lost her job, and the other, etc.

Lastly, *one another* requires simple arithmetic: *The two singers set off one another to perfection* but not *Each club has five games remaining but will not meet one another again* (but will not meet the other again).

9. Probably *which* and *this,* of all the pronouns, are most often paired off with ineligible antecedents. *It should be remembered that not many of the local workers can afford the luxury of paying for cable television, which can amount to a day's wages.* The writer may think that *which* stands for the gerund *paying,* but that would give us *paying can amount to a day's wages.* The true antecedent would be *the cost of cable television*—which is not in the sentence.

Often these pronouns bravely try to lasso a preceding, bulky idea or sentence: *Because the lottery attracts the poor more than anyone else, it has been called a regressive tax, which it is.* Here *which* has no trouble encircling a brief noun phrase that is standing nearby. A sentence may prove more elusive: *The trick we rely on to make him cheerful and talkative is to cook him a steak. But this should not be overdone.* Not the steak but the sentence should act as an antecedent to *this;* therefore reword the sentence to make it a unified subject: *Cooking him a steak to cheer him and make him talk is a trick that has always worked. But this should not be overdone.* Editorialists too often wield the unaimed, encircling *this: The State Department has said it will consider such action when the necessary legal procedures have been completed under the treaty. This is now being done* (when the legal procedures necessary under the treaty, and now under way, have been completed. On *being done,* see VOICE 2) / *Crude partisanship has on the whole been admirably restrained. The congressional leadership can take pride in this* (in this restraint) / *Countries that suffer the maltreatment of dictatorship for many years cannot recover quickly and easily. This is a part of the heavy price that must always be paid for the evils of tyranny* (this helplessness? inability? time lag?).

The dependence of modern writers on the unaimed *this* can hardly be overstated. (The unaimed *that* is only somewhat less relied on.) The author of a standard biography uses it in the third, fifth, eighth, and ninth sentences of his preface—four times in twenty lines—and often throughout five hundred pages thereafter: *He was near a crossroads in his life, and he did not know which road to take. We might guess this* (the first fact? the second? both?) *from his literary juvenilia.* The remedy is implied by the queries in the reader's mind: turn the pronoun *this* into the adjective *this* by adding the appropriate word—*this letter, this awareness, this predicament,* or whatever the true antecedent turns out to be in a backward glance.

anticipate See DEFENSIBLES.

anxious, eager In the Age of Anxiety, one should welcome chances to call by their right name feelings that are free of the blight. To say *I'm very anxious to see you* plunges us back into the pit. Surely the unwelcome emotion should not accompany the wish to see a friend. Instead of *anxious,* say: *I'm eager.* When eagerness seems excessive, there is always *I want (very much) to see you.*

anymore Once a law-abiding word, *anymore* now keeps bad company in speech. Its right place is in negative statements and in questions: *We don't shop in the Square anymore, not since the prices went sky-high / Does the train stop at Ellenville anymore? / Will J. be batting anymore, considering the condition of his knees?* The young in particular hear in *anymore* a simple synonym for *now.* Hence such statements as *It's all right to go to Carnegie Hall in jeans and a shirt anymore / Anymore we spend most of our time at the mall.* Such speakers miss the fact that *anymore* casts a glance either backward or forward in time. In the question about the train, *anymore* implies both *now* and *as the train used to do.* What *anymore* implies about the baseball player is *now and in the future.* As a synonym for *now* alone, *anymore* is wrong.

apart from. See ASIDE FROM.

apostrophe, the. Most often the apostrophe marks the possessive case (Homer's *Iliad*) or the omission of a letter in a contraction (*didn't*). Indeed, using the mark for the possessive began as a way of showing contraction: singular possessives once ended in *es* but lost the *e*, an apostrophe taking its place. By extension the mark now shows possession in plurals, after an *s* if there is one (*actors'*) or before an added *s* if there is not (*children's*); it also converts to possessive some words that have never ended in *s* or *es*: *woman's*, *Berlioz'*, *beaux'*, etc. Nouns and names whose *s*-ending is permanent take the possessive apostrophe always —and leave us wondering whether to add another *s*. Should we write *Evans' photographs* or *Evans's photographs?* The fact is that both are correct, and the writer may choose the one that his ear prefers.

The possessive pronouns ending in *s* (*its, yours, ours, hers, his, theirs*) take no apostrophe—unlike the indefinite pronouns, which become possessive by taking on both the mark and the *s*: *a room of one's own, someone else's opportunity, nobody's business.* Some measures of time are idiomatically spoken of as having the power to possess, just as if they were persons: *six months' leave without pay, four weeks' vacation, a week's extension, an hour's delay.*

The apostrophe has been stricken by fiat from the names of certain institutions and organizations: *Teachers College, Merchants Bank, Authors Guild,* etc. This departure from common habit seems arbitrary, though one can read into it a wish for a "real" name as opposed to a description. One hopes that what is gained proves worth the trouble of correcting the uninformed.

Another wide use of the apostrophe is to make plurals for special occasions: *the 1990's, the three R's / an increase in MD's / cross your t's and dot your i's.* But more and more writers find no logic in the mark in the first three uses shown; hence *1990s, three Rs, MDs,* and their like are increasingly seen— although *cross your ts and dot your is* follows logic into nonsense.

In other uses the apostrophe marks both dialect speech (*lyin' coward*) and missing letters (*sicklied o'er, e'en now*) as part of its contractive function. *O'clock* is contracted *of the clock,* and *O'Casey* is *of* [descended from] *Casey.* The mark also casually forms the past tense out of otherwise intractable words (*K.O.'d in the third round / In her youth she had been Beethoven'd and Bach'd to within an inch of her life*).

See also POSSESSIVES 1, 2, 4.

appreciate, esteem. 1. It is too late to try to hold *appreciate* to its primary and logical meaning: *measure the worth of, put a correct valuation on.* But writers who, for themselves, do hold that line will not employ *appreciate* as a loose synonym for *like, enjoy, approve, take pleasure in.* This latter use has the effect of all other heedlessness with language: it leaves better words idle, impoverishes the vocabulary, and works toward diminishing the common pool of words. This result is even more noticeable when *appreciate* is used negatively. *I don't appreciate people putting words into my mouth* is intended to mean that the speaker dislikes such presumption. *No one appreciates being interrupted when he is absorbed in his work* tries to say that the experience is annoying. Surely *dislike* and *annoy* are clearer than *don't appreciate*.

When the baggy sense is used affirmatively, *appreciate* often gathers to it quantitative words that war against its meaning. We usually *appreciate very much* or *more than we can say*. Yet once it is known that the verb means *to put a just valuation on*, such modifiers look inept; one sees better reason to use the word in its proper and unmodified sense.

That sense is unmistakable: *We appreciate the difficulties of your position* can only mean that we understand these difficulties and have taken their measure. Hence a *literary appreciation* ought to be an exact critical analysis, but it often turns out to be merely a favorable review. "Appreciation" courses in art and music have earned a bad name because the term has come to suggest conventional opinion and gush. If we mean to be clear, *appreciate* should most often be replaced by either a synonym of *enjoy* or a synonym of *understand*.

The business use of *appreciate* (= rise in value) is a specialized use, which in its context will not be misunderstood.

2. The verb *esteem* gives rise to a comparable confusion through its two meanings: (a) regard with great respect, and (b) assess, or assign a value to. The first sense is expressed in *Have much and thou shalt be esteemed much*, the second in *Mankind, by the perverse depravity of their nature, esteem that which they have most desired as of no value the moment it is possessed*. The second sense will be given unambiguously by the verb *estimate*.

See also DEFENSIBLES; PRONUNCIATION 1.

approach. See FORBIDDEN WORDS 2; METAPHOR 3.

approbation, approval. There is no wide agreement on the difference between these words. They are so nearly the same that anyone can justify preferring the second for being the shorter. Still, some careful writers reserve *approbation* to mean a favorable response on a particular occasion; they employ *approval* to denote a general favoring attitude. A man's character has our approval or disapproval, a given act of his has our approbation or disapprobation. Thus *His fiscal policy has met with widespread approval, but his most recent speech on the subject will hardly bring general approbation*.

Note that in the sense of official concurrence and ratification, *approval* is the standard and invariable word. The meaning is neutral and carries no idea of praise. Hence it would be eccentric to replace it with *approbation* in *My memorandum received immediate approval* or *In this organization many a good idea fails to win approval*.

apropos. See PRONUNCIATION 2.

archetype. See PRONUNCIATION 1.

area. See UNNECESSARY WORDS 2.

arguable. Although several centuries old, this word is flighty and should be left to its wayward ways. Dictionaries disagree over whether an *arguable* point holds up, can be argued, can withstand scrutiny—or whether it is dubious and open to argument. Able writers have long supposed that what was *arguable* stood a good chance in debate; but able readers have for just as long thought *arguable* meant *debatable* in the sense of being open to question. The careful writer today will bypass the slippery adjective and write, instead, *The point can be argued.* What is open to question will remain *debatable*—and so will the use of *arguable*.

around. The argot of the young in the latter part of the twentieth century drafted a few prepositions into unaccustomed work. The aim was vaguely poetical, as slang sometimes is. The hardiest of these bent links will probably prove to be *into*, as in *Jennifer is into exercise.* The trick with *around* is to use it where *about* might be expected: *Give us your thoughts around marriage / We're excited around driving all night to get there.* That this usage hopes to hang on is suggested by the catalogue of a museum exhibition: *Media fascination around black masculinity is always concentrated in three areas: sex, crime, and sports.* But the use of *around* for *about* has begun to do what most slang does: it dates the writer and stales the thought.

arouse, rouse. Most often *arouse* means to summon up or provoke a pronounced feeling—tenderness, pity, fury, admiration, desire, suspicion, fear. With less vivid effect, one *rouses*

oneself or another creature from apathy, sleep, or inaction. *Rouse* resembles *prod*. When the disturbance is indistinct in kind—*The dogs are gentle except when roused*—the two words are often interchanged. But the adjective *rousing* stands alone and is strong in meaning: a *rousing* cheer, never *arousing*.

See also MALAPROPS.

articulation. Some of the small English words (THE, AS, THAT, the PREPOSITIONS) act as joints between neighboring words, setting their relation to each other and thus pinning down their meaning. By itself the placement of a word or a phrase can buttress an otherwise drooping sentence. Attending to such jointing and placing is called *articulation*, and the reader will find its many forms discussed in AND/OR; AS 11; DIFFERENT(LY) THAN; DOUBT; HAVE; HOPEFULLY; IN FOR BY 2; IN TERMS OF; LIKE 1; LINKING; MEANINGFUL; RESPECTIVE; SAME; SO THAT; TELESCOPINGS; THAT, WHICH; UNNECESSARY WORDS; UP TILL; -WISE; WITH. Also A, AN, THE 5; FUSED PARTICIPLE; GERMANISMS; -ING 1; REIDENTIFICATION; SCIENTISM 4; SEQUENCE OF TENSES; SLASH, THE; TO; WHICH and AND WHICH.

as. 1. *As* for *being*. 2. Missing *as*. 3. *As far as . . . concerned, goes*. 4. *As much as or more than*. 5. *As* in negative comparisons. 6. *As of*. 7. *As regards*. 8. *As* (= since). 9. *As such*. 10. Unnecessary *as*. 11. *As to*. 12. *As well as*. 13. *As with* for *like*.

1. *As* for *being*. Some of the shortest

words make the most trouble and the most kinds of trouble. *As* may be the busiest of these, and no account of its mischief can be complete. *As* is absent where needed, present where it has no use; it occurs as a misfit conjunction; it leads to endless mismanagement in various set phrases; and it works in insidious ways to derail locutions in which it has the sense of *being, in the role of, in the capacity of.* For example: *as a tax-paying citizen, as a narrow-eyed skeptic.*

Such phrases beginning with *as* will often come at the beginning of sentences—and there inhabit a grammatical void: *As a man of peace, there could be no more effective way for him to protest.* For the subject of the phrase to go anywhere, it must be asserted again, and immediately, in the ensuing clause: *As a man of peace, he could find no more effective way to protest.* If the subject is not reasserted when the main clause begins, the *as* phrase dangles as surely (or unsurely) as any so-called dangling participle. (See DANGLERS.) The following slippages are succeeded by suitable rescues: *As a* Times *subscriber and an ardent reader of your column, kindly tell me where to write for a sample copy of* . . . (Kindly tell a *Times* subscriber and ardent reader) / *As the son of a noted sculptor-educator, his talents were fostered* (Because he was the son of) / *As a boisterous and quarrelsome youth, they foresaw that his presence would cause endless trouble* (they foresaw that the presence of this boisterous . . . youth would cause).

In letter writing, the descriptive *as* phrase must connect with the right person: *I am writing to you as the mayor* is proper from voter to politician; *As mayor I am writing to you* is the campaigner writing to his constituent. But mere propinquity does not always serve. The headline INDEPENDENCE REJECTED AS WORKABLE FORMULA FOR ISLAND leaves the formula workable but unaccountably discarded. INDEPENDENCE REJECTED FOR ISLAND AS UNWORKABLE leaves no apparent contradiction. Consider *As a completely new, responsibly edited, unabridged dictionary, no other work can rival it on its own ground.* Write the first eight words and you are irrevocably committed to *it* as the ninth—or to some other word for the dictionary in question. The main clause must be about the dictionary, not about *no other work.* A direct statement covers the subject: *This new, responsibly edited, unabridged dictionary is unrivaled on its own ground by any other work.*

2. Missing *as.* A person is known *as* So-and-so; this or that is described, depicted, characterized, or shown *as* such-and-such. With these verbs the *as* is necessary to sense and idiom—even in clauses that are already introduced by the conjunction *as.* But in these very clauses the second *as* is mistakenly omitted by writers who think the first *as* has handled the matter: *Brother Frank, as he was forever after known.* No one with an ear would want to write *Brother Frank, as he was forever after known as,* yet the sense requires the second *as.* One solution: change the verb, using *as he was forever after called.* The same alteration works with

Ginny, as she was known as to (called by) *her friends. The coach was neither so harsh nor so eager a faultfinder as he had been described* can be spared the final *as* by the simplest expedient —omit *he.*

Along with verbs of portrayal, verbs of saying or perceiving—e.g., *view, see, regard, refer to*—may also require *as* for idiomatic completion, and are maimed without it. *I view the development of a comprehensive and effective training program one of the prime duties of my office* (add *as* after *program*) / *The other question is how important his superiors regard the case* (add *as being*) / *You see young Sean Casside, as the autobiographer refers to himself, learning the pain of hard physical work and the pleasure of Shakespeare and Shaw* (use *as the autobiographer styles himself*) / *Your editorial can be seen in no other way than a spiteful personal attack on President B.* (*in no other way than as*). These wordings err by treating *regard, see,* etc., as synonyms of *consider* or *deem,* which in themselves incorporate the work of *as.*

3. As far as . . . concerned, goes. Rambling speakers stretch this idiom so far that it snaps and lets go of the verb altogether. Here the form is used correctly: *As far as I am concerned, the baseball season ended yesterday,* meaning for all I care; *As far as that* (the subject at hand) *is concerned, you can do what you like,* meaning as far as I have any say in the matter; *As far as cleaning up goes, you can forget about J.,* although cleaning up is not thought of as going far. The second and third sentences could be shortened by saying *Concerning that* in the second and *Concerning the cleaning up* in the third. But to some, *concerning* has an impersonal ring. To easily distracted speakers, *as far as . . . concerned* is an invitation to maunder. They will find such unwieldy subjects to stuff in the middle that when the verb arrives, the listener no longer remembers how the sentence began: *As far as getting the car off the roof of the Student Union and back to its owner unharmed is concerned* / *As far as putting in a full day's work after getting the children to school and dropping off the laundry and leaving the cassette deck at the repair shop goes, I think I deserve an award.* With this habit, a train of thought cannot be preserved. The speaker stumbles forward blindly and falls before uttering the verb: *We must make clear to all parties that we will hold fast as far as trade sanctions until one or another comes forward with a plan for composing their differences* / *As far as getting to Yosemite with one bald tire and a dead turn signal, the chance seemed rather a long one.* Here we see at work twin capacities for absentmindedness and wind. *Concerning* would help the first sentence a little, but *hold fast to* would help more. The second sentence ought to begin with *The chance of getting to Yosemite.*

4. As much as or more than. Were we to omit the second *as,* this skeleton would lack a necessary bone. *They had as much and possibly more influence on our history than a like number of generals and statesmen.* The writer of this sentence has unwittingly set down *as much . . . than*, perhaps from a wise but vague wish to avoid the unwieldy *They had as much as and possibly more influence . . . than*; retaining both halves of the construction produces a two-headed creature as little at home in prose as a + sign. The quickest surgical rescue is to pick the construction apart and handle its two aims separately: *They had as much influence on our history as a like number . . . and possibly more*. But this operation does not always succeed with all double forms: *A government education expert said today that some students who had taken classes over television had received grades equal to those of students attending regular classes or even better*. By the time this sentence toils to a close its meaning has disappeared. One revision might be *received grades as good as those of students attending regular classes, if not better*; here the warring *equal to* and *better than* have been banished, although *if not* is hopelessly ambiguous. (See IF NOT.) The best revision might be *grades equal or superior to those of students attending regular classes*.

It remains to suggest that most awkward juggling of two-way constructions can be avoided by not attempting to say too many things at once. Ingenuity is spared by sorting out one's ideas before putting them on paper. (See also PROSE, THE SOUND OF 4.)

5. *As* in negative comparisons. American English differs from the parent tongue in shifting from *as* to *so* when stating a negative: *This summer is not nearly so hot as last*. An English

writer would invariably use *as . . . as* —causing an American editor to pounce on a repetition that makes no hint of difference in meaning.

6. *As of*. This jargon for specifying a date has become so popular that many people think it the only way. The fact is *as of* has no use other than to assign an event to one time and the recognition of it to another. It is standard for making privileges retroactive, as in a letter dated November 1 that promotes an employee *as of* the preceding July 1. The happy implication: four months of additional salary. Academic documents refer to those who took degrees in 1996 *as of* 1995.

The phrase may also have point in a March 1995 report on the fiscal year 1994, or in a projection of current trends to some date in the future. But it is useless in *The business outlook in the Pacific Northwest as of mid-October*. Write *in* or *at* mid-October. Other common misuses: *earned $18,064,122 in this country alone as of July 12* (up to July 12) / *As of December 31 the amount received or pledged* (By December 31) / *Candidates must be under 45 years of age as of the deadline date for applications* (on the deadline date).

As of makes no sense when the time specified is the present. *I feel strongly that the league should consist of eight teams, at least as of now* (at least for the present). / *There is little doubt that, as of the moment, the Democrats are way ahead* (at the moment) / *The governor, at a news conference, asserted that as of now he did not know which candidate he favored* (did not know as yet). The prize for ineptitude in this class goes to the report in a medical bulletin: *The doctors now think that as of now he will be able to go home tomorrow.* Delete *that as of now* to discover the plain sense.

7. *As regards.* This clumsy compound preposition enhances no one's style. Ostensibly a means of singling out a subject for special emphasis, it has the actual effect of smuggling a subject in or of stealing up on it from ambush. *As regards the tenants, the implications of the law are somewhat different. For the tenants* is more lucid and direct. A like example: *As regards his competence, I am not in a position to judge* (I am in no position to judge his competence).

Variants of *as regards*—e.g., *as concerns, as relates to, as affects, as respects, as touching, as to*—display the same sidling awkwardness.

8. *As* (= since). The novice's resort to *as* with the meaning *because* or *since* is always feeble and makes trivial what follows. Notice how the link ruins emphasis on what are clearly serious matters: *It was a comparatively unproductive year, as he was dogged by ill health and by worries about his children.* For *as* read *for.* With repetition of the device, the following sentence limps on both feet: *A good business might be built up by spraying trees, as most individuals would sooner pay a fair price for this work than undertake it themselves, as it is expensive when done as individual work.* Here the important idea is merely glanced at in a subordinate clause; then a subordinate clause gives a glance at the glance

until emphasis tapers down to the vanishing point. To reconstruct: *A good business might be built up by spraying trees: most persons would rather pay a fair price for this service than undertake it themselves, for it is expensive as individual work.* The colon, which points to a following explanation, takes care of what was poorly done by the first *as;* the *for* builds up strength where the second *as* tore it down.

Some writers still employ the causative *as* precisely because it diminishes the reason assigned: *As it makes no difference to you, I will take the later train* / *They played the full chorus again, as the audience seemed to enjoy it.* But a weak link should rarely be chosen where a stronger one will do.

9. *As such.* This phrase can mean something or nothing; the difference depends on the writer's alertness. *A military expert as such has no business pronouncing on this sort of question.* This implies that the military expert may have something to say as a person of judgment, or as a citizen, or as a student of history, or as a Presbyterian, or as a New Englander, but that military expertise is irrelevant. Suppose, however, that we say: *Theology as such is helpless before these questions.* As what else, the reader asks, would theology not be helpless, and would it then be theology? *The automobile as such revolutionized our idea of a practicable shopping distance.* No one is likely to suppose that it was as a toy or as a status symbol that the automobile transformed the idea. What may have been cloudily in the writer's mind was *the automobile by itself.* A novelist who

helped a politician with his campaign speeches described his employer as *a fine writer but, as such, too intellectual.* The *as such* is difficult to construe if it means anything but *as a writer,* and in that meaning it either contradicts or says nothing at all.

The front matter of a desk dictionary has an *as such* that is baffling in both grammar and meaning: *The dictionary has combined the facts about the frequency of occurrence of different meanings that were tabulated by scholars with the judgments of experts in choosing the senses of each word that were to be discriminated and classified. As such, the dictionary utilizes the last forty years of scholarship in vocabulary selection and discrimination in the choice of senses of words to be defined.* The strangely Germanic first sentence seems to be saying that the meanings defined were chosen according to (a) their statistical frequency of use and (b) expert judgment of their importance. *As such* probably means, then, something like *in combining these two factors.* If so, why not say so?

The foregoing misuse of *as such* is not much removed from commoner botches: *Mr. R. yields to no one in his loathing of Matisse. As such, he has attracted much fire from other critics* / *I will give you my best recollection, but as such you must not assume that it is the whole truth.* Grammatically *such* in *as such* behaves like a pronoun and must refer unmistakably to a noun or noun phrase previously mentioned. It is clear in the sentences above that neither *Mr. R.* nor *no one* nor *Matisse* nor *I* nor *you* is a *such. Recollection* might

be a *such,* but so flighty are pronouns that the magnetic *you* in *but as such you* exerts its pull and all grammatical sense is sent flying. In the first passage, Mr. R. attracts fire *for this reason* (that is, for his loathing), nothing to do with *such;* in the second, the phrase *as such* has no meaning at all and should come out.

10. Unnecessary *as.* Too many *as*'s will damage a style; too few will spoil sense. (See AS 2.) But notice how the sense also escapes as the style of the following sentences collapses. *La Mancha was one region that, as she saw as soon as she began to read, they could afford to skip.* This sentence will stay on course with the *as*'s removed and one other adjustment: *La Mancha was one region, she saw the moment she began to read, that they could afford to skip. As between a bemedaled buffoon as corrupt as the Army and a self-styled economist with crackpot ideas no choice was possible* (omit *As*) / *has concluded that Great Britain might as a member emerge as more influential* (omit the second *as*) / *The failure to recognize the ambitions of other groups as being as real as one's own seems all too common* (to recognize that other groups have ambitions as real as one's own).

In the following, *as* does no perceptible work at all: *He was appointed as representative* / *You are designated as ballot clerk* / *She was elected as treasurer.* (See also EQUALLY 1.)

As can also take the place of the concessive *though*—witness the cliché *unaccustomed as I am to public speaking* and many workaday phrases: *sick as I was, much as I hate to do it, silly as it sounds,* etc. The only difference is that *though,* slipping less readily off the tongue, is more emphatic. Perhaps to give *as* the same degree of emphasis, some writers use it with a concessive sense and prominence that are no longer idiomatic: *As fond as I am of him, I think he is wrong on this issue / As convinced as they were of his innocence, the evidence given by this witness left them shaken / As busy as the Smiths were, they insisted we visit them / constantly remind us that as tiresome, as inconvenient, and as expensive as it may be, we must observe the bylaws to the letter.* Here every *as* that precedes an adjective is superfluous.

The unnecessary *as* has the further effect of derailing the reader when a proper *as* introduces a comparison. *Some of these emancipated young executives, as indifferent as they pretend to be to status* is subtly ambiguous. Are we to think them fully as indifferent as they pretend to be—a comparison? Or have we here the concessive form with a needless *as—young executives, indifferent though they pretend to be?*

The beginning *as* is necessary to a true comparison. *Glib as a candidate for office* can mean: (a) all candidates are glib; (b) glib while running as a candidate. If the intended meaning is *no less glib than,* use *As glib as . . .*

11. As to. Questions, doubts, and problems should never be *as to whether;* there is no reason why they cannot be simply *whether* or, with a following noun, simply *of.* Omit *as to* in the following: *Replying to a question as to whether there would be war / the question as to what would happen if /* *The doubt now arises as to whether this idea can be expanded / The problem arose as to whether some of the drivers might cheat and use another kind of motor oil / has put forth the question as to how much Iran dominates.* Here *of* goes with a following noun: *There is some question as to his eligibility* (replace *as to* with *of*).

Other words than *question* and *problem* call forth the stammering *as to. There was no mention as to whether the Nationalists had fired back* (no question whether) */ But the clubs in the other league have absolutely no interest as to who wins the National League pennant* (no interest in who wins) */ For the next twelve hours the mystery deepened as to what had happened to the ship and its crew* (what had happened . . . was a deepening mystery).

Clues are idiomatically *to,* not *as to.* Omit *as* in each of the following: *This article also gives valuable clues as to the items to be sold / This, in turn, will give us a clue as to the size of the universe.*

The word *doubt,* whether noun or verb, is followed by *whether* or *if* in clauses, by *of* in phrases, and never by *as to: Wright doubted if his kindness would be returned; he had doubts whether she had noticed it, and had no doubt at all of her anger.* Hints, indications, proofs, evidences, intimations, statements, opinions, confessions, etc., are normally *of.*

As a replacement for *about, concerning,* etc., *as to* should be watched; it tempts to jargon and waste. There is nothing wrong with *As to that I'm not certain / his remarks as to local police work*. But it is simpler and therefore right to say *about* in the first wording and *on* in the second. To put a subject in the emphatic leading position (*As to the selling of drugs* / *As to the distribution of this aid*, etc.) some writers find *as to* useful; at least it does not foolishly distort, as *in the case of* does (see CASE). But *as to* often drags with it *the matter of* and similar prolixities; it should be watched.

12. As well as. a. Various locutions, of which this is probably the most useful and popular, allow the writer to tuck in additional subjects before a verb in such a way that the grammatical number of the subject, and hence of the verb, remains unchanged. Other expressions of this class are *in addition to, together with, along with, besides, and not alone, like*. Any of these could be used with little alteration of meaning in this typical sentence: *The graduate school, as well as the college, is* (not *are*) *forced to increase its* (not *their*) *tuition*. Here is, in fact and in logic, a plural subject, but in grammar and usage a singular one. The phrase *as well as the college* is taken to be off the straight line running from *graduate school* to *is*, as if the sentence were written: *The graduate school is compelled . . . and so is the college.*

When the tucked-in addition happens to be plural, we discover that *as well as* does not hide the mild conflict so deftly as similar expressions do. *The Environmental Protection Administration, as well as local governments, has agreed to cooperate.* Replace *as well as* with *like* or *together with*, and the awkwardness disappears. In effect, then, *as*

well as comes closer than its substitutes to a simple *and*, which would make the subject compound and the verb plural.

One reason for this peculiarity of *as well as* is that it carries the implication of *and not alone*. In *the graduate school, as well as the college*, etc., the suggestion is given that we already knew, or expected, that the college would raise its tuition. A writer who wished to run the presupposition before the statement would begin *Along with the college, Like the college*, etc. To begin a sentence with *as well as* is unidiomatic; some expressions are unalterably sequential, not introductory, and this is one of them.

Despite the overlapping of *as well as* and *and*, the first is not to be coupled with *both*. *We have seen both an increase in cloying ads for the Postal Service, a seduction unheard of thirty years ago, as well as a measurable drop in the speed with which the mail is delivered* (omit *both* or replace *as well as* with *and* or *and also*).

b. *As well as* sometimes intrudes through absentmindedness. The following statement of parallels ought to use parallel verbs but does not: *For little if any sacrifice in comfort, I can save in miles per gallon as well as losing less per year in depreciation*. Change *as well as* to *and* and the need of *lose* becomes apparent.

13. As with for like. *As with* gives no trouble when making a straightforward parallel: *With work boots, as with shoes, you will need two pairs of socks in this weather* / *My talks with Anne, as with Barbara, were thoroughly pleasant*. In these examples, the *as with* phrases contain the following ellipses: *as* (you will need) *with shoes* / *as* (were my talks) *with Barbara.* The unwritten words—ready to hand just ahead—fall into place in the reader's mind as each sentence unfolds. Trouble starts when careless writers hastily stick a secondary subject into a sentence by using *as with* as glue: *As with France, Germany sent no troops to join the United Nations forces* / *Sherbet, as with applesauce, seems to give her a rash* / *To keep older children out of the playground, there should be a sign, as with unleashed dogs.* In these examples, no adjacent words supply the unwritten links, for nothing observable is *with* France, *with* applesauce, or *with* dogs. The logical link in the first two is *like: Like France, Germany sent,* etc. / *Sherbet, like applesauce,* etc. The third example needs *as* and a clause: *there should be a sign, as there is about unleashed dogs.*

as, connective. See SAME; SUCH 2; SUFFICIENTLY.

as, like. See LIKE 1.

as such. See AS 9.

as with. See AS 13; LIKE 1.

Asians. See CHANGING NAMES.

aside from, apart from. As idioms these two phrases are interchangeable; in fact, they are so alike that they share two radically different meanings.

To begin with, both phrases mean *besides* or *in addition to,* as in *Aside from her adroitness as an administrator, she played a game of pool that was the envy of the Austin division* / *Apart from the threat of reprisals, we must consider the chances of harming the captives.* But both phrases also mean *except for, with the exception of: Aside from his defense of the strikers, his career was commonplace* / *Apart from the abundant refreshments, the whole proceeding was a failure.* Given the ability of these idioms to slide between dissimilar meanings, the writer must ensure that context (as in the foregoing sentences) makes the meaning clear. Now consider a sentence about Texas at the turn of the century: *Apart from the one-cent piece, the dollar bill was unknown in the Southwest of those days.* The writer here means *in addition to,* but the sentence suggests *except for,* as if the one-cent piece were a kind of dollar bill. And consider this even more baffling sentence, about a seventeenth-century architect, from an encyclopedia of art: *His paintings, aside from the summary allusions* (references?) *of contemporary biographers, have been wholly forgotten.* Here *aside from* means neither *in addition to* nor *except for,* and the sentence suggests that the biographers' references (see ALLUDE) were among his paintings; in fact the sentence was meant to say that without these references we should not know that his paintings had ever existed. The writer should have said something like *His paintings, now known only from.*

Apart from and *aside from* can also point to mere separation, physical or mental. In these uses the phrases cause no confusion.

ask. See PRONUNCIATION 1.

associate. See COLLEAGUE.

assonance. See PROSE, THE SOUND OF 2.

assuming. See DANGLERS, BENIGN.

assure, ensure, insure. The second and third of these verbs are widely treated as interchangeable; but most writers prefer to reserve *insure* for protecting the worth of goods and *ensure* for guaranteeing results. Those buying or selling insurance invariably say they *insure*. The dangerous confusion arises when *assure* is thought interchangeable with the other two words. *Assure* means promise, cause (someone) to count on. In the active it takes no preposition: *I assure you that you are wrong.* In the passive it takes *of*: *assured of a fair hearing. Ensure* means make (some future occurrence) certain or reliable, and is normally followed by *that*: *His present lead ensures that he will not be overtaken*; or by a direct object, as in *Exorbitant bail ensures his appearance in court. Assure* is wrongly used for *ensure, insure* in the following: *He took steps to assure that these islands will not be a "thorn in the side of peace"* / *Richards assured cooperation on the part of the tenants by discreetly passing out small sums of money* / *Our investment in five more guards assures that the crate will travel safely.*

asterisk. See PRONUNCIATION 1.

astronomical. See CONNOTATIONS.

at about. The *at* in this phrase is usually unnecessary. *About* by itself can be (1) an adverb meaning *approximately*, and (2) a preposition meaning *near, almost at, concerning. About* acts as an adverb in the following sentences, where any urge to embellish it with *at* should be resisted: *He awoke ( ) about 6:25 a.m. and smelled smoke* / *( ) about the same time Cubs fans watched their team come from behind* / *He was negotiating with some of the regulatory agencies ( ) about the time the gifts were made. About* is a preposition in *Keep your wits about you* / *a sermon about charity.*

True, there are occasions when *about* in its adverbial sense needs *at* to make sense: *Mail this week is running at about the same rate* / *At about 100 miles, the earth's atmosphere virtually disappears.* But *at* is also used sometimes in ways that seem designed to show up its uselessness: *The additional revenue required will be at about $100,000,000.*

at its best. See SET PHRASES 2.

at risk. See VOGUE WORDS.

-athon, -thon. These bits of the place-name *Marathon* have been seized on as if they were adjectival suffixes that mean long-lasting. What then is *Mara-* thought to mean? The full word *marathon* has of course become official for a foot race of 26 miles,

385 yards—the reference being to the feat of Pheidippides, the courier who brought the news from the battlefield in 490 B.C.—and its extension to such uses as *dance marathon* is natural and perfectly clear. But when part of the word is taken as a free building block we get merely senseless hybrids. A *telethon* is supposed to mean a campaign, designed in various ways to solicit telephoned pledges to a charity. But along with such coinages as *walkathon* and *sale-a-thon* it means no more than that the coiner thinks English needs the help of mistaken Greek to convey meaning. Other scraps of Greek—see SCIENTISM—are taken as pretexts for similar formations, equally specious.

See also SPIRIT OF ADVENTURE, THE; TELESCOPINGS.

attend, tend. See DANGEROUS PAIRS.

attributed. See TRANSITIVE, INTRANSITIVE.

augment, supplement. Augmentation is the increase of something homogeneous. A supplement is the addition that results from putting a second thing with the first. Thus there need be no complaint with *He augments his height by wearing cowboy boots.* The subject's height simply increases with the enhancing boots. But no such thing can be said of statements like these: *He augmented his regular salary by occasional shrewd speculation / The hatcheries turn out 7,000,000 wall-eyed pike, to augment natural*

reproduction / a brief main text augmented by four elaborate appendixes. Each of these increases is a supplement, not an augmentation. A salary is not raised by other sources of income; natural reproduction is unaffected when artificial reproduction is added to it; a main text stays the same length no matter what other elements are added to it. In short, we do not augment one thing by creating a supply of another. The way out of the illogicalities quoted above is to find an inclusive term for the sum of things added together: he augmented his *income* by adding the gains of speculation to his salary; the hatcheries increase the *number* of pike by adding those cultivated to those naturally reproduced; the contents of a *book* are augmented by adding other texts to the main one.

autarchy, autarky. See SPELLING.

author, verb. See UNNECESSARY WORDS 1.

average. An average, in common speech, is the arithmetical mean of two or more quantities, determined by dividing their sum by their number. It is clear that if one piece of writing is four hundred words long and another six hundred, their average length is five hundred words. It is also clear that if we try to assign an average length to one of them alone, we have a contradiction: *These stories, which average about 500 words apiece* (omit *apiece*) / *Each of the travel pieces is short, aver-*

aging only three or four pages (The travel pieces are short, averaging . . .) Still, we can say that the *average story* is so many words long, or that a particular story happens to have a length which is at or near the average.

It is easy enough to guess what is meant by the foregoing examples, but what does a weather forecast mean when it states: *Rainfall during this period will total on the average over one half inch occurring as showers Sunday or Monday?* It would be hard to invent a more puzzling phrase than *total on the average* or to fashion a "scientific" sentence more resistant to analysis.

Note in addition that *average* must be treated as one of the ABSOLUTE WORDS. Two or more averages can of course be compared; but one average cannot be treated comparatively, as in *a completely average upbringing.* An average upbringing must be one indistinguishable from the general run of upbringings and therefore not more or less or completely average.

For the statistician, there are three forms of average—the mean, as defined above; the median; and the mode. These two additional forms need not concern the writer who is not dealing with calculations in science or social science.

avid. This word is short but not as sweet as journalists think. It describes an unseemly desire, a greedy hunger, a graspingness. How then to imagine *the perfect resort for the avid golfer;* or the appetite of the woman described as *an avid dog lover?* And does the col-

umnist mean what he says in describing a lawyer as *an avid supporter of the Democratic Party?*

avoid. See TRANSITIVE, INTRANSITIVE.

awed, awesome. In passing use as adolescents' slang, the adjective *awesome* is intended to describe what leaves the observer awed. But the love of an extra syllable is a powerful force, and it had its way in the memoirs of an ex-ambassador: *I gained an awesome regard for the ability of the Soviets to achieve their economic and military goals.* Since it is doubtful that his regard gave rise to awe in others, one assumes that he meant he was *awestruck.* Strictly speaking, *awesome* is the same as *awful* but has been given a benign connotation.

ax to grind. Whoever has an *ax to grind* has unadmitted purposes to serve. The metaphor was coined by Charles Miner, in his *Essays from the Desk of Poor Robert the Scribe* (1815), as follows: "When I see a merchant overpolite to his customers, begging them to taste a little brandy and throwing half his goods on the counter— thinks I, that man has an ax to grind." Our present vogue phrase for almost the same idea is the worn-out *hidden agenda* (see VOGUE WORDS). Many people think an *ax to grind* is a complaint, a dislike, an objection: *As far as he was concerned, there was no further ax to grind between him and the Browns.* This statement about the end of a feud has missed the apt metaphor *bone to pick*, which refers to outright contention, not to ulterior purpose. It is not a counsel of perfection but simple good sense to advise a writer not to make use of a SET PHRASE he does not have firmly in mind. The writer who neglects the advice risks not knowing what he has said.

See also CAKE; CRACKS; HARD PUT; RUBBER; SPIRIT OF ADVENTURE, THE; STONE.

B

babysitter. See TRANSITIVE, INTRANSITIVE.

back formation. This term refers to the modern habit of making verbs from nouns by shortening: *enthuse* from *enthusiasm*, *reminisce* from *reminiscence*, *donate* from *donation*, *convalesce* from *convalescence*, etc. These four are the most often used, but *enthuse* is the least accepted, perhaps because, unlike the others, it can claim no Latin verb in its past. *Burgle* from *burglary* and *sculpt* from *sculpture* began by being facetious, but they are frequently found with serious intent in print. The first still sounds comical and can be replaced by *burglarize* if *break in* is not satisfactory; the second should be *sculpture* (verb). *Reune*, for *have a reunion*, is low-grade American slang.

From the adjectives *groveling* and *lazy* the verbs *grovel* and *laze* were formed in the sixteenth century and have stood the test of time.

background. See FORBIDDEN WORDS 2.

bad, badly. See ADVERBS, VEXATIOUS.

balance, noun. This accountants' word should not displace the formal *remainder* or the informal *rest*. In the following sentences the natural word is *rest*: B. *drew a suspension for the balance of the racing season* / *The balance of the show was not particularly distinguished* / *replaced by United Nations troops, who remained throughout the balance of the year* / *and prepared to live there the balance of our lives.* In these sentences *remainder* would be correct but might sound stiff.

These strictures about *balance* do not apply to such standard phrases as *balance of power* and *balance of payments*, which denote not a remainder but an equilibrium.

barbiturates. See PRONUNCIATION 1.

barely . . . than. See HARDLY (SCARCELY) . . . THAN.

barring. See DANGLERS, BENIGN.

basal, basic. See ENDINGS.

based, -based. The notion that one is *based* where one lives or works derives from the military JARGON of the Second World War: forces stationed at a military base on X Island were said to be *based* there. JOURNALESE likes this *based* for its terseness, but some readers find its CONNOTATIONS distracting. Is a poet *based in Maine* battle-ready? What chain of command shipped *Chicago-based trumpeter N.* to the banks of Lake Michigan? No one would say, *My aunt is based at the Rosewood Retirement Community,* or *I understand that your grandparents came here in 1970 from their base in San Juan.*

Everyday print is cluttered with other souvenirs of carnage. Persons hoping to lend dash to an endeavor, however peaceable, mimic the wartime code names for secret armed undertakings. Titles formed on *Operation This* and *Project That* abound, and are thereby publicized, *not* kept secret. No less grandiloquent is the title *Task Force,* a group of armed forces assembled for a single task. We hear of a Recycling Task Force as often as we read of an Operation Get-Out-the-Vote. Pomposity is always out of place, and the tone is decidedly out-of-date.

based on. 1. Meaning. 2. Usage and misusage.

1. Meaning. To see why able writers shun this phrase, one must look at it with fresh eyes. *Based* is the participle of the verb *to base,* which is a synonym for *to set* and *to rest,* as in *The sculpture is set* [or *based*] *on a hollow cube of bronze* / *Wright designed the house to rest* [or *be based*] *on a lightly wooded incline.* Here we have physical things resting on physical bases. For many years, idiom has let us extend the phrase from the palpably physical to the realm of ideas and artistic creation:

I base my remarks on the report of the rules committee / *G.'s new historical novel is based on the Lewis and Clark expedition* / *Her theory is based on experiments conducted at the National Institutes of Health* / *Based on a North German folk song, the third movement features the woodwinds.* Here, in figurative usage, some remarks, a novel, a theory, and music "rest on," respectively, a report, an event, experiments, and a folk song. But note that figurative language must maintain literal relations: the imagination sees in these statements precisely what is "resting" on what.

2. Usage and misusage. Writers whose minds are not nearly literal enough flood American writing and speech with what no one can imagine. The following samples of the off-base *based on* will, by their number, suggest how broad is the inundation. *Based on my experience, seafood is the best bet among entrées* / *The crowd is young, self-consciously costumed, and most likely hearing-impaired based on the decibels they tolerate hour after hour* / *In the 1980s, the American Heart Association advised cutting back sharply on egg consumption based on the belief that dietary cholesterol raised the risk of heart disease* / *In the same novel, courtiers fall in or out of love based on the quality of a lady's penmanship* / *Based on the weather patterns of the last seventy-five years, America's farm areas may suffer devastating droughts* / *Based on your age, you can buy up to $5,000 in coverage for a very affordable cost* / *Prosecutors cannot eliminate prospective jurors based solely on their race* / *Each library will decide what time lim-*

its to impose on Internet cruisers based on demand / America's top companies will send you [discounts] *on top brands based on your answers to this survey / Based on this information, it is safe to say that the risk of transmission of HIV between prisoners is very high / The carpenter was arrested based on statements he made in confidence to fellow members of Alcoholics Anonymous / The job of Presidential spokesmen is to assert that, based on their faith in the President, nothing untoward could have occurred / "Based on their own documents and the history of medical ethics, they clearly knew that the studies were unethical," Dr. E. said.* / A headline: CORNELL DORMS BASED ON RACE ARE THE FOCUS OF AN INQUIRY / *For noise problems, inspectors use decibel meters; about odors they decide based on their noses.*

In these samples we are called on to see, among other wonders, a crowd *based on* decibels, courtiers *based on* penmanship, and inspectors *based on* their noses. To repair just these three bits of nonsense, try *The crowd is young . . . and judging by the decibels they tolerate / courtiers fall in or out of love according to the quality of a lady's penmanship / inspectors . . . decide with their noses.* Elsewhere in these sentences, the participial phrase tries to do the work of *because of, in line with, considering,* and *assigned by.* In short, *based on,* in new figurative uses, fakes a relation between two things when the writer cannot be bothered to see that relation clearly. Hence the epidemic use of the phrase in second-rate writing. (For a similar counterfeit link, see IN TERMS OF.)

One kind of sentence suggests how *based on* may first have spun free of the grammatical order: *Police have been able to draw a few conclusions based on the evidence so far gathered / The staff made an independent decision based on the facts at hand.* These writers mean that conclusions (not the police) have been based on evidence; and that the decision (not the staff) was based on facts. But to readers whose mind's eye is dull, it seems just as likely that police can rest on evidence and a staff on facts.

Based on is so overused that, as often happens, both its right and its wrong use encourage the wrong—a good enough reason for writers to give the phrase a wide berth. Some risk the literal and figurative uses set forth under 1, but with circumspection.

It may be argued that misuse and overuse have battered the figurative *based on* into what rhetoricians call a dead metaphor, i.e., one whose literal meaning no one any longer hears (examples: *branch* library, *bolt upright, cinch*). But this attempted reprieve ignores the fact that *based on* has acquired a fatal penchant for ambiguous reference. The phrase seduces lawyers (*We will discredit any such charge based on malice and deceit*) and bankers as well (*Earn up to 2 percent money back based on your annual level of purchase*). In most uses the phrase is hopeless and best left alone.

See also DANGLERS 2.

-bashing, suffix. See VOGUE WORDS.

basically. Many writers have described American speech and prose as emphatic to the point of bluster. Mark

Twain and H. L. Mencken were but two local authors who relished what they saw as the American style of "tall talk." But at present our speech displays the opposite traits, a hesitancy and meekness, of which certain adverbs and adverbial phrases give the tone. The bland VERY and *really* can hardly be called intensives, and our *pretty*'s, *sort of*'s, and *kind of*'s have never colored but only restrained the words in their charge; a *good thing* does not get better by becoming a *pretty good thing*.

More than any other adverb, *basically* marks the style of groundless apology. When it has a point to make, *basically* means *at bottom* or *fundamentally* and much the same as *in essence* and *on the whole*. Yet in speech its purpose today is mainly to dress up statements the speaker himself is afraid are wrong or dull—forgetting that few things are duller than meaningless sound. *I was basically doing my homework / Their kids basically play with my kids / She basically asked if she could come over.* It hardly needs saying that nothing in these examples is reduced to a base or an essence. Here is rather the give-and-take of our everyday lives, which requires no decoration.

Basically is likewise stuffed into speech and writing to cushion a statement the speaker thinks is too downright: *Basically, R. didn't like her family / A lot of people were just, basically, silent.* Notice the bashful stammer. Sometimes the effect of the nervous adverb is grotesque: *S. keeps up a brisk pace in various beds while, at home, M. waits, basically, to die /*

Their battle jackets were inadequate, and any flak that struck them would, basically, kill them. These are words that on the whole or at bottom would rather not be heard.

For more on self-disabling speech, see SPEAKING LIKENESS.

basis, on the; basis, on a. *On the basis of* and *on the basis that* threaten to usurp the functions of *because, for the reason that, for the sake of, on the condition that, by means of,* and simple *for* and *by*—whose work these *bases* do badly, as bureaucratic English shows. A manual issued to copy editors by a publishing house explains: *The various forms shown are recommended on the basis of clarity, acceptability, and practicality.* Why not *recommended for their clarity,* etc.? The same source warns: *Given names that are spelled out in copy should not be changed to initials on the basis of their being so shown in the catalogue*—which means *because they are so shown,* etc. In *Applicants will be judged on the basis of their grasp of first-year fundamentals,* change *on the basis of* to *by*.

If *basis* must be used at all, it should be as the basis *of* something. (See BASED ON.) But it is frequently allowed, in defiance of idiom, to introduce a *that* clause: *The candidates agreed to the debate but only on the basis that each can deliver a summation at the end of the program* (but only on condition that) / *the objection that some members raised on the basis that they had not been consulted* (some members raised; namely, that they had not been consulted).

The American shyness of adverbs

makes us depend on the windy phrase *on a* [something or other] *basis*. What happens every day can be described briefly and neatly by *daily*. What continues goes *continuously*, and the intermittent occurs *intermittently*, or *is intermittent* pure and simple. But many a pompous writer thinks qualifying adverbs and adjectives, brisk and acting alone, somehow lack the gravity of a static and abstract noun. And so we get *on a daily basis, on a continuous basis, on an intermittent basis*, and the allotted space runs out too soon or the listeners shuffle and yawn. "I'm glad you like adverbs," wrote Henry James to an admirer. "I adore them; they are the only qualifications I really much respect."

because. See AS 7; COMMA, THE 7; REASON . . . BECAUSE; SINCE, YET.

become, come to be. These two expressions seem as nearly synonymous as any pair in English; one would be hard-pressed to detect the difference between a politician who *becomes* a power in the party and one who *comes to be* such a power. Yet even as it ensures comprehension, idiom sometimes capriciously raises walls, as this illustration shows: *Such gatherings are becoming on the scale of military maneuvers* does not sound like English, but *are coming to be on the scale* goes down readily enough. The reason is obvious: *to be on a scale* is intelligible, whereas *to become on* one is impossible to imagine. In short, *come to be* can generally do duty for *become*, but the converse is not always true—one more reminder of the principle that,

under close analysis, there are no complete synonyms.

before. See AGO; NO SOONER . . . WHEN.

beg, with infinitive. See CONNOTATIONS.

begging the question. See POPULARIZED TECHNICALITIES.

beginning. See DANGLERS, BENIGN.

behaviors, plural. See POPULARIZED TECHNICALITIES.

being. Inexperienced writers are tempted to use the participle *being* as a sort of lubricant. Example: *At least eight kinds of trees will grow on the streets of New York, with Norway maple, the London plane tree, and the honey locust being the most frequently seen.* If *being* is to be kept, the sentence should omit *with* (see WITH); if *with* is to be kept, omit *being*. A disjunction would be more workmanlike than either version: *At least eight kinds of trees will grow on the streets of New York; the Norway maple, the London plane tree, and the honey locust are seen most often.* When *being* is used needlessly it acts as grit, not oil. *He lifted his right hand, his index finger being extended like a gun barrel / The whole little army, it being mostly Calabrian mercenaries, embarked in five vessels.* Omit the useless *it being* in the second example and *being* in the first. But note that *being* with a causative meaning has good, economical use: *Being* (= because he was) *a patient*

*man, he merely shrugged / The eye of
the storm being now past us, the wind
whipped around / Human nature being
what it is, this timidity might have been
expected.*

belabor. See MALAPROPS.

belie. Watch closely this useful
word for *misrepresent, contradict, deny,
give the lie to.* Lying is central to its
meaning. The speaker who says *You
come from Georgia, unless your speech
belies you* assumes that your accent
tells the truth of your origin; i.e., does
not tell a lie about you. And when
Shakespeare's Leonato in *Much Ado
about Nothing* learns that his daughter
is slandered, he says *thou hast belied
mine innocent child.* A reviewer writing
*The student singers' performance belied
their amateur standing* ought to mean
that the singing was so fine as to rule
out all thought of unfinished training,
but he may have meant *reveal* their
amateurishness. *Belie* should therefore
be made clear by its context. If it isn't,
it joins the similar word *betray* in
hopeless ambiguity. Of a man who
speaks one way and looks another, we
are likely to say, *His look betrays his
true intentions;* i.e., discloses what he
intends. But from his side he could as
well say, *My look betrayed (= falsified)
my meaning.* Because the ambiguity of
betray is now incurable, *belie* should
be kept to its first and irreplaceable
meaning of *misrepresent.*

bête noire. See FRENCH WORDS AND
PHRASES.

betray. See BELIE.

between. 1. *Between, among.* 2. *Between each.* 3. *Between . . . or.* 4. *Between . . . to.* 5. *Between adrift.*
   1. *Between, among.* The preposition
between takes a good deal of battering
from those who are too fussy about it
and those who are not fussy enough.
The underfussy too often ignore the
meaning of duality in the word: *-tween*
= *twain.* The overfussy too often want
between changed to *among.* The standard oversimplification tells us to say
between when two and only two entities are present, *among* if there are
more than two. But *between* is not
merely allowable, it is required when
we want to express the relations of
three or more taken one pair at a time.
Thus it would be overfussy and un-
imaginative to object to *between* in the
following: *the main stumbling block in
the present delicate exchanges between
Paris, Athens, and London.* The exchanges almost certainly consist of
messages from each capital to each of
the others, not of identical and simultaneous presentations from each to all.
   When three or more persons converse and each speaker addresses all
the others, *among* is accurate and
clear. *Between* is wrong in the following: *The invasion was discussed at the
house of de Tassis, the Spanish ambassador in Paris, between de Tassis, the
Bishop of Glasgow, the Duke of Guise,
and Dr. Allen.* Whoever dislikes *among*
in such a sentence can sidestep it with
by.
   2. *Between each.* As was said, *between* contains the meaning *two*

(twain); any discrepancy, agreement, difference, love, gap, bond, clash, pact, or disparity lies *between* one thing and at least one other. The distributive *each*, to be sure, implies more than one—but undertakes to consider things one at a time. For that reason *between each* is a self-contradiction, as in: *She repeated it after him, a pause between each word* (pausing after every word) / *slowly read the codicil, pausing between each sentence* (between sentences) / *given five coats of primer, and hand-rubbed between each coat* (after each coat) / *Between each meeting there had been a gap of at least two days* (between meetings).

3. *Between . . . or.* The mind's eye sees, in two improbable sentences, why this construction fails: *Jones found himself standing between the gunman or the door* / *I must have dropped the wallet somewhere between the lobby or the third floor.* In statements more abstract, such as those using *choice* or *decision*, the error is not so readily seen: *The choice was between backing Coach G. or* (and) *searching for a coach the fans liked more* / *The choice too clearly lies between an honorable agreement by the three powers or* (and) *a disagreement that could plunge the small nation into civil war* / *Given the time of night and the prairie ahead we had to decide between chili with cheese or* (and) *slow starvation.*

Note that *choice between* is often redundant; *choice* can mean the act of choosing or the alternative posed. *Between* is implied by *choice* in *a choice of red and white wine.*

4. *Between . . . to.* Writers for radio and television have particular trouble with paired prepositions like these. Many know well enough that *and* goes with *between* as *to* goes with *from*. But in the rush of reporting too many fall between idioms. *These specimens are believed to be between 70,000 to* (and) *100,000 years old* / *between* (from) *80 percent to more than 85 percent profess a belief in God* / *northwesterly winds of between forty to fifty-five miles an hour* (omit *between*). On paper, inattentive editors will approve *between 1825–50* / *flourished between 1370–1400*; the hyphen does not mean *and* (or *to* either). They will also fail to ask a careless author whether *diaries she kept daily between 1858–61* is intended to mean *from 1858 to 1861, inclusive,* or whether the diaries end before 1861.

5. *Between adrift.* Sometimes a *between* construction leads its sentence into confusion. *The President distinguished between what seemed to him permissible for the Air Force but unnecessary for the Marines.* This seems clear as far as it goes: the chief executive drew a line *between* one course of action open to the Air Force though irrelevant to the Marines—and what? We wait for the name of the service to be compared to the Air Force, but it never arrives. The distinction intended was *between what was permissible for the Air Force and what was unnecessary for the Marines.* Such perversions of sense are not rare: *the difference between handling a regular client's account, as opposed to one closely tied to a franchise or dealer operation* (replace *as opposed to* with *and*; the opposition is already expressed by *difference*).

Occasionally, by sheer absence of mind, *between* makes a passage logically or physically impossible. *Sometime between 1889 and 1890 he began to see his problem in a new light.* Query: What time did he find between those two years? A famous author of crime fiction made one of her characters hide a will between pages 79 and 80 of a book, a feat that would strain the dimensions of our world. This blunder went unnoticed through all the editing and proofreading, and to a correspondent who diffidently remarked that several hundred others must have twitted her before him, she replied that he was the fourth in the two years since publication.

biological. See OLOGIES.

bitter. See JOURNALESE.

blacks, group name. See CHANGING NAMES.

blond(e). See FRENCH WORDS AND PHRASES.

bone to pick. See AX TO GRIND.

both . . . and. Like *either . . . or, neither . . . nor,* and *not only . . . but also,* the formula *both . . . and* sets up a parallelism of grammatical elements. Consequently, the kind of word that follows *both* must follow *and*: a noun for a noun, a verb for a verb. If the parallelism is faulty, the syntax limps. *The speaker put forward the argument that it is possible both to have human freedom and economic development.*

Here *both* is followed by an infinitive verb, and *and* is followed by a noun phrase. But the infinitive after *both* requires another infinitive after *and*; e.g., *both to have . . . freedom and to maintain . . . development.* What the writer probably had in mind was simpler: two noun phrases after *to have*; i.e., *to have both human freedom and economic development.* The more complicated the wording, the more attentive to parallelism the writer must become: *designed to protect both the interests of the city and of the suburban communities* (read either *both the interests of the city and those of the suburban communities* or *the interests of both the city and* (no *of*) *the suburban communities.* The surest way through this arrangement is to watch for the parts that match and to put the *both* immediately before the first and the *and* immediately before the second. But be careful that *and*, not *or*, follows *both*. Note: *We are equally baffled both by the brainstorm that produced this break with his past or* (read *and*) *by the courage with which he accepted all that followed.* See also MATCHING PARTS.

bottom line. See FORBIDDEN WORDS 2; VOGUE WORDS.

brackets, square. See PARENTHESES, BRACKETS 2.

bridegroom is now almost never used. The second syllable stands alone, grooms of the servant kind having all but disappeared.

broadcast. See MYSTERIOUS PASTS.

bureaucrat. See CONNOTATIONS.

burgeon. See MALAPROPS.

burned, burnt. See MYSTERIOUS PASTS.

but. 1. *But* for *and*. 2. *But* for *except*. 3. *But nor*.

1. *But* for *and*. As everyone knows, *but* signals a contradiction to something preceding or offers an exception to it. *And* ushers in a second way of making a point already made or else an application that reaffirms it. When the second way offers a mild sort of contrast with the original point, a hurried writer is all too likely to mistake the contrast for a contradiction. *The reviewer completely fails to understand what the author is driving at, but substitutes a preconception of his own.* The second statement does not contradict but extends and reaffirms the first, calling for *and* to link them, not *but*. For the same reason, each *but* in the following should be *and*: *Ravens and fulmars that have eaten the flesh of newly killed sharks may sometimes be so sick that they are scarcely able to fly, but tumble about erratically* / *Catching sharks did not begin in Greenland until the early part of the nineteenth century, but only a few were caught for a long time.* Only if the second sentence is reworded so that its first clause is affirmative and its second more logically ordered does *but* become the right connective: *Catching sharks began . . . in the early part of the nineteenth century, but for a long time only a few were caught.*

A negative beginning also misleads the writer of this sentence: *There was too much snow on the ground to allow him to shop except on one stretch of street, but* (and) *this too was filling up.* For the second clause to work contrarily to the first, the first must be affirmative: *So thick was the snow that he found shopping possible only on one stretch of street, but this too was filling up.* In such compound sentences, only the exception to an affirmative statement allows a *but*. (See NEGATIVES, TROUBLE WITH.)

But, yet, still, however—all are adversatives signaling a contrary statement. When they begin a string of neighboring clauses they produce a distracting zigzag effect: *But April still permits sledge travel, even if water is to be found in some places. But when you reach Disko Bay, you find that winter still rules there. Yet even here the seals have started coming up on the ice.* The *but* of the second sentence pretends to deny the main thought of the first sentence, but actually reinforces it; this *but* should be *and*. Make it so and you leave the adversative *yet* of the third sentence free to turn off at an angle from both of the preceding sentences without causing any zigzag.

A note on *however*: some writers think this word too large and heavy to employ where *but* will do briskly.

2. *But* for *except*. Confusion reigned for years among lexicographers about the right form: *no one but I* or *no one but me*? Most chose to join battle along a grammatical line: either *but* was a conjunction requiring the nominative (*I*) or it was a preposition, a

twin of *except*, requiring the objective (*me*). Hostages in this combat were two British authors, always cited: Felicia D. Hemans, for writing *The boy stood on the burning deck, / Whence all but he had fled*; and Cardinal Newman, for stating *I am one among a thousand; all of them wrong but I*. Proponents of the conjunction theory saw spectral word-age, "understood" but not written, completing a clause after the pronoun: *Nobody came but I (came) / No one could please her but he (could please her)*.

For their part, the prepositionists advanced a subtler argument, bringing in the demands of verb-and-subject agreement. Consider: *No one but the actors has read it / All but McDonald have left the field*. If *but* were a conjunction, *actors* would become a subject and require a verb in the plural: *No one but the actors have read it*. Similarly, *McDonald*, being singular, would require the singular verb *has*. The prepositionists argued well, but the dispute, in seeking the answer in grammar or logic, had been pointless from the first. Constructions like *all but he had fled* and *if it were anyone but him who had objected* are equally right because both are idiomatic.

3. *But nor* is a blunder that spreads in silence; it could never be spoken. And spread it does, even to a page in *The New York Times*: *But seven years later, things were at a stalemate. The British could not root out . . . the I.R.A., with its 400 or so armed men . . . But nor could the I.R.A. dislodge the 18,000 British troops in Northern Ireland . . .* Comprising two adversatives, *but nor* asks you to turn about-face twice in an instant. The cause of the error is quickly deduced: the writer thought of *but neither*, as in *neither . . . nor*, yet wrote *but nor*. To be sure, *but neither* itself looks like a double reverse. In fact, it is something less, for *neither* lacks the full negative force of *nor*, an adversative quite as blunt as *but*. No such flat contradiction is needed in speaking of two forces strong enough to thwart each other. *Neither* alone would have served.

But the fact that should strike us first is that *but nor* is two conjunctions jammed together, a contraption nobody needs. Who would write *and nor*? The fact is that many people do. Can *or nor* be far behind?

See also EITHER . . . OR.

by. See PREPOSITIONS.

C

cake, eating and having. To want to eat one's cake and have it too is the age-old statement of human greed for irreconcilable good things. A man who desires public office and a peaceful life should be said to want to eat his cake and have it, too. But almost always these days the speaker or writer reverses the order and talks of having your cake and eating it too, which is no trick at all; those with cake do it all the time.

See also COULD CARE LESS; CRACKS; FORT; LAY WASTE; RUBBER; SEA CHANGE; SET PHRASES; STONE.

calculated risk. See VOGUE WORDS.

cannot but, cannot help. See HELP.

canny. See UN-, IN-, NON- 5.

capability. See SCIENTISM 1.

capable. See PREPOSITIONS.

capacity. See PREPOSITIONS; SCIENTISM 1.

careen, career. The word for rapid movement or running wild was formerly *careering*; the word for heeling or turning a ship on one side was *ca-*reening. As *careening* in American usage took over the sense of running wild, *career* all but ceased to be used as a verb. As a noun *career* properly means an occupation affording likely advancement. It is often misused to denote almost any way of making a living.

case. When it retains the Latin sense of *casus*, what (be)falls or occurs, *case* does good work briskly; in most other employments it merely idles, posing cases where there are none. For nailing down a subject at the beginning of a sentence, a quick preposition is deft beside the slow *in the case of: In the case of the Rembrandt, the museum paid a million and a half* (For the Rembrandt) / *In the case of my companion, the staff could not have been more attentive* (To my companion). There are no cases here, nor are there in the following: *Now let us turn to the cases of the other three texts* (omit *the cases of*) / *In the case of your chiseling son-in-law, experience suggests two ways to surprise him* (Concerning) / *As was once the case in St. Louis, the preservationists here have turned a blind eye* (As happened earlier in St. Louis) / *In those who look solely to their own security, as in the case of the two landlords* (Those who, like the two landlords, look solely to their own security) / *Except in the case of oysters, all seafood is assumed to have been cooked* (With the exception of oysters). Too often *in the case of* is not a chosen connection but a dodge to avoid selecting a simple and precise one. (See AS 11; IN TERMS OF.)

Where the meaning is *happening* or *occurring*, *in case* and *in case of* stand beyond reproach: *in case of fire* / *in case of rain* / *in case you find yourself at loose ends* / *Take along a can of gas in case of need* / *In any case, we stand behind him* / *In no case will I change my mind*. Similarly, *case* meaning *argument* and deriving from law is clear and direct: *Let me put the case to you* / *The prosecution's case is flimsy* / *I warn you not to overstate your case* / *R. makes a good case for going ahead* / *Considering his weakened condition, a case could be made for unlawful imprisonment*. The case against *case* does not affect its concrete uses.

See also CHARACTER; COVERING WORDS; LEVEL; NATURE.

catalogue, catalogued. Near the end of the nineteenth century the American Library Association decreed that its members would drop *-ue* from all forms of *catalogue*. The mover behind this would-be rational stroke was Melvil Dewey, who invented the system of shelving books by numbers. As the twentieth century ends, the professional linguists have mechanistically extended Dewey's mischief; otherwise reputable dictionaries gave as interchangeable not only *catalogue* and *catalog* but also *dialogue* and *dialog*,

epilogue and *epilog*, *prologue* and *prolog*, *analogue* and *analog*. In common with many reformers, these failed to foresee where plausible ideas will go bad.

Although it is true that *-ue* in all such words is not pronounced, it is no less a fact that, to fit the pattern of spoken English, *cataloged* and *cataloging* should be sounded in their endings like *massaged* and *massaging*, *managed* and *managing*—not *logged* and *logging*. Thus to those new to English, *cataloged* and *cataloging*, like *gill*, *gibbous*, and *gerbil*, are puzzlers to pronounce. *Cataloger* and *astrologer*, librarians please note, now have something in common. If the linguists shrug off this effect of their "rationality" and decline to restore the historical *-ue* to all five words, let them double the *g* for the inflected forms.

The *-ing* form finds new popularity in the earnest use of *dialogue* as a verb. Seekers after ever-new arts to pacify the office, the home, or the heart are told by counselors to *dialogue with* antagonists or fellow sufferers. Skeptics wonder how this differs from *talk with*. Careful writers follow the skeptics in shunning this verb as a VOGUE WORD.

A bewilderment similar to that stirred up by *catalog* occurs with the failure to add *k* to certain forms of words ending in *c*. One comes across *picniced* and *panicing* and *mimicing* and wonders how new users say them. No doubt those who write these clipped forms think they are making things simple.

catalyst. See POPULARIZED TECHNICALITIES.

catch-22. See VOGUE WORDS.

category. See POPULARIZED TECHNI-CALITIES.

center around. Figurative language derived from Euclidean geometry ought not to flout Euclidean sense, but this phrase does. A clear mind can perhaps imagine *center in, on,* or *at,* but not the following: *Much of this activity centered around two auto stocks / A number of them center, in one way or another, around a girl named Mariette / Right now, this enthusiasm seems to center chiefly around homes, automobiles, and bridges.* Pivot *around* is a similar way of making the core surround the apple.

challenge. See FORBIDDEN WORDS 2; METAPHOR 4.

challenged. See EUPHEMISMS.

changing names. The names by which Americans call groups of other Americans began changing in the latter half of the twentieth century as groups in pursuit of their civil rights claimed the right to name themselves —more than once if need be. Slang and colloquial terms gave way to names judged more respectful: terms like *niggers* and *colored people* yielded to *Negroes,* and *fairies* and *dykes* to *homosexuals* (for men) and *lesbians.* Women in general had been called by casual and slighting terms (*broads, chicks*), and the educated dropped these in favor of *women. Ladies* was discarded for implying a weak and impractical refinement. *Girls* became

applicable only to females under eighteen.

Soon *Negro* as a self-descriptive noun and adjective was set aside in favor of *black,* yet the matter did not rest there; some black leaders urged *Afro-American* and *African American,* both of which found favor. But some black writers decline to use either of these terms on grounds that they scant the history of blacks from the West Indies or imply an African allegiance not felt by all American blacks.

Many homosexuals, disliking the clinical and polysyllabic name they bore, adopted *gay* from an earlier homosexual argot and used it as adjective and noun. Objections were raised to this forcing of an established word into a sense new to the public, but to no avail; *gay* proved a handy descriptive for both men and women, though in some official uses it is reserved for men, and *lesbians* are specified as such. (The original meaning of *gay—lighthearted* or *bright-colored—*is right now eclipsed except in writing that is decades old.)

People of Spanish-speaking descent had long been called *Hispanics* or (for *Latin* America) *Latinos;* now Hispanic women balk at the gender of the second term and wish to be called *Latinas.* The same distinction obtains between the *Mexican Americans* who style themselves (many do not) *Chicanos* and *Chicanas.* Some political speakers and writers find it useful to bracket as *Hispanics* those of Spanish, Mexican, and Latin American descent, always omitting the Brazilians, whose native language is Portuguese, not Spanish. Some writers link blacks, Hispanics, American Indians, and people of Asian descent with the catchall *people of color*. But the phrase ignores the fact that many thousands who consider themselves members of one or more of these groups are in color as "white" as, say, a Norwegian or Scot.

The change from the general term *Orientals* to the equally general *Asians* would seem to be permanent and agreed to by all concerned. Those whose ancestry is Chinese, Japanese, Southeast Asian, Korean, Indonesian, Filipino, etc., are now grouped as *Asian* lest *Oriental* (*oriens* = *east*) place their land of origin east of a geocentric West.

The new name taken by some American Indians may also be permanent but does not displace the old. Many descendants of those who were misnamed *Indians* (by Europeans looking for the *Indies*) have claimed the name *Native Americans* as suiting their status as an aboriginal people. But *Native American* fails to satisfy Indians who make common cause with indigenous peoples outside the United States; then too, some Indian writers find *Indian* (and *American Indian*) ratified by its usage for hundreds of years. Whether Indians from the subcontinent will wish to continue as *East Indians* remains to be seen.

As this sketchy account tries to show, CONNOTATIONS cling to all of the terms discarded and to many of the terms in use; unanimous choices are rare. Some writers, black and white, now use *African American* and *black* interchangeably: *the unquestioned assumption that middle-class normalcy was aberrant for blacks and that only thuggishness and ghetto pathology were "authentically" African American.* Many writers use *black* only. Some who write historically adopt the term used during the time they are writing about: *the organizing of the Negro Pullman car porters in 1925* / *the absurd charge that* Invisible Man [1952] *lacks Negro suffering* / *In 1975 I graduated from the Harvard Law School. Out of a class of 536, there were eighty-one women, including ten black women.* Still other writers call themselves *Negro* out of pride in historical achievement: *Like his hero and mentor Ralph Ellison, he calls himself a Negro because that's where the spirituals and the jazz and the blues, and his people, came from.* Some writers use *African* (or *Afro-*) *American* or *Native American* to begin a piece of writing on a formal note, and then revert to *black* or *American Indian* or *Indian* alone.

Unanimity remains far off when humor and habit exert their natural strength. Today one hears women debonairly refer to women friends as *ladies* or *girls* (a distinguished soprano: *I'm delighted that you ladies joined me on the program today* / a leading film actress: *I'm a girl's girl*). Some black males call each other *nigger* as a term of friendship, solidarity, or admiration. Similarly, some gay men and lesbians use a range of old slang to speak of themselves and each other. And many black women and men address a woman as *girl* from long habit. But such genial usages mainly occur among members of the group and are not recommended to others.

Precisely descriptive names, unanimously agreed on and solemnly used, may elude us. The longer identifiers seem unstable, and someone is always being left out. Consider the colloquial use by educated people of *you guys* in addressing a group of males and females of all but senior years, as in *Where do you guys want to eat?* See also ANTECEDENTS 7.

character. What this word names in the human species is of bottomless interest. Yet in general use the word means nothing: *The dance was of a military character, swift, and marked by abrupt turns and halts* / *desires to establish a dictatorial and repressive regime of a totalitarian character.* No meaning is lost in writing *The dance was military, swift, and marked,* etc. / *a regime dictatorial and repressive.* *Character* need not be denied extensions to inanimate things that do show character, like workmanship, handwriting, or white oak. But as a mere synonym for *kind, sort, cast,* or *description* the word is waste. Better to use the buried adjective: whatever is *of a shabby character* is *shabby.* See also CASE; COVERING WORDS; LEVEL; NATURE.

check, verb. See AMBIGUITY; UP TILL.

chestnut. See PRONUNCIATION 1.

Chicana, Chicano. See CHANGING NAMES.

choice. See BETWEEN 3.

claim. See ALLEGE.

cliché. See SET PHRASES 1; UNNECESSARY WORDS 3.

closure. See POPULARIZED TECHNICALITIES.

clothes. See PRONUNCIATION 1.

co-. See COHORT.

cohort. In this continually misused word, the *co-* is the misleading element. Unlike many similar words, it does not imply a reciprocal combination, as in *co-signer, co[l]laborator.* On the contrary, it is related to the word *court*—an enclosed space—and denotes a multitude. In Roman usage, a cohort was a subdivision of infantry numbering from 360 to 600 men. The modern storyteller is therefore far from the mark when she writes: *She idly turned over the pages of a magazine, while in the tiny kitchen her cohort washed the dishes.* Again from a novel: *"Go ahead, boys," he said to his cohorts. "I'll meet you outside."* (The cohorts here were four persons) / *At about the same time Joe Adonis, a cohort who has since been deported to Italy, moved into a house just a quarter of a mile away.* An even more aberrant use turns up in the following passage, where the word is evidently a substitute for *counterpart: The suburbanite, riding to his job in town over a new expressway, is not much concerned by the fact that his city-dwelling cohort is sweating out his trip to work on a bus that keeps getting caught in traffic jams.*

The extension of *cohort* to nonmilitary uses is natural enough, but if the word is to retain its force it should observe two requirements: (1) it should designate members, too numerous to be conveniently counted, of some sort of united group, and (2) it should imply some sort of struggle or contest. *No one of the candidates succeeded in completely marshaling his cohorts before the first ballot / To the legion of the lost ones, to the cohort of the damned*—in such uses the sense of the word is preserved.

Note further that certain words imply the relation ordinarily marked by *co-* without any prefix—e.g., *partner, sharer, spouse.* Do not encumber them with a needless *co-*, any more than you would be tempted to say *co-friend* or *co-twin.*

collateral damage. See EUPHEMISMS.

colleague. Americans have relaxed their use of this word, none more so than the senator who regularly addresses "My fellow colleagues" (see COHORT). In England the word is used in the professions and government but carries a warning in the Oxford English Dictionary: "Not applied to partners in trade or manufacture." No such distinction is made in America, where trades and businesses have become professions, and salesmen as often as judges refer to their *colleagues.* Even in England, practice changes, and the readers of English classics will one day have to be told that a *mate* was once an artisan's or a tradesman's associate. Confusion will continue even

so, for by then all salesmen in the United States will have become *sales associates.*

See also PRONUNCIATION 1.

colon, the. 1. The colon makes a formal introduction of quotations, lists, or tables. Announcing a short quotation, it is followed by quotation marks, as in *He rose and said: "Now that you have all seen the film, I'll tell you how it almost didn't get made."* A long quotation often begins on a line below the colon and is written as a self-contained block of words (see QUOTATION MARKS).

Following a colon, a directly quoted sentence begins with its capital letter, or with a lowercase letter if only a fragment is quoted. *The note opened: "It has always been difficult for me to explain myself" / She offered her plan: "a counsel of despair," she called it.* In announcing lists and tables, the colon usually ends the line; the list or table commences on the following line in the manner of a block quotation.

2. The colon also introduces the second of a pair of statements when the first creates an expectation that the second is to fulfill. In other words, the colon unites two complementary statements. *You didn't do the best you could: you were too proud to ask questions about what you didn't understand / The remedy for this is simple: insert a briefly descriptive word or phrase / His caller was a changed man: he was fat, ill-at-ease, and tongue-tied / Let's be frank: no one has believed that story for years.*

These examples observe present usage in not capitalizing the word that follows the colon (unless, as in 1 above, it begins a quotation). In the modern view, a capital letter would trip up the eye just where the colon means to make a seamless connection.

3. When the words before the colon in either of its uses end in a group within parentheses, the colon follows the closing parenthesis. *The actors (in order of appearance): John Jones as The Receptionist, etc.*

combat fatigue. See EUPHEMISMS.

come to be. See BECOME.

comity. See POPULARIZED TECHNICALITIES.

comma, the. 1. Series, as in *a, b, c, d, and e.* 2. Adjectives parallel or cumulative. 3. Restrictives and nonrestrictives. 4. Appositions. 5. Coordinate clauses. 6. A meaningless comma. 7. With *because.* 8. Paired commas. 9. Comma splice. 10. Janus elements.

1. Series, as in *a, b, c, d, and e.* The number of items most often listed in a series is three—the pattern *a, b, and c: He had gone clandestinely to Athens, acquired a residence in Piraeus, and become one of the privileged underprivileged / a confusion of stone tombs, caves, and newish residential suburbs / He looked about nervously, dismounted, and crept forward on his stomach.* But series that go beyond three members are fairly common, too: *They wore body stockings, domino masks, gauntlets, and cloth boots instead of toe shoes / Acquire skill in your profession, be diligent in the exercise of it, enlarge the circle of your friends and acquain-*

tances, avoid pleasure and expense, and never be generous but with a view of gaining more than you could save by frugality / eager inquiry on the faces of Sonia, Chattie, Meredith, Bod, Fritz, and Virginia H. The formula *a, b, c, d, and e* represents from now on such series extended to any number.

Series can be made up of any *kind* of element, so long as the members are truly in parallel. They may be nouns, adjectives, phrases, or clauses, and of any length. Series of adverbs are common (*up, down, and sideways*) as are series of prepositions (*motion to, from, or within the circle*). Whatever the number of units, the characteristics of the series tend to be two: (1) rhetorical equivalence among the members and (2) a conjunctive word, usually *and,* which signals the arrival of the last member. Sometimes *and* is replaced by *or—Should we ask, demand, or entreat?—*and sometimes by *but.* The conjunctive word is omitted when the members reduplicate a meaning, as in *She was tired, spent, done in.*

How to punctuate these series is a question argued with considerable heat. Almost all prose writers favor the use of commas between successive members up to the last two, but there the shooting begins. Many newspapers insist on *a, b and c*—that is, they omit the last comma. Many of the most respectable book publishers stick to *a, b, and c*: they demand a comma before the cadence signaled by *and, or,* or *but.* Readers will have noticed that this book follows the latter formula.

A widely parroted dictum is supposed to settle the question: if you have the conjunction, you don't need the comma. That is bad reasoning or no reasoning at all. A conjunction is a connective device, as its name announces; but a mark of punctuation is nothing if not separative. To insist that the first perform the work of the second is to prescribe sand in the bearings.

The one cogent argument for omitting the last comma is the saving of space. In the narrow width of a newspaper column this saving counts for more than elsewhere, which is why the omission is nearly universal in journalism. But one must question whether the advantage outweighs the confusion the omission causes. Consider this series in which all—or is it only some?—of the units, being compound, call for *and* within themselves: *The agents were teamed for the search as follows: Smith and Starr, Jones and Stewart, Jackson and Wall(,) and Curtis and Snyder.* Omit, by the newspaper rule, the closing comma after *Wall* and your series ends in a hash. Was the last team made up of four agents or two?

Nor is it rare for a series to occur within a series: *The magazines were filled with such accounts of virtue betrayed, fatal infatuations of the innocent for the wicked, romantic Indians, patriotic love for old sights, relics, traditions(,) and sentimental folk tales.* Such a series, tangled at best, defies understanding if you leave out the last comma. Is it a series of three (*virtue . . . infatuations . . . love*) that eliminates an *and* before *patriotic* and makes *love* encompass *sights, relics, traditions,* and *folk tales*? Or is it a series of five (*virtue . . . infatuations . . . Indians . . . love . . . folk tales*) that omits a helpful *and* before *traditions*? One guess is as good as another.

The lesson is this: a series lacking the final comma may leave you unable to say for certain how many units it was meant to consist of. Uncertainty is assured if the last two units can be taken as forming only one: *In the following year she will be able to specialize in gynecology, immunology, orthopedics or diseases of the bone.* In this sentence *or* could be introducing an explanation of the previous item; actually, it introduces a fourth item, left floating by the absence of a comma. Omission always tends to confusion; inclusion can never confuse. Writers who wish for airtight rules will find one here.

2. Adjectives parallel or cumulative. Too many editors and writers are trained to put commas between all adjectives that belong to the same noun. The truth is that not all clustered adjectives are equal and parallel. The comma is rightly used in a construction like *this wise, farsighted policy* (a policy that is, for one attribute, wise, for another farsighted); or *a firm, forthright, unmistakable answer* (an answer having the three properties of firmness, forthrightness, and unmistakableness); and *a lazy, restful weekend.* These adjectives are coordinate, equal, and parallel qualifiers of the noun; they could be used with it separately or used in a different order (*restful, lazy weekend*) or connected by *and* (*lazy and restful*); the comma is the conventional sign of their equal status. One must likewise keep the comma in *a pretty, lush grove,*

lest *pretty* be taken as an adverb meaning *rather* and forming the compound *pretty lush*.

But are the adjectives parallel in *He was wearing his battered old canvas fishing hat*? No, because the hat is not (1) battered, (2) old, (3) canvas, and (4) fishing. Nor could the adjectives be written in a different order (*canvas, old, fishing, battered*). In meaning, the noun is not *hat* but *canvas-fishing-hat*. Does it follow that commas should go after *battered* and *old*? No again, for one of our tests would then produce *battered and old and canvas*—and something stranger still if the sequence of modifiers were changed. Adjectives grouped in this way are not parallel but cumulative, and so are distorted by commas.

It does happen that adjectives in a given locution can be construed either way—e.g., *a condensed(,) popular edition* or *a powerful(,) compact model*. But such combinations are rare, and when a question yields two right answers, neither is wrong.

3. Restrictives and nonrestrictives. Practically all language is in some way restrictive, its very purpose being to single out, to define, to limit. Hence it is remarkable that written English was slow in evolving a way to make clear whether a sentence refers to all or to only some of the class of things that forms its subject. The device, when hit upon, was simple: use the comma to set off a relative clause that is nonrestrictive, and withhold the comma from a restrictive relative clause. Secondarily, *which* became the favorite (but not mandatory) relative pronoun of the nonrestrictive clause, and *that* the pronoun of the restrictive one. (For a full discussion of the two pronouns, see THAT, WHICH, RELATIVE.)

Examples of the device: *Wild geese, which migrate twice a year, fly high* (nonrestrictive) / *Wild geese that are molting are usually unable to fly* (restrictive). The first example speaks of all wild geese and throws in a *which* clause merely to add another fact—again, about all wild geese. This fact may be pleasant to know, but it does not affect the main clause in any way; the enclosing commas tell us that the clause is optional and could be dropped. In the second example, the *that* clause cuts down (restricts) the class of geese being talked about: the sentence speaks only of molting wild geese. A restrictive clause cannot be optional; drop this one and the sentence *Wild geese . . . are usually unable to fly* will be false. The absence of commas means: "This part of the sentence you cannot do without." The presence of commas around the same part tells us: "Take it or leave it, for the meaning of the main clause remains the same."

When the relative clause ends the sentence, a single comma, by its absence or presence, tells whether the clause is restrictive or nonrestrictive: *She said slowly the words that would convict him* (restrictive) / *She slowly said the fatal words, which were followed by a silence* (nonrestrictive).

At no time is our dependence on the formula so plain as when we think it may have been neglected: *Campers should avoid the beaches where robber-*

ies have been reported. Where is a relative pronoun, and the statement as written implies that robberies have been heard of on some beaches but not on others. If this is not the case, a comma must be put after *beaches*, for none of them is safe. Again: *As a director, she had enormous success with actors who respected her.* This says that the director did well with a restricted group of actors: those who respected her. But if all actors felt this respect, the sentence cannot say so without a comma following *actors*.

It is worth pointing out that when the antecedent of a relative *which* or *who* happens to be singular, the presence or absence of a comma may not make a great deal of difference: *The novel follows the adventures of a Greek, who becomes involved in the struggle between the supporters of the prophet Elijah and the arrogant Queen Jezebel.* The *who* clause was probably meant to be restrictive, but the comma does not mislead, for the singular itself is restrictive.

4. Apposition is the placing of like things side by side, and in grammar it identifies someone or something twice: *the American writer John Updike / their favorite locale, the Olympic Peninsula.* If what is named is unique (*their favorite locale*), its second naming is preceded by a comma—or enclosed by two commas if the sentence continues (*They stayed in their favorite locale, the Olympic Peninsula, all summer long*). No comma belongs in the first example, because Updike is but one of many writers who are American.

The distinction between the two sorts of apposition is as useful as it is economical of means: a comma or its absence tells us whether something is one of a kind. Again: if a man has but one sister, she is, say, *his sister, Ellie,* the proper name denoting the only one of the kind *his sister.* If the same man has more than one sister, the phrase makes this clear by omitting the comma: *his sister Ellie* (as distinct from, say, *his sister Tara* and *his sister Carolyn*). More elaborately: *The company gave her a send-off, a party in the board room, and then she disappeared forever.* The *send-off* (given by the company, in her honor) is unique; hence the comma between the first and second version of the event.

5. Coordinate clauses. The strongest argument for putting a comma between the clauses of a compound sentence is that without it the sentence will often send the reader in the wrong direction: *My partner and I had signed a contract and a memorandum proposed to set it aside.* You think that the subjects signed both a contract and a memorandum, until you see that the latter is not a second object of *signed* —and you must reread. Punctuation alone gives warning that the words ushering in a new clause do not simply continue something in the old one.

6. A meaningless comma. It is all too easy to obey the wrong rule in punctuating before a quotation: *Answers to such questions as, "What were you like when you were a child?"* Quotations require punctuation (comma, colon, or dash) when introduced by a verb of saying (*asked, whispered, said, inquired,* etc.) but not when the quo-

tation follows a conjunction that would need no punctuating if the quotation were indirect: *He was fond of saying that the poet participates in the eternal.* Conversely, QUOTATION MARKS do not always invite the comma: *She too believed that(,) "nothing succeeds like surcease" / maintained that(,) "a door is what a dog is perpetually on the wrong side of."* Punctuate according to the structure of the sentence.

7. With *because.* Many writers are dimly aware that a comma with *because* often trips them up. To be exact, a negative statement beginning with *because* will perform perversely with an improper comma or lacking a proper one. So will negative statements beginning with *for the reason that, for the sake of,* and even *lest.* No such trouble arises from affirmative statements. *C. and B. bought the house(,) because they wanted comfort and security.* With the comma this sentence emphasizes their buying; without the comma it emphasizes their reason for buying; but either way the sentence is unambiguous. Now look at the negative version of the same statement in two forms, identical but for a comma: (1) *C. and B. did not buy the house, because they wanted comfort and security;* (2) *C. and B. did not buy the house because they wanted comfort and security.* The first means that they judged house buying an interference with comfort and security, and so refrained from buying. The second as clearly means that they did buy, but for reasons other than a desire for comfort and security.

The notable conclusion: when a negative clause is followed by a comma and *because,* the comma throws the reference of *because* far enough back to include the negative; whereas omitting the comma throws the reference far enough forward to exclude the negative and to take in the affirmative verb. In other words, after a negative the *because* clause without a comma assigns or contradicts a reason why; with a comma, it assigns a reason why not.

An example of the comma rightly omitted: *R. didn't put in years of backbreaking work because they were paying him well.* (He did put them in, but not for the reason mentioned; *because* contradicts a false reason why.) A comma wrongly omitted: *J. did not get far as a neighborhood organizer because he took all complaints absolutely seriously.* (By omitting the comma, the reason why he did not get far is presented as a reason why he might have gotten far; the *because* clause meant to state the reason why he did not.) Most errors with *because* and the comma arise on account of omission. *The sea is never completely covered with ice because of the comparative warmth of the water.* Obviously, if the sea were ever covered with ice it would not be because the water was warm. A comma is needed after *ice* to make *because* lead into a reason why not.

The ease with which meaning flips because of wrongly judged commas should warn the writer not to risk everything on so tiny and fugitive a mark when he does not have to. Negatives are themselves wayward, and in principle it is safer to assert a positive meaning than to deny its negative. Tell us what is true instead of what is not true. (For a full discussion of this point, see NEGATIVES, TROUBLE WITH.)

8. Paired commas. So many commas hunt in pairs, each partner useless without the other, that one might have thought the relationship would produce a new typographical sign: the first comma reversed so that cupping commas enclosed, like PARENTHESES, the matter between them. Had we such a device, it might prevent the careless omission of one comma in what should be a logical pair—complementary halves of a single contrivance, working together in opposite directions, like the jaws of pliers.

When one comma is omitted from a logical pair, stumbling and annoyance follow: *Although sacrifice of financial gain was once, by most candidates accepted as a condition of holding public office* . . . By the both-or-neither principle, the comma after *once* is senseless and annoying without a companion after *candidates*. We could, in a pinch, do without either, thus making a mediocre sentence read like a bad translation. It is better that we reorder the parts: *Although most candidates once accepted the sacrifice of financial gain*—an illustration of the truth that faulty punctuation often goes with badly constructed sentences. But paired commas make well-made sentences sturdy if the pair is kept intact. The second comma is perhaps most easily overlooked when the interpolation is a list: *most standard pieces of equipment, including a helmet, gloves, elbow guards, knee guards,*

and sticks will be provided. The syntactical line is *most standard pieces of equipment . . . will be provided.* Hence the whole *including* construction is parenthetical, and a comma is required after *sticks.*

Overlooking the first comma of a pair is just as annoying. *The President stopped him however, asking whether he had read the morning papers.* Connectives like *however, moreover,* and *nevertheless* are more and more often left unpunctuated; omitting the first comma is doubtless encouraged by their frequent placement at the head of sentences, but when they come later, they require both commas if given either.

It may be helpful to remember that single commas often stand for a pair. Clauses or phrases that begin or end a sentence do not look parenthetical— but often they might just as well have been put in the middle and punctuated at both ends: *Though public opinion may change later, it is practically unanimous now / Public opinion is practically unanimous now, though it may change later / Public opinion, though it may change later, is practically unanimous now.* Except for slight changes of emphasis, the meaning remains the same. Most important, the single commas of the first and second sentences have the same parenthetical function as the paired commas of the third.

The punctuation of participial elements cannot be reduced to a precept or two. Where the participle restricts or identifies, commas are usually intrusive and wrong: *pathways leading to the light / daily sessions beginning at 10 a.m. / the number of flights operated by the three airlines / the traditional welcome accorded by the port to new vessels.* Where the participle offers supplementary facts that could be omitted without changing the sense, commas are often necessary: *Persons doing demanding intellectual work, editing textbooks or teaching English to immigrants, now make one half the money of licensed electricians / They acknowledged that their boat, stationed at the entrance to a channel leading to the fuel-tank area, had been unable to . . .* The punctuation or nonpunctuation here parallels that of nonrestrictive and restrictive clauses (see 3).

9. Comma splice. Many teachers and grammar books still put the label "comma splice" or "comma fault" to a disjointed pseudo-sentence like *This engine is hard to start, the timer needs adjusting.* But such specimens do not offend punctuation as much as they deny the idea of what a sentence is. For that reason the discussion of this error is taken up in SENTENCE, THE 1.f.

10. Janus elements. Janus, the Roman god who protected gates and doors, was portrayed with two faces turned in opposite directions, hence the use of his name for an expression left adrift between what precedes and what follows. The unmoored phrase often floats between two commas, one of which should be dropped or changed to something else. *Although many of these letters are dull, taken as a whole, they are interesting as the record and signature of an artist.* What is to be *taken as a whole,* their dullness or their interest? If the second meaning is intended, the second comma should disappear, despite what was said about setting off participial phrases. No generalization should be allowed to interfere with clarity.

Janus elements come in all lengths. *Although Imagism and Spectrism were both programs of revolt in the field of expression, Mr. M. maintained in his introduction, they were diametrically opposed.* If Mr. M.'s maintaining belongs with the final clause, the sentence should read: *Mr. M. maintained in his introduction that, although Imagism . . . ;* if it belongs with the opening clause, *Although Mr. M. maintained . . . that Imagism . . . ;* if with both, *Mr. M. maintained . . . that both Imagism and Spectrism were programs of revolt . . . but that they were diametrically opposed.*

See also PARENTHESES; SEMICOLON, THE.

commiserate. See PREPOSITIONS.

commission, omission. See PRONUNCIATION 1.

commit. See TRANSITIVE, INTRANSITIVE.

common. See DEFENSIBLES.

communicate, communication(s). The drift toward abstraction and the use of COVERING WORDS has left *communication,* with its verb and cognates, empty from overuse. Nevertheless, *communications* is now a university subject, elementary and advanced, and is the ruling idea of several divisions of universities, e.g., the S. I. Newhouse School of Public Communications at Syracuse University; following the *communications industry*, these teaching bodies may soon adopt the *media* label.

We think we compliment a President by calling him *the great communicator*, as if what he says were of secondary interest. Small wonder that through the haze of abstraction we hear on every side about a *lack of communication*. The prevalence of the impressive noun drove a *Washington Post* editor to deplore one headline use: "*Communicate* is being used illegitimately and pompously, generally in connection with our own profession of journalism . . ." The editor went on to complain: "The story under the head incidentally said *Motivated by the desire to communicate* . . . Why not simply *Wanting to communicate* . . . ?"

Why not simply *Wanting to speak* or *tell*? The word *communication* does not elevate the concrete bearers of ideas—newspapers, broadcasting, movies, speech, presidents—much less the ideas themselves. Like hundreds of other words ending in *-tion*, this one should be reserved for the abstract and general.

communications skills. See SKILL(S).

companion. See EUPHEMISMS.

compare, compared. To compare something *to* another thing is to imply a premise: you believe the two are at least roughly similar. The speaker in Shakespeare's sonnet asks the rhetorical question *Shall I compare thee to a summer's day?* and then makes a comparison in which his beloved not only resembles such a day but also gloriously surpasses it. Most often comparing something *to* something else is an easy gesture; it does not doubt the likeness: *Onlookers compared him to a maddened grizzly / The writer compared you to the grasshopper in the fable.* It is also likely that a comparison *to* will be figurative. By contrast, to compare one thing *with* another implies work, a perusal of specific similarities and differences: *The instructor compared the advantages of steel bracing with those of concrete buttresses. / B. noticed that, in comparing the youth's alibi with the doctor's, he had left out the older man's nearsightedness.*

In haste, nothing is easier to write than a false comparison. The fatal first step is generally *compared with* or *as compared with* (see AS 9). A typical example: *Her new salary will be $125,000, compared with her present salary of $100,000.* Clearly her salary will still be $125,000 if *not* compared with her present salary or with anything else. The two facts are independent, and good sense requires that they be stated separately and the comparison left for the reader to make. Or else the writer should propose the comparison rather than hint at it. *Her new salary will be $125,000; her present one is $100,000* would give the meaning accurately; so would *will be $125,000, $25,000 more than she is getting now.* The variants of this faulty coupling are many and widely found, as the following specimens show: *A crop of this size compares with last year's small production of 10,964,000 bales* (This crop is x bales larger than last year's, which was) / *He placed earnings at $4,542,000, or $2.85 a share, compared with a loss of $2,542,000 the year before* (He said that this year's earnings were . . . and that last year's loss was) / *The power of the captured device was less than one kiloton, as compared to the twenty-kiloton bomb that leveled Hiroshima* (less than one kiloton; it was a twenty-kiloton bomb that) / *The cost of a weekend for two will be $435, compared with $525 in season* (will be $435; the cost in season is) / *estimates that placed the need for new social workers at 15,000 by next year, as compared with the 11,000 earlier estimated* (by next year; an earlier estimate had been). Note that several of these examples use *with* where, if *compared* were applicable at all, the preposition should have been *to*.

A further caution is in order. No right way exists for comparing incommensurable things. *E.'s attainments in American letters over a lifetime cannot be compared, in scope or daring or mastery of forms, with Y.* Two records of attainment may lend themselves to comparison; so may two writers; but to compare attainments with persons is to couple ideas at random.

See also PREPOSITIONS.

complicit. This invention is increasingly favored by those who like LEGALISMS, of which it is not one. Lawyers and others employ the adjective *complicitous* to describe an accomplice, one who is a partner in an evil action. Non-words often imitate genuine words, and *complicit* mimics the sound of *implicit* and suggests the moral tone of *illicit*; neither fact warrants its use.

component. See SCIENTISM 2.

compose, comprise. The whole is composed of its parts: the whole comprises the parts. The parts compose the whole and are comprised in it. *Comprise*, the word that produces most of the trouble, expresses the relation of the larger to the smaller, not the other way around. If we think of *comprise* as meaning *take in*, we shall escape the pitfall into which even good writers manage to stumble. *The suburbs of large cities also are avoided . . . because their booming populations are comprised mainly of white-collar workers.* Not so: the booming populations are *composed* of white-collar workers, and these workers are *comprised in* the booming populations. *The denomination is comprised of three sects.* On the contrary, it is *composed* of three sects, and it *comprises* them. For *the new poems which comprise the present volume* read: the poems compose the volume (or the volume comprises the poems). *The politicians comprise* (compose) *most of that shrill group.* (The group comprises the politicians.)

Speaking mnemonically:

The whole comprises the parts;
The parts are comprised in the whole;
The whole is composed of its parts;
The parts compose the whole.

comptroller, controller. See PRO-
NUNCIATION 1.

computerese. See PERIOD, THE; SCI-
ENTISM 1; TRANSITIVE, INTRANSITIVE.

conceding. See DANGLERS, BENIGN.

concept, -ion. The vogue of *concept*
as a word that will dignify any idea
from a passing fancy to a full-fledged
plan has blurred—probably forever—a
useful distinction. But those who like
to call things by their right names continue to mark a difference between
concept, the abstract, general notion of
any entity, and *conception*, the particular image, shape, or set of features
with which the empty *concept* may be
filled. Thus the *concept* God is the
idea of a supreme ruler of the universe.
The several religions propose different
conceptions. For any namable thing
there can be only one *concept*, but the
conceptions are many. It would follow
from this formerly well-understood
difference that the statement PANEL
WEIGHS MAN'S CONCEPT OF GOD IN
AN UNFOLDING UNIVERSE should read
MAN'S CONCEPTION. The panel members could not have discussed various
definitions of God if their *concept* had
not been virtually the same and thus
defined their problem; i.e., with what
new or changed *conceptions* should
we now fill the unchanging *concept*
God?
   The negative *misconcept* (CHINA
MISCONCEPT HELD CAUSE OF RIFT) is so
far only a headline word.

concern(ed). See COVERING WORDS.

concerning. See DANGLERS, BE-
NIGN.

concocted. See CONNOTATIONS.

concur, concurrence. See PREPOSI-
TIONS.

conditions. See UNNECESSARY
WORDS 2.

conferee. See -EE, -ER.

conform, conformity. See PREPOSI-
TIONS.

connect. See PREPOSITIONS.

connive. The first and indispensable
meaning of this very old verb is *wink
at, avert one's eyes from, pretend ignorance of.* One *connives at* what one
secretly sympathizes with or cannot
prevent. No synonym exists for the subtle action and motive the word denotes; for that reason the careful writer
will protect this distinct meaning
firmly. A second and slapdash definition, wholly unneeded, crept into use
during the Second World War; *connive* did duty by impressment for *plot*
and *conspire*, words already provided
with synonyms enough for a feast. No
doubt *con-*, the Latin prefix meaning
with, suggested the wrong preposition:
one *connives at*, not *with*.

connotations. Through literary or
vernacular use, words and phrases may
acquire a particular slant that qualifies
their literal meaning. This nuance limits the purpose such words and phrases
can serve. Only by close listening and

extensive reading of good writers can one learn connotations, for they stick in the mind only through frequent repetition. To rely on literal meaning, ignoring the shaping hand of tradition, will mislead or distract one's readers or listeners.

Thus *to have words with* someone does not mean *to chat* but *to quarrel.* A few more examples may induce readers to think twice before using a familiar SET PHRASE while uncertain of its ambit. One can only put a convict *at hard labor,* not the neighbor's boy digging up stumps. It is still useful to know that *pleasantries* are light, bantering jokes, not simply amiable conversation; that *well-spoken* means polite, not elegant in speech; that a *visitation* is not a mere visit but a tour of inspection to discover errors or defects; that *bureaucrat* is a disparaging word; and that *literate* is a left-handed compliment to pay to the college-educated, let alone to an author or a book. Then, too, though few will complain, the letter that begins *I am pleased to send you* (*give you; tell you*) is condescending in tone. Only sovereigns and puissant lords should say that they are *pleased* to do what the rest of us are merely *glad* or even *very glad* to do. Nor should we, in this day and age, *beg to acknowledge* another's good turn or compliance; after all, when we *beg to differ,* we are standing our ground, not being ornately gracious.

Connotations follow no rules, and no laws exist to enforce them; they embody an awareness of what others say and have said, hence what people assume. Good writing observes connotations like modest good manners, without a fuss, but the effect of their detailed observance upon the reader is like moving through bright, clear air.

For searchers and to spur attention, here is a short list of connotations that are sometimes ignored:

abrasive: that which wears down by rubbing; hence not *the abrasive questions of a newspaper reporter.*

allure: benign and enjoyable attractiveness; not interchangeable with the neutral or entrapping *lure*: hence not WOMEN WHO SURVIVED THE ALLURE OF SUICIDE as a headline.

astronomical: large, but for distances only; hence not *an astronomical price.*

concocted: means *cooked together*: hence not *clad in a uniform concocted of odds and ends.*

emanate: for the invisible and impalpable only—an idea or a fragance *emanates*; hence not *The draft treaty emanates from a government on its last legs.*

feisty: spirited in a touchy and quarrelsome manner; hence not *a feisty squad of cheerleaders.*

heritage: a concrete or abstract legacy received by a person or a people, not by an object or a place; hence not *Whitehorse, with its colorful Gold Rush heritage.*

meritorious: always of persons; hence not *a high school with a meritorious record of integration.*

Nemesis: the goddess of retributive justice; in lower case, not an enemy or something feared, as in *Stagefright is her old nemesis,* but someone who seeks to avenge a wrong.

Nirvana: the extinction of the self and all sensation and desire; hence not *a tuna salad to put your guests in a state of Nirvana.*

notoriety: the state of being widely known for unfavorable reasons; not a simple synonym for *fame*; hence not B. *first gained notoriety for his triumphant recording of the Beethoven Opus 61.*

plenitude: always abstract; never a synonym for *plenty*; hence not *"Plenitude from Petroleum"* as the title of an article.

stance: the place or position of one who is standing, as for instance a golfer; by extension someone's mental attitude or intellectual position; the very sound of the word and the literal use of *stance* in sports will always summon up a standing figure, making figurative use risky; hence not STANCES IN SENATE SEEN TO BE HARDENING as a headline.

verbiage: always in a bad sense and improperly used for *language* or *wordage*; hence not *in honor of three modern masters of judicial verbiage.*

-conscious. See FORBIDDEN WORDS 2.

consciously. Writers recognized conscious and unconscious motives well before nineteenth-century psychologists took up the subject. But it was surely Freud's hold on the popular mind that propelled this adverb to its present favor over *deliberately, intentionally, purposely, on purpose, by design,* and *designedly* to describe the alert will at work. The trouble with *consciously* is that it pretends to make a point from knowledge we do not

have. Who but an omniscient narrator in fiction could know how aware or unaware were the subjects of the following statements? *He consciously did all in his power to impede the committee's work / They consciously avoided the newcomers until winter got here in earnest / The dancers had not consciously expected the reception European audiences gave them.* The speakers of the first two examples could guess, at most, that some actions were *deliberate.* In the last sentence *consciously* either describes the unknowable or means nothing at all. For a situation hard to imagine, this from *The New York Times: The museum has been consciously seeking to increase its holdings of women's photographs.* There is doubtless no remedy for this tic-like usage until the users become conscious of it.

considering. See DANGLERS, BENIGN.

consist (in) (of). *Consist in* states a definition or identity: *In a good world, bravery will consist in showing your good sense instead of your willingness to fight / Her refusal consisted in no more than failing to appear / In what does this famous kindness consist?* Name the material of which something is made and you say *consist of: R.'s program consisted of songs sung better by others and tedious anecdotes of which she was always the star / What was called bread consisted of no more than flour and water / His story consisted largely of lies.* When something is made wholly or chiefly of one material, a moment's confusion of *in* and *of* may arise. Keep in mind that behind *consist of* lurks the idea *made of*, and behind *consist in* lurks *is*.

See also PREPOSITIONS.

constant(ly). No one minds the use of *constant* to mean *continual*. The link between the two is the idea of steadiness. But the awareness of *constant* as meaning, more exactly, *faithful, unchanging* will tell the alert writer when to prefer *continual*. There is more than a touch of the comic in *He was constantly fidgeting* when one thinks of *I am constant as the Northern Star*, which twinkles but does not fidget. And the exaggeration in *She was constantly bearing children, each less welcome than the last* would be as effective (and not distracting) if the writer had used *continually*.

See also CONTINUAL, CONTINUOUS.

consul. See COUNCIL, COUNSEL, CONSUL.

contact, verb. 1. Writers old enough to remember their elders' dismissal of *contact* as an ugly makeshift have long since conceded that nothing can stop its career. It is used almost everywhere now, and the valiant resisters have almost died out. Meanwhile, the trouble with the verb has grown worse.

The essence of the noun, as all electricians know, is *surfaces touching*. But the verb carries no such meaning and in its vagueness adds to the plague of COVERING WORDS; *contact* pretends to do duty for *consult, ask, approach, sound out, report to, complain to*—not

to mention such physical actions as *meet, write to, telephone, fax*, and, since the spread of computers, *access*. The question gapes wider than ever: What action are you describing?

Predictably, the vagueness of the verb seeps back to infect the noun. If, in a case under inquiry, *J. had contact with R. in 1992*, what exactly took place? A veterinarian writes of a cat that has undergone radiation therapy: *Upon discharge your cat will still be minimally radioactive; until radioactivity disappears through decay and excretion over two to three weeks, we recommend avoiding close contact.* Does the doctor mean *handling* or mere proximity?

2. Two other nouns converted to verbs by continual use are *implement* and *process*. They resemble *tool up* and *retool*, standard verbs for preparing a factory to undertake new production. *Implement* and *process* strive for this same allure of the technical, even though their meanings comprise only commonplace business actions. A plan is *implemented* when supplied with the practical apparatus—money, staff, schedule, and whatnot—needed to carry it out. One *processes* an application, request, or other document by putting it through a usual sequence of consideration, approval, and execution. Those willing to forgo the appearance of fierce efficiency may prefer *carry out* to *implement* and *handle* to *process*.

Note that all three of these words— *contact, implement, process*—belong to the mechanistic lingo of bureaucracy rather than the language of conversation or literature.

contemporary, modern, postmodern. The ease and grace with which a language may be handled by skillful riters depend largely on the vigor of single words that denote complex relations. If instead of *a contemporary* one must say *a person who was living at the same time as the other person we have been speaking of*, elegance collapses. Accordingly, when such words have been shaped, it is in every writer's interest to maintain them in working order. For centuries *contemporary* has been a relative term meaning *existing or occurring at the same time with* or *as*. *Contemporary witnesses say that the child was delivered just before dawn* / *Contemporary with the king's illness, certain curious conditions were noticed in the heavens* / *Writers contemporary with the spread of factory machines turned out tales of machinery run amok.* / *L.'s last days were contemporary with the onset of the Great Depression.* The adjective *contemporaneous* likewise means *belonging to the same time*, but it is overweight and is, moreover, used only for things and events. The last example above could read *L.'s last days were contemporaneous with the onset*, etc.

Contemporary has been saddled of late with the absolute meaning *of our time*: *Five floors of contemporary furniture to suit the toughest budget* / *He put a contemporary spin on "Too Late Blues" that rendered it unrecognizable.* This use invites confusion. The phrase *our contemporaries* is clear enough because the time relation is pinned down by *our*. But if after discussing events that occurred, say, a century ago a writer says *Consider contemporary conditions*, meaning *conditions now*, he will leave some readers a hundred years behind and further weaken an indispensable term. To repeat: *contemporary* is a relative term, often made clear by *with*. Hence the headline CONTEMPORARIES AT THE X GALLERY SHOW VIVID CONTRAST may be true but does not, as written, designate living artists. For *contemporary art* is not of itself synonymous with *the art of today*.

Of today is best conveyed by the simple words *present, now, current, new, today, at present, at the moment, at this time, present-day, of this time*, and so forth. It is also made unmistakable by names and dates and known occasions; e.g., *since the end of the twentieth century*. Until recent times that century was covered by the adjective *modern*—though historians date the modern period from 1500, and the phrase *modern art* denotes movements begun in 1879, 1900, 1920, and later. How will the adjective *postmodern* fare? Much depends on whether people understand it as saying only what the times are *not*; or as telling, with a hint of pride, what we think we have gone beyond.

content(s). Teachers' colleges seem to be responsible for the change of *contents* (what is contained) into *content* which, with the accent on the second syllable, also means *contentment*. Where is the gain? Long ago, T. H. Huxley could unambiguously write, *I have only begun to learn content and peace of mind since I have resolved to do this* [follow wherever nature leads]. Modern readers hesitate an instant at *learn content*, which at first sounds familiar from the Parent-Teacher meeting. They would be in no doubt if *contents* had retained its *s* in the schools as it has in the kitchen, where bottles and cans state their *contents* on a label. Critics who like to analyze multiple meanings in works of art might also like to resurrect *form and contents* to describe what fills the containers of art.

context. The figurative uses of this word are rapidly dissipating its important literal sense, which is: the words surrounding a term or phrase or sentence and making it clearer. It presupposes *text*. *Context* for things more abstract or miscellaneous is most often wind. *Giving everyone orders may work in your family, but in a neighborhood context people won't put up with it.* Why not simply *in the neighborhood*? *The dispute over fishing rights, unimportant in itself, arouses concern in the context of the tariff negotiations.* The same point is made with *arouses concern on account of.* *Context* is not synonymous with a location, a landscape, other people, or what else happens to be going on. It denotes adjacent words that assist interpretation.

continual, continuous. No careful writer fails to observe the distinction modern usage draws between *continuous* (going on without interruption) and *continual* (recurring at frequent intervals). Normal breathing is *continuous*, a chronic cough *continual*. A lifetime is *continuous*; the surprises it affords are *continual*. The distinction has not always existed, and old dictionaries list *continuous* as a secondary meaning of *continual*. But the difference once seen cannot be done without, and modern writers jealously preserve it in practice. Violations stand out: *It must be remembered that in December the Arctic is continually* (continuously) *dark / She has been chief or deputy almost continually* (continuously). Most readers would find *almost continually* (= almost again and again) a self-contradiction; *almost continuously* (= with infrequent interruption) raises no doubts. Presumably doubts did arise when a noted rhetorician made the opposite substitution: *But there is no doubt that a continuous use of* miracle *to describe any coincidence or amazing happening is vulgar.* Whatever occurs repeatedly, with intervals, is *continual*, not *continuous*.

See also CONSTANT(LY).

continue. See PREPOSITIONS.

continuum. See POPULARIZED TECHNICALITIES.

contractions. See I'D, I'LL, I'VE; SHALL (SHOULD), WILL (WOULD).

contradictory. See CONVERSE, OBVERSE, REVERSE.

contrariwise. See ON THE OTHER HAND.

contrary. 1. *Contrary* does duty as an adjective (*The contrary opinion is also outspokenly held*) and as a noun (*Only* *the credulous can believe the contrary).* In either form it is easy to use, only giving pause to some in the choice between CONTRARY, ON THE or TO THE, and raising occasional problems in logic where it overlaps *opposite* and CONVERSE. The commonest trouble with *contrary* as a noun occurs in the standard locution *to the contrary notwithstanding*; this expression is now often found in a mutilated form that lops off *notwithstanding*. Doubtless the shortening defers to a feeling that a four-syllable, fifteen-letter word is something to avoid if you can. But can you? *She even believed, all previous experiences to the contrary, that her new book would restore her to favor / The runaway victory in the pennant race to the contrary, this was no smashingly superior effort by a smashingly superior team / The declining number of two-parent families—movies and television plays to the contrary—was recorded in a report released on Thursday.* Unfortunately, in all these examples the omitted *notwithstanding* is the word that does the work. Without it the idiom is empty; some word must negate *all previous experiences* or the meaning disappears. Writers unwilling to handle *notwithstanding* had better give up *to the contrary* as well. The locution can perhaps be replaced, with a gain in brevity, by *in spite of* (or *despite*) *all previous experiences.*

2. *Contrary* also maintains its credentials as an adverb, though weakly. For its meanings, dictionaries give *contrarily* and CONTRARIWISE. *Contrarily* works well as an adverb (*behave contrarily*) where *contrary* (*behave con-*

trary) usually does not; and *contrariwise* spells full opposition where all that is wanted is a reverse inclination. Is *contrary* not an adverb when we say, *He is acting contrary?* No, it is a predicate adjective describing *he.* The adverbial *contrary* in C. *argues contrary to logic* modifies *argues* awkwardly and vaguely. Say it outright: C. *argues illogically.*

See also CONTRARY, ON THE, TO THE; CONVERSE.

contrary, on the, to the. These wordings of the same idiom deserve mention because *to the contrary* seems to be gaining ground, jarring readers accustomed to the other version. *Staff members fear that the station has lowered its standards. "To the contrary, we are seeking variety while maintaining the quality of our broadcasts,"* Mr. M. *said last week / They remarked that he was not good-looking; she, on the contrary, thought him perfectly splendid.* Over time good writers have signaled the opposed or *contrary* position with *by, for, in, of, on,* and *to,* leaving little ground for preference. Still, some writers prefer to avoid giving momentary pause to those readers who for years have supposed *on the contrary* to be short for *on the contrary side.*

See also CONTRARY 1.

control. See PREPOSITIONS.

controversial. What expresses memory we call *memorial;* what sets forth testimony we call *testimonial;* what exhibits emotion we call *emotional.*

These pairs show by analogy how politics skewed and cheapened the word *controversial* in the twentieth century. It was skewed to mean possibly likely to attract controversy rather than (its historical meaning) setting forth contention. By rights a *controversial* book is one intended to change minds; all arguments *about* it must be referred to by some other adjective. *Controversial* has been cheapened, most often at the hands of journalists, by the looseness of its new application. It has become a safe-playing label, warning those who approached the *controversial* entity (person, work, idea) that they might be distressed, but not telling them why. This usage seems designed for messengers who fear being killed for bringing bad news. The effect is a muted alarmism that leads to discrediting all but the bland.

Whether the adjective can be rescued from this low employment will depend in part on the willingness of writers to observe its first meaning and to describe the controversy at hand.

converse, obverse, reverse; opposite, contrary, contradictory. 1. In logic, the *converse* of a proposition results from transposing the subject and the predicate. Here care must be taken to preserve for each term the degree of generality that it had in the original form. Thus the converse of the proposition *All Canadians are North Americans* cannot be *All North Americans are Canadians*, because the original proposition does not tell us anything about *all North Americans*; what it really says is *All Canadians are some*

North Americans and the correct *converse* therefore is *Some North Americans are Canadians*.

2. The *obverse* is the negative counterpart of an affirmative proposition or the affirmative counterpart of a negative proposition. If we start with *Everyone is fallible*, an affirmative, then the obverse is *No one is infallible*. Both propositions must make the same assertion, but with the affirmative and negative terms changed each for each. (See also 5 below.)

3. Still in logic, *contrary* propositions are those in the relation of affirmative and negative within the same degree of generality: *All men are honest* and *No men are honest* are contraries. So are *Some men are honest* and *Some men are not honest*. In the first pair, both cannot be true and both may be false. In the second pair, only one can be false and both may be true. Now if we relate No. 1 of the first pair with No. 2 of the second pair and No. 2 of the first pair with No. 1 of the second pair, we get two new pairs of propositions, which form *contradictories*. In contradictory pairs, one must be true and the other false. If *all men are honest*, then it cannot be true that *some men are not honest*; and if *no men are honest*, it cannot be true that *some men are honest*.

4. These logical relationships are grouped together under the heading of *opposition*; and as everybody knows, ordinary language calls *opposite* both contraries and contradictories. Similarly it uses *reverse* for both *obverse* and *converse* propositions. There is no need to refine on ordinary usage except when formal argumentation might make it convenient to separate two kinds of opposition or of conversion, in which case it would be best to use the established terms of logic. As for the common phrase *diametrically opposite*, it has no logical significance; it is merely emphatic. By vaguely suggesting opposite points on a circle or sphere, it applies equally well to *contraries* and *contradictories* and to *obverse* and *converse* propositions.

5. In speaking of coins or medals, the *obverse* is the main surface—say, that depicting a head or figure; the *reverse* is the other side.

convict, verb. A suspect is charged *with*, indicted *for*, and convicted (or acquitted) *of* something. He may also be convicted *on* a charge. There is a tendency, especially in newspaper writing, to borrow for *convict* the preposition that belongs to *indict* and thus to pervert an idiom. *Two suspended patrolmen were convicted yesterday in Special Sessions Court for* (of) *soliciting business in behalf of a lawyer* / *A. had once been acquitted for* (of) *a burglary charge and B. had been convicted for* (of) *bookmaking.*
See also ACCUSE.

convince, persuade. Winston Churchill (as quoted by Theodore M. Bernstein) contrasted his wartime powers with those of Josef Stalin and Franklin Roosevelt: "They could order; I had to convince and persuade." Churchill knew that the latter two verbs were not exact synonyms; *convince* means to bring about conclusive belief or con-

viction; *persuade* shares this definition but also means to win someone over to a course of action.

We can *convince* or *persuade* someone *that* a statement is correct, and we can *convince* or *persuade* him *of* its correctness. Thus the statement *He tells us too much and convinces us of too little* could read *persuades us of too little.*

But *convince* refuses to take an infinitive. We cannot *convince* someone *to* believe a statement or *to* act on the belief, though we can *persuade* him *to* do either or both. Moreover, we can *persuade* him *to* stop, *to* go, *to* try again, *to* do all sorts of things. But we cannot *convince* anyone *to* do anything. *Convince* stops at the mind; only *persuade* can lead on to action.

coordinates. See SCIENTISM 2.

core. See METAPHOR 4.

correctional facility, correctional officer. See EUPHEMISMS.

correlate, noun. Since T. S. Eliot coined the scientific-sounding phrase *objective correlative*, the second word has flourished in critical journals. It is worth remembering that there is a noun *correlate*, meaning either side of a relation. *Precipitate, cancel,* and *carouse* are other verbs in good standing as nouns. By storing up for later use such single acquisitions, one can help to reduce the crowd of words ending in *-ment, -tion,* and *-tive,* the plague of modern prose.

correlation. See SCIENTISM 2.

correlative, noun. See CORRELATE.

correspond. See PREPOSITIONS.

could care less, couldn't care less. To the generations of world-weary young, the avowal of indifference *I couldn't care less* is ever new. To others it is trite and glib, but at least its logic is clear: one cares so little about something or other that caring less is beyond one's powers. Speakers who mean to convey this but change *couldn't* to *could* are not jaded but deaf to LOGIC. To say *My boss could care less* (about something) implies unmistakably that the boss takes an interest. All that remains in doubt is the degree of that interest, which may be the highest possible.

It is striking that those who say or write *could care less* leave logic intact in the comparable expression *I couldn't agree more.* Perhaps the greater mental emphasis that falls on *agree* in the second expression keeps their minds on the sense.

See also CAKE; CRACKS; LAY WASTE; RUBBER; SEA CHANGE; SET PHRASES; STONE.

council, counsel, consul. The ability to spell, pronounce, and use these three words is no longer the test of literacy. Light on the mystery is as much needed by Ph.D. candidates as by stenographers. The main point to bear in mind is that the first two words should be held separate from the third, in pronunciation and in meaning. Concentrate first on the consular (*con*, not *cown*) service of the United States. Its *consuls* are persons working in *consu-* lates, who deliver passports, compile statistics, and serve as business agents. The ancient Roman *consuls* were like prime ministers and worked in pairs. Bonaparte made himself First Consul in 1799, and he was the last. The connections between the roots of *council, counsel,* and *consul* no longer affect our usage and had best be forgotten by those who get entangled in the words.

Counsel, as we know from marriage *counselors,* school or camp *counselors,* and lawyers in court (= *counsel* as a plural collective noun or *counselor* as a singular title), means to give advice: *The doctor counseled him to take a long rest / If you come to me for counsel, I'll give you some, but on condition that you don't follow it. Counsel* in the second sentence is advice itself.

A *council* is a public body or committee of persons set up to make policy or advise others about making it. It is clear that a *council* counsels and that a *consul* may also counsel. But the differences are no less clear. The *City Council,* a group sitting at home; the United States *consul,* someone sitting abroad; and the commodity furnished by doctor, lawyer, rabbi, and priest are distinct and, once understood, easily kept apart. The annoying fact that lawyers, singly or in groups, call themselves *counsel* is an irregularity we can forgive when we have got thus far.

counterproductive. See DYSFUNC-TIONAL.

couple, missing *of.* From an exhibition catalogue published by a great art museum: *A couple blocks away, on Eighty-sixth Street, there were bakers, butchers, commuters, and housewives at their marketing in the striated shadow of the elevated train platform.* From two editorials in *The New York Times: Liberal bias creeps into, perhaps, a couple dozen of the 2,600 sample lessons / When a couple hundred veterans of New York City's last fiscal crisis gathered last week* . . . From an expensive advertisement by an environmentalist group: *As for your windows and doors, a couple packages of $3 weatherstripping should do the trick.* This clipped version of the informal phrase *a couple of* sounds to some ears like a ruralism, to others like immigrant dialect; it is both. When used in serious writing, it affects a folksy naïveté. Pedants will say that *a dozen of* lost its preposition a long time ago, except in uses like *I'll take a dozen of the blue ones.* True enough, but the fact makes no point. If consistency governed language, we should have the hard work of remembering to write *a pair puppies, a flock geese, a school fish, a bunch flowers, a handful dust.*

For other ruralisms, see GROW, TRANSITIVE; LOOKING, KNOW WITH INFINITIVE; OF A.

covering words. The respect for abstraction that we have learned from science encourages us to befog our prose with obscure generalities. We avoid concrete words and active verbs as being too particular to be quite serious, and favor featureless abstraction as if describing interstellar events. CONTACT and COMMUNICATION illustrate the point. The verb *contact* is used everywhere because it covers *write, speak, fax, wire, access, phone, visit*; it may

wind up meaning *I'll ask your assistant to remind you. Communication* is similarly substituted for *letter, fax, memorandum, report, summons, money order, E-mail,* and even *chat.* These uses remind one of French classical tragedy and pre-Wordsworthian poetic diction, in which *charms* and *flames* and *bonds* repetitiously covered the numberless incidents and feelings of love.

In the modern vogue, one notes the direction in which the abstractness inexorably moves. *Communication* has always meant the abstract idea of conveying information, a purpose for which we still need the word. But when it is made to stand for the actual letter or message (*Our communication made this point clear*), the abstraction is seeping downward to engulf particulars that should be stated in concrete words. How are you to know that when the train conductor asks that you *please take your transportation with you* he means your ticket?

True enough, precedents abound for using the abstract to say the concrete. *Conversation, definition, imposition* become specific as *a conversation, an imposition,* etc. Generalities require abstract words, e.g., *Evil communications corrupt good manners.* But the language lumbers with too many *-tion* words to make it easy to write agreeably; we need not use more to replace good words like *ticket* and *letter.*

Our names for our feelings sound false, for we more and more replace good adjectives and nouns with three or four battered and imprecise terms. Are we *worried, uneasy, curious, bewildered,* or *in the dark*? If so, what comes out is that we *are concerned* or, more awkwardly, *have a concern.* The once-forceful *shocked* now covers for *surprised, amazed, taken off-balance, disappointed, startled, astonished;* thus overworked, *shocked* has no force and no meaning of its own. And there is scarcely an unwelcome feeling, from *fury* to *resentment,* that is not denatured by the all-purpose *-tion* word *frustration.*

Some covering words are new singulars from old plurals: *a facility* for *a building and its equipment, an amenity* for *a meeting room,* etc. Here *facility,* a general term for *ease of doing,* is stolen to dignify an already respectable concrete object, such as a tennis court, now *a recreational facility.* (A proposal to a foundation assures the directors that *no special facility is required for pianists.*)

The original *facilities* was a covering word too, but it frankly disclosed its generality by the plural mark of indefiniteness. Phrases like *kitchen necessities, writing materials,* and *men's furnishings* are obviously useful, but who would want them to displace *pot, pen,* and *necktie,* as *communication* and *facility* are displacing *memo* and *building?* (See also *infrastructure* under POPULARIZED TECHNICALITIES.) Very rarely indeed does the complexity of a plan or business require covering words. *Work floor* is clearer and more practical than *central personnel station.* The vague *essentials, basics, components, roles, specifics, accessories, coordinates,* and *environments* clogging workaday prose are just so many wrenches in the works. (For more on *environment,* see TRANSITIVE, INTRANSITIVE.)

Nothing more clearly shows the yen for abstraction than the recent vogue of *product* to cover whatever comes out of a place of work, be it movies, reports, or paper cups. These are, to be sure, all *produced,* but the verb itself is abstract. It is both sad and confusing to hear that which requires craftsmanship, intellect, or imagination being called by the word for what only requires a template.

Similarly, *processing* is a word that covers *doing whatever is necessary.* We will process your application, your medical history, your old raincoat, your sinful soul. Why not simply say: *We will consider your application, study your case, repair your raincoat, purge your soul?* For the unspecifiable *processing,* it is better (because less pompous) to say *handling.* Speakers or writers who can summon up a clear idea of what is supposed to happen (not *eventuate*) will not need to repeat *structure* (verb), *motivation, orientation, development, expansion, potential, realistic,* or *activity* (*leisure-time activity*) for the steps or qualities they have in mind. And having exerted themselves to say what they mean, they will find the work of the expensive *communications facilitator* partly done.

See also CASE; CHARACTER; DEVELOP; FISCAL; FORBIDDEN WORDS 2; IMPACT; LEVEL; MINORITY; NATURE; SCIENTISM; VENUE.

covert operation. See EUPHEMISMS.

cracks, fall through the. The purpose of a figure of speech is to call up an image that shows instantly what might take several words to describe.

But too often those employing such shorthand do not trouble to see with the mind's eye what they are saying. In the figure at hand, an object drops on a surface of boards, and negligence allows it to slip out of reach through spaces between them: the object *falls through the cracks*. The unseeing will continue to say that something or other *fell between the cracks* until someone points out that what lies between the cracks is the boards.

See also CAKE; COULD CARE LESS; LAY WASTE; RUBBER; SEA CHANGE; SET PHRASES; STONE.

crafted. See UNNECESSARY WORDS 1.

crave. See PREPOSITIONS.

crazy. See METAPHOR 4.

creative. See TRANSITIVE, INTRANSITIVE; VOGUE WORDS.

credible, credibility. See VOGUE WORDS.

critical mass. See POPULARIZED TECHNICALITIES.

critics' words. Nothing is more difficult than writing about the arts, literature included. To do so daily, weekly, or even monthly has proved a strain that the minds best endowed for this sort of work can withstand for only a few years. One ought therefore to be lenient with those who tell us every morning what the play or concert was like or what the gallery exhibition expressed. But critics tend to ease

their labors by fashioning vocabularies which are neither technical nor plainly descriptive, and which must therefore be called jargon.

The generic fault lies in the adjectives. The recurrent ones are metaphorical, or at least transferred from common use, and they soon cease to mean anything except approval or disapproval. The reader will recognize such thin figuratives as *crisp, layered, resonant, dazzling, sensitive, sophisticated,* MASTERFUL, and *structured*; as well as the phrases *imaginative control, dominant insights, shifting context,* and *richly textured*. Not everyone has met *utter dispassion* or *efflorescent ambit,* but it makes no difference: none of these terms means much. Still others, which begin by having a meaning, do not keep it long when turned to daily use: *apocalyptic, decadent, empathy, epiphany, evocative,* IDENTIFY, MEANINGFUL, *perceptive, ironic, irreverent, outrageous, transgressive, stimulating, stylish,* etc. Faced with this devalued currency, British writers in particular overstate beyond reason; many years ago, they gave us *riveting* and *compulsively readable*; the progress of inflation is shown by a recent reviewer who finds a novel "compulsively delicious" and "one of those explosive reads that hooks you from the start."

The best critics are those who use the plainest words and who make their taste rational by describing actions rather than by reporting or imputing feelings. Walt Whitman's advice to critics still stands: "Nothing is better than simplicity . . . nothing can make up for lack of definiteness."

See also SAKE, FOR ITS OWN; VOGUE WORDS.

crucial. See FORBIDDEN WORDS 2; JOURNALESE.

crushing. See JOURNALESE.

cryptic. See JOURNALESE.

culminate. See TRANSITIVE, INTRANSITIVE.

culture. See POPULARIZED TECHNICALITIES.

cusp. See POPULARIZED TECHNICALITIES.

cutting-edge, adjective. See FORBIDDEN WORDS 2.

cynical, skeptical. We might as well interchange *murder* and *surgery* as mix up these two descriptives. They have strayed far from their sources in Greek philosophy, but in modern use neither is replaceable, least of all by the other. The *cynic*'s outlook—jaded, suspicious, without hope or belief—needs its traditional name. The *skeptic*'s outlook, by contrast, withholds allegiance or belief until a good case is made. The cynic we presume to be a cynic for life; but the skeptic, like the Missourian of folklore, says, "Show me," and waits to be shown.

D

dabbling. See PREPOSITIONS.

dangerous pairs. Words similar in both look and sound (*pair, pare*) are mastered in childhood; but words that are also related in meaning (*intense, intensive*) can be confused for a lifetime. What sends the educated writer most often to the dictionary is not an unknown term but the wish to avoid or shake off an habitual error. It follows that the ablest writers consult the dictionary more often than other people do.

Some look-alike English terms differ in the root lodged between shared beginnings and endings. But English more frequently uses these prefixes and suffixes to stamp distinct meanings economically on a shared root. The most confusable words may be those whose only difference is in the suffix.

A random list of such words would include at least the following, of which those in small capitals are discussed elsewhere in this book. All on the list can be differentiated with the aid of a dictionary; a few are followed by comments that may aid memory.

abjure, adjure
acceptance, acceptation
ADHERENCE, ADHESION

adjudge, adjudicate
ADMINISTER, MINISTER
ANXIOUS, EAGER
assured, insured (see ASSURE, ENSURE, INSURE)
autarky, autarchy (see SPELLING)
BELABOR, LABOR
bi-, semi-(weekly, etc.)
COMPOSE, COMPRISE
compulsive, compulsory (the first is from within, an obsession)
CONCEPT, CONCEPTION (the first is not for daily use)
confound, confuse
CONSTANT, CONTINUAL
contemptible, contemptuous
CONTINUAL, CONTINUOUS
COUNCIL, COUNSEL, CONSUL
decry, descry
defer, delay
definite, definitive
DELINEATE, delimit
deprecate, depreciate
diffidence, indifference
DISCOMFIT, DISCOMFORT
DISINTERESTED, UNINTERESTED
distinct, distinctive
elemental, elementary (see ENDINGS 1)
emanate, emulate
ENORMITY, ENORMOUSNESS
EUPHEMISM, euphuism
EXCESSIVELY, EXCEEDINGLY
exhausting, exhaustive

exposure, exposé, exposition
feasible, possible
FELICITOUS, FORTUITOUS
flout, flaunt
IMPLICIT, EXPLICIT
IMPLY, INFER
import, importance
inchoate, incoherent (the first means only *beginning* or *not fully formed*)
infest, infect
ingenious, ingenuous
intense, intensive
intent, intention
JUDICIAL, JUDICIOUS (the first requires a bench)
LIBEL, SLANDER
luxuriant, luxurious (see MALAPROPS)
mantel, mantle (the first sits above the fireplace; the second covers all over).
militate, mitigate (the first fights against, the second softens)
nauseous, nauseated (what is described by the first will cause the feeling named by the second)
necessary, necessitous
offending, offensive
perspicacious, perspicuous
PRAGMATIC, practical
precipitate, precipitous (see ENDINGS 1)
primal, primary (see ENDINGS 1)
principal, principle (the first, adjective and noun, means *most important* or someone who is just that)
PRIOR TO, before
PROSELYTE, proselytize
remediable, remedial
seasonal, seasonable
sewage, sewerage
stratagem, strategy
stricture, restriction
subject (to), subjected (to)

tortuous, torturous (the first means *sinuous* or *devious*)
visit, visitation (see CONNOTATIONS)

Failing to distinguish words that bear a family resemblance can leave one blind to what one has written. For example, one *attends* to something—cooking, a repair—by giving it attention. *Tend to* says the same thing informally—but also means *be disposed toward*: *He tends to arrive late / The ship tended toward the South.* But one *tends* or *attends* (no *to*) the young, the sick, or the disabled in giving them care. *The New York Times* distinguishes the East Side from the Lower East Side among Manhattan locations but mixed *tend* and *tend to* in a headline that justified those whom hospitals depress: STUYVESANT POLYCLINIC, AT 100, STILL TENDS TO LOWER EAST SIDERS.

danglers. 1. Anything that dangles is attached at one point while elsewhere hanging free. But in language study, *dangling* is most often used to describe a participle that is unattached to anything. A proper participle fastens to the subject of a main clause, as in this example: *Already hurtling toward the corner, the truck seemed to pick up speed.* The *truck* is clearly doing what the participle says: *hurtling.* But a participle that refers to a noun outside the main clause, or fails to refer to any visible noun, would be better called unanchored, unmoored, unlinked, adrift, floating, disconnected, loose. Consider this tennis report: *J., whose position plummeted after suffering a wrist in-*

jury, could benefit from a low draw. What did the *suffering*? The *position*? Not likely. Fowler sensibly calls such a participle *unattached*. But *dangling participle* is a byword in American grammar books; hence *danglers* is used in this book to denote not only participles of faulty reference but also other constructions that evade the lawful bonds between words.

The language is always loosening in some departments and tightening in others; in the late eighteenth century, most now-classic authors, writing an introductory phrase, would set down a participle if it referred to a noun present anywhere in the sentence that followed—or referred to a noun not present but easy for the reader to supply. An anecdote written in the time of Richard Brinsley Sheridan shows the freewheeling practice: *Sheridan was once staying at the house of an elderly maiden lady who wanted more of his company than he was willing to give. Proposing, one day, to take a stroll with him, he excused himself on account of the badness of the weather.* It was the lady who did the proposing, but she is present only in a subordinate construction in the first sentence. Today, all writers except the most heedless would feel that the second sentence must begin *When she proposed*, thereby connecting the action to its author; or, to forge the same link, that the subject of the second sentence should be *she*, not *he*. The doctrine which codifies this modern feeling insists that a participle at the head of a sentence shall affix itself to the subject of the following verb. If the two will not connect, the writer

must trade the participle for some other construction. A modern example of nonobservance comes from an interview in *The New York Times: Clutching a white linen handkerchief, her eyes fill again.* Recast in one way, this might read: *Clutching a white linen handkerchief, she seems about to weep again;* in another way, *As she clutches . . . her eyes fill again.*

Writers often dangle the present participle in laying down a premise swiftly. A letter to the editor of a magazine begins: *By presenting apparently contradicting views on the subject of world population growth, it appears that there exist just two diametrically opposed camps.* With *presenting* the sentence promises to tell who or what put forth the views in question, and then cheats the expectation raised. The writer could have fixed his subject in place by speaking directly of the editor (*By presenting . . . you make it appear*) or by naming the author of the article (*. . . Smith makes it appear*).

Important facts attached to a participle will drift if the participle drifts. After a sentence about the Englishman Henry Bryan Binns, a literary biography continues: *While in this country collecting material, an admirer of Whitman in California told Binns his theory of the poet's being the father of some children in New Orleans.* It was Binns, not the California admirer, who was in this country collecting material. But the whole phrase surrounding the dangler *collecting* is alike unmoored. One way to tie things up: *Binns, while in this country collecting material, was told by an admirer of Whitman.*

A participle does not have to precede the subject in order to dangle. *Should we win our fight in the courts, thus permitting us to use public funds* shows the point. The participle must join with a noun that answers the question Who or what permits? There is no such noun here, and the participle behaves like an adjective trying to modify the verb *win*. The meaning is: *Should we win . . . and thus become entitled to use*. Again, from a book review: *Moreover, major developments in medicine have occurred without understanding their theoretical underpinnings . . .* Since no one is named who might or might not understand, one can only clarify this sentence by making the participle into a noun: *without an understanding of their*, etc.

The participle *including* receives particularly rough treatment from those who broadcast the news. It means *inclusive of* and its work is adjectival. But announcers will state that *protesters marched in several cities including here in Washington* or *we're expecting showers including in the morning*. No noun is *including* another noun here. *Including* is used in these statements as paste to join the unjoinable. The makeshift works no better in this sentence from an historical work. *He . . . frequently wrote tenderly of children—including his perennial campaign against the cruelty of teachers in the classroom.* Who or what is *including* what? Neither *children* nor the subject *He* can include his campaign; nor can the adjectival *including* modify the verb *wrote*. One way to revise would drop *including*: *He often wrote tenderly of children, and [he] kept up his perennial campaign . . .*

2. Up to now the participles treated have been active verbs ending in *-ing*; that is, words denoting actions. But quite as easy to dangle are passive descriptives, such as *questioned, followed,* and *written* in the following sentences. *He believed that the Smith woman had lied, but until questioned by the police or at any rate followed, no one could guess at her reasons.* Since it is the woman who should be questioned or followed, *she was* must be inserted after *until*. *Written by one of T.'s friends and filled with touching anecdotes and never-before-told incidents, no account could come closer to the truth.* Clearly, only *this account*, not *no account*, will fit the description given; the writer must end with something like *this account must come close to the truth*.

Put, when it means *phrased, described, stated*, can almost always be counted on to dangle. *Put another way, the speed of upper-class English speech precludes good manners / Put another way, New York winters should be spent in the company of a loving family or a sizable checking account.* Notice that each dangling *put* refers to something outside the sentence. To take account of such outlying elements one does well to substitute *in other words, that is to say*, or some other nonparticipial expression.

But for every *put* that fails to tell what is put a hundred uses of BASED ON duck the question What is based? *Based on information from M., police focused a records search first on Knoxville, Tenn., and then on Riverside,*

Calif. We are asked here to imagine police who are *based on information.* What would they look like? Consider the following consecutive sentences in a respected newspaper: *G. was convicted of murdering his mother based on a confession that was later shown to have been false. In the film* [made from the case], *a local boy has been convicted of bludgeoning the prominent town doctor to death based on circumstantial evidence at the murder scene.* In this passage, what is *based on a confession* is the convicted man, or the verb *was convicted,* or possibly even the murdered mother. Soon we find that either *death* or the verb is *based on circumstantial evidence.* The writer has not asked himself, What is based on what? More often than *including, based on* is used as a means to couple elements whose relation the writer ignores. The first sentence might begin *Working with information from M.* The second means to say something like *G. was convicted of the murder of his mother, his conviction resting on a confession that was later shown to be false.* The third might end *bludgeoning the prominent town doctor to death in a case that turned on circumstantial evidence at the murder scene.* Notice that these recastings make no use of *based on* at all. Even handled properly, the phrase is so worn from overuse that those who want to write well tend to shun it.

3. Bad participles are by no means the only danglers which disregard sense. The antonyms *like* and *unlike,* if not bonded to the main subject, compare the incomparable. Thus a much respected writer in an intimate essay: *Like numerous marriages of the era, one could argue with equal cogency that adultery splintered ours or preserved it.* Here two nouns need linking but the first is linked to a wrong second. The *marriages* spoken of are not *like* the subject *one* who could argue cogently; the author means to compare other marriages with his marriage, not with himself. He could do this with *ours was either splintered or preserved by adultery; one could argue either way.* Sometimes the fact that two terms look alike will deceive a writer into thinking them properly compared. In the following sentence, two men's names gave such an appearance: *Like another Philadelphian, Benjamin Franklin, Dr. Squibb's interests were catholic.* What has in fact been described as *like* are *Benjamin Franklin* and *interests.* To hitch the right noun into a comparable pair, say: *Dr. Squibb's interests, like Franklin's.* (See LIKE 2.)

4. *As,* in its comparative meaning, gives rise to danglers, most often because a writer chooses it over the *like* he wants but distrusts. *As everywhere else, Massachusetts will be holding elections Tuesday / As with the dog in the yard, something was upsetting the children / As in baseball, professional hockey is due for a shakeup.* Massachusetts holding elections as everywhere else? Something upsetting the children as with the dog? Professional hockey is due as in baseball? Such statements stop being gibberish when *as* is exchanged for *like: Massachusetts, like other states / Like the dog in the yard, the children were upset by something /*

Like baseball, professional hockey is due for a shakeup.

But *as* need not be a changeling for *like* to disrupt a sentence. A speaker at a women's college declares: *As a woman, your B.A. and the income it represents don't belong to you alone.* Neither degrees nor incomes being women, a revision is called for: *As (or Being) a woman, you should not think of your B.A. and the income it represents as belonging to you alone.* For similar troubles with *as* meaning *in the capacity of*, see AS 1.

5. A descriptive noun or phrase in apposition to a main subject can also go adrift. When you read a sentence beginning *Daughter of a millionaire, transformer of philosophies, passionate politician,* you assume that the inevitable next word is *she.* Alas for the inevitable, the sentence goes on: *a wit of the day said of her . . .* The heralded subject likewise fails to arrive in *A chef's chef, his staff would have followed him anywhere.* True enough, the strongest position for such appositives is at the beginnings of sentences. But to keep this one at the head of the statement will take rewriting: *A chef's chef, he had a staff that would follow him anywhere.*

danglers, benign. Some participles ending in *-ing* have varied their adjectival function so as to perform at times the work of adverbs, prepositions, or parts of prepositional phrases. For example, *considering* may act as a preposition and mean *in view of* (*Considering the deficiencies of his education, his career has been amazing*); or it may remain a common participle modifying the subject of a following clause (*Considering the jig to be up, he packed for a hasty departure*).

According may be less versatile, but it is still a respectable participle: *According perfectly in their fundamental tastes, they achieved a remarkable collaboration.* Many think this use odd, and certainly it is now rare. More often *according* (with *to*) acts as a preposition very much like *by*, as in *the Gospel according to Mark* and *according to my way of thinking. Concerning* resembles *considering* in having taken on the prepositional task; it does the work of *about* or *on the subject of: Concerning the exact terms of the contract I have no opinion / It was all that the boy could do, in such a family hubbub, to hide his knowledge concerning the events of the night.* The likewise altered *owing (to)* in the sense of *because* is useful in doing well what should never be asked of the grammarless DUE TO.

There is no limit to the number of participles that writers try to enfranchise for similar purposes. Any list of such transformed words would include the following: *acknowledging, admitting, allowing, assuming, barring, beginning, conceding, depending, excluding, granting, including, leaving, looking, meaning, providing, reading* (as in *reading from left to right*), *reckoning, recognizing, regarding, speaking* (as in *broadly speaking*), *taking* (*account of, into account*), and *viewing.* Here are examples of some of these words at work: *Acknowledging the force of what you say, it is necessary to point out what you fail to say* / *Admitting his competence, there is reason to distrust his general attitude* / *Allowing for the usual delays, the job should be done by April* / *Assuming that the plane is on time, there will be an hour in which to get lunch* / *You can count on it, barring accidents* / *Conceding all that, there is no getting away from the fact that* / *Granting that in thought one may travel far from one's own center* / *He looks down on everybody, including his betters* / *Leaving the High Arctic and going south, the weather is likely to show only gradual change* / *Viewing it from this distance, such fears seem at least exaggerated.*

The reader will notice that many of these converted participles denote some way of thinking or perceiving. But some mean no such thing, and in fact no generalization fits them all. Each is merely on its way to assuming prepositional or adverbial use. The word *looking* is so unsure of its versatility that it strikes the reader as drifting in this example: *Looking seaward . . . eleven lighthouses are visible.* Lighthouses are said to look out to sea; but are these looking, or is an observer doing so? Writers who only hope that certain participles have attained new functions invite such puzzles into their prose. The best prevention is twofold: a dictionary, which may note a tendency but is unlikely to give a verdict; and the writer's eye on guard against ambiguous relations and faulty links.

Taken one by one, the sample sentences above will excite diverse opinions. The loose constructionist will accept all such uses as welcome expansions of linguistic opportunity. The purist will deplore a good many as being loose. Among moderates who pick and choose, most would defend *You can count on it, barring accidents* but draw the line at *Leaving the High Arctic . . . the weather is.*

Some quasi-participles offer room as well as reason for maneuver. The active *granting* is best replaced by the crisper passive *granted* in what is called the absolute construction: *Granted that in thought a man may travel.* A similar briskness is gained by *His competence admitted* / *Reasonable delays allowed for* / *his betters included.* The writer who has qualms about *Reading from bottom to top, the table shows* can rest easy with *The table, read from bottom to top, shows.* Then too, in many statements the participles veil a conditional edge that may be opportune; the meaning is *if* one considers, acknowledges, assumes, begins, concedes, etc. To refine exactness, replace a suspect participle by *if* with the simple verb.

The careful writer who uses a converted participle must consider whether its participial meaning could possibly modify the subject of the main clause; if such a mismating is possible, he will firmly change the subject. *Assuming this document to be authentic, the authorities will have to revise the previous interpretations of B.'s motive.* The structure here tells us that the authorities make the assumption named. But what if the writer does not mean this and intends his first phrase to convey no more than *if it is assumed* or *on the assumption that?* With *Assuming,* he will do better to leave the authorities out of it and continue with *the previous interpretations . . . will have to be revised,* whereas if the authorities do in fact think the document authentic, this can be said in due course. The point is to keep each particular sentence from saying two things at once, of which one is not meant.

dare say, daresay. Whether as two words or one—the choice is the writer's—this expression introduces, not a startling conviction, but a strong hunch: *I dare say her charm has not increased with the passage of years / You, I daresay, will be wanting four days off.* As a pocket-size idiom, *dare say* brings with it certain restrictions: no infinitive *to* (*dare to say*), and no ensuing *that,* as in *I daresay that your father will get the idea.* Then too, the expression nowadays only appears in the first person and in the present tense. The examples above show the way.

dash, the. 1. Keats used the dash with abandon in punctuating his letters, but writing today gives the mark only one purpose: to set off. The dash does this singly or as half of a pair.

A single dash sets off the final part of a sentence to give it particular force or suspense, or to mark it as an afterthought or summary: *Suddenly she had money to burn and time on her hands in this glorious city—and not a soul did she know / Ten years of research, each fact double-checked, and now you have rejected my book—and with a printed form! / C. had questioned everyone who* had seen the shooting—but did he know for certain who owned the gun? / *Continuity and recall need the most definite signs available, and these in turn are best fixed by visible marks—writing.*

Paired dashes, like parentheses, set off a thought that interrupts the main sentence. The interruption may be a word or a clause but should not run so long that the reader forgets the unfinished business the sentence began and will resume. Whatever is enclosed, many writers count on paired dashes to lend it a note of definiteness; by contrast, parentheses are seen as signaling a modest aside. *That he always disappointed her—that he disappointed everyone—persuaded him that life was tragic and therefore ennobling to all / The reporter's account was honest—that is, he thought it was true—and so boring that nobody cared / They came to agree—how inconceivable they hadn't felt it sooner—that they were unsuited to each other.*

2. Parentheses show by their posture that they open and close, but dashes mark only breaks. Thus three or more dashes can fragment a sentence, as they do in this example: *The provincial leaders are hoping—not for the first time—and given the likelihood that the regime will fail—to convince the rebels of their real strength.* A sentence with four dashes gains no clarity for being symmetrical: *I knew for a fact—not that it mattered—something I never told Smith—that the lawyer had dated Smith's wife years before—she had been one of many.* What is the relation of the first five words to the final six? And did the narrator never tell Smith that it did not matter? The sentence must be punctuated in a way that will show the relative importance of its several cascading ideas: *I knew for a fact (not that it mattered) something I never told Smith—that the lawyer had dated Smith's wife years before (she had been one of many).* Perhaps better still, the last clause should drop its parentheses and let a semicolon link it to the rest.

To type a dash with a machine that lacks one, hit two hyphens, not one.

See also PARENTHESES, BRACKETS; SEMICOLON, THE.

data. "On the evidence," said the first edition of this book, "it is too soon to say that *data* is slowly turning into an English singular." It is still too soon to say so, for the evidence has not changed. True, we continue to read statements here and there like *Additional information . . . will be reported as the data is transmitted;* and the following from an elegant magazine, mocking statisticians: *"The results* [of certain calculations] *could then confirm the Statistician's Law: "If you torture the data long enough, it will confess."* But Americans for the most part seem at home with the Latin neuter plural of *datum.* Incongruous plurals—*datas, datae*—are rare.

See also AGENDA; LATIN AND GREEK PLURALS.

de, du, des (French). See TITLES AND PROPER NAMES 5.

decease. See EUPHEMISMS.

decimate. See MALAPROPS.

decisionmaking. See VOGUE WORDS.

deep. See *in-depth* in VOGUE WORDS.

defensibles. Many who consult books on usage know the standard warnings about some half dozen words in common misuse. The thoughtful must decide for themselves whether they will heed the warnings or follow the crowd. Will they write *mutual friend* for *friend in common?* Do they APPRECIATE a favor done for them? And what about *aggravate, anticipate, (self-)deprecatory,* and *meticulous?*

Calling these *defensibles* implies that their longtime misuses have themselves become useful enough to be accepted. Of those listed, *aggravate* may seem the least needed in its transferred sense, for which *annoy, irritate, put upon, rile,* and *vex* have long performed well. If the former useful meaning of *aggravate* is given up, we are left with only *worsen* and the unlovely *exacerbate* to handle that meaning.

For *appreciate* in the sense of *value* (not the business sense of *increase in value*) there is no ready substitute. Many Americans are uncomfortable with the directness of *I valued your sending those kind words / I value your point but must disagree with it.* Hence, *appreciate* seems here to stay. Similarly, *anticipate* in the sense of *looking forward* is a great convenience. It means both more and less than *expect,* and neatly fits polite locutions: *Every day we anticipate your arrival.* The cheerful word slips lightly between the sense of *counting on* and that of *jumping the gun*.

In the sense of *praying against*, *deprecatory* took a passive stance, earnestly hoping to *avert* or *ward off*. Having now displaced *depreciatory*, it actively *devalues* or *dispraises*. Similarly, *meticulous* has lost its sense of *timid* to rest in the simple meaning of *extremely careful about details*.

As for *mutual interest, mutual distrust*, and other pairings where *mutual* means *common*, the latter remains the adjective to prefer. *Common interest* is heard as often as the other phrase, and no one supposes that *vulgar interest* is meant. But to say M. *is, I think, our common friend* might not be similarly clear. Dickens's *Our Mutual Friend* has fastened the error of one of his lowlife characters upon the English-speaking world; it will not be shaken off.

define, defining, re-define. See VOGUE WORDS.

definitely. See ABSOLUTELY.

delicious. See VOGUE WORDS.

delimit, delimitate. See VERBIAGE.

delineate properly means *to trace the outline of*, as in *Officials are awaiting a United Nations report delineating the famine area*. By extension, the word means *to sketch* or *to draw*. Many misuse *delineate* as a substitute for *mark off, separate, distinguish, draw a line between*: *The board cannot delineate* (distinguish) *the yearly mainte-

nance costs from the supervisor's private expenses*.

See also CONNOTATIONS.

dentures. See EUPHEMISMS.

deprecatory, depreciatory. See DEFENSIBLES.

despicable. See PRONUNCIATION 1.

destabilize. See EUPHEMISMS.

detention center. See EUPHEMISMS.

deter. See TRANSITIVE, INTRANSITIVE.

develop. Some VOGUE WORDS outlive the depletion caused by overuse and pass into a kind of death in life; they mean everything and nothing. People say that they *develop* an idea, a plan, a photograph, a melody, a species of plant, a plot of land (by building on it), a movie script (by changing it), a cold (by catching it), a feeling (by heeding it), and so on forever. Universities and other institutions in need of gifts say *development* for *fund-raising*. In business *develop* acquired an honorific sound which attracted those who had trouble saying what they were doing. Since the wraith still walks among us, it is useful to recall that it once meant *unwrap, unroll, unfurl*, as *envelop* meant *wrap*. *Roget's International Thesaurus* gives eleven nontechnical classes of meaning for the word as used today, and synonyms in the hundreds. Those who prefer to use fresh diction please note.

See also BASICALLY.

developing countries. See EUPHE-MISMS.

devil to pay. Curious things happened to the lingo of wooden ships when it came ashore. This expression, for one, was wholly transformed. At sea, *devil*, associated with difficulty and mischief, was applied to a seam that was difficult to get at and likely to spring leaks. It had often to be *payed*; that is, waterproofed with pitch, tar, tallow, or resin. (*Pay* = Latin *picare*, from *pix* = pitch; unconnected with *pay* = reimburse or give money.) Hence, the marine expression for an impossible predicament, a hopeless fix: *The devil to pay and no pitch hot.* To modern ears *the devil to pay* refers to bargains made with Satan that exact dire payment in the end. See also POPULAR-IZED TECHNICALITIES.

dialogal. See SCIENTISM 5.

dialogue. See CATALOGUE, CATA-LOGUING; VOGUE WORDS.

dichotomy. See POPULARIZED TECH-NICALITIES.

diction. Though often used for *speech, articulation*, or *enunciation*, this word is best reserved for the meaning *choice of words, vocabulary*. Even then, the context must make the meaning clear; ambiguity is otherwise too easy and too frequent. *It was the force of his diction that persuaded her* — enunciation or choice of words? *Improved diction is often the key to social or political success.* Are we to use exact words or stop saying *twenny* for *twenty*?

differ. See PREPOSITIONS.

different, various. The friend who says he made *four different phone calls* to your house in your absence must be versatile on the phone. If he says instead that he *called four different times*, the statement is, given the nature of time, redundant. As everyone knows, he means only that he made four calls or that he called four times. But so often is *different* used as a mere intensive that in many contexts one can no longer tell whether real difference is meant—let alone what is different from what.

Worse, *different* is so often meaningless that writers may fail to examine it when using it in earnest. *Two major studies seeking detailed information on sexual behavior, like how frequently different sex acts are performed by many different kinds of people, were cancelled.* More troubles plague this sway-backed sentence than its two misuses of *different: how* is equated with *information* (see LIKE 2), *like* should be *such as*, and the main verb pops in at the end like an afterthought (see PROSE, THE SOUND OF 2). But notice that *different sex acts* raises the question: Different from what others? The writer's point in fact is not difference at all but particularity; he means *certain sex acts*. His second *different* is redundant; it modifies *kinds of people*, a phrase which itself means people unlike. He could omit either *many* or *different* with no loss of meaning. Three paragraphs later: [A psychiatrist] *said that while there had been some studies of different sexual practices, there was little information about the frequency of different sexual behaviors in some groups and in the general population.* The misuse of *different*—even twice—is not what caused this fall into chaos. But we can both get rid of the word and recover the meaning of the sentence by careful recasting: [A psychiatrist] *said that some sexual practices had been studied but that their frequency, within certain groups and in the general population, remains unknown.* By noting that *frequency* is an absolute (it is either known or unknown), we have also erased an unhelpful *some* (see ABSOLUTE WORDS).

On the subject of *some*, it should be added that adjectives of number—*several, some, many*—are often shoved aside by *different* and by its cousin *various. Jones opened the door and saw that Smith had brought various friends.* It is unlikely that the point of this statement is that Smith brought a banker, a big-game hunter, and a nun. More probably Smith's friends were *several, many, a few,* or *some.* So too, the sentence *I spent the morning going to various barbers* most likely means less than it says.

different(ly) than. British usage has swung between *different to, different than,* and *different from*—and may not yet have come to rest. In the United States *from* has been standard in writing, while speech has chosen *than* increasingly often. The British *different to* sounds simply wrong to American ears.

To choose between *than* and *from* after *different* and *differently,* the careful writer looks from several directions. On grounds of logic alone, the reasonable choice is *from. Than* compares degree, as in *warmer than May* (is warm), *shorter than you* (are short), *older than baseball* (is old), *richer than Fred* (is rich). Logic throws an odd light on *We could not get over how different Wyoming was than Nebraska.* By contrast, *from* compares nouns, separating sheep *from* goats.

Not that logic alone shapes idiom; history and habit affect it too. To the American eye, there is something "off" about *Her nature is so different than mine.* This example raises the point that in weighing possibilities, one often finds that only one of them invites trouble; few readers would puzzle over *different from* but many over *different than.* Still, some writers might fairly object that *different from* can lead to a wordy outcome. *The dog's behavior now is very different than in June* becomes prolix if we make it *different from what it was in June.* But all sorts of constructions lead to flabby excess and must be changed for that reason alone. To make the point about the dog as swiftly as possible, forget about *different* and say *has markedly changed since June;* it is often better to side-step a thicket than to push one's way through it. *Flooding streams caused the family to move to a different hillside in the fall from the one on which they had lived in the summer* is too big a mouthful. Drop *different* for *caused the family to forsake their summer hillside for another in the fall.*

Differently than and *different than* can often be replaced by *otherwise than* or *other than. Apparently polar bears behave differently* (= otherwise) *here than elsewhere in the Arctic / The cousins all wanted something different* (= other) *than what they had ordered the last time.*

To sum up: in simple sentences the remedies for *different than* are (1) keep *than* but use some word that goes with it, such as *other;* or (2) keep *different* and replace *than* with *from. For reasons different than Bonaparte's, Necker also was pressing for a settlement* can equally well be written *For reasons other than Bonaparte's,* or *For reasons different from Bonaparte's.* If a sentence is too long or complicated to be fixed by these remedies, rewrite it from its root meaning.

See also PREPOSITIONS.

differential, noun. See UNNECESSARY WORDS 1.

difficult. See PREPOSITIONS.

dilemma. Should the meaning of this word be lost through careless misuse, we would have no replacement. A *quandary,* a *perplexity,* the colloquial *fix*—none are inescapable, as a *dilemma* is, and none implies two evils (and only two) requiring a choice. *It was not possible either to advance or to retreat without disaster* is the statement of a true dilemma. But consider the following sentence: *The dilemma facing the government was whether to trust the rebels' assurances.* This states a dif-

ficulty, a *predicament,* or, as we say daily, a *problem.* It is not a *dilemma* and does not suggest the two horns long associated with that word.

See also ALLUDE; OXYMORON.

dimension. See FORBIDDEN WORDS 2.

dis-, prefix. See DISINTERESTED.

disadvantaged. See EUPHEMISMS.

disassemble. See UNNECESSARY WORDS 1.

disassociate. See UNNECESSARY WORDS 1.

disciplinary, discipline. See ENDINGS 2.

discomfit, discomfort. The first of these verbs is so often misused in place of the second that some writers wonder if the second is a verb at all. It is, and its self-evident meaning is *to deprive of comfort* or *to distress.* This definition is mild indeed beside *to utterly defeat, to rout, to undo completely,* which are meanings of *discomfit.*

See also ABSOLUTE WORDS.

discussant. See RESOURCE PERSON.

disinclined. See DISINTERESTED.

disinterested. Some wise and some weary writers on language have declared the battle for *disinterested* lost to those who think it a synonym of *uninterested.* This verdict gives a single meaning to a pair of words with a common root and dissimilar prefixes while throwing the meaning of one word out the window. At best, one could say that *disinterested* has swung back to an earlier meaning. But should it have? It has done invaluable service in a post where at present no replacement is in sight.

That service was to describe an act or a person devoid of self-interest. The arbitrator in a dispute, the judge in court, the official making appointments or awarding contracts should be *disinterested*: unmindful of possible selfish gain to himself or others from the choices at hand. Such adjectives as *just, fair, impartial, equitable, dispassionate, impersonal, unprejudiced, moral, ethical,* and *high-minded* do not hit the mark. They do not make particular the *getting rid of* and *being free of* (= *dis-*) interests which affords a presumption of fairness, justice, and the rest. Those who sense this vivid difference will continue to use *disinterested* for what it has meant in its hardy period.

Those who make it a synonym of *uninterested* have always invited confusion. The writer looking for the opposite of the noun *interest* (= concern, attentiveness) will use *indifference*. To be sure, *uninterestedness* can be found in dictionaries, but the word is unwieldy and almost never used. The noun *disinterest* will stop the reader who sees two possible meanings—and it is in any case not the name of a lack, which is what our writer seeks. *Is one of the consequences of good times a disinterest in bad news?* Here *disinterest* is a mistake, and *uninterestedness* would be clumsy. *Indifference* (with *to*) is in-

evitable if we insist on a single word. (Those whose space or leisure can afford a phrase will prefer *lack of interest*.) *Indifference to* also belongs in both of the following: *Allan saw only widespread disinterest in the warning the scout had brought back / The division between city and suburb goes deeper than a mere apathetic disinterest in each other's problems.*

The adjective *interested* has the self-evident antonym *uninterested*. *The hound remained completely uninterested as long as no one approached the porch.* Make the hound *disinterested* and its drowsy condition is likened to the scrupulous work of a good presiding judge.

To come full circle: *interested* in another meaning has *disinterested* as its antonym. *Interested* in this sense stands for *involved, having something at stake,* as in *an interested party* or *interested testimony.* This use, which explains itself in context, causes no difficulty. Trouble arises only when one tries to equate the negative prefix *un-*, generally passive, with the negative prefix *dis-*, generally active. For example, to be *uninclined* is to merely lack inclination, but to be *disinclined* argues a positive aversion. *Uninterested* denotes only the absence of interest, but *disinterested* (= free from the influence of self-advantage) is a highly affirmative word.

dislocate. See LOCATE.

disputant. See RESOURCE PERSON.

district. See PRONUNCIATION 1.

dive, dove, dived. See MYSTERIOUS PASTS.

divergent. See PREPOSITIONS.

divest. A transitive verb, *divest* has one meaning in the financial press: *to sell off*. But in common usage elsewhere, it means *to undress* (someone), *to take away* (something), *to deprive* (something or someone) *of*. It became a POPULARIZED TECHNICALITY in the 1970s when pressure was put on institutions and businesses to get rid of holdings in unlovable industries or nations. So used, the verb, still transitive, was also reflexive, its object the agent of the action; thus *Corporation W. is being urged to divest itself of factories in South Africa / H. University divested itself of stock in Hellspawn Inc.* Soon writers dropped the reflexive pronoun required by common idiom, producing statements like this: *J. Corporation, according to a Supreme Court ruling, must divest R. Associates, its Cleveland subsidiary / N. Publications Inc. will divest its paper suppliers.* The reader of ordinary English can only imagine undressed associates and suppliers spirited away. See also TRANSITIVE, INTRANSITIVE.

division. See *dichotomy* under POPULARIZED TECHNICALITIES.

do, do so, done so. See VOICE 2.

Doctor. See TITLES AND PROPER NAMES 3.

double-duty construction. See PROSE, THE SOUND OF 4.

double entendre. See FRENCH WORDS AND PHRASES.

double passive. See VOICE 3.

doubt, doubtless, no doubt. American usage expresses two shades of meaning by the choice of conjunction to follow *doubt*. The statements *I doubt that I can go* and *I doubt if I can go* mean *I probably cannot go*; the speaker is nearly certain. *I doubt whether I can go* is a less certain statement; the possibility of going is slightly stronger. *I am in doubt whether* evens the odds; the speaker may go or not go. (For *doubt* with *as to*, see AS 10.)

The idiom *I do not doubt that* gives exact weight to the provisional nature of *doubt*. The expression concedes a point while minimizing it. *I do not doubt that you are sincere, but you have broken the law / I do not doubt that you would recover damages, but what good would that do you?*

The *-less* in *doubtless* is not so sweeping as the suffix in *pitiless, witless, helpless,* and like compounds. Indeed, *doubtless* covers a narrow range from meager certainty (*They were doubtless glad to see you, but you cannot change their minds*) to polite hope (*You will doubtless want to settle this bill at once*). Similarly, *no doubt* can stand for *probably* but advances no further than *very likely*. It almost never means *there is no doubt*. (For *doubting*, see DOUBTFUL, DUBIOUS.) See also ADVERBS, VEXATIOUS.

doubtful, dubious. A person or thing described as *dubious* is the object of others' doubt: *He was regarded as a man of dubious honor* / *"Your so-called cure," she snapped, "seems to me of dubious value"* / *What a collector has called a newly discovered Willa Cather story is described by scholars as "of dubious authenticity."* In these examples other people have doubts about the man's honor; the speaker doubts the value of a "cure"; and scholars question the authorship of the story. Substitute *doubtful* for *dubious* and the cloud of mistrust only darkens; to describe a man as being of *doubtful* honor is to politely call him a scoundrel.

But those who impute doubtfulness to the objects above are themselves *doubtful* in a different sense; that is, they are doubting. The difference in usage implies a shift of attention from object to subject which must not be ambiguous: *The couple were doubtful that a child so young could learn to read music* / *Of our wisdom in taking this step I am doubtful.* These sentences would keep their meanings if recast with *The couple doubted* and *I doubt* (omitting *of*). Ambiguity is fatal in *My colleague's assessments of our chances of winning are invariably doubtful.* Do the assessments themselves express doubt or are they of doubtful value? Either or both could be true.

Some dictionaries approve both objective and subjective uses of *dubious.* Such latitude encourages sentences like this: *Police said he was dubious in his description of the boy.* Do the police doubt his words, or does the describer himself have doubts? The careful writer will reserve *dubious* for the object. Applying it to the subject can be called a dubious use.

See also TRANSITIVE, INTRANSITIVE.

doubtlessly. See OVERLY.

down the tubes. See VOGUE WORDS.

downgrade. See FORBIDDEN WORDS 2; ONGOING.

downsized. See TRANSITIVE, INTRANSITIVE.

downscale. See ONGOING.

drastic. See JOURNALESE.

dreamed, dreamt. See MYSTERIOUS PASTS.

drink, drank, drunk. See MYSTERIOUS PASTS.

-driven, suffix. See FORBIDDEN WORDS 2; SCIENTISM 1.

due to. Everybody agrees that an effect is *due to* a cause. Hence, a disease is *due to* an infection, exhaustion *due to* overwork, success or failure *due to* aptitude or inaptitude, and so on. One thing is *due to* another thing. In such uses, *due* is an adjective modifying the nouns *disease, exhaustion, success,* or *failure.*

But the logic of cause and effect is flouted by those who say *Due to the President's speech, the scheduled program will be delayed* / *Juan succeeded due to his natural gifts.* In these statements it cannot be said that one thing is *due to* another. *Will be delayed* is not the effect of *speech*, though *delay*, a noun, would be: *The delay of our scheduled program is due to the President's speech.* Nor is *succeeded* the effect of *natural gifts*, though *success,* another noun, would be: *Juan's success is due to his natural gifts.*

Not that logic invariably dictates usage; rather, usage is established and changed by wide practice over a long course of time—becoming, sometimes, illogical. Since the 1920s, watchers of American English have warned that *due to* was changing from a compound adjective to a prepositional phrase. Yet the very terms of the warning may have puzzled its hearers, to whom a phrase like *due to* does not look prepositional. Tell students (many teachers have told them) that the prepositional phrases *owing to, because of,* and *on account of* will serve in place of *due to*—and they may go right on using *due to.* To them, *because of* and *on account of* do not look prepositional either, and *owing to* sounds British. *Thanks to* will also serve, but only with an object for which one could be thankful (*thanks to a loan from my mom*) or in a statement meant ironically (*we won, no thanks to you*). Broadcasters seem to think that the dangling *due to* sounds more refined than *because of,* but they are mistaken. (See DANGLERS.)

The editor Theodore Bernstein settled the matter for now: "There can be little doubt that *due to* used as a prepositional phrase will ultimately become thoroughly established in the language. But the careful writer, who does not wish to be suspected of negligence, will in the meanwhile use *be-* *cause of,* which has a less casual flavor and is above suspicion grammatically."

durable, durational. See ENDINGS 2.

dysfunctional. In the JARGON of physiology, what is *dysfunctional* either fails to work or works badly; the term is ambiguous but helpful to those who observe, test, measure, and alter tissue by physical means. As an adjective it suits the scientific purpose of classifying: it is general, not precisely descriptive.

What is served in the social sciences by calling a violent or sad or fearful group of humans *dysfunctional* is less clear. But sociology took the word in the 1950s, and from there it has passed to the cults and cranks that pick over the campsites of thought. It has also slipped into speech and public print, thickening the fog of pseudo-science and diminishing color, exactness, and force in American English. DYSFUNCTIONAL FAMILY REDEFINES THE CONCEPT. This headline precedes a favorable review of a play about a mad, divided, and criminal family. Concealing all vivid particulars, the headline writer gives us instead the boilerplate of SCIENTISM. Similarly, in a column about a despondent teacher who gives up teaching, the writer tries to engage our feelings by writing of *dysfunctional classrooms.* What, in plain English words, does he mean?

The abstract mind that thinks *dysfunctional* vivid has probably tired of its rusty forerunner *counterproductive.*

See also CONCEPT, -ION; POPULARIZED TECHNICALITIES.

E

each, every. These words are alike in their singling-out effect; both imply a plurality but take its members one at a time. Both have kinship with the idea in *apiece. You are to have three guesses apiece* can be said as: Each *of you is to have three guesses* / *You are to have three guesses* each / Every *one of you is to have three guesses.* Thus *each* and *every* call for singular verbs and for representation by singular nouns and pronouns—generally pronouns in the third person. *Each showy dog in the park has its rapt owner in tow* (not *their;* not *owners*) / *They shall sit every man under his vine and under his fig tree* (not *their;* not *vines;* not *fig trees*) / *Each of us* (*Every one of us*) *is required to feel that he is in some sense his brother's keeper* (not *are required;* not *we* or *they;* not *our* or *their;* not *keepers*). *Each of you* (*Every one of you*) *is going to be asked if you knew her* (not *are* and not *they*).

Everybody and *everyone* likewise call for an array of singulars coming after: *Everybody has to make up his own mind* (not *have to;* not *their;* the figurative *his* is discussed in ANTECEDENTS 7). The notion that *everybody* and *everyone* might be plurals ignores the fact that people persist in saying: *Everyone does it* (not *do*) / *Everybody goes there*

(not *go*) / *Everybody has it* (not *have*).

When *each* is not a subject but only follows a subject, it no longer dictates number in the nouns and pronouns to come; instead, the reigning subject lays down the ensuing pattern of both number and person: *We each have our* (*You each have your* / *They each have their*) *own difficulties.* Note that the paired singulars *his or her* make hash of such plural constructions: *We each have his or her own difficulties* amounts to *He or she have.*

Move *each* so that it follows the verb and you find that idiom offers a choice in the first person: either *We have each his* or *We have each our own difficulties.* Second- and third-person statements are formed as before: *You have each your own* / *They have each their own.* But this placement of *each* is little used now, and the reason is readily seen: when *each* stands after the verb, it is difficult to know whether the object of the verb should agree in number with the singular *each* or with the plural subject: *We have each his own difficulties* (*difficulty?*) / *You have each your own destinies* (*destiny?*) / *They demand each their own place* (*places?*) *in the sun.* Neither the form nor the problem is so alluring as to take up a writer's time. Substitute a form that raises no question of number: *All of us (you, them) have our (your, their) own troubles.*

Each other was once *each the other,* and many believe that it still implies only two, and that *one another* suggests three or more. But usage has by now made the phrases interchangeable—without affecting their exclusive allegiance to single items. This strict concentration rules out the plural possessive *each others'* and any plural noun to follow. *Each threatened to break the other's neck* (not *others',* not *necks*). Put another way: *Each threatened to break the neck of the other* (one other, possessing only one neck).

Each other can be the object of a verb but not the subject; that is, we may *like* or *dislike* or *listen to* or *put up with* or *helplessly adore each other;* but we cannot *know what each other wants for Christmas* or *hope that each other is pleased.* Instead, we *each know what the other wants,* and *each hopes that the other,* etc. The nonsense is factual rather than rhetorical in *Two men walk behind each other, keeping step.* In our world, if A. walks behind B., B. cannot walk behind A., and the two must settle for walking *one behind the other.*

For *between each,* as in *sixty seconds between each signal,* see BETWEEN 2.

each other. See EACH, EVERY.

ear, play it by. Musicians of whatever quality can be presumed to know what is wrong with the current use of this phrase. If they do, they should point out to their heedless neighbors that to play a piece by ear means to

reproduce a composition from memory, without the score. The use of the image in everyday life implies a different situation, which is illustrated by *It's too far ahead for us to plan; we'll have to play it by ear.* The meaning here is *we shall have to improvise:* there is no score; the piece not only has not been composed but in the present circumstances it cannot be.

The point of this trifling observation is that when a word exists that means exactly what you mean—in this case *improvise*—use it.

echelon. Borrowed from the military during the Second World War, *echelon* is now suffering from the overuse that invariably goes with misplaced extension. An *echelon* is a step in a scale. The French Army has ranks or groups of ranks that form *échelons,* the *échelons supérieurs* being what we know as the *top brass.* It might at first seem odd that in the United States, where hierarchies are not well thought of, *echelon* should have caught on so well. But a moment's thought shows that its purpose is precisely to avoid saying the blunt words *grade, rank, class.* This evasive use is clear in the headline LOW ECHELON WOMEN FOUND MORE NEUROTIC, which doubtless echoes the wording of the survey thus announced. The kindly intention of *echelon,* at once pretentious and genteel, does not keep the word from being an avoidance of plain fact. See EUPHEMISM.

eclectic. Perhaps this VOGUE WORD, because it comes from Greek, sounds impressive. Its strict meaning is *selected* *or selecting from diverse sources*, as in *Their eclectic furnishings told the guest that this was a family of travelers / So broad a range of musical quotations bespeaks a composer of eclectic taste or little original thought.* In these examples, the ideas of both selection and diverse sources are clear. But vogue use reduces *eclectic* to a pedantic replacement for simpler terms like *mixed, varied, dissimilar, unlike.* An *eclectic bowl of fruit* is probably only *a bowl of mixed fruit.* An *eclectic list of excuses* will do well enough as *a varied list.* But the columnist who offers to *raise one or two eclectic issues* defies correction. He may mean *two dissimilar issues*, but surely two issues already differ. As for *an eclectic potpourri of songs*, both writer and editor failed to consult a dictionary for *potpourri*: petals from diverse flowers mixed with several spices to perfume a drawer or a room. Their phrase is redundant.

-edly, adverbs in. See REPORTEDLY.

education. Originally the sum of anyone's intellectual and moral acquirements, *education* is now loosely used to mean *instruction, information, propaganda, advertising* (e.g., *a campaign of consumer education*), and even *course* or *curriculum* (*We offer a comprehensive yet well-balanced two-year education on the college level*). As a result, in place of teachers' colleges and departments of pedagogy, we have schools and departments of *education*. Pedagogy is in bad repute, both as a word and as a branch of knowledge, and the ubiquitous and quite unteachable *education* reigns in its stead.

There are two divisions within *education* so conceived: *methods* and *subject-matter disciplines*. Those who profess the former are *educationists*. Those who profess the latter are *disciplinary faculty* (see ENDINGS 2). Writers who are careful of their diction will hesitate to use *education* in its new senses and will avoid most of its derivatives.

educationese. Special terms, known in law as terms of art, naturally arise in every trade or profession for the convenient discharge of its duties. The terms may be words not used in the vernacular or common words used in a different sense. Some of these words are borrowed from the trade by speakers in other trades, often with a mistaken meaning.

One would imagine that the profession of teaching, presupposing in the practitioners wider knowledge than is usual in the laity, as well as a greater sensibility to meaning, accuracy, and logic, would have produced for itself an admirable technical vocabulary. One would be wrong. The language of education is the worst of all trade JARGONS, perhaps because it is one of the most recently contrived, certainly because it is overstocked with ill-considered metaphors. (Consider the sound of *a college prep program that targets students in the seventh grade and tracks them for six years.*) Compared with the sailor's vocabulary, which is much older and one of the best, the teacher's supplies no evidence for a belief in progress.

The faults of educationese are excessive abstraction and intentional vagueness, coupled with a naïve faith in the power of new terms to correct old abuses. It would be tedious to illustrate these faults in their unremitting variety. It should suffice to mention the shifting terms by which the contents of education themselves have come to be known. They used to be *branches*, on the analogy of the tree of knowledge. When the notion of change and movement replaced that of fixed, eternal knowledge, the tree seemed inappropriately static and the *branches* became *fields*, which the scholar or pupil was said to explore or discover for himself. So far reason was still in her seat. Then came the wish to express the lack of boundaries by replacing *field* with *area*. Areas could be anything known or unknown. Several researchers could *concentrate on* (in?) *one area*, or one person could choose an *area of concentration*. But in the phrase *area studies* the areas are actual portions of the earth's surface—i.e., geographical regions. The looseness of *area* was sometimes felt, so it required the aid of a *framework*. Nowadays few academic enterprises can be discussed or curricular reforms instituted without recourse to a *framework*, and any set of remarks about it or them is made *in terms of* (see IN TERMS OF) a *frame of reference*.

All this effort is arduous: to suggest how arduous, the subjects of learning—traditionally known as *subject matters*—had to become *disciplines* (see ENDINGS 2). English, mathematics, and the rest are now *disciplines*—except that their rudiments for young children are SKILLS. In the confusion of proliferating skills and disciplines

and the talk about them, it proved necessary to discern some parts that were more important than the rest—something to FOCUS on. These nuggets were quickly baptized *nuclei*. In groups they formed the *core curriculum*. Classes or periods in the schoolday became *modules*. Meanwhile, slices of each skill or discipline had to be marked off for orderly presentation. They obviously could not be called *lessons*; they had to be *units*, absorbed in successive *learning situations* with the aid of *clinics*, *workshops*, TOOLS, and *audiovisually qualified personnel*.

By the end of this ordeal, *teaching* and *instruction* had well-nigh disappeared. All that was left was EDUCATION.

See also JARGON; METAPHOR.

-ee, -er. The extension of the suffix *-ee* from legal terminology (*donee*, *grantee*, *vendee*, etc.) into general English has had mixed results, some of which are verging on the absurd. The original scheme was to denote agents and the objects of their action. *Lessor* and *lessee*, *assigner* and *assignee*, *mortgager* and *mortgagee* are readily explained by their relative positions. The *-er*, *-or* denotes one who acts toward another who receives the benefit or is the object of the deed. The extension of this device has been influenced by the belief that the form in *-ee* will stand for any French past participle in *é* doing duty as a noun—e.g., *employee*, which English might have chosen to render as *an employed*. We do say, in a collective sense, *the unemployed*, and less frequently we also say *the employed*.

Both the *-ee* and the *-ed* forms convey a passive meaning, the agent bearing the correlative name in *-er* (employer).

The application of this reasoning has given us some standard and inescapable words, such as *debauchee, devotee, referee, employee,* and *refugee.* But the *-ee* does not play the same role in all. In some we find the normal passive meaning, which points to the direct or indirect object of the action. In others the suffix is, as the Shorter Oxford English Dictionary calls it, "arbitrary," as in *bargee* (British for a *bargeman*). In *devotee* it is possible that the notion of one devoted to a cult (i.e., given or assigned to it as by a higher power) subsists in the *-ee.*

But whether this explanation holds or not, what makes these words with "arbitrary" endings acceptable is that, being familiar, they no longer cause us to think of the meaning of *-ee.* In words newly coined the trouble can be serious—as when persons who pledge funds to a charity are called *pledgees.* They are *pledgers* if they are anything, and the charity is the *pledgee.* The same objection applies to *attendees* for *attenders* and *conferees* for *conferrers.* As for those whom an understandable wanderlust entices away from a prison or an asylum, they are surely *escapers,* though now unreformably called *escapees*: COURTROOM ESCAPEE GETS PRISON TERM.

The false analogy that leads to such paradoxes must be held in check when we coin new names; one already comes across examples of *resignees* and *relaxees.*

For parallel active-passive confu-

sions in new coinages, see -ABLE, -IBLE; TRANSITIVE, INTRANSITIVE.

effect. See IMPACT.

effective. This adjective must be pinned to whatever noun answers the question: What goes into effect or is brought to bear? American business English pretends that *effective* is an adverb, with the result that the question requires for its answer some noun that is not there: *The price of a first-class accommodation will be increased effective November 30.* What is effective here, and what *effective* modifies, is the *increase*—not mentioned. The cure will generally be, not to supply the missing noun, but to abolish *effective*; in the foregoing sentence, there is no reason not to say *on.* In the following, other substitutes are suggested: *would replace it with another program, effective October 30* (there being no *replacement* to be modified, *effective* might well be *to begin*) / *ordered the Norfolk schools closed effective Monday* (from Monday on) / *It will be seen at 8:30 p.m. on Thursdays, effective this week* (beginning this week).

See also AS 5.

either . . . or; neither . . . nor. 1. A complete diagram of all the kinks and turns possible with these four words would occupy a large part of any such book as this. *Either* and *neither* are adjectives (*on either hand / Neither applicant can be taken seriously*), pronouns (*Either is well qualified / Neither deserves consideration*), and adverbs (*Not that we can fully accept this prop-*

osition either), besides being conjunctions that characteristically hunt in pairs—*either* with *or*, *neither* with *nor*. They also serve uses that grammarians are at one in approving while quarreling about their classification. Nevertheless the perplexities that bother a modern writer are comparatively few, and they occur within a fairly narrow range of the conjunctive uses. *Neither* and *either* as adverbs raise hardly any problems. As adjectives and pronouns they require us only to know that they presuppose two subjects of discourse but treat them (as EACH and EVERY do) one at a time and therefore call for statements in the singular number. *Neither candidate has a chance* tells us that two are under consideration, but separately. *Neither of them has a chance* tells us the same, and the number of the verb is unaffected by the intervening plural. All aberrations being possible, we find an occasional sentence in which the alternative subjects are handled like a plural: *Neither the President nor the Secretary of State were* (was) *informed* / *Neither Helen nor Paris were* (was) *in Troy when the Greeks attacked.* The last example, which occurs in a serious work, exemplifies a rare blunder. The feeling that *either . . . or* and *neither . . . nor* introduce separate alternatives is strong and is generally obeyed.

2. It is also rare to find in modern writing a combination in which *neither* is acceptably correlated with *or*, or *either* with *nor*. When we read: *one he could neither cow, browbeat, or intimidate*, we think at once of a misprint, or else of carelessness. (In older and state-lier prose one might have found *She did not blanch; neither did she weep or cry.*) The coupling raises the question whether *either* and *neither* may be used of more than two items—a license now sanctioned by dictionaries and other authorities.

3. As for what might be called the disguised confusion of *neither . . . nor* with *either . . . or*, it is common enough and it brings up subtle considerations of emphasis and logic.

The common form of the practice substitutes *nor* for *or* in sentences where a *neither* is imagined at work though physically absent. The force of *neither* is fallaciously ascribed to some other negative word that is actually there—usually *not* or *never: Can't ever dent, rust nor tarnish* results from the impression that *can't* (cannot) is the equivalent of *can neither*. Modern English argues that it is the equivalent of *cannot either*, the sequel of which is not *nor* but *or*.

Still, the argument is not conclusive. George Bernard Shaw, who was steeped in Elizabethan and biblical English, was much given to this questionable *nor* and used it often but not invariably. He wrote: [Tchaikovsky] *never attains, nor desires to attain, the elevation at which the great modern musicians . . . maintain themselves.* Analyzed, this says *nor never desires to attain*; though Shaw might reply that *never attains, nor desires* is equivalent to *not either attains or desires*, which can be converted into *neither attains nor desires.* Modern usage responds as to a double negative in *never . . . nor*, and feels that they cancel each other.

Shaw similarly writes: *and think, not of his own safety, nor of home and beauty, but of England,* construing *not . . . nor* as the equivalent of *neither . . . nor,* or as if *not . . . or* limped as badly as *neither . . . or.* An American example of the same false *nor: The most important item . . . was not the title poem nor the other six poems he included.* (Among classic American writers, Ambrose Bierce is a partisan of the Shavian *nor,* but he has not generally been followed.)

Lesser writers often make their uncertainty graphic by using both *nor* and *or* in the same construction after a negative: *He does not need to become a Pangloss nor a Pascal . . . he does not fancy himself, or any philosopher, a revolutionary or teleological planner.* The *nor* and the first *or* are parallel; the *nor* should patently be *or.*

4. This type of confusion is compounded by the existence of a functionally quite different *nor*—the separate conjunction that means *and not* and introduces a totally disjoined independent clause, generally with subject and verb inverted. Several of the foregoing examples could be recast in this independent construction by retaining the *nor* that was a miscue as written; and indeed the two constructions have so beguiling a resemblance that the authors may have thought they were writing elliptical forms of the clausal construction. *G. never acknowledged any boundaries between these, nor did she acknowledge any between public and private life:* this correct though wordy version has the radical difference that its *nor* cannot be correlated with any preceding word mistakenly assumed to perform the task of *neither.* Similarly, *There is no point nor honesty in pretending* uses a false *nor* for *or,* but might with entire correctness be written *There is no point, nor is there any honesty.*

As a connective of simple nouns, *nor* is sometimes substituted for *or* where it suggests an almost calculated effort to be wrong. *The shrewd seal always keeps his blowhole open beneath a protruding piece of ice where no bear nor harpoon can strike down at him.* Obviously, here is an option of *no bear or harpoon* and *no bear and no harpoon* —the second so superior in emphasis as to be worth the extra monosyllable. For aberrant uses of *or* for *and* see BETWEEN 3; also EQUALLY 2.

5. *Neither* and *either* are subject, like other negative and alternative words, to careless misplacement, with resulting imbalance: *Americans so far have neither been permitted to learn their names and records nor their beliefs.* This becomes grammatically tenable if we put *neither* after *learn.* Note, however, that on the principle of giving a negative meaning a negative form the sentence would be better if written *Americans so far have not been permitted to learn either . . . or . . .* Written as first quoted, it implies a quite different kind of matched structure: *have neither been permitted to learn . . . nor been* [some construction balancing *permitted*— e.g., *enabled to know*] *their beliefs.* Likewise *The size of my contribution is neither a measure of my indebtedness nor of my belief in the significance of the program* becomes tolerable with

neither after *a measure* instead of before it, but would be still further improved by writing *is not a measure of either . . . or . . .* Such examples have no bearing on the force or meaning of *neither;* they concern the order of modifiers and the general question of the misplaced negative.

6. *Neither . . . nor* does not combine two singular subjects into a plural but emphasizes their disjunction; hence the following verb is singular when each of the subjects is. Some grammarians encourage writers to make the verb agree in number with the nearest subject; but the clash will be felt by thoughtful readers. *Neither Judaism nor its voluntary adherents possess the characteristics of a race or a nation.* This is defensible, but a workmanlike writer may put his pride in not writing sentences that need defending. Nor need he, in the interest of grammar, go in for such a dotting of *i*'s as *Judaism does not possess, nor do its voluntary adherents, the characteristics . . .* He could always write: *Judaism and its voluntary adherents do not possess the characteristics* (or *lack the characteristics*) *of a race or of a nation.*

A typical mismanagement involving *neither . . . nor* occurs in such sentences as *Neither the experience of 1994 nor this year—two years of record snowfalls—has conclusively shown . . .* Here we have another form of the false comparison, the second year being matched, not with the first, but with the experience of the first. The interpolation in dashes reasserts that the experience of 1994 is a year. Perhaps the intention was *The experience of neither 1994 nor this year . . .* Much better to scrap *the experience of.*

See also AND / OR; MATCHING PARTS.

eleemosynary. See PRONUNCIATION 1.

elemental, elementary. See ENDINGS 1.

ellipsis. 1. Also called *ellipsis dots, ellipsis points,* and the *ellipsis mark,* this device is the familiar three dots that show an omission of a word, phrase, sentence, paragraph, or more from a quoted passage. Try not to be confused by the fact that *ellipsis* denotes both this punctuation and an implied repetition of words; a discussion of the latter ellipsis can be found under WHAT IS "UNDERSTOOD"?

At its most elementary, the ellipsis announces an omission within a quoted sentence or between two such sentences. If the words you are omitting end with a period, question mark, or exclamation point, put that mark after the dots. In general, the aim is to make a simplified passage clear and faithful to the author's meaning, not to hint at how many or what kind of words you have omitted.

You need not put dots at the beginning or the end of a quotation even though words have been left out fore or aft. The reader assumes that other words originally preceded and followed those you have quoted.

2. Three dots (not more) are also used to suggest the trailing off or abandoning of a thought. *When I imagine all the good that a little money might*

have done her, I could just . . . This device makes for lifelike utterance but also ever so slightly teases the reader. If used more than sparingly, it will annoy.

emanate. See CONNOTATIONS.

emerging nations. See EUPHEMISMS.

empathy. See POPULARIZED TECHNICALITIES.

emphasis. It is a commonplace that the emphatic parts of a sentence are the beginning and the end, but this generality is subject to important exceptions. In the periodic sentence—that which begins with a subordinate clause and makes one wait for the meaning held in the main clause—the first emphasis falls somewhere in the middle of the utterance. *Although he fought a series of brilliant battles across Europe, Napoleon in 1813 could not hope to prevail over so many enemies massed against him.* Here and in all similar constructions, the expectant rush toward the subject—*Napoleon in 1813*—heightens the emphasis on it. The end of that sentence, however, is weaker than it need be because *against him* is filler made necessary only by rhythm. If the sentence had ended *prevail over such a host of his massed enemies* the chief idea in the predicate would have gained prominence and therefore emphasis.

There is no decree that all sentences should begin and end with emphatic bangs. LINKING often depends on quiet

endings or beginnings that reserve a single emphasis for the most important thought within the paragraph. A succession of emphatic sentences tires the mind. They resemble maxims or aphorisms, which do not develop an idea but rather compress it into a final utterance. If it is indeed final, there should be nothing more to say; a chain of final statements is a contradiction in terms. Hence no good paragraph can come out of recurring hammer-stroke emphases.

If a writer or speaker has thought enough about his subject to be aware of its main parts and of their interconnections, his discourse will probably find the right moments and the right expressions for the emphasis he desires. What he has to guard against is inadvertent emphases in the wrong places, for these can occur in many small ways, easily avoidable if tagged in advance and steadily remembered. Here are a few types of this common fault that will open the alert reader's eyes to other types equally damaging:

1. Muffed climax. In a progressive series there should be a logical order of increase or decrease: *We were bored, exhausted, beyond all caring.* Though there is no established scale for such intensifications of feeling, a little thought shows at least which is the term that should come on the highest rung of the ladder (= scale = climax). This natural rule of oratory has been forgotten in the otherwise acceptable reversal *After years of gambling and winning, he had lost by the merest fluke, by a careless shake of the head, by inattention.* As the least emphatic,

because most general, term, *inattention* should come first, *shake of the head* last.

2. Making a point of the subordinate. The statement of an objection or a conclusion or any other affirmation must not be obscured by its surrounding details. *What is damnable about these personnel tests is that only the men who give nonconformist answers fail to get a job.* This clearly implies that the writer wishes other people would also fail, whereas he means that the tests *unfairly weed out the nonconformists*—or some such phrasing.

3. Misleading intruders. Words like *always, both,* and *whenever* can impart a stress that throws the sentence out of shape and will sometimes puzzle the reader: he looks for a nuance that is not clear since it was never intended. For example: *The locking up was systematically done, without hurry—each door, each drawer, each window latch whenever he came to it* (substitute *as* for *whenever*) / *I will sign an affidavit that they both attacked me, both inside and outside* (inside and outside the house) / *At times he would go over the whole sequence in his mind invariably after the gap, the clue, to the mistake he had made.* This needs recasting: *At . . . in his mind. What he sought persistently was the failure that would be a clue to the mistake,* etc.

4. Emphasis by exaggeration must be sparingly used. It wears itself out just as quickly as understatement or OXYMORON. Nor should one count on the obviousness of an exaggeration to impart a light humorous touch. The sign repeated on every floor of a first-

class hotel on the West Coast fails of whatever effect may have been intended: *Incredible confusion, indeed needless dismay, can develop if you do not study this timetable* [of restaurant hours].

5. The use of italics will emphasize words that ordinarily would be slurred over and hence would not convey the right meaning. But one must make sure, by hearing the words spoken actually or in the mind, which word needs the stress. In the exclamation *She doesn't need him!* any one of the four words could conceivably be italicized, according to the context and the intention. The *locus classicus* of unintended emphasis by means of italics is the following biblical quotation as it is printed in versions that italicize words supplied by the translators: "He said 'Saddle me the ass.' And they saddled *him*."

See also PROSE, THE SOUND OF; SENTENCE, THE.

(de-)emphasize. See FORBIDDEN WORDS 2.

empower. See VOGUE WORDS.

enable. See TRANSITIVE, INTRANSITIVE.

encroach. See PREPOSITIONS.

end product. See SCIENTISM 2.

endings. 1. Alternative. 2. Misdirected.
1. Alternative. Although the difference between *basic* and *basal, supplementary* and *supplemental* is for most

purposes negligible, similar differences in other pairs embody important distinctions, and their neglect can blur meaning. The most persistent modern confusion of this sort has been that between *precipitous* and *precipitate*. The former refers to a sharp downward slope: *The descent for the next three hundred yards is precipitous. Precipitate* as an adjective means *hasty.* It follows that the action of the chairman of the board is *precipitate,* not *precipitous.* The decline in the company's profits is *precipitous* and cannot be *precipitate,* no matter how suddenly it occurred.

Two similar pairs must be treated with a like attention to differences. *Elementary* refers to the simple parts of a subject or a compound, and hence to the beginnings of schooling, study, explanation, as well as to the products of analysis, as in the *elementary* particles of physics. *Elemental* has the special connotation of power and a further suggestion of first in point of time: the *elemental* forces of nature, the *elemental* passions of men. (A special usage in chemistry reserves *elemental* for the free, uncombined substance—e.g., *elemental phosphorus*—while phosphorus in general remains one of the *elementary* substances.) Very nearly the same distinction separates *primal* from *primary*: the *primal* brute, the *primary* school; our *primal* parents (Adam and Eve), our *primary* needs—food, clothing, and shelter.

Generally speaking, the urge to change the endings of established adjectives should be repressed. Such changes are not necessary and may lead to trouble. The usage of a profession (e.g., *basal metabolism* in medicine) should be respected, but it is an affectation of singularity to change the *basic texts* of some years ago to the *basal readers* that some publishers now bring out. See also -ION, -NESS, -MENT.

2. Misdirected. The modern desire to bestow special names that are anything but transparent on the objects of our concern often leads to absurdities that involve the meaning of suffixes. Thus a study of the law's delay found, and dealt with, a group of *durable cases*—that is, cases that lasted an inordinately long time. It may be useful to speculate that the authors, in their wish to be technical, first suggested and rejected *enduring* and *durational* and then fastened on *durable,* blind to the common meaning of that word and to the force of -ABLE. As a result, cases that should *not* endure are denoted by a word that proclaims their power to do so. One may surmise that if *long* (or *long-lasting*) *cases* ever occurred to the legal experts, the phrase was discarded as insufficiently technical. The desire to tell all in a single somewhat abstract modifier is strong; it has inspired the awkward and needless *societal, dialogal,* and others; but it should be resisted.

A related but different type of error is to name an act or function by means of an accepted and well-formed adjective, yet one that singles out the wrong feature and sets up an ambiguity with an established meaning. The commonest instance is that of *disciplinary* and, by extension, *interdisciplinary,* as these words are used in the academic world. In the 1940s, *discipline* became a synonym for *subject matter*; then questions arising in research became *disciplinary problems*, on a par with naughty boys; finally links between subjects or "across disciplines" generated *interdisciplinary*. To restrict *discipline* to its original meaning is a desirable but probably utopian goal. See also EDUCATIONESE.

enormity, enormousness. These nouns have in common the roots *e* (= outside, beyond) and *norm* (= a mason's pattern, a standard). That said, the partial likeness gives way to the gravest of differences, which careless speakers or writers ignore when they use the words interchangeably to denote great size.

An *enormity* is a monstrous wickedness or crime, evil being no less potent in the definition than magnitude. *The enormity of Herod's slaughter of all the children of Bethlehem two years old and younger* names an action marked by more than its scope. Modern life notoriously abounds in illustrations of the word, from death camps to forced migrations. The often used *atrocity* is a vaguer word, since it denotes the horrific done to many or one. To speak of *the enormity of that lawn when you come to cut it* verges on the ludicrous. *Enormous* the lawn may be, but *enormousness*, though correct, is a clumsy word. *Immensity, hugeness,* and *vastness* are fitting terms.

ensure. See ASSURE, ENSURE, INSURE.

entropy. See SCIENTISM 2.

environment. See COVERING WORDS; TRANSITIVE, INTRANSITIVE.

envisage. See TRANSITIVE, INTRANSITIVE.

epic. See LEGEND(ARY).

equally. 1. *Equally as.* 2. *Equally with.* 3. *Equally . . . or.*

1. *Equally as.* This may be the shortest redundancy in English. We can either call one man *as tall as another* or call the two *equally tall*; what we must avoid saying is that one is *equally as tall as* the other. The remedy for *equally as* is to omit the *equally* or the *as*, a correction as small as the error. Occasionally the construction turns up in disguise: *I was entitled to it equally as much as him* (*equally with him* or *as much as he*). (See also AS 10.)

2. *Equally with* is underused, considering its handiness in adverbially linking a description or an action to a pair of subjects: *We were given the run of the grounds equally with the paid-up members* / *Young G. sways her audiences equally with the most practiced speakers.* Vocal emphasis naturally falls on *equally* here, making the idiom particularly apt for statements in which the idea of equality may be unexpected.

3. *Equally . . . or.* It should go without saying that *equally*, when it introduces a two-part alternative, takes the sequence *and*, not *or*, by a logic as inexorable as that which requires *and* after *both* and *or* after *either*. But to let the point go unmentioned would be to overlook the propensity to forget one's intention on setting out. *It was equally*

hard to imagine that he was unaware of these details or that he could be aware without doing anything about them. Obvious patterns for the thought are (a) *equally hard to imagine* [this] *and* [that]; (b) *as hard to imagine* [this] *as* [that]; (c) *hard to imagine either* [this] *or* [that]; (d) *hard to imagine both* [this] *and* [that]. A mixture entails the usual disadvantages of swapping horses in midstream.

See also PREPOSITIONS.

ergonomic. See POPULARIZED TECHNICALITIES.

essence, of the. See POPULARIZED TECHNICALITIES.

essential. See JOURNALESE.

esteem. See APPRECIATE 2.

et cetera. See ABBREVIATIONS 2; PRONUNCIATION 1.

etymology. For some time the experts on language and stylistics have inveighed against making pupils aware of etymologies. The old practice of noting derivations is said to be pernicious because it ignores the detailed history of each particular word and sets up between ideas barriers that usage has broken down. Etymology is thus reserved as the exclusive province of the professional linguist, and professional writers are told once again that they know nothing about language, except now and then how to use it.

It is true that words lend themselves to plausible but false derivations and that to discover the actual ones re-

quires painstaking work which writers lack the time and the knowledge to pursue. But the fact remains that writing without a sense of the interconnections or repulsions arising from the meaning of roots is likely to produce prose that is deficient in some way. It will lack the inner cohesion that comes from the linking of complementary ideas by means of those hidden meanings; or it will fall into tautology—as when someone speaks of *eradicating the root of the trouble*; or it will overlook mixed METAPHOR—as in the sentence *It was the governor's veto of this measure that ignited a race of unsurpassed bitterness.* Obviously the last writer took *ignite* to mean *set off, start up*, recalling the *ignition* mechanism of a car. That the word is inseparable from the idea of *fire* can of course be learned unconsciously from usage if one reads widely and attentively; but the knowledge is also obtainable direct, from looking into etymologies. It was one of the advantages of studying Latin that it disclosed the meaning of many roots in common words. For those who never had a brush with Latin and Greek one can recommend the etymological dictionaries by Skeat and by Weekley, and the admirably organized *Origins* by Eric Partridge. They should be the bedside books of the many persons who invent or baptize products and processes with Greco-Latin coinages of their own. See SCIENTISM; TELESCOPINGS.

euphemisms are mild or ingratiating words or phrases meant to veil disturbing ideas. They are, for example, essential to diplomacy, as when it is announced that a certain step by another nation will be regarded as *an unfriendly act,* meaning a deliberate affront that could lead to war. In this instance, avoiding plain words gives time for second thoughts and the saving of lives. Euphemisms have their good applications.

But nice words are also employed to conceal the gravity or purpose of an action taken. Such euphemisms change over time, but few periods in history have been so steadily unwilling to call things by their right names as our own. In the realm of espionage, a *covert operation* is anything from a burglary carried out for political ends to toppling (*destabilizing*) a government. In war, the old phrase *air raid* was replaced by *air strike,* which sounds briefer and more precise. Following this line, *precision bombing* in the Second World War bragged of its merciful limits; *surgical air strike* in the Vietnam War sounded almost therapeutic. Meanwhile, the phrase *collateral damage* was invented to cover what even exquisite bombardment hit by mistake.

The euphemism for a war that goes on undeclared is *conflict,* as in the mid-century *Korean conflict.* A *retreat* is called a *withdrawal,* and *invasions* have become *incursions.* To *neutralize* or *pacify* means to conquer by force, perhaps by a *pre-emptive strike,* which is a surprise attack. Enemy troops that are spoken of as *accounted for* are disabled or dead; and sending refugees back where they came from is called *involuntary return.* Forced labor and indoctrination take the high-minded name of *re-education.*

The trouble with euphemisms is that they are quickly seen through and become as distressing as the words and ideas they mask; another screen must be raised. What was called *shell shock* in the First World War became *combat fatigue* in the Second and still later *post-traumatic stress disorder.* The triumph of medical technique is implied by the change from *madhouse* to *insane asylum* to *mental institution* to the victorious *mental health center*—to which, presumably, only the carefree go.

In the course of such tiptoe progressions, sense can be discarded long before it is missed. Technologically backward countries were once called *undeveloped countries,* which was found offensive and so replaced by *underdeveloped countries.* A taint of reproach still lingered, and within a short time we heard of *developing countries.* But this phrase in many contexts implied that Japan, the United States, Germany, and others were not *developing countries,* whereupon their cousins became *emerging nations.*

No matter where, the *poor* know who they are, but politicians and the press scarcely know what to call them. For a time the adjective and noun *underprivileged* implied that they were privileged but less so than some; *disadvantaged* likewise accented the root and modified it with a prefix. The recent *underclass* is more downright, although it uncomfortably implies that the poor are always with us, whatever we call them.

The euphemisms of commerce cater to vanity and fear, and might better be called genteelisms. For example, the fat man and woman shopping for clothes are no longer willing to be called *portly* and *stout*; he goes to a *big man's* store, and she is shown clothes for the *full-figured*. *Secondhand stores* are *thrift shops*, and their goods are not *secondhand* but *previously owned*, or worse, *pre-owned*. Airline passengers who want a *life preserver* handy may find instead a *personal flotation device*, their fear giving way to wonder.

By nature, some occupations see a greater need than others for pastel language. Your dentist does not design *false teeth* but *dentures*, and the *undertaker* wants to be known as a *mortician* or a *funeral director*, who does not *bury* but *inters*, or else *inurns* if the body has been cremated. No longer does the veterinarian *destroy* an animal he cannot cure; it is *put to sleep*, or even more vaguely, *put down*. Prisons are *correctional facilities* or *detention centers* presided over not by *guards* but by *correctional officers*.

Euphemisms in the private life are by now too many to count. The child past monosyllables learns to use the *toilet* (itself a code word from French that means to groom oneself), and, in growing, learns to go to the *bathroom*, the *restroom*, the *john*, the *men's* or *ladies' room* (*women's* has not caught on), or to *conveniences* too coy to mention. Love may or may not leap into marriage, but if it does not, unmarried lovers may introduce "my *companion*," "my *partner*," "my *significant other*" (now mainly facetious), or simply "my *friend*," which leaves nobody any the wiser.

Euphemisms are newly in fashion for mental or physical failings, whether early or late. Formed on the adjective *challenged* (as in *orally challenged* for afflicted with a speech impediment) or on the suffix *-impaired* (as in *hearing-impaired*, meaning *deaf* or *partially deaf*), they manage by vagueness and wind to attach new dread to the problem. Cancer and tuberculosis once inspired such terror that their names were rarely printed or spoken; the ban has been lifted long since.

Senior citizen must have been inspired by a fear of aging accompanied by the wish to appease a newly large class of consumers and voters. But that class of *elderly, retired, aged*, or *old people* may have bridled at having its citizen status noticed quite so archly. Many will tolerate *senior* as a noun today, but many others insist on being *elderly* or *old*.

Euphemisms meaning *to die* seem to be limited now to *decease, pass away, pass over*, and *pass on*.

See also DEVELOP; *downsized* under TRANSITIVE, INTRANSITIVE; EDUCATIONESE; FISCAL; FORBIDDEN WORDS 1; IMPLICIT, EXPLICIT 2.

-ever. See WHATEVER, WHOEVER, INTERROGATIVE.

every. See EACH, EVERY.

everybody, everyone. See ANTECEDENTS 7; EACH, EVERY.

every day, everyday. The two-word phrase is made up of an adjective and a noun (*Every day she has a new sug-*

gestion); the single word is a compound adjective (*Overwork is his everyday lot*).

exception. Usage dictates that all exceptions must be *to* a noun that is placed nearby. The *to* may be omitted as being understood, but *exception* can have no meaning unless the larger entity from which it stands apart is named. *Mr. A. acknowledges that his troupe has adopted austerities; but, with one exception, these were not apparent on stage last evening.* Ask the question: *Exception* to what? The answer is: *these* (pronoun standing for *austerities*). *With one exception, I can enjoy the Shakespeare comedies. Exception* to what? Answer: *the Shakespeare comedies.* Notice that in the following examples from a national newspaper, a respected biography, and a library journal *exception* hangs in a void: *M. found writing excruciating, and* [his] *book was no exception* / *She did less drinking in those days, with a few exceptions* / *It is always a revelation to listen to a poet reading his or her own work, and this* [recording] *is no exception.* These three sentences alike collapse into talk of *exceptions* at the point at which the subject slips the writer's mind. The first sentence should stay with what it is talking about and end *his work on the book was no different.* The second should keep its subject (*she*) in view and end with something like *though she had lapses.* (For the fumbling *with*, see WITH.) In the third, *revelation* is clearly meant to apply to the recording at hand: *this recording affords that experience.*

excerpt. See PREPOSITIONS; PRONUNCIATION 1.

excessively, exceedingly. This is one of the numerous pairs (see DANGEROUS PAIRS) whose differentiation is helpful and not to be given up. *Excessively* tells of an unwanted surplus; *exceedingly* merely carries a stated quality to its highest point. So we should expect the dentist to be *exceedingly* careful in her work on us; but if she is *excessively* careful, the work will drag on forever. The common phrases are *I am exceedingly grateful* / *He is exceedingly quick* (*tender, sharp, clever, friendly*) / *She is exceedingly kind* (*sweet-natured, muscular, rich*). And again: *He is excessively polite* (= obsequious), *excessively forthcoming* (= gushing), *excessively rich* (= too much so for his own good). Note that a quality that may be supposed regrettable takes *excessively: excessively shy, poor,* or *stupid;* but that words of absolute import (see ABSOLUTE WORDS) cannot take *excessively: excessively fatuous, excessively mature* go against reason.

exciting. This by now ridiculous word needs no illustration from current sources: it is ubiquitous and nearly always empty of meaning. It has not yet displaced its equally empty companion, *fascinating,* so that a comparison of the two is still possible and instructive. *Exciting* implies agitated motion; *fascinating* implies frozen immobility. The two are used interchangeably to say: *admirable, new, excellent, practical, pretty good, not half bad.*

exclamation points. See QUESTION MARKS, EXCLAMATION POINTS.

excluding. See DANGLERS, BENIGN.

execrable. See PRONUNCIATION 1.

execute. Ambrose Bierce, a vigorous fighter in intellectual rearguard actions at the end of the nineteenth century, bridled at the use of *execute* to mean *put to death by law.* Bierce insisted that it is the judicial sentence that is executed, not the criminal. By Bierce's time the extension of the word to the new meaning was beyond reversal. But *execute* still retains its etymological and primary meaning of *carry out, fulfill, pursue to the end, follow through.* A writer who reports that *the sentence of five years' banishment was strictly executed* shows knowledge of what the word originally meant and commits no archaism. This sense is kept in the noun *executive,* one who carries out decisions, and in *executive* as an adjective describing the branch of government which does the same.
See also PRONUNCIATION 1.

exhibition. See PRONUNCIATION 1.

exigent. See PRONUNCIATION 1.

explicit. See IMPLICIT, EXPLICIT.

exponential. See POPULARIZED TECHNICALITIES.

expound, expatiate. To expound is to set forth in a systematic way—to explain, make clear, elucidate—and the word calls for a direct object, with no preposition. One expounds a doctrine; one does not expound *on* it. *Expound* is often confused with *expatiate,* whose somewhat pejorative meaning is to expound at too great length: to go on and on. Fittingly, one expatiates *on* one's subject, or tries not to. *V. opened the discussion by expounding what he called "the iron law of diminishing literacy," as it affects recruitment* / *A volunteer was chosen from among many to expound the people's grievances.* Contrast with the foregoing statements: *T. was given to expatiating on the unfairness of assignments, changes in the roster of courses, and limitations on student aid* / *My colleague expatiates on this single instance as if it had no parallel and we no other claims on our time.* See PREPOSITIONS.

express, adjective. The modern craving for speed—our demand for the express package, the express bus, the express messenger—overlooks or distorts the distinct other use of this modifier. *The President's express purpose* does not mean an intention rapidly uttered or meant to be instantly carried out; it denotes a purpose clearly and unmistakably stated with something definite in mind. *Against the old lady's express dislike of Mother's Day, all four sons conspired to take her on the trip of her life.* To some, *expressed dislike* might seem more reasonable here, as might *expressed purpose* in the phrase about the President. But to say only that the purpose or the dislike was expressed does not say as much about either as the adjective *express* does.

People state things with more or less clarity—and their hearers or readers may partly understand, or get the vague idea, or miss the point. *Express* describes what not only leaves no doubt in its wording but also unmistakably means what it says.

exquisite. See PRONUNCIATION 1.

extraordinary. See PRONUNCIATION 1.

extrapolate. See POPULARIZED TECHNICALITIES.

F

fabulous. See LEGEND(ARY).

facilitator. See RESOURCE PERSON.

facility, fluency. To praise the eloquent speaker or writer, mention his *fluency*. This gift is not the same as *facility*, which comes from *facile* and implies the merely glib. *Facility* and *fluency* are increasingly confused, the former being, in a quite different meaning, a hugely popular COVERING WORD; *facility* leaps to mind as some weeds leap over fences.

factor. See SCIENTISM 1; / UNNECESSARY WORDS 2.

faculty. This word is and should remain a collective noun, like *company*, *senate*, *college*, and so on. Too often one comes across statements of this sort: *I could see a little knot of men talking heatedly on the edge of the grass; two were faculty and about five were students / No plan can succeed in an institution with good morale unless enough faculty are behind it.* One says, correctly, *Three company employees* (not *three company*) *reported feeling symptoms / Two members of the Senate* (not *two Senate*) *voted "Aye" / College students are not immune to fads* (not

College are not). Hence, *three faculty members* or *three members of the faculty*; also *Dean of the Faculty*, not *Dean of Faculty*.

fail in. We may fail in an attempt to do something, or we may fail to do it; but to say that we fail in doing it is self-contradictory. *They have notably failed so far in convincing Spanish or foreign businessmen here of their thesis* is such a contradiction. The failure is in not convincing them; convincing them would be success. It should be put: *They have . . . failed . . . to convince.*

faintly. See UNDERSTATEMENT.

fault, verb. See VOGUE WORDS.

feisty. See CONNOTATIONS.

felicitous, fortuitous, fortunate. *Fortuitous* (occurring by chance) elbows out *felicitous* (apt, successful, agreeable) in more places than it should. *It was not a fortuitous* (felicitous) *moment for you to begin telling jokes / This is a particularly fortuitous* (felicitous) *book for the summertime / Her remarks after the annual dinner were thought especially fortuitous* (felicitous). Aptness, not chance, is the point of these statements. A fortuity may be felicitous, but the context should make clear that this is the case: *A fortuitous break in the weather allowed our plans to go forward.*

Fortunate means lucky, auspicious, marked by good fortune; *fortuitous* is often mistakenly used where *fortunate* was meant. Indeed, in the previous sentence, the break in the weather was an agreeable (*felicitous*) event, the result of chance (*fortuitous*), and a piece of good fortune (*fortunate*), all three at once. And those unwilling to blame an infelicity will speak politely of *P.'s unfortunate figure of speech* or *the waiter's unfortunate manners*. Probably to limit the overlap, Americans neglect *felicitous*. Writers unsure of their choice among the three words will trust the dictionary, not lucky coincidence. See DANGEROUS PAIRS.

fewer, less. *Fewer* is by nature a word applicable to number; *less* is applied to quantity as bulk. Hence in making numerical comparisons, *fewer*, not *less*, is required: *We drew fewer people last night than a week ago / Investigators have fewer clues to the cause of this crash than they had in the Korean disaster.* But we speak of *less tonnage, less sugar, less wine.*

An occasional construction in which the ideas of quantity and number are hardly distinguishable will take either *less* or *fewer*: *The million seasonal farm workers normally work less than 150 days in a year.* Here *150 days* can be felt as either a specified number of days or a unitary measure of time (as *less than half a year* would be). *Search-*

ers have fewer than forty-eight hours to find the couple alive could employ *less*, though with a loss of dramatic effect. Sometimes an ostensibly numerical statement is unmistakably a unitary measure and, as such, excludes *fewer*. We take *a million dollars* as a sum of money, not as a measure of units; *fifty feet* as a measure of distance, not as one foot added to forty-nine other feet; *thirty minutes* as a stretch of time, exactly like *half an hour*. Such unitary expressions not only take the quantitative *less* but also require a singular verb: *A million dollars is more easily accumulated than it used to be / Fifty feet is too short a distance.*

The antonym of *less*, which is *more*, applies either to number or to quantity. When applied to a number, *more* ought not to be paired with a word that properly applies only to quantity—e.g., *much* or *little*. *Little more than 1,000 old people in a county population of 17,000* does better with *scarcely more than* or *hardly more than*. The SET PHRASE *more or less* invites the confusion of quantity and number: *Two dozen people, more or less, passed by as the crime was in progress.* Those who wish to can substitute *Some two dozen*, since *some* serves for both quantity and number.

See also NONE.

fiction. See UN-, IN-, NON-.

field. See EDUCATIONESE; UNNECESSARY WORDS 2.

figuratively. See LITERALLY.

finalize. See -IZE.

financial. See FISCAL.

first of all. Enumerating reasons, causes, or arguments often requires a trumpet call to arrest attention. Usually *first, second, third,* and so on are adequate. If one wants still greater emphasis for the first item, the subtly impatient *first of all* will do the trick. But one overdoes emphasis and brings on tedium by following suit with the frequent and foolish *second of all.*

Save *firstly* for sojourns in Great Britain, where it is still much loved and leads on to *secondly, thirdly,* etc. If an American adverb is wanted, remember that *first* is as much an adverb as *firstly: Maria first made sure to notify all her neighbors.* The sequence *first . . . secondly . . . thirdly* is mere nervous affectation.

fiscal. The pirating of one word after another to give a fresh look to old routines has become a mania among business people, from whose statements in the press civil servants, academics, and the common man pick up the habit. Within living memory, sensible people spoke of *money matters* and *money troubles.* If they were a bit Micawberish, they referred more loftily to their *pecuniary situation,* and in so doing they remained within the limits of reason. But at some later point, private citizens began to refer to their *finances,* which was at once inaccurate, pompous, and genteel. *Finance,* as *financier* still suggests, is properly the management of large sums by profes-

sional money handlers. But it is doubtless impossible to recapture this useful distinction. Every schoolchild who overspends his or her weekly allowance is in *financial difficulties* and hopes to secure *refinancing.*

For larger entrepreneurs and corporations, *finance* (noun and verb) has grown commonplace; they now speak of *fiscal* measures to be taken by the board or *funding* arrangements to be made by the treasurer. But *fiscal* refers only to taxation and government budgets, and *funding* means *pay* or *appropriate* into a reserve.

That first slipcover on the old reality has a plausible justification in the accepted use of *fiscal year.* But *fiscal* in that phrase simply records the fact that business adopted the government "year," which was *fiscal* because that is the name appropriate to governmental money matters. *Fiscus* is the Latin word for the public chest, derived from the meaning *wicker basket.*

A late arrival among the euphemisms for *money* is *resources.* This COVERING WORD already does duty in official prose for everything from crayons and chalk to nuclear missiles; its currency should not be accepted.

See also EUPHEMISMS; LIMITED.

fit, fitted. See MYSTERIOUS PASTS.

fixation. See POPULARIZED TECHNICALITIES.

flammable. See UN-, IN-, NON-.

focus (on). See METAPHOR 4; SCIENTISM 1; VOGUE WORDS.

folk(s). See PERSONS 2.

for free. See FREE GIFT.

forbid. See PREPOSITIONS.

forbidden words. 1. By reason of obscenity. 2. As an aid to writing.

1. This heading will bring to mind what were known as "four-letter words" and "good old Anglo-Saxon" when this book first appeared. In 1966 most publishers still forbade such terms except in works of a presumably literary kind, but change was already occurring in the code of manners that the educated practiced in public. Since then, policy may have outstripped manners, though not by so much as appears. The famous words now sport freely in all sorts of books, in movies, on recordings, in some magazines, and on cable television. But most newspapers, magazines, and commercial broadcasters still prohibit a few.

The lingering power of these terms derives not from what they name but from their old and widespread use in expressing hatred, disgust, and contempt; voiced in one spirit, they are still heard or read by some as voicing another: a hostile desire to shock. It remains to be seen whether as time goes on our acceptance of the "natural" leaves us hankering for the forbidden: whether new words will be launched in the hope of replacing the waning power of the old.

2. Many are the books and systems that promise to enlarge and invigorate one's vocabulary. But none is so effective as the practice of denying oneself the use of fifty or a hundred words that are overworked by the persons and machines that address us every day of our lives. The words listed below are not to be banned forever, nor are they all disreputable in themselves. But their abuse has turned them into mere plugs for the holes in our thought. As such they block the way to finding the exact word—one of several possible words. Removing these stoppers and putting the mind firmly on its subject will release the words kept imprisoned by the habit of thinking in disposable lingo. Of the following sixty-seven, those printed in small capitals are discussed elsewhere in this book.

NOUNS: ACCESS (noun and verb), *approach, background, bottom line, challenge,* CONCEPT, CONTEXT, *dimension, essentials,* FACTOR, FOCUS, IMPACT (noun and verb), *input, insight, issue* (subject), *mode* (preceded by participle), MOTIVATION, NATURE, *needs, picture* (situation), *potential, process, (re-)evaluation,* ROLE MODEL, SCENARIO, (my, your) THINKING.

VERBS: CONTACT, *downgrade,* (de-) *emphasize,* FINALIZE, FOCUS ON, *formulate,* HIGHLIGHT, IGNITE, INDICATE, INTERFACE, *maximize,* PINPOINT, PROCESS, *research, spark, target, update, upgrade.*

MODIFIERS: *basic,* CRUCIAL, *cutting-edge,* DRASTIC, ESSENTIAL, INITIAL, KEY, MAJOR, MEANINGFUL, *mini-, overall, ongoing* (continuing), *realistic,* SIGNIFICANT, WORTHWHILE.

LINKS: *as of* (see AS 5), *-conscious, -DRIVEN, -free,* IN TERMS OF, -WISE, WITH.

foreword, introduction, preface, etc. The vocabulary to designate the elements of front matter in books has long been in disorder, and there is no prospect of putting an end to the confusion. To this, *foreword* is a chief contributor. The word existed in English well before German philological scholarship became fashionable, about the end of the nineteenth century; but it is as certain as anything unprovable can be that *foreword* was reinvented late in the nineteenth century as a transliteration of *Vorwort*, in German the standard word for *preface*. So reinvented, *foreword* flourished until it has become as common as *preface* itself, a word at home in English for many centuries. We have, then, the paradox that the Latin *preface* is sound old English, whereas the upstart *foreword*, with two Anglo-Saxon roots buried in it, is foreign and relatively new.

A multiplicity of words for the same kind of composition, or a multiplicity of meanings for the same term, is a liability, not an asset, when technical details are to be distinguished. And though the components of a book are not parts that work with the rigidity of a machine, there would be some value in having the designations such that the reader or buyer of a book might know the scope and purpose of the sections designated *Preface, Introduction,* and so on. Of course an exact use of these terms can never be enforced. A logical hierarchy among them is suggested here only as a guide to the growth of a possible convention.

At the present time the *preface* to a book may be by the author or by somebody else; it may be one paragraph or forty pages; it may be either an integral and necessary part of the preliminaries to the subject or a mere note on the

author's purpose and point of view. *Foreword* is similarly noncommittal; and *introduction* may designate a puff contributed by someone other than the author, or an editor's preface to an edition of someone else's work, or the author's indispensable survey of background matter, or a mere prefatory comment or acknowledgment. Scholarship and instruction might be better served if it was agreed that:

1. A *preface* is a brief explanatory statement by the author; it is about the book, but not an integral part.

2. An *introduction* is a statement by someone other than the author—either a tribute included as reinforcing the claim to attention or an expository essay by the editor of a work.

3. An author's preliminary exposition—in effect an indispensable opening chapter of his work—may well be called an *Introductory*, and it should be folioed as belonging to the main text, not in the lowercase roman numerals given to front matter.

4. When the editor of another's work finds it desirable to include, in addition to his own introduction, a prefatory explanation about his part in it, this explanation ought to be called the *Editor's Preface*.

5. Ornamental or quasi-poetic terminology such as *prologue* or *prelude* could be restricted to such special classes of works as epic drama and long narrative poems; units so labeled should be treated as text, not as front matter.

Foreword finds no place among these suggestions, the need for it being slight or nonexistent except as a variant of *preface*. Its one possible excuse for being is as a companion term to *after-word*. But this pairing, under the suggested scheme, could be effected less obtrusively by matching *Introductory* with *Conclusion* (or *In Conclusion*). For the occasional work in which an editor's hand supplies comments after the death of the author of the book, *Editor's Note* can be used, or—on loftier occasions—*Epilogue*.

format. Originally a French word spread abroad by way of the printers' international jargon, *format* properly denotes the size, shape, and general design of a book or magazine. By a dubious extension, the word has been taken over, first by the producers of radio and television programs, and next by anyone who finds *arrangements* or *program* too ordinary for his taste. *The format is this: cocktails at seven, dine at eight, then a short two-mile drive to the auditorium where this unrivaled entertainment awaits you / The format displeased him. He would have to sit there with nothing to do while all the lesser lights crowded him out of the limelight.*

formulate. See FORBIDDEN WORDS 2.

for starters. See VOGUE WORDS.

fort, hold the. Many unschooled in the lore of battle hold an odd idea of forts. For more than a century, the idiom, commonly figurative, has been to *hold the fort*—that is, to retain possession of a place against all threat or contention: *C. is holding the fort in the art department while H. is away.* Those who have taken to saying *hold down the fort* would never say *hold down an odd idea of forts.*

See also CAKE; COULD CARE LESS; CRACKS; LAY WASTE; RUBBER; SEA CHANGE; SET PHRASES; STONE.

fortuitous. See FELICITOUS.

framework. See JARGON.

Frankenstein. In 1818 a young prodigy named Mary Wollstonecraft Shelley published a horror story called *Frankenstein; or, The Modern Prometheus*, about a German student, Frankenstein, who fabricated a monster that ultimately became the agent of his creator's destruction. The aptness of the fable and the success of a 1931 movie popularized the plot among many who never saw either. The well informed have often felt it necessary to correct those who thought that Frankenstein was the monster, and in any direct reference to the story this correction is still in order. But in alluding to situations in which the creature undoes the creator—e.g., man and his machines—it seems permissible to many writers to transfer the maker's proper name to his invention. The change follows the natural process of acceptance. Thus *a mackintosh, a Ford, a silhouette*—to say nothing of *a Rembrandt, a malaprop*, or *a sandwich*—are familiar extensions that legitimize *a Frankenstein*.

-free, suffix. See FORBIDDEN WORDS 2.

free gift. Advertisers coined this redundancy in the apparent belief that the common reader cannot absorb either word by itself. The phrase advertises a victory of desperation over common sense. *For free,* on the model of *for nothing* or *for a dollar,* is no better; *nothing* and *dollar* are nouns, but *free* is always an adjective.

French words and phrases. A British writer on usage offers the incidental suggestion that it would not be desirable to adopt the American habit of countering *I beg your pardon* with *You're welcome.* This example shows what pitfalls lie in the path of those who would use unfamiliar expressions borrowed from abroad. What is worse, it is not enough to know the foreign language in order to know how to use (and spell) in English the indispensable borrowed phrase, nor is it always clear what amount of agreement (by means of endings) should be shown in the foreign word playing a role in the English sentence.

Still, despite the difficulties, there are certain spellings and relationships that are cast-iron and must not be tampered with. Of the French phrases used in American prose, the one most liable to error in print is *bête noire;* the final *e* is compulsory whether the application is to a man or a woman, the feminine *noire* modifying *bête* and not the person in the given instance. Since *bête noire* means only *bogey* or *obsession,* use one of these if the feminine spelling of *noire* bothers you. It is a good rule to use foreign phrases only when no native equivalent is to be had.

Force majeure follows the same pattern as *bête noire:* the *e* is invariable and the phrase, unnecessary in English, means *compulsion, coercion, duress.*

But what of this sentence from a work of criticism? *The incident reminds us of the hero of Lermontov's novel and of his fatale attributes.* What coursed through the writer's mind was the phrase *femme fatale,* of which he thought the second part adaptable to his purpose. It is not. The phrase is an all-or-none affair. With the *e, fatale* cannot apply to a hero; without it, *fatale* loses its French connotation. The way out of the dilemma is to write simply *his fascination, his powers of fascination, his irresistible qualities* (or *features*). There is always a way to say what one means if one has to give up a conventional figure of speech, because figures only embellish what can from the outset be stated literally.

Two pairs of French locutions that give trouble may look as if they were too tangled to sort out: *à fond* and *au fond,* and *à point* and *au point.* The first pair is the easier to keep clear: *à fond* means *thoroughly,* and says it by saying *to the bottom;* the other means *after all* or *when all is said and done,* and it does this by saying (as we also do in English) *at* (the) *bottom.* In the second pair, *à point* is the absolute phrase, as is shown by the absence of the definite article. Anything properly cooked is *à point. Au point* occurs only with words preceding or with a situation understood. [*La*] *mise au point* is *the final adjustment, correction,* or *improvement.* The full phrase just given thereby comes to mean a meeting between contending parties in which everything is to be set straight. In English there is no conceivable sentence in which *au point* could by itself be rightly substituted for *à point*. The former is always a mistake for the latter.

Au naturel is used in French for an article of food prepared without a sauce, though menu French often reduces this to *nature*. By extension *au naturel* is sometimes used in English for *naked*, with the emotional grade of elegance of *in the buff*.

Double entendre is not French at all but is by now excellent English to denote a play on words whose secondary meaning is risqué or suggestive of some impropriety. The French original is *double entente* and it covers a wider range of hidden meanings—threats, allusions to the past, or anything insinuated, not necessarily off-color.

In the previous paragraph the word *risqué* illustrates the recurrent question of spelling. Should the word become *risquée* when the writer has used a word that he thinks would be feminine in French, such as *remark*? The answer is that the text is not in French and *risqué* is invariable. Who could tell what French word might lie behind the English noun? *Remark* might be translated *propos* (masculine) instead of *remarque* (feminine). The gender of the imported word is therefore best forgotten. This goes for *blond* as an adjective applicable to girl or boy. *Blonde* and *brunette* are nouns denoting women but only rarely men. The pseudo-masculine *brunet* is a figment of the pedantic mind.

Spellings and connectives in certain French phrases often used in English must be mastered by the writer who would not be thought amateurish. The spontaneous, revealing exclamation is *le cri du coeur* (not *de*); the happy afterthought that comes too late is *l'esprit de l'escalier*; violence between lovers is a *crime passionnel* (two *n*'s, no final *e*); high society is *le haut monde*—not *haute*, which belongs to *couture* and *cuisine*, both preceded by *la*. Apropos of cuisine, all designations for special dishes are in the feminine, to agree with *à la mode* understood. So it is *boeuf bourguignonne* and not *bourguignon*. *Chaise longue* is a long chair and should not be rationalized into *chaise lounge*. And *de rigueur*, meaning *obligatory*, needs two *u*'s whether as French or English.

A word finally about shades of meaning to be aware of when using French words. Most important, perhaps, is the connotation of the contraction *M'sieu* for *Monsieur*, which appeals so strongly to novelists who want to create local color. No educated person in France reduces the two syllables to one in addressing another; and, a fortiori, no such person uses the popular combined form *m'sieu-dame*. Writers who portray church dignitaries and high civil servants need to be aware of these distinctions, of which habit, not snobbery, is the cause.

Arrière-pensée does not mean *afterthought* but *ulterior motive* or, occasionally, *hesitancy*. The *arrière-pensée* is a thought, as it were, spatially behind the present thought, not after it in time. *Vis-à-vis*, which is nothing but the literal equivalent of *face to face*, should be used in English with a clear sense of this root meaning. There are other linking terms for use when faceless elements are joined, and the following should be recast as suggested: *Article 6 taken vis-à-vis Article 9 leads one to conclude that the authors of these by-laws were not models of consistency* (Article 6 taken together with Article 9) / *If the officer chooses to postpone the payment of tax vis-à-vis his retirement* . . . (until, when, considering his retirement) / *Vis-à-vis what you were saying last night, I've thought it over and I accept* (Apropos of, As to, About).

friend in common. See DEFENSIBLES.

frustrated, frustration. See COVERING WORDS; SCIENTISM 2.

-ful, suffix. See MASTERFUL, MASTERLY; MEANINGFUL.

full-figured. See EUPHEMISMS.

fulsome. See MALAPROPS.

fund(ing). See FISCAL.

funeral director. See EUPHEMISMS.

fused participle. The so-called fusion in this construction occurs between a participle and the noun or pronoun which performs or undergoes what the participle names. Consider the words *me doing* in *I see no point in me doing all the hard work if no one appreciates it.* Consider also the less jarring *proposal being accepted* in *He was certain of his proposal being accepted.* When Fowler denounced this construction in 1926, he correctly described it as a compound in which the parts bore no grammatical relation to each other but were simply fused. In the sentences above, the objects of the prepositions *in* and *of* are not *me* and *proposal* but the compounds *me doing* and *proposal being accepted.* If only because compounds like *me doing* seem so strange, many writers itch to undo all such fusions by using the traditional possessive construction: *I see no point in my doing,* etc. But as Follett wrote in the first edition of this book, "There is room for both constructions."

This allowance does not, be it said, relieve the writer of choosing between the two constructions with care. One sort of statement, for instance, calls for a pronoun and excludes a possessive adjective: *The idea of me standing in the pulpit in my uncle's robes and delivering his sermon was too much, and I began to laugh.* Here *me* insists upon being the central idea; *my standing* would give a misleading emphasis to *standing,* the action expressed by the participle. By the same logic, when the statement requires more stress on the action than on the agent, the possessive should be used: *In What I cannot stand is some journalist calling a politician "Bob,"* it is clear that the speaker's objection is not to journalists but to what one sort of journalist says, the *calling.* Hence *some journalist's calling a politician "Bob."*

But there are statements in which the possessive would simply be foolish. For instance: *The likelihood of that ever happening is slight.* No one of sense would say or write *of that's ever happening.* One might of course write *the likelihood of its ever happening;* or one could retain the original *that* by inverting the noun and rewriting: *Imagine the unlikelihood of that ever happening.*

But neither construction will serve when one is juggling compounded terms: *What the Justice feared was the Constitution of the United States becoming a shield for the criminal.* What the Justice feared was obviously not the Constitution but its becoming; hence the stress that falls on the former, as the sentence stands, is wrong. But an apostrophe after *United States* would be both wrong and absurd. Again the writer must recast: *What the Justice feared was that the Constitution . . . would become.*

A fused participle can make a sentence seem to say one thing until, with a bump, the remaining words say something else. *I take no pleasure in organ music being out of favor* appears to say that the speaker dislikes organ music—until the participle launches the opposite thought. The same surprise awaits in *He could not bear a child having too little to eat.* To ensure against misreading, one changes *child* to the possessive *child's.* But a similar alteration will not work for the first example; except for a handful of idioms, possessiveness is a strictly human trait, and *music's* defies sense (see POSSESSIVES 1).

Some writers seem to lack all feeling about what may or may not own something else. But when we confront a sentence such as *The argument arose because of pacifism's claiming a greater following than it could show,* many will feel that personifying a doctrine is ludicrous and clumsy. *Pacifism* does not claim; its partisans do. The sentence should be rewritten in any of several ways to show the actual proponents claiming *for* pacifism (or for themselves as pacifists) the condition later named. Abstractions and inanimate objects will make the unfused participle sound affected and the fused one mistaken.

fusion. See SCIENTISM 2.

G

gambit. This is a move in chess by which one player gains an advantage by sacrificing a pawn or some other piece. An *opening gambit* is therefore something cleverer but more costly than what is implied in its cliché use as a substitute for *opening remark*, adroit or not. Note that *opening* is a good noun and will serve without *gambit*: *His opening was friendly, even diplomatic; he spoke of friends they had in common*.

gay, adjective and noun. See CHANGING NAMES.

gender. See SEX, GENDER.

Germanisms. Under the influence of advertisers, American English has slipped into a construction deeply at odds with the genius of the language and more akin to German, in which compounding is normal practice. Early examples included *easy-to-read books* for the children and *ready-to-bake food* for the whole family. This agglutination of ideas into complex phrases requiring hyphens to make them into adjectives goes against the normal articulation of thought, which is *food ready to bake* and *books easy to read* or *easy books*.

One wonders why the habit has taken hold, after centuries in which the utmost adjectival compounding was a handful of common expressions such as *would-be, all-or-none, so-called, long-drawn-out*, etc. Perhaps our minds have been prepared by reading the algebra of the headlines and the pseudo-science of the ologists. From the former we get NEW BUS STRIKE PEACE HOPE and from the latter we get *non-age-discrepancy sex offenses*. In both, the insult to reason consists in the failure to articulate. The reader must unscramble the ideas for himself. In the headline it is only the *hope* that is *new*, though the adjective stands before *bus* and *peace*. The consequence is that we learn to think of a *strikepeacehope*, a single notion quite close to the *easy-to-read book*. In the *non-age-discrepancy sex offenses* one cannot even apply the same factoring formula, and that is what condemns the practice. We are not to look for *non-age sex* but for a tangle of relations nowhere expressed and no less ridiculous than the *exceptional all-butter Paradise fruit cake*.

All these locutions can be uttered, but sound does not give them meaning. When in advertisements for a directory we are promised 4,000 *hard-to-find biographies*, and in a dictionary we are asked to note its concern for *hard-to-say words*, we have reached a point where agglutination sounds like baby talk. And indeed the advertiser's view of his public confirms this impression. Hear the tone of addressing tots in *no-iron sheets / an easy-to-carry bag for many uses / a not-for-profit solicitation /* an *easy-order form*. It is small wonder that fairly well-written prose catches the trick and produces: *overpasses of more or less look-alike appearance* and *inflexible, difficult-to-change statutory language*.

The counterpart of this device in the realm of social science is the discussion of such topics as *the non-tax-paid liquor supply traffic, the life-lethal concentration of nitric acid oxide,* and *a family-centered alternative to hospital-based birthing*. From here it is but a short step to the adjectival SCIENTISM of auto advertisements: *four-speed automatic overdrive transaxle* and *12-function memory profile system*. These multiple collisions of words look as technical as chemical compounds. The same look of technicality has made incomprehensible the titles of honorable jobs: the head of security guards becomes the *loss prevention operations coordinator*; the ex-wrestler who stays by the vice-president is a *dignitary protection agent*. (See EUPHEMISMS.)

The language has no need of such fallacious compressions. They save no time; they corrupt both style and thought; and they leave the user unable to imagine how his meaning is read. Would one give house room to what an advertiser calls *a virtually*

unbridled channel reception capability?

If we wish to protect ourselves from this assault on our wits, we must begin by avoiding every form of easy compounding—e.g., *flight-conscious, career-* and *action-oriented, accident-prone, plot-driven, budget-wise* (see -WISE), and all other lumpings of words in which the relation is not either established by usage or controlled by rule. *Parking lights* deceives no one into thinking of lights that park, because the phrase is formed on a regular pattern; the same is true of *hairdresser, lantern-jawed, housebroken, bowling alley,* and *secretary bird*—in all these we know how the elements affect each other to denote a fact or idea. (The coiner of *facial tissue*, when the phrase was still noticed, was lucky to sell one box.) But in *budget-wise* and *crisis-oriented* the juxtaposition merely suggests some relation, as in the still lower perversions *tidescapes, guesstimates, blaxploitation,* and their like.

These last were called by Lewis Carroll *portmanteau words*. Except for humorous effects that can soon turn tedious, they sound commercial or pretentious. For that reason they should not usurp the place of older terms or of complete sentences that explain what part of experience has so far been overlooked and unnamed. It is a mistake to think that because everything is classifiable everything must be classified. And Germanisms in English are but clumsy attempts to make labels of arbitrary groupings: *never-before-told incidents / drop-dead-stunning shoes / a sweaty-gym-clothes-over-one's-shoulder kind of chance meeting / a let-the-devil-*

take-the-hindmost attitude, to which we may add the multitude of definitions by *non-* (*nonfiction, nonviolent, nonreligious, nondenominational*). Some of these last may be necessary, but most of them only pretend to define.

See also TELESCOPINGS.

girl. See CHANGING NAMES.

glamor, glamour. No one has yet proposed leaving the *u* out of *amour,* and we do not find *dour*—like *glamour,* a Scottish word—spelled *dor.* But *glamour* has a delusive resemblance to a class of words in which the British keep the *u* of Old French where American spelling since Noah Webster has omitted it, as in the Latin *favor, honor, labor,* etc. *Glamor* is now so common in the United States that dictionaries have taken to recording it as a variant. As a result of this misunderstanding, our Anglophobes fume at *glamour* on the assumption that its intention is Anglophile. They might as well reserve their ire, for the spelling is the normal Scottish one. Note, however, that the adjective *glamorous* does drop the disputed *u.*

A separate question is whether, or when, a judicious writer can afford to use *glamour* at all. The word needs to recover from the battering it has taken from perfumers, advertisers, and every kind of designer. Before these fell upon it, the word meant formidable magic, enchantment, a spell to be reckoned with, not sexual allure or expensive finery.

got, gotten. See MYSTERIOUS PASTS.

graduate, verb. Someone who *graduates* or *is graduated* from a course of instruction deserves attention and credit. Why, then, say *Natalie graduated Harvard? Graduate* means *step forward,* and she is the one who moves on. The college stays where it was. The verb *graduate* may be active and take an indirect object (*Natalie graduated from Harvard*) or active and take a direct object (*Harvard graduated Natalie*) or passive (*Natalie was graduated from Harvard*). But in each case, Natalie is the one affected; Harvard is not graduated by her or by anybody else.

See also TRANSITIVE, INTRANSITIVE.

grammatical error. A few stuffed shirts will always contend that this expression is a contradiction in terms and itself in error, since *grammatical* means *conforming to the requirements of grammar* and hence, by definition, *free from error.* To such remarks one is permitted to listen with half an ear, for *grammatical* quite as readily means *pertaining to grammar, belonging to the province of grammar.*

The phrase, moreover, is but one specimen of a very large class: e.g., *logical error, diplomatic blunder, theatrical tedium*—all these failures being readily understood to occur in the domains designated by the adjective. *Logical, diplomatic,* etc., when they stand alone, denote rightness. To condemn phrases that are perfectly clear and have long been accepted is pedantry.

granting. See DANGLERS, BENIGN.

grievous. See PRONUNCIATION 1.

grow, transitive. Americans scorn affectations except for the ones they adopt. For instance, the well-educated like to show off the occasional rural expression, which, besides seeming novel, shows how unaffected they are. When Governor Bill Clinton of Arkansas, in his first campaign for the Presidency, spoke of wishing to *grow the economy,* journalists noted—and began to repeat—the transitive usage, for which the linguist's term is *dialectal. Grow* has long been transitive in a few idiomatic uses. Anyone can *grow vegetables, fruits,* or *flowers,* men can *grow whiskers,* and both sexes nowadays *grow their hair long.* But about the first three we only mean *make a crop of* or *plant and tend,* nature doing the lion's share of the work. In speaking of hair we mean the quite passive *letting it grow.* To liken these idiomatic and natural *grow*ings to inducing the growth of an economy goes against common sense. So does the journalist who, ignoring idiom, adopts the rural vogue word: *Mr. W., who took over in June, said he would shy away from acquisitions but would seek to grow the company from within.* A second violation of sense: one cannot *shy away from* the initiating act of acquiring.

For other ruralisms, see COUPLE, MISSING OF; LOOKING, KNOW WITH INFINITIVE. See also TRANSITIVE, INTRANSITIVE; VOGUE WORDS.

H

had rather, would rather, would sooner. 1. Some writers think that for modern use *would rather* is to be preferred to *had rather*. *I had rather you didn't take the time to answer this letter and be fully organized for the trip / I would rather be hanged for a sheep than a goat.* Of the two constructions, *would rather* has come into use more recently. But *had rather* recommends itself by sidestepping the question of when to use *would* and when to use *should*; considering the American reluctance to use *shall* and *should*, this avoidance is an added point in favor of *had rather.* See SHALL (SHOULD), WILL (WOULD).

2. In the two constructions discussed above, *rather* expresses the idea of *prefer*; it shows the speaker's desire in a particular situation. Both *had* and *would*, by being in the SUBJUNCTIVE mood, show the statements to be imaginings; the situations have not in fact occurred. Likewise subjunctive are *I would sooner* (which requires *than*) or *would as soon* (which requires *as*); these forms too express preference but place it ahead of something else in both time and desire: *I would* (not *should*) *sooner cut my hand off than sign such a document / as soon cut my hand off as*, etc. We construe such sentences as meaning *I would cut my hand off before I would sign*, etc. Again, no question need arise as between *would* and *should*: the occasion for amputation or signing has not in fact occurred. The British use *sooner* in such exclamations as *Sooner you than I!* meaning *You do it. I wouldn't!* Most Americans would use the latter version rather than choose between *I* and *me*.

hands-on. See VOGUE WORDS.

hanged, hung. Since the sixteenth century, those who are killed by hanging have been *hanged* (past tense and past participle of the verb *hang*), and pictures, tinsel, tapestries, etc., have been *hung*.

hardly. See FEWER, LESS; NO SOONER . . . WHEN.

hardly (scarcely) . . . than. The conjunction *than* is a chronic producer of idiom trouble (see DIFFERENT[LY] THAN). It is, in fact, nowhere completely foolproof except after adjectives and adverbs in the comparative degree (*safer than / more safely than*) and after *other* and *otherwise*. It is continually being asked, in defiance of both idiom and its inherent tendency, to follow the almost indistinguishable synonyms *barely, hardly,* and *scarcely: Barely had the first Europeans landed at the Cape in 1652 . . . than they clashed with the Bushmen / Hardly was he dead than Nxou and Bauxhau started skinning the bull / The Frenchman had hardly uttered his antiwar remark than W. dived in to investigate / They had hardly got settled at the new address than F. was assigned to the Seattle office.* The idiomatic and grammatical word in each of these examples is *when.*

Apart from idiom, this type of sentence is open to criticism because it subordinates what is logically the main clause and puts the rhetorical emphasis on the subordinate clause. On principle and in practice *He had hardly gotten home when the phone rang* is open to a reservation that does not apply to *As soon as he got home the phone rang.* And the sentence about the man who was sent to Seattle will profit by being rewritten: *Almost as soon as they had gotten settled at the new address, F. was assigned,* etc.

hard put. The full idiom is *hard put to it,* and *to it* is so nearly the efficient phrase that the expression loses more than half its meaning when shortened. The original figure probably derives from putting a horse to the jump. Latterly, the idiom appears less often intact than in its mutilated form. *The government appears to think that even a militia of three thousand will be hard put to protect it from the rebels.* Here it is possible that the writer thought it better to clip the idiom than to tolerate

it repeated in a different sense, but he should have avoided the repetition in some other way. The writer of the following sentence may have wanted to avoid repeating *to,* but here again rewriting could have done the trick. *Mayor C., a Democrat, says he is hard put to pin down why local employment is moving in the opposite direction from the nation's.* Saving two syllables does not justify distorting a standard idiom. The frequency of the abuse suggests that many writers are unaware what the standard idiom is—or confuse it with *hard-pressed,* whose meaning is practically identical. The unsure can stop doing damage by using *hard-pressed* when something of this sort is needed.

See also SET PHRASES.

have, noncausative. You have yourself photographed for a passport; your neighbor has her car repaired; the coach has the outfield shift to the left. These are causative expressions, and the actions are rightly reported as proceeding from a human will. But forms of *have* crop up in sentences whose subjects show no will and perform no action; they are subjects only acted on. The Oxford Dictionary quotes a use of this disputed construction by Daniel DeFoe: *Another had one of his hands . . . burnt.* And a present-day journalist writes: *Democratic candidates might have their positions seriously jeopardized if the city administration opposes community wishes.* Some authorities fiercely object that such constructions wrongly attribute improbable acts to the will of the subject. Would a man undertake to have his hand burned? Would candidates arrange to have their positions jeopardized? We know these cannot be the writers' meanings, and in conversation, the form being familiar, we transpose ideas rapidly as we listen. Changing such statements for print takes a bit more ingenuity: *The Newark team had six of its fifteen games rained out last spring* (Six of the . . . team's . . . games were rained out) / *It is obviously unfair both to Mr. L. and to those who paid to hear his new work to have it presented in such shabby, self-defeating circumstances* (unfair both to Mr. L. . . . to present it in) / *The Tennessee Williams play has had its engagement extended at the Arts Theater* (The engagement of . . . has been extended) / *Lillie Langtry had a town in Texas named for her* (A town in Texas was named for).

Quotations in the Oxford Dictionary show this noncausative construction in use since the sixteenth century; Shakespeare is quoted three times, and Oliver Goldsmith is cited with *We often had the traveler or stranger visit us to taste our gooseberry wine.* Another writer quotes Shakespeare's Falstaff in defending the usage: *The other night I fell asleep here behind the arras and had my pocket picked.* The matter comes down to the difference between hearing and reading the language. Reading *I had a horse run away with me* (1860) or *John had his father die unexpectedly* (1995), one can take from the page a wholly wrong idea. This is the dread of the careful writer. Another argument against this usage points the way to better prose in general. The first

edition of this book observed: "The trouble with every such *have* is that, active in form, it is passive in meaning; it gives somewhat the effect, nearly always feeble . . . of narrating action in the passive voice. The simple cure is generally a truthful active verb with a different subject."

he or (and) she. See ANTECEDENTS 7.

height. See PRONUNCIATION 1.

heinous. See PRONUNCIATION 1.

help for avoid, prevent. We often use the idiom *I cannot help doing it* to express the idea that we cannot refrain from (avoid, prevent ourselves from) performing a certain action. *I cannot but do it* once served the same purpose but now sounds literary. Not so the popular muddle made of the two: *I cannot help but do it.* We read: *A novel that cannot help but hold the attention* / *O'Neill could not help but suspect that his writing days were over* / *Given her insanely adoring mother, she cannot help but be all wrapped up in herself* / *Her last two films cannot help but remind us* . . . Notice that the first and last samples use subjects incapable of will or influence over the action named. The verb *help* should not be used of an unconscious or impersonal subject. But all versions of *cannot help but* lack both clarity and thrift: *help* functions as *avoid* or *prevent* leaving *but* to signal a contradiction that never in fact arrives. The trouble with *cannot help but* is its waste of a potent word.

Some writers feel uneasy about another idiomatic use of *help: Don't take longer than you can help.* It seems to mean *Don't take longer than you can't help taking*—but only a contentious purist would insist on such logic here. Idiom does and should prevail, though it can be pointed out that for the same price the same thing can be said compactly and without apparent illogic: *Don't take longer than you have to* or *longer than you must.* Anyone bothered by an idiom that does not feel right can recur to a principle bred in the richness of English: When in doubt, sidestep.

And yet this same idiom is capable of another interpretation. To say that *more than you can help* is an illogical compression of *more than you cannot help* is true only if we limit the special meaning of *help.* If it is negative only to the extent of *avoid,* then the wording is illogical. But if it goes as far as *prevent,* then the idiom follows logic: *I can't help it* = I cannot prevent it; *I can't help myself* = I cannot prevent myself from. By logical extension: *I don't spend more than I can help* = I don't spend more than I can prevent myself from spending. This interpretation is borne out by the following dialogue from a novel whose tone is naturalistic throughout: *"Too much action but you can't help it." "I should have helped it."*

heritage. See CONNOTATIONS.

Hispanics. See CHANGING NAMES.

historic(al). That is *historic* which holds an important place in history. Thus Napoleon's return from Elba was an *historic* event, President Monroe's doctrine of 1823 an *historic* utterance. All things *historic* are also *historical* in the sense that they belong to authentic history, but the great mass of *historical* figures and events have nothing *historic* about them: *historic* = remarkable; *historical* = actual. It is thus possible to use *historical* to affirm or deny the truth of a supposed event. *The great terror of the year 1000 is not historical.* Had it in fact taken place, the occurrence would have been both *historical* and *historic.*

hitherto. See AGO, BEFORE.

homosexuals. See CHANGING NAMES.

hopefully. The German language is blessed with an adverb, *hoffentlich,* that affirms the desirability of an occurrence that may or may not come to pass. It should be translated by some such periphrasis as *it is to be hoped that;* but hack translators and people more at home in German than in English persistently render it as *hopefully.* Now, *hopefully* and *hopeful* can indeed apply to either persons or occurrences. Someone in difficulty is hopeful of the outcome, or a situation looks hopeful; we face the future hopefully, or events unfold hopefully. What current misusage wants *hopefully* to convey is the desirability of the hoped-for event. College, we read, is *a place for the development of habits of inquiry, the acquisition of knowledge and, hopefully, the establishment of foundations of wisdom.* No one and nothing is here identified as being hopeful; *it is to be hoped* is the natural way to express what is meant. *The underlying mentality is the same, and, hopefully, the prescription for the cure is the same* (let us hope) / *With its enlarged circulation—and hopefully also increased readership—the magazine will seek to* . . . (we hope) / *There is now no obstacle to Senator L.'s nomination and, hopefully, his election this fall to the Presidency* (I hope).

The particular badness of *hopefully* is not alone that it strains the sense of *-ly* to the breaking point; it also appeals to speakers and writers who do not think about what they are saying in general and pick up VOGUE WORDS by reflex action. Indeed, the misuse of *hopefully* is a nearly infallible warning of unarticulated thought fore and aft.

How readily the rotten apple will corrupt the barrel is seen in the similar use of transferred meaning in other adverbs denoting an attitude of mind. For example: *Sorrowfully* (regrettably), *the officials charged with wording such propositions for ballot presentation don't say it that way* / *the "suicide needle" which—thankfully—he didn't see fit to use* (we can be thankful). Adverbs so used lack point of view; they fail to tell us who does the hoping, the sorrowing, or the being thankful.

See also TRANSITIVE, INTRANSITIVE.

hospitable. See PRONUNCIATION 1.

however, interrogative. See WHATEVER, WHOEVER, INTERROGATIVE.

human, noun. The word *animal* is equally satisfactory as adjective (*the animal kingdom*) and as noun (*the lower animals*). But for a large part of the twentieth century this double use was denied by many to *human*, which had somehow lost its credentials as a noun. Authorities labeled the noun sense "jocular," "affected," and "colloquial," favoring instead the stately *human being*. Follett thought the noun *human* "a stylistic blind spot," and was certainly right in 1966 to describe it as out of favor. But he also conceded that the history of the noun was long: the Oxford Dictionary finds Chapman using it in the sixteenth century to translate the *Iliad* (*Mars* . . . *smear'd with the dust and bloud* / *Of humanes, and of their ruin'd wals*) and Conan Doyle three hundred years later writing, *You will often see it in humans.* Other reputable authors upheld the usage until its curious banishment. That exile now has ended, and the noun sense of *human* turns up often. It serves the science writer as a counterpart to *animal*, and it aids those whose feminism continues to war on *man* and *men* as designating the species.

humanism, humanist, humanity, humanitarian. A speaker at a public meeting praises the guest of honor for his *liberalism and humanism, practiced through a long career*. It seems probable that the speaker is thinking of the guest's *humanity* or *humaneness*—a kindly disposition toward his fellow humans—rather than of his possession of a particular cultural heritage (*humanism*). *Humanity* is something that one can indeed practice through a long career; *humanism* describes what one believes rather than what one practices. *Humanism* is accordingly applied to various philosophies that make man the measure of all things.

The confusion between *humanism* and *humanity* is frequent and easy, because the plural *humanities* signifies neither humane practices nor any particular philosophy, but the branches of learning that make up the liberal-arts curriculum—literature and the arts, history, and the branches of philosophy. The name for one who cultivates the humanities is *humanist*, not—as one sometimes hears and reads, even in academic places—*humanitarian*. This last term is reserved for those whose career or public doctrine serves the object of *human kindness*, which is *humanity*.

hyphen, the. 1. This little sign is most often used to show readers that the end of the printed line is not the end of a word. But before examining the splitting of words, consider how, in the middle of the line, the hyphen joins them.

First, it joins almost all two- and three-word adjectives that come before a noun: *stick-shift convertible* (but *Her convertible has a stick shift*) / *single-bed sheets* (but *Put sheets on the single beds*) / *eighteenth-century music* (but *Our class is stuck in the eighteenth century*) / *out-of-print book* (but *a book out of print*) / *the hoped-for settlement* (but *not the one we hoped for*) / *six-pound trout* (but *weighing six pounds*) / *head-on collision* (the adjective is hyphenated regardless of position). Prose is often ambiguous without this aid (*I can't find a single bed sheet*) and is incompetent when the hyphen turns up where it does not belong. It never be-

longs between an adjective and an *-ly* adverb that together modify a following noun: *a serenely unconscious man* / *a verbally incompetent proposal* / *a remarkably pleasant day*.

Hyphenating ahead of a noun warns the reader that he must fuse two ideas before he understands how they apply to the subject, whereas ordinary adverbs signal that fusion by means of *-ly*, as in *serenely unconscious*. But when adverbs like *well* and *free* and *safe* modify a participle coming before a noun, the hyphen is required: *a well-liked coach* / *a well-intentioned fool* / *a well-turned phrase*. A *safe playing bureaucrat* and *a free ranging consultation* are at once ambiguous and vague without the binding hyphen following the adverbs *safe* and *free*. (See AD-VERBS, VEXATIOUS.)

In general, two-word modifiers that are capitalized do not have hyphens: *Air Force general* / *Commerce Department memo* / *Cathedral Valley vacation*.

A suspended hyphen is fastened firmly to a word or prefix that applies to a word farther on in the sentence: *These were second- and thirdhand reports* / *Some dolls were hand- and some machine-carved* / *They watched the pro- and antigovernment forces fill the square*. The space after the first hyphen is imperative.

Some terms made up of two words will probably always be hyphenated: nouns like *hangers-on* and *set-to* will be mispronounced if made into one and will collapse if the halves stand alone. Other nouns (like *housekeeping*) have gone from two words to one, then to a hyphen, and then back to one. No rules govern these changes, and the writer in doubt consults a dictionary for the current spelling—or spellings; at the moment, the American Heritage gives *lunchmeat* and *luncheon meat* as well as *house painter* and *housepainter*. Do not distract your reader with impulsive collisions like *picturegallery* or *exexecutive*; wait until a dictionary can be blamed. (See also GERMANISMS.)

2. From speaking of the way separate words are joined, we turn to the use of the hyphen in dividing them. The division of words into their syllables is called *syllabation, syllabication, syllabification*, and even, absurdly, *syllabism*. To perform the task is to *syllabize, syllabicate, syllabify*, or *syllable*. One would think that an aspect of language so reinforced with synonyms ought to be as nearly systematic and settled as anything about living language can be. But the syllabification of English has been a chronic annoyance to linguists, who seem to suffer equally under the British system, based on etymology, and the American system, based on pronunciation. The common reader is in turn confused by alternate exposure to American books and to the British books we import. One system marks a difference between the noun *prog-ress* and the verb *pro-gress*, the noun *proj-ect* and the verb *pro-ject*, but the other system does not; one system divides *photog-raphy* phonetically but the other sticks to etymology and *photo-graphy*. The clash becomes particularly graphic in the parallel words *signif-icant* (American division) and *magni-ficent* (British division).

Some software for word processing

has a built-in lexicon and will automatically syllabify if the user adjusts it to do so. But many writers will not relinquish to a machine a matter so vexed by bad luck and in need of literate judgment. They know that any system of division, given its way, will come up with correct but disruptive splits.

In general, a division is bad if it ends a line with the letters of an unintended word. The broken-off portion causes a mental mispronunciation and thus requires the reader to retrace his steps. For example, *face-saving* is a good division, but *face-tious* is bad though correct; make it, if possible, *fa-cetious*. Similarly, *tar-ry* is a good division of *tarry* meaning *covered with tar* but a bad one of *tarry* meaning *dawdle* or *linger*. There are many such misleaders in English; among the most common are *char-acter, reap-pear, read-just, coin-cidence, opera-tion, bar-rier, fun-erary, pale-olithic, cog-itate, mate-rial, tar-iff, scar-city, pane-gyric, car-amel, par-agraph, par-amount, par-allel, rein-force*, and *rear-range*. All but one of these can be divided elsewhere than at the point of false lead, and, if the spacing permits, should be. In proofreading his text, an author sensitive to wayward divisions might add or delete a word or syllable to ensure a reading without a break or with a better break. The editor of a text not his own has, of course, no such option. And writers for the narrow measure of a newspaper column often find no cure.

Unless adjusted to syllabify, most software for word processing will only end a line with a hyphen that always belongs to the word—that is, the hyphen of *first-class* or *first-born* or *first-rate*, which the compositor is bound to set regardless of its place in the printed text. But the software will not split *first-hand* with a hyphen at the end of a line but move the word intact to the beginning of the next line. The expedient splitting of words is by this means left to the compositor. Judgment and repair of the result is left to the proofreader and the writer.

See also RE-CREATE, RECREATE; STYLE, TYPE 2.

I

I. See WE, EDITORIAL.

-ible. See -ABLE, -IBLE.

icon. The day when tabloid head-lines relied on short, vague terms like *bid, ban, woo, rift* seems to be waning. Meanwhile, headlines in the serious press try to temper vigor with sub-stance. But writers of headlines are still enticed by a brisk and novel usage. Soon terms like *drug lord* and *kingpin* pass from the large type above to the article below, whether or not the words correspond to demonstrable facts or entities.

The progress of *icon* through one great national newspaper, from head-lines to text and from front to back, shows that words used chiefly for snap or swagger may end up meaning ev-erything and nothing. For centuries, *icon* has denoted an image of a sacred being, the image itself deemed worthy of worship. Technicians abducted the word to make it stand for the small pic-tures that represent options in a com-puter program. This kidnapping may have encouraged the newspaper in question to exempt the word from any set meaning at all: headlines and arti-cles referred, without explanation, to the following as *icons*: the Coney Is-land boardwalk, wooden water tanks, alumni clubs, women in general, plas-tic bowling pins, a sculptor, plastic picture frames, lamps, a skyscraper, a civil-rights leader, a clothing store, Goethe and Wagner, Coca-Cola bot-tles, several movie actors. Also paper cups, beanbag chairs, a radio commen-tator, artificial Christmas trees, a poli-tician, a painter, the British theater, an acute accent, a nun, a singer, an alu-minum magazine rack, a composer, an office chair, Jacqueline Kennedy Onassis, a saxophonist, popcorn, and the Monroe Doctrine. The word caught on elsewhere and was used to denote, among many other things, the atom, the Internet, a murderer, and a washing machine. Now and then mod-ifiers were employed like tongs to hold the word still: *generational icons* (two actors), *cultural icons* (a skyscraper, Goethe, Wagner), *suburban icons* (the bowling pins), *an intellectual icon, icons of style—our ideal; a kind of icon, an icon more than a sex symbol, an icon of suffering and authenticity; a public icon.* But there is no restraining a word that has become a popular toy.

The writing of headlines and the working of crossword puzzles both fit broadly approximate meanings into an arbitrary space. Neither teaches much about writing, where meaning should be respected.

See also JOURNALESE.

I'd, I'll, I've. No American would say or write *I'd no money* or *I'd a few thoughts left, not good ones.* In these statements the contracted *I had* (meaning *I owned, I possessed*) is a British locution and too unemphatic for American taste. Similarly, we would not say *I've to bathe and dress* but would insist upon the full emphatic *have* in the sense of *must.*

For the belief that *I'll* can stand equally for *I will* and *I shall*, see SHALL (SHOULD), WILL (WOULD). See also HAD RATHER, WOULD RATHER, WOULD SOONER; SEQUENCE OF TENSES 5.

identical. Americans practically never say *different to*, an extremely common locution in British English; but they often say *identical to*, which is unidiomatic in both the United States and England. *The sequences filmed in Hollywood were shot on a set identical to the Paris apartment, which has long since been remodeled / the present currency system, which is identical to the British / A watch identical to the one you are wearing was found on the wrist of the corpse.* In each example, idiom calls for *with*; a thing has identity (sameness) with, not to, another.

See also DIFFERENT(LY) THAN; PREPOSITIONS.

identify, identification. These words cause much more trouble to those learning English than their incessant use might suggest.

1. In the jargon of business, we *identify* problems in a financial plan. This is a pretentious way of saying that we *find* or *name* or *point to* or *pick* them *out* (see JARGON).

2. The act of *identifying* an unconscious man as one's uncle comes close to the Latin meaning, *making the same.*

3. Intending a different sense still, bosses want their employees to *identify* their interests *with* those of the corporation. Akin to this sense yet somewhat distinct from it is a reader's meaning in saying, *I identify with Jane Eyre. With* is inseparable from both these uses, and the second use at one time required a reflexive pronoun in order to express the fullness of the sympathy felt: *I identify myself* [not my looks or my income] *with Jane Eyre*['s]. This denotation of feeling oneself the same as another gained extensive use with the translation of Freud's work into English. But as early as 1940 the reflexive pronoun was already slipping out of the construction. (George Orwell: *Sam Weller, Mark Tapley, Clara Peggotty . . . identify with their master's family.*) The disappearance of the pronoun from present usage leads to statements so casual as to be meaningless: *I identified with the way he kept feeling that he had to watch his language / We certainly identify with other couples who can't stick to a budget.* All that such statements require is *sympathize with, feel sorry for*, or *act like.*

idiosyncrasy. See POPULARIZED TECHNICALITIES.

if and when. The conjunctions *if* and *when* have different meanings when separately used; when put together, as they continually are by automatic speakers, they duplicate or contradict. *Let us know if and when you hear from her* says no more than *when you hear from her* or *if you hear from her;* whichever is said, the hearer is to report on receipt of a message and not to report if no message is received.

Sometimes we get this double-barreled LEGALISM in the shape of *if or when.* With *and* it is an unconscious use of duplication; with *or* it records awareness that the conjunctions have different meanings—which the user seems helpless to choose between. The AND/OR type of nonsense is avoided by the simple expedient of keeping *if* and *when* apart.

See also UNLESS AND UNTIL; WHEN AND IF.

if not. This modest phrase seems ready-made for LINKING but is in fact a snare that waylays even the vigilant writer and speaker. Consider: *His departure from his native land is but one more sign that life there has become hard, if not unbearable / It will be difficult, if not impossible, to send you the check by the end of the month.* If life is *hard* in the country of the first sentence, it may nevertheless be borne; if it is *unbearable,* the population must emigrate or revolt. But which is it? What does the reporter's *not* rule out? Similarly, will the check be sent by the end of the month, or is that *impossible?* In both sentences *if not* stands as a wholly equivocal substitute for either *though not* or *perhaps;* meaning hovers between the two. Do these writers intend to state a negative (*though not* or *but not unbearable; though not* or *but*

not impossible) or an alternative (*perhaps unbearable, perhaps impossible*)? Given its habit of flirting with almost opposite meanings, *if not* is avoided as a matter of course by many writers. Taken up by one reporter for *The New York Times,* it managed this double betrayal: *What made the comments riveting, if not a bit remarkable, was . . .* Did the writer mean *though not . . . remarkable* or *perhaps . . . remarkable;* or did *not a bit remarkable* mean *not remarkable at all?*

ignite. See FORBIDDEN WORDS 2; TRIGGER.

illegal. See PRONUNCIATION 1.

illicit. See PRONUNCIATION 1.

illy. See OVERLY.

imbue. See TRANSITIVE, INTRANSITIVE.

immodest. See UN-, IN-, NON- 5.

impact. 1. Meanings. 2. Noun. 3. Verb. 4. Confusion with *affect* and *effect.*

1. Meanings. This VOGUE WORD has been aptly called a blunt instrument. Overuse years ago dulled its sharp dictionary meanings, which are, for the noun, *the striking of one thing against another* and, for the verb, *to pack firmly together.* Thus two cars can collide *with a terrific impact* and two teeth can be *impacted,* dentistry being the only endeavor in which the verb still has clear meaning.

2. Noun. *Impact* is incessantly used

by those who believe it sounds businesslike. It only sounds vague. When you speak of the *impact* of something-or-other you may have in mind any one of such diverse ideas as *importance, effect, power, influence, bearing, pressure, consequence, upshot, significance, impressiveness, implication(s), value.* Only fatigue or the copycat habit chooses poor old *impact* ahead of a noun whose meaning is clear at once.

But vogue words do worse than put a blur where meaning should go; their triteness bores the reader. Such words have been reduced to mere sound, and the reader instinctively tries to ignore their repetitious faucet-like dripping.

3. Verb. A worn-out noun makes an even worse verb, for we cannot envision the action attributed to it. More important, a bad verb robs the whole sentence of movement. *There can be no doubt that the absence of deductibility will impact our work in the coming year.* This statement warns of some sort of trouble ahead, and a good verb would tell us what kind or how much. But who can guess whether *impact* has stolen the place of *curtail* or *cripple* or *force suspension of* or *make altogether pointless*? And any one of these verbs would not only inform us but also make the sentence *move*. A faint awareness that the verb is a dud has led to the stilted *impact on*, which only enlarges a waste of good space.

4. Confusion with *affect* and *effect*. *Impact* may have been perverted by those who fear mixing up *affect* and *effect*, with which it faintly rhymes. Certainly the sample above implies

no more than *affect our work in the coming year.* The verb *affect* means *to influence* (or else *to assume ostentatiously*), and the verb *effect* means *to bring about*, a very different matter. The noun *effect* (*good effect, bad effect, no effect*) could hardly be simpler, whereas the noun *affect* is a term in psychology, where it should stay.

impact on. See IMPACT 3.

-impaired, suffix. See EUPHEMISMS.

implant. See INCULCATE.

implement, verb. See CONTACT 2.

implicit, explicit. 1. These descend respectively from the Latin for *entangled* and for *unfolded. Implicit* means *unstated, with nothing in evidence,* as in *We had his implicit agreement. Explicit* means *laid out in full, with everything clear,* as in *I spent a half hour giving explicit instructions.* The words seem perfect antonyms—but for the unexpected fact that they join in implying that what they describe is undoubtable. *Implicit trust* is as firm as *explicit trust* because quite as real. Note that *implicit* makes its point absolutely but that *implied* requires telltale loose ends (see IMPLY, INFER). For a promise to be *implied*, there must have been a word, a look, a gesture that made the implication. *Tacit* is often used in the same way as *implicit*. A *tacit* reconciliation is one that both parties acknowledge and act upon without speaking of it.

2. *Explicit* and *mature* are EUPHE-

MISMS for *obscene*. For the difference between *explicit* and *express*, see EX-PRESS.

imply, infer. These two verbs illustrate the pitfall of using the historical meanings of words as the sole guide to their right use today. *Imply* and *infer* seem to be of about equal age. Both were well established early in the sixteenth century but were mainly used in senses remote from what is thought natural now. *Imply* meant, among other things, *to ascribe* or *to attribute*: you implied a motive or a quality to a person—meaning that you thought of him as having it or asserted his possession of it—or you implied a given result to a specified cause. And *infer* commonly meant just what *imply* means now: *to suggest strongly, to mean without saying*. So it is used when John Milton in the seventeenth century writes: "Consider first, that Great or Bright infers not Excellence."

Small wonder, then, that various dictionaries neglect to make the sharp differentiation that the New International makes when it says that *infer* is "loosely and erroneously" used for *imply*. When dictionaries neglect the distinction, the loose and erroneous speaker can feel justified in what is today an outright mistake. For usage has built up a clear difference here—one as clear as that between *give* and *take*. *Imply* is a word for the transmitting end, and *infer* a word for the receiving end, of the same process of deduction. The relation is that between a rubber stamp and paper: an implication delivers an impression; an inference re-

ceives one. *When you say that you did all that needed doing, you imply that we did nothing / Walker's silence implied his stern disapproval / I infer from your glowing demeanor a victory over the forces of right / Don't infer from a single sentence that he has changed the belief of a lifetime / "When I said that the price seemed high, I wasn't implying that I had lost interest." "Oh, I inferred that you had."* Smoke, according to the proverb, *implies* fire. On your side, when you smell smoke, fire is what you *infer*. *Imply* means *fold in*; *infer* means *draw out*.

These examples have been corrected in parentheses: *The defense is trying to infer* (imply) *that the prosecution is concealing something / We know that you did not actually say it, but you have plainly inferred* (implied) *it.*

impracticable. See PRACTICAL.

in-, prefix. See UN-, IN-, NON-.

in addition to. See AS 11.

in for by, of, etc. 1. Noticeably on the increase is a peculiar use of *in*, usually followed by an *-ing* form of some verb, in a way that sometimes befogs the intended meaning and often contradicts it. *Our political leaders are not fulfilling their responsibilities in illuminating and arousing concern in the public.* This *in* seems to concede that the leaders are illuminating (enlightening?) the public and arousing concern in it, but not sufficiently to discharge their responsibilities;

whereas the writer was probably trying to say that the leaders are failing to enlighten the public and arouse concern. Using *of* (and in some other constructions *by*) would avoid the false implication; or better still, substitute the infinitives and thus avoid a cascade of participles. *We must restore America to its position of world leadership in achieving universal peace!* This demand probably means that universal peace is not being achieved because America has lost her world leadership, but it seems to say that universal peace is being achieved under other leadership. If we substitute *in order to achieve* for *in achieving* we express the probable intention. *There will be problems in construction of some types of shelters in complying with existing building codes* (in constructing some types . . . if builders must comply) / *Specialists have contributed both in determining what words were to be included and in framing accurate, precise definitions* (replace each *in* with *by*).

2. Less paradoxical but no less slovenly is the journalistic use of *in* to suggest a connection without naming it: PRESIDENT IN SURPRISE VISIT HERE / STUDENTS IN PROTEST / MARRIED WORKING WOMEN IN JOB SURVEY, and so on. The meaning is perhaps sufficient for a headline, but the abuse of prepositional vagueness ends by breaking down both the sense of idiom and the particular power of the small word itself. What we need in the examples above is a *survey of women*, a *surprise visit* from *the President*, and a *protest* by *students*. A proof that articulating ideas correctly is on the wane may be

found in almost any scholarly bibliography. The titles are certainly long and lumbering enough, but the prepositions used give the impression of having been scattered at random. No distinction seems to be felt between *Air Disinfection in Large Rural Central Schools*, where *in* is literal and right, and *Recent Developments in Diarrhea of the Newborn* or *Group Attitudes in a Polio Vaccine Program*, where *in* is figurative and wrong. Clearly, the developments are *in the study of* the subject, hence they are *about* [the subject of] *diarrhea*; the attitudes are likewise *about* the program, not *in* it. (See WITH.)

3. When describing the material of which an object is made, *of*, not *in*, is idiomatic: *I want the shelving made of teak* / *The small bust of Napoleon was of plaster* / *a robe of richest silk*. The temptation to substitute *in* arises from the shopper's natural query *Have you the same model in green? In velvet?* Here *of* is impossible because of the effect of *same model*. But this variation does not authorize *He treated himself to a huge tomb in marble*, for nothing is more partitive than the making of objects out of materials, and the partitive requires *of* or *out of*.

in order to. The use of this phrase can be a kindness to readers. Consider: *Rachel thought it best to accept the young man's offer to clear the air.* Who or what will clear the air—Rachel, the young man, an acceptance, or an offer? The use of more than one infinitive in a sentence will often raise such questions. From the context one sees the author's meaning: *to accept the young man's offer in order to clear the air.*

in part. See PART, IN.

in terms of. The craving to express everything *in terms of* something else is a disease traceable to college-catalogue English. For a long time now, a college course has hardly been respectable if it did not offer to present literature in terms of its social effects, an author in terms of his or her influence on the development of this or that form, history in terms of underlying economic forces, geography in terms of transportation and commerce, and so on. By now academic writers find themselves unable to finish a paragraph without using *in terms of.* Small wonder that their grown-up students spread the blight in business, law, and elsewhere. The phrase is a ready substitute for the common prepositions *at, in, for, by,* and the rest, and it also supplies a loose coupling for ideas whose exact connection has not been thought out by the speaker or writer.

The professoriate has undoubtedly borrowed the phrase from the sciences. In formulas and equations you do express one thing in terms of another—distance as a function of rate and time, earnings as a product of volume and price, etc. But in an equation the terms are named and numbered; they are the components of the problem—visibly there. As the phrase is used in general discourse no one is thinking of converting anything into anything else. The phrase is evoked to lend an air of intellectual strictness to statements that in fact have none. *The author examines the purposes, history, works, and effects of the Bauhaus school of design in terms of Gropius's career both in Europe and in America.* In what useful sense can a career be said to have terms? The statement means simply that Gropius's experience and works are used as a narrative thread. *By recounting Gropius's career,* etc., makes the point.

Here is a purposely long list of examples showing the extent of the blight; parentheses suggest how they might be rewritten to advantage. *The seating arrangements, while excellent for music, are far from ideal in terms of drama* (for drama) / *the industrial charters, if construed in terms of the guarantee of exclusive craft jurisdiction, could not mean very much* (construed as guarantees) / *Wilson, with his passion for decentralization, had set up operations in terms of independent local corporations* (set up operations as a system of local corporations) / *looked at the future of world affairs in terms of the key forces and events of the past decade* (as a sequel to) / *Hardships have been diminished in terms of food and clothing* (The shortages of food and clothing have been reduced) / *The industrialization programs are showing results in terms of factories going up and in terms of actual production* (omit *terms of* in both places) / *His major political task was to designate a new Premier, but this designation was always in terms of what was thought might be acceptable to an elusive majority of the Assembly* (was always dictated by) / *Al-*

though the Communists remained the second biggest party in terms of the popular vote (in the popular vote cast) / the culturally shaped notions in terms of which people organize their views of themselves, of others, and of the world in which they live (notions with which) / advised newspapers "to tell advertisers of your reach in terms of circulation and area coverage" (your reach in circulation) / consider the Halloween of yesterday in terms of a great equalizer (as a great equalizer) / her gifts as a critic of movies in terms of their sheer energetic entertainment, in terms of their openness to ordinary, present-day experience, and in terms of the particular and expressive personalities of the actors in them (a critic of movies who values them for their sheer energetic entertainment, for their openness to ordinary, present-day experience, and for the particular and expressive personalities, etc.).

See also ABOUT; LINKING.

inasmuch, insofar. These trisyllables, which almost always lead to an excess of as's, should be reserved for situations in which the idea of proportion or measurement is needed. Insofar as he could see into her character he thought her a woman of honor / Inasmuch as the old storekeeper had relied on the other's political influence he was bound to be disappointed. The implications in this pair of sentences are, in the first: insofar—and not one inch further; and in the second: to that extent, but not more than that. It is waste to pepper the page with inasmuch when since or because would do as well or

better; and with insofar when so far is enough.

include for are. It is apparently easy to confuse the idea of inclusion with that of identity. Witness this assertion: Some of the thirty or more scientific and technical disciplines which this vigorous research-based organization is applying in its pioneering effort include [a list of eighteen items]. The whole thirty, of course, include the eighteen: but some of the thirty are the eighteen named. The writer incurred the usual consequence of saying something in two ways at once; he started by restricting his subject to a part of itself, but chose a verb that can go only with the unrestricted subject.

For an even more common confusion of a like sort, see REPRESENT.

including. See DANGLERS 1; DANGLERS, BENIGN.

incredibly. See TRANSITIVE, INTRANSITIVE.

inculcate. This unlovely-sounding word denotes the instilling of ideas, principles, or habits in the mind of someone else. Indeed, the Latin root means to stamp in with the heel. Picture a child on a warm day driving a penny into the asphalt and you see the direction of the action. No habits of thrift having been inculcated in the heirs / If you ask me, it was his mother's way of blowing hot and cold with him that inculcated the fickle habits we see in the man today / Their boast is that they inculcate pride as well as self-restraint in the members who stay the course. These examples say *inculcate in*, but *inculcate into* is still considered idiomatic by some; *inculcate on* and *upon*, once common, are no longer used.

The spreading *inculcate with* carelessly changes the direction of the action: it suggests that the child inculcates the pavement with the penny instead of the penny into it. The third edition of the American Heritage Dictionary approves without comment the use of either *in* or *with*. But it also gives *teach* as a synonym for the verb in the example *inculcate the young with a sense of duty*; to speak of teaching the young with a sense of duty is absurd. Webster's Third New International Dictionary likewise mutely approves the *with* construction, but with the curious proviso that "a person" do the inculcating.

Meanwhile, statements like the following have become commonplace: *Any youngster who has been inculcated with the "dictionary habit" has taken a giant step toward self-education / By adulthood they have been inculcated with a sturdy cunning and have lost all curiosity / She had been inculcated with her mother's kindliness long before she saw where it could lead.* Both Fowler and Follett noticed this altered usage and suggested a confusion with *inoculate* (as in *inoculate with serum*). Follett further warned that the same confusion might overtake *instill, inject,* and *implant*: "A philosophy is *instilled into* the mind, not the mind instilled with the philosophy; a new idea is *injected into* a discussion, not the dis-

cussion injected with the idea; an ambition is *implanted in* a person, not the person implanted with the ambition." Given the slippage of the dictionaries, it may well be that *inculcate* will lose its straightforward sense of *putting in.*

See TRANSITIVE, INTRANSITIVE.

incursion. See EUPHEMISMS.

in-depth. See VOGUE WORDS.

Indians, American, East, West. See CHANGING NAMES.

indicate. Bad American English lurches between the overdecorated (see, for example, POPULARIZED TECHNICALITIES; QUOTE, UNQUOTE; THIS KIND) and the vacuously general (see, for example, COMMUNICATE; DEVELOP). Thirty years ago Follett complained that *indicate* had become a word-of-all-work, ever more general, "doubly damned by the frequency of its occurrence and by the number of more expressive words that it displaces"; these he listed as *hint, suggest, insinuate, imply, disclose, intimate, reveal, convey, announce, affirm, assert, specify, stipulate, insist, protest, proclaim, propose, advocate, recommend, urge, note, point out, show, signify, profess, particularize, report, write, admit, concede, grant, confess, testify, state, declare, remark, say.* Good writing, today as then, draws from a similar range of choices to characterize ways of speaking or writing; it limits *indicate* to its modest function as a synonym for *signify, point out, be-*

token. The senator's presence on the dais indicated an end to his year-long feud with the chairman / Americans stationed in the capital say that the general's statement indicates his readiness for war. These are proper uses for *indicate,* whose root is *index,* a pointer.

The most intemperate users of *indicate* talk and write for the federal government. Their duties require them to quote and paraphrase daily, but habit apparently makes them avoid the common verbs listed above. The resulting Potomac drone of *I indicate, you indicated, he, she,* or *it indicates* makes for discourse both inexact and monotonous: *The Secretary has not indicated that he will accompany the President / Nowhere in this bill are indicated the exact conditions under which the EPA would intervene / As I indicated yesterday, my opposition to this candidate arises from her apparent mishandling of three cases / As I indicated to the press last week, my vote waits upon two conditions being met.* Note the pointlessly vague effect of the verb in these seemingly downright statements.

One specialized use of *indicate,* adapted from the standard medical vocabulary, has become a piece of parlor slang. In a given patient's condition, such-and-such a treatment is *indicated*—i.e., rendered logical or necessary, prescribed by the circumstances; in the opposite circumstances it is *contraindicated.* Whence such remarks as *A time-out is indicated* or *A good stiff drink is indicated.* Some find this borrowing arch.

indict for. See CONVICT.

indifference. See DISINTERESTED.

infer. See IMPLY, INFER.

inflammable. See UN-, IN-, NON-.

informant, informer. See RESOURCE PERSON.

infrastructure. See POPULARIZED TECHNICALITIES.

infringe. See PREPOSITIONS.

-ing. 1. Hostility to. 2. When to omit.
1. Hostility to. It is shown under A, AN, THE 5 that depending unduly on nouns linked by a definite or an indefinite article can be avoided through the use of a present participle acting as a noun. Instead of writing *The law also called for restoration of the ban on parking,* one can write *called for restoring the ban,* etc. Similarly, one can be in favor of *stabilizing the peso, reducing taxes, discussing peace terms,* and *protecting rain forests.* These verbal nouns (gerunds) happily stand for *stabilization, reduction, discussion,* and *protection,* which not only require joints to their neighboring words but also add to the *-ion*'s and *-tion*'s that disfigure English.

Many writers shy from the participial *-ing* noun in the mistaken belief that the form is weak. The modern temper likes abstractions—in the arts, the sciences, and daily life—and consequently feels most secure when it is offered a grand process labeled with a noun. *Reduction, discussion, protection* seem less human than *discussing,* etc., and therefore surer, more abstract and scientific. It may be rash to quarrel with the feeling, yet it must be pointed out that as between the *-tion* and the *-ing* forms, the *-ing* is closer to the verb, hence more active, concrete, direct, real. *Our discussion of the film went on for hours* is not so strong as *We sat there discussing the film for hours.*

The aversion to *-ing* also expresses itself in the shortenings *frypan, swimsuit, walk shoes,* etc., which, as they multiply, change radically the principle of compounding nouns and verbs into new terms. We shall soon have *dine rooms, run tracks, win teams,* and *dress rooms* if we go on finding our adjectives in amputated infinitives.

Writers hostile to *-ing* resort to other dodges as well. The distaste often leads to making up new words: *To minimize crowdage, spectators are requested to remain behind this line* (crowding); or to the misuse of old ones: *The noted British scientist who studied the Yenisei River's annual dissolution* (melting); or to pseudo-technicalities: *Substituting an all-civilian review panel would result in falloff in departmental efficiency* (in a falling-off of); or yet again to ambiguity: *He cannot blame anyone else. The rumor is of his own generation* (generating).

The preference for the infinitive over the participle also interferes with idiom. Ear and mind insist that we say *I look forward to going away,* not *look forward to go away.* But less common

parallels to this construction are repeatedly mangled; e.g., *In his early years, Mr. H. did everything from set type to solicit advertising to reporting* (from setting type to soliciting—just like the final *reporting*) / *She was accustomed to take a little nap after her lunch* (to taking). The one idiomatic exception is: *You are welcome to go or stay* (not *to going*).

2. When to omit. Perhaps by way of compensation, the contrary taste—equally bad—has popularized *my (your, her) thinking;* presumably, *thought* lacks the hum of process.

Overfondness for *-ing* also mismatches verbs: *The lecture adds much to the required reading rather than repeating it* (rather than repeats it) / *He must simply assert facts and judgments rather than proving them to doubters* (rather than prove them). These are parallel or balanced constructions, whose signal is often the linking *but, than,* or *rather.* Give such constructions parallel verb forms. *She saw no reason why she should continue to stand there rather than being* (be) *swallowed up by the earth* / *The officer indicated by a nod that he was willing to keep silent rather than turning* (turn) *in a report* / *They did not quite raise the roof but neither were they lowering* (did they lower) *their voices.* See LINKING and MATCHING PARTS.

Where *-ing* does sound weak, a different verb form can usually be found, bringing with it a gain in clarity. *He bought the pictures hanging on the wall* is both weak and ambiguous. A relative clause is always stronger than a pivoting participle, which in this case is not a verbal noun but a verbal adjective. Say instead, *He bought the pictures that hung on the wall,* and you will feel definiteness and strength return. No style is worse than that which slithers down a series of *-ing's: They spent that summer lazily, the house going slowly dilapidated, they not caring. In the village nestling far down below they could see men and women trotting like ants about their business depending on the hour of the day, waxing and waning with the heat oppressing them all alike.* Except for *trotting,* all these participal adjectives need a second look and a pruning knife.

inherent. See PRONUNCIATION 1.

initial, adjective. See SCIENTISM 4; VOGUE WORDS.

initialese. Scientists early discovered that their work was aided by the use of symbols—letters or arbitrary signs, which could be more readily associated with numbers and postulates than words could. Chemistry and mathematics were the first sciences to make the practice systematic. Thereafter engineering and manufacturing invented their own kinds of shorthand with two ideas in mind: the systems were to be understood within the profession and convenient as well for the public, which would use them on rare occasions: we can order Model N–ooF66498 whether or not we know that the letters and the figures denote and connote the type of object, its main features, and perhaps the date of its making.

Chemistry took notation further. As chemical compounds increased in number and their names became longer, chemistry resorted to abbreviation by initial letters. Instead of *trinitrotoluene,* chemists said *TNT;* instead of *dichloro - diphenyl - trichloro - ethane,* they wrote *DDT.* Other sciences followed suit to gain the same convenience.

But note: in each of these activities, the symbols and abbreviations were distinct—unique to that industry or science. Those engaged in the work readily learned the shorthand, because they needed the knowledge it conveyed and because the system was intelligible.

The extension of this clear and intellectually decent arrangement to public matters—to organizations, social programs, classifications, routines, proper names, and other identifiers— is quite different. It lacks system, clarity, intellectual fitness, and a proper respect for mankind, and so becomes a menace to the memory as well as to the rational mind. A trifling instance of its irrationality: consider the way in which the initials *PIN,* for *personal identification number,* are usually referred to. The ordinary citizen, assigned a *PIN* by his bank, almost always calls it *my PIN number,* even though *number* is the last of the three abbreviated words. It need make no one smile that people prefer to call a number a *number* and not a *pin.* Had clear minds in banking noticed that *personal* has no meaning here, they might have adopted the extant initialese for *identification* and given the customer an *I.D. number.* Everybody knows what that is.

Everybody also knows that there are

two types of denotation by initials: the one in which they stand for an ordinary descriptive name—e.g., the American Medical Association becomes the A.M.A.; and the one that begins in reverse with a word or near-word whose letters then become the initials of a name or phrase—e.g., *CARE* is made into the *Cooperative for American Remittances to Everywhere*, and *CORE* becomes the *Congress of Racial Equality*. (The pattern is sometimes varied by forming a pronounceable near-word out of syllables; e.g., *radar = radio detection and ranging system* / *motel = motor hotel*.)

No one can object to a group, professional or other, making the abbreviations it wants; it knows the meaning of the shortenings and the ease they provide when members address each other. But the world is large and the alphabet finite. To teachers, *NEA* is supposed to stand for the *National Education Association*. Yet, as many teachers know, it also stands for the *National Endowment for the Arts*, the *Nutrition Education Association*, and the *National Economic Association*. Each of these associations has dealings with journalists, many of whom know the syndicate called the *Newspaper Enterprise Association*. Judge then the confusion of interests among these groups when someone speaks of the *NEA*. What do the letters mean?

There were, by a recent count, twenty-nine *NEA*'s and forty-six *STD*'s. The New York State Department of Health sponsored an ad on buses which warned, "Sex is risky. It can lead to unwanted pregnancy, AIDS, or other STDs," the latter initials refer-

ring to *Sexually Transmitted Diseases*. But a rider who looked up only the medical definitions of *STD* would find that it also "officially" stands for *Short-term Disability, Skin Test Dose*, and *Standard Test Dose*. Confusion is made perfect by the fact that *dose* is an old slang term for the sexually transmitted disease gonorrhea. Again, what do the letters mean—and to whom? To people buying tickets at a theater, *SRO* means *Standing Room Only*; to a social worker, the same abbreviation means *Single Room Occupancy* (describing a building for welfare clients) —and *PINS* refers to *Persons in Need of Supervision*.

Names contrived from initials or syllables are called *acronyms*, and the supposed ingenuity required to invent them leads to the devising of elaborate names for very simple things. Thus an apparatus for breathing underwater is called a *scuba*, from *self-contained underwater breathing apparatus*. If ingenuity needs exercise, it should be employed in the traditional way, which is to find the old word that best describes the new object. There has long been a word for *self-contained underwater*, etc., and that is *gills*. Fins and *flippers* already serve for what some swimmers wear on their feet.

Initialese pretends to precision, uniqueness, and easy reading, but delivers their opposites. Though a game, it fails to imagine the other player, the hapless reader, whose understanding it may only blunt. The moral person should not get used to *BW* and *CW* for *biological* and *chemical warfare*, and there should have been public protest when the dread disease *Ac-*

quired Immune Deficiency Syndrome was called by the cozy term *AIDS*. One feels only embarrassment for organizations that freely call themselves *JOIDES* and *NASDAQ*; the latter sounds like a duck. And do pancakes or chicken appeal more to diners when the restaurants serving them are called, respectively, *IHOP* and *KFC*?

In short, there is no reason why our minds and our prose should be cluttered with letters and baby talk which, unlike the symbols and abbreviations of science, neither denote precisely nor connote anything whatever.

For a passion akin to initialese, see COVERING WORDS. See also PERSONAL(LY); SCIENTISM.

inject. See INCULCATE.

input. See FORBIDDEN WORDS 2; SCIENTISM 1.

inside. See PREPOSITIONS.

insight. See FORBIDDEN WORDS 2.

insigne, insignia. In 1966 Follett urged that we keep the Latin singular *insigne* (pronounced *in-sig-nee*), though he granted even then that it was almost never used. There is no law that requires a writer to give up a well-loved word. Today the Oxford English Dictionary still finds *insigne* correct but "less frequent" in British English than the plural *insignia*. By contrast, Americans thought *insignia* a singular a century ago. Follett and the Oxford agree that the plural of the plural, *in-*

signias, an American invention, is something to avoid.

Given a little-known singular and a silly plural, how should the American writer proceed? Usage supplies the answer: *insignia* is becoming both singular and plural, like *sheep, asparagus,* and other familiar nouns. Like these, it will rely on its context to indicate its number to the reader. *The scepter, the seal, and the crown remain the insignia* (plural) *of the monarch / The bullet had torn away the Air Force insignia* (singular) *from his cap.*

See also LATIN AND GREEK PLURALS.

insofar. See INASMUCH, INSOFAR.

instill. See INCULCATE.

insure. See ASSURE, ENSURE, INSURE.

integrity. See VOGUE WORDS.

inter. See EUPHEMISMS.

interact. See PRONUNCIATION 1.

interdisciplinary. See ENDINGS 2.

interested. See DISINTERESTED.

interest groups. See VOGUE WORDS.

interface. See SCIENTISM 1.

Internet. See PRONUNCIATION 1.

into, in to. 1. The two forms are not interchangeable; the second, in which the words are separated, conveys a meaning quite distinct from that of the first. In technical language, the first is a preposition, the second an adverb followed by a preposition. Failure to distinguish them is common and damaging to sense. *While the Prime Minister leads his guests into the reception* (in to; *in* = inward to another room; leads *in* his guests *to*) / *The growling sound of angry men in the streets outside reached into* (in to; *in* = inside) *them* / *For a time he had resisted this enchantment, only in the end to give into it* (give in to; *in* is an integral part of the verb phrase *give in*) / *late drivers who pulled into* (in to) *the curb, glancing apprehensively over their shoulders* / *where he could see the excursion boat coming into* (in to—otherwise it is a catastrophe) *the pier* / *The farmers* [in a blizzard] *just couldn't get into town.* The last is a borderline case; *get into town* is often idiomatic, but the author probably meant that the farmers were failing to reach town from the environs—*get in to.*

2. A slightly different trouble appears in *Then she placed the phone into its cradle.* For some logic-defying reason we *put* things either *in* or *into*, but *place* them *in*; she placed the phone in its cradle. This inflexible idiom runs counter to the general rule that we use *in* for simple containment without motion (*This volume is in the history collection*) or for motion within (*He was pacing back and forth in the corridor*), and *into* for motion toward (*She tiptoed into the bedroom*).

invaluable. See UN-, IN-, NON- 5.

inversion. See A, AN, THE 3; NUMBER, TROUBLE WITH.

invested. See TRANSITIVE, INTRANSITIVE.

-ion, -ness, -ment. No clear distinction *exists* between *precision* and *preciseness*, or between similar roots that can take both *-ion* and *-ness* without making either derivative seem artificial. Perhaps a distinction would be desirable, and sometimes one suspects in reading the best writers that they consciously or unconsciously mark a difference between these two endings. When they do, or seem to, the difference appears to be that *-ion* describes the abstract act and *-ness* the concrete quality. One might say, for example: *The exercise of concision will bestow conciseness on a piece of writing.* And likewise of course for *precision* and *preciseness.* A number of words, however, do not follow the same simple pattern and form the *-ness* compound from the longer adjectives ending in *-ive* (or *-ate*). We say *derision* and *derisiveness, division* and *divisiveness, intrusion* and *intrusiveness, decision* and *decisiveness, persuasion* and *persuasiveness, deliberation* and *deliberateness,* etc. As a result, the distinction sought appears more clearly, because the adjective that generates the longer noun points more emphatically to *the quality of,* which leaves the *-ion* form more abstract. Surely everyone feels—or can come to feel—the difference between *consideration* and *considerateness.*

What works against establishing this distinction is the need to avoid stuffing sentences with words ending in -ion, which are so numerous and, for some writers, so hard to escape. The whole question is one of style rather than of usage, and it illustrates how style must effect a compromise between contrary demands. The ear wants fewer -ion words, regardless of meaning; the mind wants cognate words with different endings to convey different nuances. Both are right, and we face here a dilemma akin to the one produced by the wish to make *that* the restrictive and *which* the nonrestrictive relative pronoun. (See THAT, WHICH, RELATIVE.)

In spite of what has just been said about the difficulty of absorbing more than one or two -ion words into a sentence agreeable to the ear, there is no warrant for seeking novelty by the substitution of -ment in old words that end in -ion. The campaign in the 1960s for the abolition of capital punishment made some journalists grow weary of *abolition* and introduce *abolishment*. Most of them had a good enough ear to use this new creation next to *death penalty* and so avoid the sequence *abolishment . . . punishment*, though it may well be that the jingle inspired the change in the first place. In any case, the -ment ending has not enough life in it to displace -ion, except where -ion has been pre-empted by the same root for another meaning. We have to say *containment* because we cannot say *contention* without ambiguity. But we say *detention* and find *detainment* affected.

What is more, there are occasions when the established word in -ment

has another meaning than the one intended. *Confinement, retirement, assignment, impressment,* and *advisement* have not the same meaning as the verbal nouns *confining, retiring, advising,* and the differently formed *impressiveness* and *assignation.* Purpose and context decide which is to be used, and the resistance to words ending in -ing (see -ING 1) should not cause the placing on -ment of a burden it cannot bear.

ironic. See JOURNALESE.

irony. See UNDERSTATEMENT.

irregardless. This is *regardless* changed by mistake to resemble *irrespective,* its cousin in meaning. *Regardless* says *without regard, unmindful,* and is usually followed by *of,* as in *Regardless of drops of rain, they continued to climb.* By adding the negative prefix *ir-,* the careless produce the meaning *not being without regard.* This notable nonsense is just what *regardless* does not mean.

issue(s), noun. See FORBIDDEN WORDS 2; UNNECESSARY WORDS 2.

issue, verb. See PREPOSITIONS.

-ize. The Greek suffix *-ize* has proved so useful in modern science for designating a process (*electrolyze, polymerize, hydrolyze*) that speakers and writers make up new *-ize* words to give a technical air to everyday goings-on. *-Ize* has the sound of dispatch; it says that we know just what we are doing (see also EMPOWER). But the words that we make with it are rarely needed, and most of them are badly formed. A scholar who is asked how he composes his books says that until he starts to write he *folderizes his ideas* (= files notes). Businessmen no longer *strike a bargain* or *make a deal,* they *finalize an agreement.* Musicians *concertize in Europe and Latin America* instead of *playing, singing,* or *performing.* Faced with the multiple blazes of a terrible fire, the professionals who fight it do not *make choices* but *prioritize.* Librarians and clipping bureaus *permanize* documents by covering them with a transparent adhesive sheet. Corporations which sell off subsidiaries announce (with difficulty) that they are *deconglomeratizing.* City planners worry aloud, not about more and more cars, but about an *increase in automobilization.* On television a commercial claims that one make of car has *optimized the placement of controls,* the best news since safety was *maximized.* As for the child who was referred to a diagnostician as *grossly undernasalized,* it is impossible to say whether the trouble required a plastic surgeon or a speech improver. These absurdities and those not yet born call for only two comments. If the itch to *-ize* a common word is irresistible, make the addition to a clear-cut fragment; *permanize* looks amputated and like a misprint. Better yet, delay invention until after a review of existing words. The business that sells doctor's records to medical researchers need not, as it vows to, *anonymize* them but *disidentify* them instead. The word may not be lovely, but it commits no malpractice with English.

See also JARGON; SCIENTISM.

J

jargon. Properly the special vocabulary or phraseology of an art or a profession—and as such acceptable—*jargon* has by a metaphor become the pejorative name given to certain faults of modern writing. It would be more exact to call the corrupting influence *pseudo-jargon*, for the badness consists in the pretense of using technical words when these either have no currency or are not appropriate to the present setting. Sometimes the writer makes them up as he goes; at other times he picks them up from an art or science without a sufficient awareness of their use and tone. With this obscure diction goes a heavy syntax that strings together abstractions and noun clusters with *of*'s and *in*'s, so that the sentences lack rhythm, clarity, and force (see NOUN PLAGUE). Here are two examples, the first and milder one being from an essay called "Plenitude from Petroleum"; the pseudo-jargon is marked by roman type: *In the energy* field *during the next twenty years the* overall position *of petroleum will not be affected other than* marginally, *although the* fuel pattern *is likely to change. The use of nuclear reactors in electric power stations and in ships may check the* growth rate *in the use of heavy fuel, and cheaper electricity may well cause the* growth curve *for domestic petroleum fuel for central heating to* flatten out; *but on the other hand there is likely to be steady growth in the utilization of petroleum in metallurgy, particularly for reducing iron ore.* (This last phrase startles by being straight English and not *iron-ore reduction.*)

The second is from a report by an industrial engineer: *After trying* a variety of methods of operations (various ways of conducting it) *this year the seminar* operated against the framework *of an outline the chairman prepared and presented at the opening meeting* (the seminar used an outline I presented at the outset). *While the various presentations did not follow, or indeed* in many cases tie into, *this outline* (Although some of the reports diverged from the outline), *yet it* definitely provided a greater coherence *to the seminar* as a total operation *and I am grateful for the distinct contributions which were made to* my thinking (yet the outline helped, and I am grateful for what I learned from the discussions).

By dint of repetition, pseudo-jargon of this sort infects all our minds until it seems impossible to express ourselves without recourse to its battered elements—*motivation, framework, time factor, calculated risk, positioning, structuring,* and dozens of others (see EDUCATIONESE; CRITICS' WORDS; POPULARIZED TECHNICALITIES; SCIENTISM; and VOGUE WORDS). Since the manufacture of jargon goes on at an accelerating pace, the seeping of the output into one's mind and speech must be steadily resisted. In writing, the only cure is to deny oneself the use of an ever-enlarging list of terms; or, rather, the use of them in their jargon sense (see FORBIDDEN WORDS 2).

journalese. The best writing is done by professional writers, of whom a great many are journalists. Hence much good prose, free of the faults discussed in this book, is to be found in newspapers and magazines and on the air, despite the rush and distraction that go with daily writing that is tied to events. But every profession is liable to certain failings. It is these failings that have given rise to the name *journalese* for a kind of fault in writing which, owing to the public's daily exposure to it, is particularly contagious.

In general, the tone of journalese is the tone of contrived excitement. Consider this opening paragraph from a well-known travel magazine: *Rising from the postmodern ashes of the eighties, New York's East Village precociously retains its cutting-edge spirit. Aquarius Central in the sixties, feisty and punk-nacious in the seventies, the neighborhood is still a cacophony of countercultures, reflected in a dizzying range of fashion, food, nightlife, art, and shops.* This mess of illogical images and misused words is extreme, to be sure, but it presents in short compass the sort of careless violence that ends by injuring the language. What are postmodern ashes, and how is something precociously retained? When the facts alone may not make the reader exclaim, the journalist thinks it his duty to apply the whip and spur of breathless words and phrases. Since these exist only in finite numbers, they get repeated, and repetition leads to their weakening, their descent into journalese. That is how we have worn out the adjectives *drastic, cryptic, crucial, essential, crushing, bitter, ironic,* and others that a scrupulous writer will now use only with caution. What sense of danger (or, more properly, of a turning point in a dangerous situation), for example, is left in the poor abused word *crisis*? Through frequent and automatic repetition such words find themselves in contexts where they do not belong, hence where their meaning does not come into play except as a signal to routine excitement. Thus *drastic* rightly used implies a violent action involving a sacrifice, a loss. The Massacre of the Innocents was a drastic decision of Herod's, because a king does not like to deplete his population. The storekeeper who announces drastic reductions in all his prices suggests that he is going to lose by your gain. But there is nothing drastic in the suddenness and violence of a riot, an explosion, or a decision to move a factory to a better site. Similarly, *cryptic* implies a teasing mystery, a provocative concealment, not just a secret. A document marked *Top Secret* is not cryptic. As for *irony* and *ironic*, the idea of an opposition of meaning between the thing said and the thing intended must be present to make the words applicable. By extension they can be applied to events, and that is why journalese has annexed them. From the *irony of fate*, which consists in the contrast between opportunity and circumstance (you have a chance to cruise around the world—you should be happy, but you are ill and condemned to bed for six months), journalese came to use *ironic* for all disappointments and defeats, regardless of their connection with some contrary appearance.

The desire for excitement tempered by sophistication leads writers to commit other faults classifiable as journalese. Most common is the abuse of superlatives—*the most, the first, the only*. These are rarely true, or provable if true; and even if true and provable, they generally do not add much to the interest of the subject. It is enough that the gift of a piece of furniture for the White House be genuine and of a suitable period; it need not be the oldest, most expensive, or rarest of its kind. It is enough that the giving of a prize to a scatological novel has raised angry objections; these need not be called *a full-scale furor*, a phrase that leaves the reader wondering how lesser furors are measured. Headline words overemphasize as a matter of course. *Bar, ban, score, quash, rap* (BISHOP RAPS PRIEST) and their kin suggest a very primitive form of debate; just as the corresponding words for actions that are not hostile (*scan, see, urge, tie*) reduce a great

variety of attitudes and acts to a very few. This overemphasis and reduction establish the atmosphere of journalese, which is melodrama.

As if tired of one kind of artifice, more and more journalists try to spice their prose with the merely strange or surprising. An actor, M. is interviewed after the play in which he had performed has closed: *The Roy Cohn character is slowly peeling away as a finished accomplishment, and M. is restless at the molting.* (The lame *as a finished accomplishment* admits that the metaphor of actor as snake is already failing before it has been spelled out; see METAPHOR 3 and 4.) An article on car engines recalls that in *the distant days of leaded gasoline . . . engines produced tremendous horsepower while combusting great quantities of fuel.* (The curious verb *combust* belongs to the nineteenth century; see SPIRIT OF ADVENTURE, THE.) A film festival makes an unexpected choice of films, and they are called *fiercely eclectic selections* (see ECLECTIC; PROSE, THE SOUND OF 2). A number of editors, all on dry land, who have left the book business for software publishing, become *a flotilla of young editors* (consult a dictionary). No longer content to be overemphatic, headlines strain to be odd as well: NOT LETTING AN AMNESTY TURN INTO A TRAVESTY: BUCKS OR BOOKS, IT'S A SHORT SHELF LIFE; this puzzle heads an article on the effects of "amnesties" for those who neglect to pay traffic tickets, return library books, etc. SIX ENVIRO-MYTHS amputates the *n* of the French root *environ* to join it to a word it has nothing to do with.

Extravagance comes in all kinds in the pages devoted to clothes, cooking, and interior design. A dress or a model is *a fashion sensation,* desserts are *sinfully fabulous,* and it is meant as praise for a chef that *the complexity of his recipes pushes the limits of culinary sanity.* The reader of these verbal coercions soon doubts that what they point to has much intrinsic interest.

Routine overstatement can insidiously affect the imagination. For example, journalese has adopted the phrase *mass murderer* for a killer of six or a dozen persons. More likely he or she is a *serial murderer,* and the acts are *multiple murders.* (The killer, being only one, is not a *multiple murderer.*) If ten deaths in a terrorist attack in the Tokyo subway are *mass murder,* by what phrase shall we remember Joseph Stalin and Adolf Hitler? How to describe Tamerlane in the fourteenth century with his pyramids of 80,000 skulls? The return of a sense of proportion will perhaps be signaled when every good book, play, or film need not be *riveting, brilliant,* or *scathing.* Meanwhile, it is our bad luck that journalese, when it seeks to excite regularly and routinely, ends by dulling interest—an outcome that might be called ironic.

See also CONVINCE, PERSUADE; DYSFUNCTIONAL; EXCEPTION; EXCITING; GROW; ICON; IF NOT; LEGENDARY, FABULOUS; LOOKING, KNOW; MINORITY; POPULARIZED TECHNICALITIES; REPORTEDLY; SCIENTISM 1, 2; SEA CHANGE; TRANSITIVE, INTRANSITIVE; UNNECESSARY WORDS; VENUE; VOGUE WORDS. For broadcasters' misuse of prepositions, see PREPOSITIONS.

K

---

key. Overindulging in figurative language tends first to denature the common words used and then to undo the figure of speech itself. (See META-PHOR.) This change in two steps has affected the word *key*. For centuries it has conveyed the image of a device, idea, or person that unlocks. The "lock" is an obstruction, a refusal, or some other form of difficulty. *The key to cumbersome East–West trade was the building of a railroad / The key to the stalled peace talks was the prince himself / When the fifth case* (of a disease) *was reported, it was plain that the key to survival for the rest of us was some device for catching rainwater.* In each example the imagined key opens a way by turning an imagined lock. By extension, the term came to be used as an adjective: *the key passage in the document, the key player in the game, a key invention.*

But once the indefinite article could replace the definite—*a key* for *the key* —the metaphor was dying: common locks have only one key, any others being mere copies. The idea of resolving a difficulty by a single instrument began to disappear or to become its opposite: FALTERING FUEL CELL A KEY TO SPACE FLIGHT. Here the key is the obstacle, not the means of removing it.

Having lost, with the definite article, the connotation of *unique*, the adjective *key* was doomed to join *vital, essential, significant* as yet one more stand-in for *important, noteworthy,* or *useful*. Accordingly, many writers now omit even the indefinite article: *Ninety percent of the executives questioned said a sense of humor was key to advancement / In her plans, his splendid cheekbones and excellent mind were key.*

The interests of good writing suggest that we leave *key* in actual or conceivable locks and reinstate the simple qualifiers *chief, main, prime, important, outstanding, indispensable.*

kind (sort, type) of. See THIS KIND, THESE KINDS, THOSE KINDS.

knack. See PREPOSITIONS.

know, with infinitive. See LOOKING, KNOW.

knowledge, to my. The idiom *to my knowledge* refers to what the speaker knows positively, perhaps at first hand; it is a shortened version of the older idiom *to my certain knowledge. They*

*have not had, to my knowledge, a visitor
in the last six months / To my knowledge, you were the last to see her in her
right mind.* The idiom for expressing
the tentative is *to the best of my knowledge,* which means *as far as I know* and
concedes that different information on
the subject may turn up.

knowledgeable. See -ABLE, -IBLE.

known (as). See AS 2.

L

labor, verb. See MALAPROPS.

lackadaisical, adjective. This oddity is all that remains of the ancient exclamations *alack* (= shame on, woe for [something or someone]) and *lack-a-day* (= woe for the day [on which something has happened]). In British usage, the adjective means affectedly drooping and spiritless; it derides the sort of person who once would cry *Lack-a-day*. American usage imputes no playacting and takes the condition at face value: *Spring weather makes me lackadaisical / She's so lackadaisical that she must be on a diet.* By association with *laxness*—or through laxness in reading—many wrongly pronounce the first syllable *lax-*. See PRONUNCIATION 1.

ladies. See CHANGING NAMES.

last, latest. The distinction between these has virtually disappeared, with odd results in usage. One may now speak to a writer of his *last* book without his taking the remark for a death warrant. He knows we mean his *latest*. Again, although no one would confuse the *last news* from a friend who died suddenly with the *latest news* from him if he is alive, yet the custom is to refer to this latest news as the *last*, as in *the last I heard from him was ten days ago*. And certainly *last week, month, year* are the only possible expressions, even though those times are only the *latest*.

Latin and Greek plurals. As is shown in INSIGNE, INSIGNIA, usage wobbles like a run-down top when it tries to fit into common prose the Latin and Greek that the modern mind uses freely but professes not to need. The chief difficulty occurs when the writer has to decide whether a Latin word ending in *-a* is a singular or a plural. The college *alumna* is visibly singular, since the plural *alumnae* is well known for causing a confusion in pronunciation with the masculine plural *alumni*. But beyond this point all is *terra incognita* (singular). Of television one hears regularly *This media eats up material*—an error encouraged by the fear that the correct *medium* might suggest a soothsayer. The label on an expensive gadget says, *This cartridge is equipped with a diamond and sapphire styli.* Is this pretentious plural of *stylus* due to the two precious stones that make it up? Or is some vague notion abroad in the world that Latin (and Greek) endings are at once euphonic and optional? Certainly one often hears *a phenomena, a criteria* in circles where these words are used with the right meaning in mind. But then, when a learned musicologist writes in the Encyclopaedia Britannica of *canti fermi*, obviously unaware that *cantus* belongs not to the second declension but to the fourth and forms its plural with *-us*, the less learned may permit themselves their lapses. For writers and speakers who prefer to observe the forms of the original language, the following short list may prove useful.

NEUTER SINGULARS (Latin in *-um*, Greek in *-on*)	PLURALS (original or anglicized)
addendum	*addenda*
(no singular)	*agenda*
animalculum	*animalcula*
candelabrum	*candelabra*
criterion	*criteria*
datum	*data*
(no singular)	*marginalia*
medium	*media*
memorandum	*memoranda*
miasma	*miasmas* (Eng.)
	miasmata (Gr.)
nostrum	*nostrums*
(no singular)	*paraphernalia*
pendulum	*pendulums*
phenomenon	*phenomena*
stratum	*strata*

FEMININE SINGULARS	PLURALS
alga (rare)	*algae* (pron. *-jee*)
alma [*mater*]	(no plural)
alumna	*alumnae* (pron. *ee*)
bona [*fide*]	(no plural: *fides* is a singular nominative sometimes used with *bona* instead of the ablative *fide*.)
persona [*non grata*]	*personae* [*non gratae*] (rare)
propaganda	(no plural)
phantasmagoria	(no plural)
sequela	*sequelae*

Masculine Singulars	Plurals
alumnus	alumni (pron. -eye)
bonus	bonuses
cactus	cactuses, cacti
calculus	calculi (medical only)
coitus	(no plural)

Note that *opus, lotus,* and *octopus* are not masculines ending in *-us,* and they give (in English) *opuses, lotuses,* and *octopuses.* (For *cantus fermus,* see above.) *Opera* is the regular *Latin* plural of *opus* (= work, as in *magnum opus*), but *opera* in the sense of a musical play is from another Latin word, singular, that means *noble effort* or *enterprise.* In English the plural is of course *operas.* AGENDA is now singular and takes *s* in the plural. *Viscera* is plural and has no English singular. *Aborigines* is plural, and its infrequent singular is *aborigine* (pronounced *jinee*).

Latinas, Latinos. See CHANGING NAMES.

lavish. See MALAPROPS; PREPOSITIONS.

lay, lie. It is a pity that the eighteenth-century freedom of usage which permitted Byron still to write *There let him lay* did not persist and bring about a useful amalgamation of these overlapping forms. They trip up careful speakers and cause more trouble than they are worth. What is still more confusing is that careful writers, who are not tripped up, recognize as correct

the inconsistent form *lay of the land,* at least in its figurative sense; the rarely used *lie of the land* suggests more directly terrain or topographical features. For the rest, what we do with our bodies is *lie, lay, lain;* what we do with objects is *lay, laid, laid.* A hen, of course, both *lies* and *lays.*

To this, one must add the caution that the prefixes *over-* and *under-* seduce into error. *Seventeen centuries of violence overlay the bloody Balkans* means to speak in the present tense, which requires *overlie,* as in *violence lies over.* Yet the ear is annoyed because the mind thinks of a layer of violence covering the country. *Underlying cause* is standard, as in *An unpaid debt was the underlying cause of their feud;* but here again the contrasting standard *underlayer*—of clouds, fur, skin, etc.—tempts the unwary to the wrong form.

lay waste. In use since the sixteenth century, this transitive idiom, meaning *devastate, ravage,* uses *lay* as a verb in the sense of *render* (as in *lay bare, lay open*) and *waste* as an adjective. In the book of Ezekiel, God announces succinctly, *I will lay thy cities waste.*

Sleepy writers and editors frequently serve up sentences like *The rebels have laid to waste the farmlands in their path* and *The measure in question would lay to waste forty years of progress.* Whence this pointless *to*? No one would write *She threatened to lay to bare the entire scheme* or *With one stroke he laid the melon to open*; rather, we write that she may *lay bare the scheme* and he *laid the melon open*. The preposition *to*, besides being unidiomatic, weakens the force of the phrase. Its source may be a mental echo of the idiom *lay to rest*, but there *rest* is a noun.

See also CAKE; COULD CARE LESS; FORT; RUBBER; SEA CHANGE; SET PHRASES; STONE.

leaving. See DANGLERS, BENIGN.

legacy. See VOGUE WORDS.

legalisms. See ABSENT; ADDRESS, SPEAK TO; AND/OR; AS 5; IF AND WHEN; PRIOR TO; RIGHT, IN HIS (HER) OWN; UNLESS AND UNTIL; VENUE; WHEN AND IF.

legend(ary), fabulous, etc. Advertisers and coiners of slang have long used the names of certain literary forms as terms of praise. Since these names will outlive careless borrowing, we should recall what they mean.

Legends were once accounts of the lives of saints and are now regarded as traditional but embellished stories. What is *legendary* arises from such fictions, e.g., the boy George Washington admitting to chopping down a cherry tree. In careless usage, *legendary* is used to describe something that is at least well known and at most to be admired for that reason. More confusingly, the word is applied without discrimination to things past or present and to persons living or dead. It follows that when the press calls a living person *the legendary* M. or S. or Y., the subject cannot be distinguished from *the legendary Balzac* (dead) and *the legendary Paul Bunyan* (never alive). The adjective defies understanding in *the reportedly legendary performance of* T. *in the first New York production* and in *Tennis has lost one of its true legends.*

What is *fabulous* or *fabled* can be found in a *fable*, a similarly made-up story, usually short, that offers a moral lesson. "The Grasshopper and the Ant" is a *fable*; it thus makes *fabulous* the fictional insects it describes. In present popular usage this descriptive is supposed to mean worthy of great admiration. A journalist does not mean *fictional* when she refers to *the actor's fabled kindness*, nor does a reviewer invoke an old tale in saying that P. *is a fabulous dancer.*

A *myth* in the literary sense is another fiction, but a narrative once believed; it serves, in M. H. Abrams's words, to explain "why the world is as it is and things happen as they do." Supernatural events or persons figure in *myths*. The myth of Oedipus is often said to mean that no human being escapes his fate, as Oedipus cannot fail to do what the Delphic oracle predicts. In casual use *myth* has come to mean a mere untruth, *mythic(al)* describing what has never happened or existed.

What appears in a *proverb* is *prover-*

bial. "A stitch in time" might be called the *proverbial* precaution that "saves nine." Only the foggiest of minds would refer to a governor's *proverbial* (or *fabled*) *caution,* or to *Niagara's proverbial* (or *fabled*) *falls.* The governor's caution is probably *characteristic* or *famous;* the falls at Niagara are also *famous, well known,* or, in a figurative adjective, *trademark.*

Most difficult of all to distinguish from publicity use are *epic* and *saga.* Strictly speaking, an *epic* is a narrative poem celebrating the deeds of one or more heroic persons, historical or imagined, e.g., the *Iliad, The Song of Roland.* By contrast, a *saga* is a work in prose which tells the story of an ancient Icelandic family or a Norwegian king. Advertisers of movies have reduced these technical terms to vague betokeners of grandeur, elaborateness, and expense.

See also POPULARIZED TECHNICALITIES.

lesbians. See CHANGING NAMES.

less, lesser. See FEWER, LESS.

lesser light(s). See SET PHRASES 2.

lest. See SUBJUNCTIVE.

level. When a hierarchy of rank, authority, or power is discussed, *level* may be the appropriate or even the inevitable word; it can denote one among several ascending figurative planes. But *level* has acquired a vogue in uses unconnected with either literal or figurative elevation; one *level* stands in no relation to others named, implied, or imaginable. In such settings the word has no meaning and is among the most dispensable VOGUE WORDS. The form *on a something-or-other level* also wastes as many words as the form *on a something-or-other* BASIS, with which it is usually interchangeable. Both are, moreover, as vague as IN TERMS OF. To escape from any of these traps, one must search for the useful word that affords a concise rewriting. Consider these everyday statements: *I tried to discuss it with him on a rational level* (or *basis*) / *I tried to discuss it with him in terms of rationality.* Cleared of verbiage, these sentences mean only *I tried to discuss it with him rationally.* The following examples show how varied uses of *level* can be trimmed away to reveal a concrete meaning. *Sales increases at the retail level have led to greater optimism among manufacturers and distributors* (Increases in retail sales) / *On the conversation level, we get along just fine* (In conversation) / *You can criticize Dr. C. on an ethical level and find some agreement from his peers* (criticize Dr. C.'s ethics) / *You say that he must have been crazy, but I think that on some other level he knew exactly what he was doing* (I think that in some way or other) / *They opposed the watering down of the Ph.D. program as a way to get more teaching candidates at that level* (get more teachers who hold that degree) / *At the junior-high-school level, 58 percent of the students are involved in foreign-language study* (Fifty-eight percent of the junior-high-school students study a foreign language) / *a manifestation at* *the local level of the all-embracing love of Christ* (a local manifestation) / *The betting is good on a tripartite conference at the foreign ministers' level* (on a conference of the three foreign ministers) / *if the level of military activity was substantially raised* (if military activity were considerably intensified) / *Many laundering problems can be avoided if they are anticipated at the manufacturing level* (anticipated by the manufacturers) / *conviction that "neither party was worth a damn" on civil rights on the national level—and, in some cases, on the local level* (in the nation at large *or* in the towns and counties).

See also CASE; CHARACTER; COVERING WORDS; NATURE.

level playing field. See VOGUE WORDS.

levied. See MALAPROPS.

libel, slander. In legal definition, *libel* can result from injurious remarks that are circulated in writing, *slander* from those that are spoken, including those broadcast over television or radio. But with the proliferation of devices for reproducing either writing or speech, the technical distinction has become blurred. A videotape, a CD-ROM, or an audiotape is at once speech and a form of magnetic or electronic writing. Since the difference between the fugitive voice and the permanent script had made the difference in law, and it no longer holds, many legal scholars recommend that the two classes of tort be reduced to one.

lie. See LAY, LIE, verb.

lifestyle. See POPULARIZED TECHNICALITIES.

like. 1. *Like* for *as*. 2. *Like, unlike*. 3. *Like* as filler.

1. *Like* for *as*. According to modern usage, most comparisons involving two clauses should be joined with *as* or *as if*, not *like*. For example, the educated ear knows at once that such statements as *He went on like he was crazy* and *I don't sing like I once did* do not belong on paper unless they are quoted speech. For the first *like*, use *as if* and change *he was* to *he were* (see SUBJUNCTIVE); for the second, use *as* alone to join the two little clauses.

Linguists tell us that *like* was used as a conjunction in the formative stages of English and that it has tried to work as a conjunction ever since. In casual American and British speech, it often does. But written English leaves the conjunctional use to the advertisers, who have made it a mark of their guild. A cigarette company bragged for years that its product *tastes good like a cigarette should.* An auto maker likewise boasted of *cars that can do what they look like they can do and they look like they can do more than other cars on the road.* Here again, *like* should be *as* in the first construction and *as if* in the second. Today a photo ad for an investment bank has an elegant woman saying in the caption: *Sometimes* [my mother] *holds me like she did when I was a child.* Such English is not a product of advertisers' ignorance but an expensive effort to be folksy. Yet the substitution of *like* for *as* makes the elegant woman sound slovenly rather than artless. A business writer who adopts the argot of those he reports on cannot help mimicking the chatty tone of an ad: *The firm responded like it had been set upon by pirates.*

Like does appear more and more as a conjunction in one sort of written comparison. When the verb in a main clause is repeated in a second clause, many writers now prefer *like* to *as* and *in the way that.* The old popular song that says *If you knew Susie like I know Susie* may have strengthened the usage; the popular witticism *I need [something] like I need a hole in the head* almost certainly did. Nowadays statements like the following are increasingly found in print: *The governor is waiting like he always waits to see which position is safest / L. felt like she had felt on the first day of Passover ten years before / He treated her like he had treated me.* But writers uneasy with this construction should use *as he always waits* and *as she had felt* and *as he had treated.*

Some writers are so confounded by the choice between *like* and *as* that they fall into the opposite error of substituting *as* in comparisons between substantives where *like* is needed: *This stairway, as the one in the hall, was uncarpeted / There was nothing left to do: he was utterly baffled, as I / She hoped to appeal to his better nature, as her predecessor Jennifer / He decided* that, as his cousin, he must make an appearance at the ball. The last two examples imply subjects in disguise, *she* as *Jennifer* and *he* as *his cousin.* In all these comparisons, *like* is required —and in the second one, *as I* must be changed to *like me.*

In blind fear of misusing *like,* some writers fall back on *as with,* even when *with* turns out to be meaningless. *As with most things here in Moscow, etiquette is politics / The Greenland birds, as with the mallards, remain in the country in winter.* Both statements make clear sense with *like: Etiquette, like most things here* and *The Greenland birds, like the mallards. Like* joins equivalent things or ideas where *as with* is an empty gesture: *And as with so many people, mere abstract ideas were not nearly as disturbing to M. as immediate actualities.* Here there is no equivalence between *people* and abstract ideas. Recast so as to join *people* and M.: *Like many people, M. was not nearly as disturbed by abstract ideas as by immediate actualities.* See also AS 13; LINKING.

Writers who think they can do without *like* do not know their business. The grammatically scared end up writing silliness: *Her breath came fast, as a small animal's;* or more elaborately: *We must not behave as children or coax them to lie down as seemly ghosts in quiet graves* (like children; like ghosts). The chancellor of a university declares: *I have spent my life among the private corporation, the government office, and the campus, and I understand that each of these is, as are the church and the press, a prime source of strength and thought and aspiration.* Here the correct but awkward *as are* manifestly represses the spontaneous *each of these, like the church and the press, is.* A popular novelist writing as a masculine narrator produces: *The words just came tumbling out; I spoke as her mother.*

Some traditional examples encourage modern confusion. When we read that Jesus spoke *as one having authority,* we cannot be sure from the diction alone whether the Bible translators were saying that he possessed authority or simply that he talked as if he did. Today the second meaning would require *like one having authority.* Again, *They fell upon the supplies as men starving* would mean that they were actually starving men; *like men starving* should mean that had they been actually starving they could not have seemed more voracious. The rule of thumb is: *As* tells in what role or capacity the deed is done; *like* introduces a comparison between similars: *He spoke as an innocent* implies that he is an innocent; *spoke like an innocent* compares him to one. (Note the logic in *spoke like the innocent that he is.*) See also SUCH 2.

2. *Like, unlike.* As is shown by the examples above, language is continually called on to say that *this* is like or unlike *that.* If such statements are to make clear sense, we must understand precisely what the *this* and the *that* are. But precise thought takes effort; it is easier to say that something indefinite resembles or does not resemble a nearby something else, and to hope that two vaguenesses, once they have

met, will bring forth a concrete meaning. The twin adjectives *like* and *unlike* are exact antonyms but exact equivalents in grammar. Put them at the heads of sentences and they dangle as often as the so-called dangling participle. (See DANGLERS.) Moreover, they can blandly assert resemblance or difference between incommensurables.

In the following examples we see the flouting of syntax and the comparison of incompatibles: *Like Emerson in his mystical experience on a bare common in wintertime on a cloudy day, the setting of this poem would seem at first glance to be unpromising.* One who begins a sentence with *like* is committed to answering the question: What is like what? The only possible answer requires that the first half of the comparison be the subject of the following main verb. The sentence above tells us that Emerson is like the setting of someone else's poem—a wrong answer to what is like what. To supply the right answer, we need an overhaul. One might say: *The setting of this poem, like that of Emerson's about his mystical experience . . . would seem.* This is no pearl of a sentence, but it does compare the setting of one poem to the setting of another, it does say what is like what, and it does pin the descriptive matter to the right subject. If one wants to keep *Like Emerson,* one must reorganize the main clause, and the opening must read: *Like Emerson in his poem about his mystical experience . . . T. gave this poem a setting that,* etc.—a spate of words, but at least Emerson is like another poet.

3. *Like* as filler. American speech

may have always used fillers—*uh / um / y'know*—to take up the pauses when thought lags behind the unstoppable tongue. The reason for the speaker's fear of an instant of silence lies beyond a discussion of usage. But there are fashions in fillers, and of these the most disruptive do damage to words that have meaning elsewhere. It goes without saying that the speaker means nothing by *like* in: *I was, like, desperate / Like, what did he mean? / You seem, like, depressed.* After decades of this dithering fashion, one longs for a moment's silence or a well-placed *uh*.

For *like* as a sentence demolisher, see SPEAKING LIKENESS. See also OKAY; UNNECESSARY WORDS; VERY, MUCH, REALLY.

-like. See STYLE, TYPE 2.

limited. Those who shrink from plain words about money often decline a request for it on grounds of possessing *limited funds*. But all funds are limited; the usage is euphemistic for *meager, scant, insufficient, inadequate.* An adverbial dressing gown like *relatively limited, strictly limited, sorely limited* (see UNNECESSARY WORDS 3) makes nothing clearer. Conversely, an advertiser who is offering a premium (or FREE GIFT) only states the obvious by saying that *supplies are limited.* Everything is.

See also EUPHEMISMS; FISCAL.

linking. 1. If there is one principle that may be said to govern the whole art of writing, it is the principle of linking; that is, joining what should be joined and separating what should be separated. Put in these terms, the principle remains abstract and does not take us very far. That is why many separate suggestions are made in this book about the best ways of joining and separating the several parts of speech as well as their clusters—phrases, clauses, and sentences. The injunction to give parallel form to parallel ideas, the advice about placing adverbs and commas—all these particulars relate to the craft of correct or adroit linking, which is the prerequisite of good prose.

It is easy to choose from good writers examples of skillful linking; the reader alert to the difficulties of framing a complex sentence can pick out such passages and study them. Here all that will be done is to draw attention to the subject and illustrate a few of the common blunders.

The first care of the writer who would be clear is to connect modifiers and their objects in such a way that the resulting phrase slips into the mind without effort. He need not be pedantic and try to glue each adverb or adjective to its verb or noun (see ONLY), but he must avoid outlandish combinations such as *permanent artists' oil colors* (in which it is the oil colors that are meant to be permanent and not the artists) or *Ask for our cup of complimentary coffee* (when it is the cup of coffee that is complimentary). All accumulations of qualifiers without proper links between them are liable to this fault (e.g., *the non-tax-paid liquor traffic*, which attempts to squeeze ideas into a narrow space) as are all mismatings of locutions (e.g., the bank slogan *Help to people with money since 1792*, where one would expect the help had been given to people *without money*). In each, the reader must unscramble and rearrange the elements for himself, and even if he succeeds in doing this correctly every time, he is halted and annoyed by having to do work that should have been done for him.

Parallelism of thought and of form is discussed at several places in this book, notably in MATCHING PARTS and under COMMA, THE 1 and SEMICOLON, THE 2, where precepts are given for managing a list that concludes with *and*. The failure to observe these pieces of advice leads to poor linking, by which the reader is jarred. For example: *The victims were surprised at night, threatened, tied up and gagged with transparent tape and their cash—nothing but cash—carried off.* Finding no pause after either *tied up* or *tape* (nor before the banefully verbless phrase that follows), we are forced to imagine people not only bound but also gagged with both tape and cash.

Equally obstructive of sense is the linking of parts that need to be separated if they are to be understood correctly. Sometimes a comma will do the trick: *When I got through the table at the end of the room was ready for the meeting* (comma after *through*). But often punctuation will not help or cannot be used: *Its significance in headaches is not clear, but by providing relief from an external application it holds intriguing possibilities.* The author of this editorial did not mean *relief from an external application*; he meant *providing relief by an external application*. And what makes the sentence worse is that only a few lines earlier he had led us to link the same two words that should now be unlinked. He had written: *If we can get relief from pain.*

Similar trouble frequently occurs in subordinate clauses in which *that* can be taken either as conjunction or as relative pronoun. For instance: *It was 4 p.m. and they were all turning in, but I persuaded the second taxi driver that I stopped to take me downtown.* On a first reading the mind runs: *I persuaded him that I stopped* (e.g., along his route), whereas the sense is *the second taxi that I stopped.* Unless strictly controlled, the ever-present *that* can be a flighty connective.

2. As in evolutionary theory, so in writing there are missing links. Commercial jargon has always been known for a tendency to leave out the necessary and put in the unnecessary—a curious form of fair trade. But the same tendency works throughout the realm of print, in an effort to be brisk or allusive. In the following sentence from a novel, the effect is pointedly literary: *It was good to be far, to be a continent, from the meaningless sprawl of Los Angeles.* Between *continent* and *from* we need a link, such as *away*, because *to be a continent* is no synonym for *far*; it is in fact much more "meaningless" than the sprawl of Los Angeles. A more confusing example calls for a structural remedy: *R. . . . shot and killed a former beauty queen who had once been his stenographer and then took his own life.* As it stands, the *once* and the *then*

make a false link. One correction would be *his stenographer; then he took his own life.*

The greatest difficulty in linking is the one that comes in the arrangement of a number of circumstantial details. There are no rules for the order in which time and place and the other bits and pieces of the full situation should come. Their length and rhythm often determine their place, and so does the emphasis desired. But the comic collision of parts is fatal to sense, as is the dangling remnant: *Some passengers jumped out of windows while the train was still moving to escape the fire.* The fire being in fact aboard the train, rewrite: *To escape the fire, some passengers jumped out of windows while the train was,* etc. Even in the absence of deliberate linking, good or bad linking takes place: *The philosopher B., ninety-three, disclosed that the meeting took place last month in an article in the newspaper* Liberation *on Friday morning.* But the meeting did not take place in an article; rather, an article disclosed that the meeting had taken place. Hence: *The meeting took place last month, the philosopher B., ninety-three, disclosed in an article,* etc. All that said, it must be admitted that placing will not work if the parts fail to dovetail, as they fail in *Two people were killed and three seriously wounded early yesterday when gunmen burst into a Brooklyn home during a robbery attempt, the police said.* The failed link here is *during,* which puts a robbery in motion before the gunmen broke in. Change *during* to *in.*

See also ABOUT; IN TERMS OF; WITH.

literally means *actually; without exaggeration; not metaphorically; factually.* It has long been misused by those who want another all-purpose and meaningless intensive like *really.* (See VERY, MUCH, REALLY.) *She was literally heartbroken* announces no fatal breakage, just as no hit by a ball is implied in *I was really bowled over. Really* will not soon be restored to meaning; yet it can be done without, for it seldom contrasts with *unreally,* present or implied. But a rightly used *literally* insists that the speaker intends no hyperbole or figurative meaning: *She was literally penniless when they found her / With one blow he was literally struck dumb for the rest of his life / That was one movie that literally put me to sleep.* These statements mean precisely what they say.

litmus test. See METAPHOR 4; VOGUE WORDS.

livelong. See PRONUNCIATION 1.

locate often runs the risk of ambiguity. The secretary says, *I'll try to locate her at the terminal,* meaning, *I'll try to find her* there. The owner of a new business may use the word intransitively to say, *I am thinking of locating on West Broadway* and mean *renting* quarters there. *Locate* is least questionable in the passive mood, when it becomes an adjective synonymous with *situated,* as in *The last public horse trough is located in front of a building on West Street;* though in most sentences where the passive *located* occurs, *at* will suffice: *The house F.W.D.*

bought is located (is at) . . . *Locate* is often needlessly elaborate and so is favored by broadcasters. But its antonym, *dislocate*, is indispensable. *Relocate* is business jargon for moving people to a place they may or may not want to go to.

logic. Writers who do not bother to think about the interrelations of the words they use, and who take these relations ready-made in the form of clichés, often fall into the habit of referring to *a fine toothcomb*, and sometimes just *a toothcomb*. This instrument is found especially often in crime fiction, where it is called into play for every systematic search. Now, it does not take much reasoning power to discover that (1) the very essence of a comb is to have teeth and (2) what serves to make a sifting particularly close is *the fine tooth* of the comb. In short, the battered metaphor is about a fine-tooth(ed) comb—a comb with fine teeth—not a tautological toothcomb, fine or coarse.

This brief demonstration, which could be supplemented by many others, defines the place of logic or reasoning in the use of language. Educated people are often heard to say that "logic has nothing to do with language—usage and idiom are all"; and they illustrate their dogma with telling instances of common sense defied. They are right about those instances, and every book about usage confirms and extends them. But for one piece of arbitrary arrangement in the language, recorded as idiom or anomaly, there are hundreds of thousands of expressions, ordinary and familiar or new and strange, in which the application of reason is implicit or required. Only by thinking about what we mean can we decide whether to say *M. threw a punch* or *C. was hit; She likes me better than he* or *She likes me better than him; to eat your cake and have it, too* or the reverse (see CAKE). The form of words known as an Irish bull (*If you could see the molecules in this piece of matter, they would be moving so fast you couldn't see them*) embodies the failure or refusal to make words accord as they should with the dictates of logic. The effect is comic in the bull, ambiguous or irritating elsewhere.

For example, the writer who tells us that *the absence of a preplanned strategy strongly impacted upon the board's thinking and left management without a loophole* is a writer we come to resent after a very few pages, because his neglect of logic forces us to do his work for him as we read. What is a strategy, if not planned, and what is the point of the extra remove in time denoted by *pre-?* How can an absence hit upon thinking and, having done so, leave no loophole? (See IMPACT; ON, UPON, UP ON; and *thinking* under VOGUE WORDS.) The illogicality here is due to the loose coupling of metaphors; but the penchant for metaphorical writing in prose very often comes from a weak sense of logic. (See METAPHOR.)

Yet the exercise of logic where it will make for tight and clear sentences is no warrant for forcing it into situations where it has been given up by the language in exchange for the convenience of mental shorthand. For example, English does not bother to analyze and to articulate the relation of many modifiers to the nouns they modify: a *hairbrush* is a brush *for* the hair; a *hair shirt* is a shirt *made of* hair; a *hairline* is a line *as thin as* a hair or else the line *where the hair begins*; a *walking stick* does not walk, but a *walking delegate* does. We have a *literary critic*, not a *literature critic*, but also a *dance critic*, because a *dancing critic* would be another kind of wonder altogether.

The upshot of this discussion is that when one has eliminated everything that idiom and usage clearly command, one must apply one's logical faculties to what remains. And this in turn is a warning that without a knowledge of idiom and usage gained from reading there is little chance of good writing.

long, hard look. See UNNECESSARY WORDS 3.

long-lived. See PRONUNCIATION 1.

looking. See DANGLERS, BENIGN.

looking, know with infinitive. In conversation, ruralisms may seem good-natured, but on paper and in political discourse they are at best affectations and at worst subverters of clarity. Movie Westerns for decades spoke in such rural forms as *fixin' to go to town, lookin' to buy a horse, studyin' to be a lady*. Strictly speaking, no fixing, looking, or studying was meant by these, but *preparing* or *getting ready, hoping, trying, expecting,* or

doing the best I can. Too many educated writers have lately adopted the ruralism common to the following examples: *As a child psychiatrist, Dr. G. was looking to find out how the Hispanic way of life was transmitted to children* / *The Supreme Court is obviously looking to narrow the uses of* (the doctrine called) *affirmative action* / *Whether you're looking to buy or sell used books* / *Executives of N. Airlines were looking to strengthen their frequent-flier program by offering a credit card* / *B. spent much of his year looking to build a new empire on his acquisition of P. Communications Inc.* In each specimen, *looking to* is counterfeit for *hoping to, trying to, preparing to, expecting to, planning to,* or *bending every effort to*—diverse meanings among which the reader is left to choose.

Know with the infinitive is a clipped form of *know enough*, as in the mock-compliment *He knows enough to come in out of the rain. Know enough* implies strictly limited knowledge: *Kathryn knew enough not to answer the door but could not imagine how to get help* / *He knew enough Spanish to order in a restaurant and to read the traffic signs.* As the following examples show, the idea of limited knowing has nothing to do with statements where *know to* now creeps in: *The owner knew what people wanted to hear, and audiences also knew to trust his taste* (trusted) / *Smart shoppers know to return to the bargain racks several times in the course of their stay, because new items tend to pop up every fifteen minutes* (omit *know to*) / *I know, unlike the authors, not to expend much effort defining excellence in teaching* (Unlike the authors, I do not expend).

For other ruralisms, see COUPLE, MISSING OF; OF A; GROW, TRANSITIVE. See also VOGUE WORDS.

loose (un). See UN-, IN-, NON-.

lost causes. Everyone knows that the meanings of some words change, although such words are few in relation to the full lexicon, and the change takes a good many years. In a sense it is never complete, for the great, indispensable works of the past stubbornly assume that we know what the words meant when they were written. And so we have footnotes to Shakespeare and to many others, recalling earlier meanings. Meanwhile, for the best of reasons the careful writer views with alarm the words that change in his lifetime. Here are earlier meanings of a handful of terms that decisively changed in the twentieth century.

The adjective *hectic* once meant *flushed, as with tuberculosis,* not *hasty* or *confused; volatile* described what was able to *fly or flit,* not the *changeable* or *explosive; mundane* was the *earthly* as opposed to the celestial or divine, not merely the *ordinary* or *dull; via* meant *by way of (flying to Los Angeles via Denver)* not *by means of;* what was *restive* was *rebellious* or *mulish,* not *fidgety* or *restless; epoch* denoted a *turning point,* not an *era;* schoolchildren worked at *arithmetic,* not *mathematics;* and *trivia* were *crossroads,* not *trifles.* For the popularity of this last bit of Latinity, Logan Pearsall Smith, a scholar and lexicographer, is indirectly responsible, having chosen the word as the title of a series of essays not at all trivial but suggestive of traveled roads and chance meetings, like the verses of John Gay called *Trivia, or the Art of Walking the Streets of London* (1716).

For good causes not lost, see DATA; DISINTERESTED; DUE TO; OBLIVIOUS OF (TO).

lotus. See LATIN AND GREEK PLURALS.

luxuriant, luxurious. See MALAPROPS.

luxury. See PRONUNCIATION 1.

-ly, suffix. See ADVERBS, VEXATIOUS; HOPEFULLY; MASTERFUL, MASTERLY; OVERLY; PROSE, THE SOUND OF 2; REPORTEDLY; SENTENCE, THE 7.

M

major, minor. In JOURNALESE every novelist's new novel is a *major event*, and troops incur *minor casualties*, of which nobody wants to be one. The standard of comparison is in each case assumed to be known to all. Since this assumption cannot be true, we are all of us free to magnify our doings and diminish our errors until the visible world teems with *major figures* performing *major work* and suffering only *minor setbacks*. The solemn overuse of *major* led to its adoption as satirical slang for *large, important,* or *impressive.* (*I gave them a major piece of my mind.*) But even this extra duty has failed to earn *major* and *minor* the rest they deserve. The careful writer can speed that retirement by using simple terms like *great, large, important, big,* and *small, unimportant, few.*

majority, minority. 1. The occasions of democratic practice impel us to overuse these correlative words. They are most often (not *in the majority of cases*) substituted for the simpler *many* and *most, few* and *some.* From such misuse, *majority* acquires the incorrect connotation *nearly all,* and *minority* the likewise unwarranted sense of *a negligible few.* Yet everyone knows that one unit more or fewer than half is

enough to permit the use of these technical terms.

2. Politicians rise or fall by the will of a *majority,* hence some have the word on the brain, using it with singular nouns only technically made up of units. There is no such thing in good usage as *the majority of the money* or *the majority of timber.* (See TOTAL, TOTALLY.)

3. The distortions of magnitude visited on *majority* and *minority* are often worked upon *maximum* and *minimum* but in reverse. The latter two are made to stand for *much* and *little,* instead of *the most* and *the least,* which are their proper meanings. To write clear English today one must use the neglected small words, among the first to be learned and still as good as new.

See also MINORITY, collective noun.

malaprops. The aunt in Sheridan's *Rivals* requests that the conversation contain *no delusions to the past,* meaning of course *allusions.* By making a habit of such blunders, she has given her name to those mistakes in language which consist in using one word for another that it more or less resembles. Some linguists maintain that native speakers of a language cannot make mistakes—they merely incarnate the spirit of Change; but most people continue to believe that Mrs. Malaprop's *delusions to the past* still produce delusions in the present. *Fortuitous* for FELICITOUS and COHORT for *companion* are discussed in their alphabetical places. Here are a few more malaprops often encountered in talk and print.

A *stickler* is not a puzzle but a *precisian*, a *fussbudget*.

To *decimate* is not to utterly destroy or kill off but to kill in a large proportion; it applies only to persons.

To *burgeon* means to put out buds; figuratively to come out in a small, hopeful, modest way, not to spread out, blossom, and cover the earth.

Gertrude Stein and Ernest Hemingway were not *ex-patriots* in Paris but *expatriates*, out of (= *ex*) their native country (= *patria*).

Costive has nothing to do with *cost*; it means *constipated*.

To *wrest* a purse from its owner requires two hands, but to *wrestle* it is to engage it with all one's torso and limbs in order to subdue it.

Scarify has to do with *scratch*, not *scare*; figuratively it means to deliver a slashing attack, to flay and leave the scars with which the word begins.

A *prerequisite* is a necessary condition to some occurrence that is to follow; a *perquisite* is an advantage or gain attached to office or status.

Luxuriant and *luxurious* are related but distinct. The first means *of abundant growth*, as applied to vegetation, hair, imaginative power; the second denotes the same copiousness, but of comfort and showy things. The jungle is *luxuriant* but not *luxurious*; the upholstery of a car may be *luxurious* but should not be *luxuriant*.

The woman writing her memoirs and rarely going out is not in fact *leading a hermetic life* (= given over to alchemy and magic) but a *hermitical* one (= like a hermit's).

Difficult or technical wording is probably not *obtuse* (= stupid, thickheaded) but *abstruse* (= remote from ordinary understanding).

The art critic who promises not to *belabor a point* refrains from beating it with a stick; he means instead not to *labor* it.

A *pitched battle* is one fully prepared for on a ground deliberately chosen; a *pitch battle* would be conducted, if at all, with *pitch*, a viscous substance distilled by boiling turpentine.

A *testament* (with an *a*) is a will disposing of property after the testator's death or, by extension, a statement of belief left to posterity: e.g., Richelieu's "political testament." The Old and New Testaments partake of this meaning as being the words of the Deity. But a *testimonial* (with an *i*) is a statement or gift expressing thanks or respect. *Testimony* is confession or evidence of a fact. Too often in JOURNALESE the award of an honor or of praise is called a *testament*—wrongly, since neither bestows property or solemnly expresses a body of beliefs or commands. The dinner in honor of P. is *testimony* to the esteem in which he or she is held.

I feel a repulsion against bearded men confuses the outward act of being repelled (*repulsion*) with the inward feeling of being revolted (*revulsion*).

The too amiable man who was accused of *languishing praise on all his friends* did not in fact languish (= grow anemic, have a lingering illness); he *lavished* praise, like a too generous (lavish) spender.

That same man was doubtless to be described as *fulsome*, a word that turns into a malaprop when intended for *complete* or *satisfactory*: *We want to give these young people a fulsome education.*

Again, *noisome* will mislead if interpreted at a guess. *Noise* plays no part in its formation, which draws on the root meaning stench. What is *noisome* is evil-smelling.

The causes of our shaky grasp of words today are not all obscure: language is freer, less bound by convention and timidity than it was a hundred and fifty years ago. Besides, modern literature—especially poetry—plays with words: Joyce's later prose is a mass of deliberate malaprops. Then, too, language-making with an eye to surprise and simple punning has long been the advertiser's sport. All these laxities, real or apparent, confuse the ear and the mind and encourage innovation on the part of ordinary citizens. They are no longer guided by wide reading in good authors and are often misled by analogy, true or false. The result is the endemic malapropism of the college-bred.

See also CONNIVE; DANGEROUS PAIRS; DELINEATE; PRISTINE.

manner. This civilized word has moved, over time, through several uses. Dictionaries mainly agree that it no longer means *condition*. Thus the posted request *Please leave the toilet in the manner in which you found it* was properly answered underneath: *You mean by groping around?* The penman aligned himself with the majority view among writers on usage that *manner* chiefly means the way in which something is done or takes place: *style, mode, fashion. No one complained of his judgment, his timing, his grasp of the problem; all agreed that the cause was lost by the manner of his announcement / When you say they were kidnapped, I trust it is only a manner of speaking.*

But American usage preserves a second sense of manner: *kind* or *sort. She had a mannish manner of mind and face, able to feel hot and think cold* (Joyce Cary); *And all shall be well and / All manner of thing shall be well* (T. S. Eliot); *What manner of man is this, that even the wind and the sea obey him?* (Mark 4:41); *Of that there is no manner of doubt* (W. S. Gilbert). These are all English voices, but the Oxford Dictionary finds this sense archaic in British English.

mantel, mantle. See DANGEROUS PAIRS.

market. See PREPOSITIONS.

massive. See VOGUE WORDS.

masterful, masterly. If writers go on ignoring the difference between these words, we shall lose the second one. The first means dominating, overmastering, even enslaving, and is therefore silly when applied to the creation of a lyric poem or a mathematical formula. One who has mastered an art or skill or mode of reasoning does not by that fact overbear or rule; he or she does *masterly* work. Virginia Woolf, who did such work, wrote of her sister with the other idea in mind: *How masterfully she controls her dozen lives; never in a muddle, or desperate or worried; never spending a pound or a thought needlessly; yet with it all free, careless, airy, indifferent.*

Many writers favor *masterful* for all occasions because it alone has the adverb: *masterfully*. *Masterlily* is impossible. But there is a lust these days for single words, however contorted, in place of phrases, however simple and brief. *Like a master, in a masterly way* are wrongly thought to be verbose. Hence a gate-crashing *masterfully* turns up everywhere.

But what can we say when the work of master musicians, actors, or others so overcomes us that the *-ly* and the *-ful* forms seem equally apt? *Mr. Bergman's staging is masterfully direct, plain, and unfancified.* A second thought would maintain the distinction here recommended: *Mr. Bergman's masterly staging is direct, plain, unfancified.* Thoughtless speed is always the enemy, making for nonsense such as *a pale, shimmering, altogether masterful watercolor.*

matching parts. This heading is borrowed from Le Baron Russell Briggs (1855–1934), onetime teacher and dean at Harvard. It was his shorthand for the principle that similar thoughts in the same sentence should be put into similar constructions.

Only those afflicted with a tin ear will fail to respond to the clarity and force this precept ensures. It guided Macaulay's prose from first to last, as in his famous sentence about Frederick the Great: *In order that he might rob a neighbor whom he had promised to defend, black men fought on the coast of Coromandel and red men scalped each other by the great lakes of North America.* The translators of the English Bible achieved glorious cadences by putting matching ideas in parallel forms: *Canst thou bind the sweet influences of Pleiades, or loose the bands of Orion? / If I ascend up into heaven, thou art there; if I make my bed in hell, behold thou art there / The Lord gave, and the Lord hath taken away.* Such graceful phrases seem to the reader foreordained by the thoughts they express. But in the act of writing, few of us strike off a lean and cogent parallelism until faced with a mess of a sentence that demands recasting. We should then try pairing words and mating phrases to see whether parts can be matched. *Thus he belonged to neither group, for he had outlived his status as a former husband and lagged behind the pack of second-time suitors.* Matching calls for *and he had lagged behind the . . . suitors,* which puts *he* before each of the verbs. *R. was thinking about the date of his departure and that he must work harder.* Matching calls for *and the need to work harder,* which puts *need* in the same position as *date,* the two ideas he thought about. *Something subtle and powerful in this luminous darkness suggested a vast and open landscape and that the station was situated higher up* (suggested that the landscape was vast and open and the station higher up) / *She began to talk about herself as the most depraved of all mankind, never to share in the heavenly grace* (to talk about herself as if she were the most depraved . . . and could never share).

It is fatal to arouse an expectation of matched parts and then to disappoint it. *Picture my amazement at the government's argument, all prejudicial bluster and relying on circumstantial evidence* (all prejudicial bluster and circumstantial evidence) / *It was he who made the case for opportunism and she who made the case that we should watch and wait* (case for opportunism and . . . made the case for watching and waiting). A different sort of aroused expectation is the false match: *The buttons seem to be vulnerable to ultraviolet light and to deteriorate* (buttons seem to deteriorate under ultraviolet light). Two verbal formulas are hard-and-fast promises of parallel construction: *not only . . . but also* and *either . . . or* (*neither . . . nor*). The promise of the first is broken most often by the misplacing of *not only*. *Viewers will find that they are experiencing not only the process of scientific discovery but reliving also the last fateful years of the war* (not only experiencing the process . . . but also reliving the last . . . years) / *The agency stood ready to place not only the laid-off loggers but also to supply their families with the costs of resettlement* (ready not only to place . . . but also to supply . . . with the costs) / *Not a thing has been done either to ease the mother's suffering or for getting food to her children* (has been done to ease the mother's

suffering or to provide food for her children). Notice that parallel infinitives improve this sentence but do not perfect it. The direct objects *suffering* and *children* work here as paired nouns but are unbalanced by the modifier *mother's*. Good writing gives modifiers to each of paired nouns or to neither (*a greeting and a smile* / *a warm greeting and a reassuring smile*). Then too, the idea of *mother* all but demands to be paired with *children*. Recognize this natural tie with *Nothing has been done to ease the suffering of the mother or the hunger of the children*.

See also BOTH . . . AND; EITHER . . . OR; NEGATIVES, TROUBLE WITH.

maximize. See FORBIDDEN WORDS 2; -IZE; SCIENTISM 2.

maximum. See MAJORITY, MINORITY 3.

may, might. See SEQUENCE OF TENSES 3.

me. In each generation, an American knocks at a friend's door and, on hearing the call *Who is it?*, chokes on the natural answer *It's me*. But American usage long ago licensed the colloquial *It's me* despite the purist preference for the grammatically chaste *It's I*. Follett noted that "*It's me* and *That's me* are indispensable to friendship and domestic life."

But *I* is in turn indispensable when the sentence carries the subject into a relative clause: *It was I who insisted that no more lawyers be consulted* / *It's I who need this favor*. For reasons of both grammar and idiom, suppress any sentence that tries to begin *It is me who.*

meaning. See DANGLERS, BENIGN.

meaningful. It seems a long time ago that Follett showed patience with this empty word and with the American love of adding the suffix *-ful* to nouns. *Meaningful,* when applied to most intellectual experiences and to nearly all understandable statements, adds but a feeble emphasis. To say *He found their discussion meaningful* tells us merely that the talk did not seem to him gibberish. Perhaps only the presence of the antonym *meaningless* can save the word from hopeless infirmity. Thus when works on logic and literary theory speak of a *meaningful statement* as opposed to a *meaningless statement,* the *meaningful* has what the other lacks. But to say that is not to say much.

Properly used, *meaningful* does not make something *full* of meaning. It says only that meaning is there to be found. Someone *beautiful, youthful, and slyly deceitful* possesses or is characterized by *beauty, youth,* and *deceit* but cannot, logically speaking, be full of one trait, let alone all three.

It may be this false sense of *-ful* that drives the advertiser and the potboiling author to hawk their wares with *meaningful, flavorful, heartful, impactful, insightful,* and worse. The crowning cliché of our time is *meaningful relationship;* no one knows exactly what it means.

means, noun. Like INSIGNIA, *means* is at will singular or plural. *He proposed as a means to that end the buying up of all outstanding shares / The means are ready to hand.* By itself, *means* almost always refers to money. *A man of means was a rarity in that outpost of civilization.* In *They wanted to move, but did not have the means,* the writer must have in mind lack of cash, not lack of a vehicle or of suitable housing.

median. See SCIENTISM 2.

meet. See PREPOSITIONS.

meld. This word entered common speech to mean a declaring or a showing forth. In that sense it formed part of the JARGON of the card games pinochle and rummy, wherein one *melded* or showed combinations of cards. Through much of the twentieth century, strict speakers insisted on the meaning *declare,* having in mind the derivation of *meld* from the German *melden: to announce.* But *meld* came to be used more and more as a synonym for the verb *combine.* Winston Churchill so used it when he told the United States Congress in 1952: *What matters most is not the form of fusion, or melding—a word I learned over here.* Helped less by that splendid orator than by the sound of those other verbs *weld* and *merge,* usage was probably bound to prevail and did. The change is not grievous. English retains, after all, a good store of verbs with which to *declare, announce, report, proclaim, assert,* etc.

memento. See PRONUNCIATION 1.

meritorious. See CONNOTATIONS.

message. See VOGUE WORDS.

metaphor. 1. Mixed. 2. Metaphoric
style. 3. Causes of the style. 4. Pervasiveness of the style. 5. Damage to
sense. 6. The term misused.
1. Mixed. By now all who write have
heard of the mixed metaphor and intend to avoid it. The experienced can
always have a laugh at the expense of
the doctoral candidate whose disserta-
tion stated, *This field of research is so
virginal that no human eye has ever set
foot in it*. But even the experienced
can write in a metropolitan newspaper
that *the First Lady is repeatedly described as keeping a low profile* [but]
*remains a one-woman flying fortress,
jetting around the country beneath the
radar to scores of media markets, pop-
ping up here on* Oprah *and there on*
CNN. Or can say of a President: *In
this clash of opinions* [he] *is following
his gut;* or of a former President: *The
old competitive juices that might have
gotten* [him] *into the 1992 campaign
seemed to have lost their edge.*
But the trouble today is not that
kind of absurd yet rhetorically tempting mixed metaphor. Indeed, the scorn
which mixing is met with often over-
shoots the mark and calls mixed metaphor what is only a succession of
parallel images. The prime instance,
easily remembered, is the eulogy of
England by John of Gaunt in Shakespeare's *Richard II*, where the *scepter'd
isle* is also the *seat of Mars, a precious*

stone set in the silver sea, and thirteen
other discrete metaphors. It is not a
mere succession of incompatible images that offends reason but the joining
of these images (*competitive juices* losing an *edge*) into one unworkable
device. When this is not attempted,
credulity is not strained; and to the fer-
tile mind that thinks up a series of
comparisons one gives admiration—
and defense against those who misunderstand the ban on mixed metaphor.
2. Metaphoric style. Far worse than
any laughable mixing is what might be
called the metaphorical style—to suggest its continuity and its difference
from the decorative metaphor. That
style is nowadays found everywhere. It
is characterized by a steady reliance on
images so overused or vague that they
no longer strike the speaker or writer
as figurative but often leave the hearer
or reader perplexed as to the meaning.
In the early twentieth century, there
lived in Scotland a woman of modest
circumstances named Amanda Ros,
who wrote and found a publisher for
several novels written entirely in this
metaphorical style. A sentence from
her fiction will show how she joined
images without analyzing them and
managed to give an impression of
meaning where there is none to be
found: *Every morning, at the same
hour, mistress and maid were at their
respective posts, the former, with bright-
ened eye, mounted on her favorite ped-
estal of triumphant account and gazing
intently on the object of rescue; the latter, casting that grave and careworn
look in the direction of the niched signboard of distress, stood firmly and faith-*

fully until she received the watchword of action and warning.

No power on earth can help us to follow this author; the pictorial confusion is too great. And only our willingness to supply tentative meaning creates the illusion of sense in a letter from an executive placement bureau that describes its client as *one who seeks sharper challenge in his preferred sphere.* A succession of such loosejointed and half-conceived images makes a page or even a paragraph so woolly that the reader's mind ceases to respond at all.

Yet much day-to-day prose of the supposedly practical kind—business reports, political statements, departmental notices, news releases—consists of just such series of unconsidered images. For example: *The company overextended its operations in hopes of stimulating its liquidity position, but the disastrous end product was not hard to foresee / The road to the American Dream is littered with task-force reports that were lightly read, widely ignored, and then as messily discarded on the roadside as empty beer cans / This book on the news media is useful, partly for the simple reason that its target resonates at the grass roots / Supporters maintain that he is drawing a much more concrete line in the sand / The agency's track record nurturing talent is . . . / It is our hope that the contents of the brochure form a launchpad for dialogue / Folded into this reversal of fortune is a window of opportunity for anyone of limited means who is new to the co-op market / Some say that the candidate has embraced the mantle of*

change. And for a prime instance of visual carelessness, in a novel in the James Bond series: *Bond's knees, the Achilles heel of all skiers, were beginning to ache.*

3. Causes of the style. The widespread habit of writing in images rather than saying in direct fashion what one means has a number of causes. The most important is the desire to make one's activities or one's thoughts about them interesting in a world otherwise felt to be dull. Those who work in business and advertising are continually framing new metaphors with this in mind. They want to sell ordinary products by throwing over them the enchantment of an implied comparison, or they want to seem dashing by coining sophisticated phrases about their own doings. To understand what is going on at meetings and conferences, one must accordingly learn the meaning of dozens of metaphors, such as *take a bath, wear two hats, roll* [money] *over* (which mean respectively: *incur a loss; have two jobs or sets of duties; defer payment or reinvest funds or renegotiate terms*).

The dangerous effect of these pictures when joined to others is to suddenly give new life to the literal meaning of common words and professional terms of art. Thus in the bank report quoted above, *liquidity* is a technical term. *Liquidity position* is already a combination that brings much too vividly to the mind's eye the literal meaning of *liquid*, and when to this are added the idea of a stimulus and the sight of an *end product*—a physical object—the mind refuses to follow;

reason revolts and asserts that positions cannot be stimulated and that liquidity is a state, not a position.

It is important to remember that this revolt is not deliberate, this objection not the response of a hairsplitting mind. Both are spontaneous, and both express immediate feelings; the mind's eye has been opened to these conflicting sights by the writer himself; it is he who has interrupted the flow of meaning through carelessly putting together pictures that clash. Since the writer wishes above all for the reader's close attention, he cannot complain when that attention is interrupted by his own fault.

The writer may object that he has not intended to write metaphorically; that in putting down *Tensions in the negotiations are heating up* he did not wish to be "taken literally." He is truthful on both counts, but the metaphorical style has become so contagious that many who use it think they are writing straight English. The reader who takes them literally does so at his peril. He must instead guess at the meaning behind the verbal cosmetics. When a city official writes, *The budget gap must not be closed on the backs of our schoolchildren,* the competent reader is vaguely aware of a series of subdued comments within himself: "A *budget* is a list. How can you close a list on someone's *back,* let alone on the backs of thousands of children? Would they have to be bending over for this to be done?" While this soliloquy takes place, the intended meaning escapes.

A second cause of the metaphorical style is the careless use of VOGUE WORDS whose literal meaning is no longer attended to on account of their vogue. For instance, a high-school teacher writes to a newspaper that he is glad to learn *that Superintendent G. is about to make life more viable in the Paper Castle which has so long imprisoned the school staff.* Lately *viable* has displaced *feasible* as the omnibus word to express an unspecified possibility; the writer did not see that the one thing that cannot be made *more viable* (= capable of living) is life itself.

Since the modern vocabulary borrows heavily from the professions in order to be up-to-date and solemn at once (see POPULARIZED TECHNICALITIES), it perpetually transfers meanings instead of speaking direct. Metaphor begets metaphor without check, even in the writing of those whose task it is to improve writing. One of the incessant figuratives in education is *approach,* a metaphor that hardly suggests a coming to grips; in order to give it force, writers often link it with the word *functional.* The phrase sounds imposing but remains vague, even though we are assured that *such a functional approach is of immeasurable benefit to the student and will be particularly important in future years when swollen enrollments make individual attention difficult.* In that sentence from the chairman of a department of English, no person is named, no action shown, no result defined. All is abstraction, everything floats. In this regard there is little to choose between educational prose and commercial: [We] *announce the opening of a shop with complete facilities for the production of individually designed handmade frames to compliment and embrace all art. Personalized services to individuals, artists, and interior designers.* Here *facilities, production, compliment, embrace, personalized services,* and *individuals* have only the cloudiest meanings. Compare the clear naming of *handmade frames* and *the opening of a shop.* (See also EDUCATIONESE.)

4. Pervasiveness of the style. It is of course true that "all language is metaphor" and that the growth of language, as of literature, depends on the extension of literal meanings. The word *crazy* comes from an earlier word meaning to crack or shatter, and the cracking of a pottery surface is known as *crazing.* But to justify this or any other extension there must be a better motive than blind habit or silly affectation. The extension must meet a need expressive or evocative or both. None such appears in the large mass of metaphors that are made today, which may be why almost all are so inexact. They lack the proper intention. For example: *Dear Developer* (first vague image): *The World Conference of the Society for . . . Development is just weeks away* (*weeks* is an image for *a few weeks*—the time would still be weeks even if the conference were five years away). *Your help is needed in making this conference a useful tool* (third image; see TOOL) *for international, social, and economic development* (it is difficult to know what *international* stands for here, since it does not parallel or exclude *social* and *economic*). It makes no point to protest that the foregoing passage is not the

work of a professional writer. Turn to a professional who writes in the self-same affected manner: *Mr. K. and Mr. H.'s company, Film Preserve, can walk the shaky line between the two hostile parties, plumbing the studio archives and library collections with one hand and reaching out to the underground network of collectors with the other.* Or go from business and journalism to the head of a learned society: *The issue has taken on such an ideological fervor that votes, Presidential and otherwise, are hanging in the balance. In the fray, the image of African-American college students has taken a beating.* An *issue* is an abstraction and can have no *fervor,* which in turn need not bring about *votes.* These are being weighed in a *balance,* which becomes a *fray,* and so on.

No doubt the search for bright, arresting headlines and broadcast words contributes to the perpetual extension of meaning which is the principle of metaphor. But as metaphor is now practiced everywhere, both the principle and its application have been lost sight of. Thus in the metaphoric headlines BABY-PROOFING FOR A SAFE HOME and AIR OF CONFUSION GROWS IN BRAZIL, the verb forms misdirect the reader: the house is not to be proofed against a rampaging baby but the baby protected from dangers in the house; the second headline forgets that although *confusion* can grow, *air* cannot. One might imagine that poets still know how to use one of their traditional devices, but a celebrated poet begins a public statement thus: *The young people represented here have chosen to channel the complex cornu-copia of their world—their hopes and ambitions, dreams and fears, niggling doubts and urgencies—through the an-nealing fire of art.*

For one first-rate metaphor such as *moonlighting* (holding a second job, perhaps at night) or *kneeling bus* (it lowers a ramp to let in a wheelchair), we use fifty that are so foolish or tired that the reader takes in nothing: *bottom line, focus, litmus test,* IMPACT, *thrust, evolve, core, package, challenge, context,* etc.

5. Damage to sense. The harm metaphor does to the power of concentration is less insidious than the harm it does to thought. Indeed, there is a domain of fact, namely scientific fact, which metaphor has lately invaded, and where it has visibly weakened the hold of common sense. For example, many scientists and laymen believe that computers think, have memories, learn, translate, make errors and correct them, and succeed each other in "generations." Likewise, scientists and laymen have been seduced into believing that the formative elements in genetics constitute a *code,* which *transmits information* and thus helps determine the shape and growth of living things. Finally, some theorists have come to look upon science itself as a metaphor or a series of metaphors. All this is dangerously unclear thought.

Whether the doctrine that science is a metaphor explains why scientific hypotheses succeed one another without cease is not the point. The point is that metaphor, by definition, is something different from a literal statement. In order to say, as in the old grammar books, *He was a lion in the fight,* lions must exist, and *lion* must be the common, literal name each lion goes by. Now, if science is "only a metaphor," what are the literal *words*—not things —that it is a metaphor of?

6. The term misused. Metaphors are words or combinations of words, nothing else. But the general grasp of this fact has become so weak that attempts are made to extend the very term itself: *Dresden has become a metaphor of wartime death and destruction.* It would be news to those who lived through the bombing of Dresden in 1945 that their city was a figure of speech. In bald fact it was not and cannot be now. No truer are statements like *The strain in Ms. D.'s usually splendid voice acted as a metaphor for her character's hopeless endurance* or *The cost of the film is a metaphor for Hollywood today.* Hoarseness could *parallel* or be *expressive of* or *suggest.* And the expense of making a film might, if the writer's thought were no fresher, *tell us* something or even be *emblematic.* But the writer is giddy who says that laryngitis or money are literary conceits.

See also CONNOTATIONS; SPIRIT OF ADVENTURE, THE.

methodology. See OLOGIES.

meticulous. See DEFENSIBLES.

Mexican Americans. See CHANGING NAMES.

mimicking. See CATALOGUE, CATALOGUED.

-minded. See LINKING 3.

mini-, prefix. See FORBIDDEN WORDS 2.

minimum. See MAJORITY, MINORITY 3.

minister, verb. See ADMINISTER.

minor. See MAJOR, MINOR.

minority. See MAJORITY, MINORITY 1.

minority, collective noun. Like *crowd, congregation, family, team,* this noun names a group, not any one man, woman, or child. Before the twentieth century, it denoted only abstractions: (1) the condition of being under age (hence a legal *minor*), and (2) the lesser of two portions, the greater being the *majority*. Persons were said to be *in* a *minority*, but the noun implied no kind, no size, no social place, and no human feature.

Only after the First World War did politicians speak of racial, linguistic, and religious *minorities*, which corresponded to what the social scientists called *minority groups*: aggregations of people, each group distinguished by race or religion or language. With time, other minorities, each identified in its particular way, have claimed a right to public attention. But as the word became everywhere used, some writers and speakers failed to grasp its collective nature. The following examples are quoted from radio, television, and print: *Fourteen new minorities were elected to the House this year:*

nine blacks, three Hispanics, and two Asians / Three students complained that because they are minorities their grades did not correspond to their achievement / The lawsuit concerns the hiring of fifty-three minorities in training positions / A headline: STUDIES SHOW RECORD NUMBERS OF MINORITIES RECEIVING PH.D'S. Each statement mistakenly assumes that *minority* means *one member* of a minority group.

Everyone is, to be sure, unlike the *majority* in his or her combination of history, genes, and characteristics; in this obvious sense, each of us amounts to what Herbert Spencer called "a minority of one." But Spencer's phrase depends for its wit on contrast with the age-old convention that *minority* is a collective noun.

Two of the examples above raise the kind of questions this misusage leads to. How many people around the world might be included in the *fifty-three minorities*? And how can the *record numbers* the headline reports be squared with the article running below it, which reports on Ph.D.'s earned only by Asians, Hispanics, and blacks?

mischievous. See PRONUNCIATION 1.

mistake, verb. See PREPOSITIONS.

mixed metaphor. See METAPHOR.

mode. See FORBIDDEN WORDS 2; SCIENTISM 2.

modern. See CONTEMPORARY, MODERN, POST-MODERN.

modest. See UN-, IN-, NON- 5.

money. See FISCAL.

moonlighting. See METAPHOR 4.

more. See FEWER, LESS.

mortician. See EUPHEMISMS.

motivation. See JARGON.

Ms. See TITLES AND PROPER NAMES 1, 3.

M'sieu. See FRENCH WORDS AND PHRASES.

much. See VERY, MUCH, REALLY.

mutual friend, mutual interest. See DEFENSIBLES.

mysterious pasts. To American speakers and writers, certain verbs offer a choice between equally apt past tenses, or a true past and a defective one, or a true past and a false one. An American who knows British usage, which often diverges, will find choosing even more difficult.

Among the interchangeables, *proven* is now seen as often as *proved* in American usage: *She has proved* (or *proven*) *her point / The allegation was never proved* (or *proven*). Writers make their choice according to sound and the sentence rhythm they prefer. (See PROSE, THE SOUND OF.) But when a noun needs the adjective form in front of it, American usage dictates *proven*: *a proven remedy / a proven liar*. Simi-

larly, *pled*, which only Americans use, has equal rights with *pleaded*.

Dived and *dove*, too, are on a par, except that *dived* is preferred for diving as an athletic event and is alone correct for the past participle (*having dived*).

The literal making of baskets or cloth calls for *wove* as the past tense. But merely figurative weaving requires that the writer judge how alike are the literal action and its metaphoric use: *They wove* (weaved?) *in and out of traffic / The storm lit up the beach, where wet clothes weaved* (wove?) *ghost-like from an improvised line.* These examples seem clear as written and not to be improved by the alternative verbs in parentheses. But note that no football player ever *bobbed and wove* down the field.

Both *dreamed* and *dreamt* are used as the past tense, as are *spilled* and *spilt*, *burned* and *burnt*, and *thrived* and *throve*. But *learned* has far overtaken *learnt*, which now seems old-fashioned, as does *thriven* as a participle; *thrived* is preferred. Dictionaries give *strove* as the past and *strived* or *striven* as the past participle, although *striven* too seems quaint.

For a long time *got* and *gotten* troubled Americans, the rumor being that one or the other was coarse. But *got* is the simple past tense in both British and American English: *A. got the point / I got home Tuesday / We got a snack at the hamburger place.* Both idioms likewise make *got* an intensive for *have* and *has* (*I've got two tickets / G. has got to go / You've got no right to complain*), though British speakers think this use informal. Only in American usage do the present perfect and past perfect tenses take *gotten: We have gotten fifteen wrong numbers / He has gotten his haircuts there for years / I've gotten steadily worse since I saw the doctor / Hasn't the sky gotten lighter?* Only the British use *got* in all past tenses.

Both *fitted* and *wedded* have lost their old sway as past and participle. *Fitted* has always been favored in New England and in British English: *He fitted the police description / Both boys have been fitted for glasses.* Midwesterners are more likely to say *He fit the description*—but they would never say (nor should anyone), *Both boys have been fit for glasses.* By now, several dictionaries approve both *fit* and *fitted* as the past tense, as in *I doubt that her words fit their expectations* and *I thought the music fit the occasion.* Writers who prefer to use *fitted* should prepare themselves for overeager editors.

A like wavering between *wed* and *wedded* is being resolved by the sure replacement of the connubial meaning by *married.* Headlines still favor *wed* for its shortness, and the traditional ceremony still prescribes *With this ring I thee wed.* But few any longer write, *I wed* [or *wedded*] *the first woman I fell in love with;* and almost everyone now says, *They are no longer married.* But *wedded* (not *wed*) flourishes in figurative uses: *wedded to one idea / wedded to his work / the set and costumes are perfectly wedded.*

Drank is the past tense of *drink,* and *have* or *has drunk* the past perfect. Why then do so many Americans, perfectly sober, say *I have drank?* They may be half-aware that the adjective *drunk* now rivals *drunken* in common usage and law; and that the noun *drunk* has all but replaced *drunkard.* Perhaps *drunk* no longer seems quite respectable as part of a verb.

Showed (past) and *shown* (past perfect) likewise get in each other's way, perhaps put awry by *shone,* which is both the past and past perfect of *shine.* Statements like *She had showed* (shown) *them every courtesy* crop up all too often.

A special case arose when broadcasting came into being. Grammarians argued for the past *broadcasted,* because, by convention, verbs that consist of two words compounded will end in *-ed.* But *-cast* proved uncommonly strong, and *-casted* has not survived in speech or writing. It is *broadcast* throughout present, past, and past participle.

myth(ical). See LEGEND(ARY).

N

name, verb. See PREPOSITIONS.

Native Americans. See CHANGING NAMES.

nature. As the immortal mother of mortals, nature deserves and generally receives a good press; but in many of its uses, the word is degraded in the same way as *character*. Indeed, in these uses the two are interchangeable. Both become pretentious substitutes for *sort* or *kind*, both can almost always be replaced by a noun (often ending in *-ness*), and both bear the taint of JARGON. Those who want to say that So-and-so has a cheerful or a saturnine nature, meaning disposition, do no harm; but to permit the word to mean nothing at all is to waste space and time. *State and city officials stressed the continuing nature* (the persistence) *of the threat to the water supply / The following varied events helped to picture the country's divided nature* (for *divided nature* read *division* or *disunity*) */ Because of the fickle nature of the breeze, there was a twenty-minute delay beyond the appointed deadline* (for *fickle nature* read *fickleness* or, even better, *Because of the fickle breeze*). A biologist seems to pun perversely when he writes, *I see modern man enjoying a*

unity with the trilobites of a nature more deeply significant than anything at present understood in the processes of biological evolution (for *of a nature* use *of a kind*, or omit altogether).
    See also CASE; CHARACTER; COVERING WORDS; LEVEL.

nauseated, nauseous. See TRANSITIVE, INTRANSITIVE.

necessity. See PREPOSITIONS.

née. See TITLES AND PROPER NAMES 2.

needs. See FORBIDDEN WORDS 2.

negative, proving a. Someone sets down a statement that sounds like a newfound and important truth, and if it is tersely enough put, it will be unthinkingly copied by the legion of authors. Aping them in turn, the public repeats the original nonsense. Such has been the history of "You can't prove a negative." A tenth of a second's thought would have shown that if A. thinks she did not bring her umbrella home from the office, all she has to do is walk to the coat closet and by inspection prove or disprove her negative proposition. In law every alibi is the

202 • NEGATIVES, DIVERGENT

proof of a negative: *I was not at the scene of the crime; I was 500 miles away.*

What is probably intended by the false maxim is the suggestion that in matters of fact a *universal* negative is difficult or at least laborious to prove. To try to prove *There are no snakes in Ireland* or *No fifth gospel exists* or *No one suffers as much as I do* is a tall order. Even to define what would constitute proof would be difficult, let alone carry out the search for contrary instances.

But take note of two further truths. First, universal positives are equally difficult to prove: *All rabbits have long ears* seems an established fact until some are found or bred with short ears. Black swans and white crows have turned up to confound the positive generalizers. Universal propositions are the same whether positively or negatively framed. Second, universal negatives not about concrete matters are readily proved: *There is no whole number that is the square root of 2.* This leaves us, then, with a tenable statement: "Proving empirical generalities is usually difficult."

negatives, divergent. See UN-, IN-, NON-.

negatives, trouble with. For many reasons, negative statements have to skirt more grammatical pitfalls than do affirmative statements. An affirmation is usually a simple whole and thus resistant to slippage; whereas a denial often applies only to a part, sometimes an unimportant one. Nothing but careful thought before writing will clearly answer the question: What is being denied? Every writer knows how easy it is to deny the wrong thing.

Of the slips to avoid, the most common are four: (1) misplacing the negative so that what is meant to be denied is affirmed or what is meant to be affirmed is denied; (2) stating an affirmative meaning in a negative form; (3) stating a negative meaning in an affirmative form; and (4) stating antithetical or alternative meanings that require the reader to guess at words left unexpressed or expressed in an unrepeatable form. To avoid all four errors, one must start by asking: Where does the negative element belong?

1. The misplaced negative at its simplest occurs in connection with the word *all* and its synonyms. From a timetable: *All Saturday buses do not stop at Park Street.* This seems to say that none stop—but meant to say, *Not all Saturday buses stop at Park Street.* From a scientific article: *All of these acids are not found in complete form in protein foods.* The meaning: some of the acids are found, some not. But as written, the sentence flirts with the meaning that none are found. Rewrite with the negative foremost: *Not all . . . are found.* The author of a questionnaire sent to some three hundred people testifies: *All of them did not reply. But we found twenty-seven persons in Paris who . . .* Patently, *Not all of them replied* is the shape the first sentence needs. *All of the Founding Fathers may not have acknowledged a formal faith, yet all of them profoundly respected spiritual belief* (Not all . . . may have

acknowledged). *Our entire stock is not included in this sale* (This sale does not include our entire stock). If the warning were meant as written, there would be no sale.

The word *any* is as sweeping as *all* and can as readily capsize a negative sentence. From a prominent book-review supplement: *Any young child, and any parent who has threatened and cajoled at the dinner table, will not be immune to the appeal of* The Boy Who Ate Around. This is inside out, and should read, *No young child, and no parent . . . will be immune,* etc.

The *not only . . . but also* construction requires careful placement of its negative lest *not only* prevent rhetorical balance. The form (like EITHER . . . OR, NEITHER . . . NOR, and BOTH . . . AND) explicitly promises that what follows its first member will be equal and similar in grammar to what follows its second.

2. Statements of affirmative meaning in negative form are an inviting trap. *The fight was a quarrel between two Muslim groups. It was not believed to be connected with the recent political crisis but with a family feud.* The important part of the second sentence is what is believed, not what is not believed. Hence: *It was believed to be connected not with . . . but with . . .* The same pattern of cure will nearly always apply. *The cornetist does not consider himself a representative either of the revived Chicago style or of the new classical style but of pure New Orleans style* (considers himself a representative of neither the revived Chicago style nor the new classical style

but of) / *In this film the actor is not used for his famous charm but as the quiet object of a desperate murder plot* (is used not for his . . . but as the) / *It is not included in this dictionary because we think that someone might need to know these facts but simply in order to make the list complete* (It is included . . . not because we think . . . but simply).

The very tone of constructions that discriminate—that say, "Not *this* but *that*"—can induce the belief in writer and reader that what is said makes sense. Consider: *The problem, therefore, is not one just for railroad management but for the good and welfare of all of us and our progeny.* No mere shift of a negative from here to there will illuminate what this speaker thinks he is saying. He presents a *problem* as being *for* management and *for* the good of all; moreover, what follows *but* concerns not the problem but its unnamed solution. Only radical reconstruction can produce a possible meaning: *Solving the problem is not merely a responsibility of railroad management but a necessity for the welfare of all of us and our children.*

3. In the preceding cluster of bad sentences, negations of unimportant parts were made to negate important parts. What follows is a negation tucked away in an unimportant part that ends up negating the whole: *I can, neither as a friend nor as a lawyer, recommend that you accept the money.* The main clause *I can . . . recommend* runs counter to the actual meaning, which is *I cannot recommend.* Once again, put the negative foremost: *I can-*

not, *as either a friend or a lawyer, recommend.*

4. The second part of a complex sentence often requires, quite legitimately, that the reader supply a word that has already appeared in the first part: *I began the long drive home, and she* (began) *a lecture long-prepared*—crystal-clear meaning. But we cannot legitimately ask the reader both to summon up a verb and to change its negative form into an affirmative: *R. did not embarrass new acquaintances with questions as much as her former husband had but more than our circle of friends was used to.* Logic requires that after *but* the reader supply *did so*; but the sentence as written has given the reader only *did not embarrass.* A recasting is needed to give the affirmative verb in full: *R. did not embarrass . . . as much as her former husband had but did so more . . .* Nor should we expect the reader to supply *always* from a sentence that comes no nearer to that idea than *never. We are never assured that anything is a "bed of roses" but that it is not* (but always that it is not).

In the examples that follow, the needed elements not present in the originals are suggested in parentheses: *Thus his reports would not be consistently truthful and the increasing losses impossible to explain* (would be impossible) / *V. never really mentions it, or only to remark that C. will have no priest at his deathbed* (or mentions it only to remark) / *For a moment neither spoke, but sat mute, gazing across the current at distant Manhattan* (but both sat mute) / *stated that there appeared to be no references after 1564 to the* Queen's own hair, only to her wigs (that all references after 1564 appeared to be to the Queen's wigs, not to her own hair) / *Washington stopped making sense to me one month after I got here, and it never has since* (never has made sense since) / *The Midwest wanted none of it. He wasn't so sure he did himself* (wanted any of it himself).

A negative will often lead one into a snarl from which there is no escape but to abandon the position and start afresh. Consider: *as though confronted with a problem for which there was no solution; as indeed there wasn't.* The author has without noticing it produced *there wasn't no solution.* The cure is not to supply an affirmative verb in the first phrase but to make the verb negative: *confronted with a problem for which there wasn't any solution.* Conversely, the verb in the following must be made affirmative: *There has not been a recurrence of thefts, no revival of late-night shopping, as we had come to call it* ('There has been no recurrence of . . . no revival of.) Still another kind of adjustment is needed to take care of *No one had told him to his face what he was, not knowing what effect this would have.* Here the author has written unawares, *No one . . . not knowing.* The simplest escape: *No one had told him . . . for no one knew . . .*

See WHAT IS "UNDERSTOOD"? for more about unexpressed elements to be supplied by the reader. See also HARDLY . . . THAN; UN-, IN-, NON-.

negotiation. See PRONUNCIATION 1.

Negro. See CHANGING NAMES.

neither . . . nor. See EITHER . . . OR; MATCHING PARTS.

nemesis. See CONNOTATIONS.

neurotic. See POPULARIZED TECHNICALITIES.

neutralize. See EUPHEMISMS.

Nirvana. See CONNOTATIONS.

noisome. See MALAPROPS.

non-, prefix. See GERMANISMS; UN-, IN-, NON-.

none. Some newspapers lay down a rule that *none* is to be treated as a singular at all times. Lexicographers, who know as well as journalists that *none* = *no one*, point out that modern usage more commonly treats it as a plural meaning *no ones*, as does colloquial speech. Literature shows both usages and no clear preference: *None but the brave deserves the fair* (Dryden) and *All are / naked, none is safe* (Marianne Moore) by no means prevail over *None of these finally satisfy* (Whitman) and *There were none who could work at it* (Southey). That two examples of each use are American and two British is apt; both nations seem evenhanded in the singular and plural usage.

The point is not statistical, for statistics on the incidence of words are vain when they take no account of meaning. The fact is that in some contexts *none* means *not a single one*, making singularity emphatic, whereas in other contexts it means *no two, no few, no several, no fraction of many*. In *None*

of us is entitled to cast the first stone the singular meaning is hardly mistakable; in *None of the commentators agree on the meaning of this passage* the plural meaning is equally clear. *None*, then, is freely either singular or plural according to the sense suggested by its context. Often the number we give it makes no difference. As style, as grammar, and as meaning there is little to choose between *None of these opinions seems to be held with much conviction* and *None of these opinions seem to be held.*

Obviously *none* should be given a plural verb wherever a singular one would produce awkwardness. Contortion and absurdity result when the rule prescribing an invariable singular fights with the plain sense, as in *None of these authorities agrees with one another.* Here *none* is trying to be both singular and plural at the same time. Sometimes *none* will lead into a trap from which there is no escape but by abandoning the word. *None of the cities or towns in this sprawling region . . . are* (is?) *connected by road* is uneasy either way. At the cost of wordiness one might write: *None . . . is connected with any other by road;* the trim repair seems to be *Of the cities . . . no two are connected by road.*

None is often balanced against *some: Some of them may have been eccentric, but none of them was* (were?) *crazy.* The natural procedure here is that of MATCHING PARTS; otherwise the shift to the singular calls attention to itself. When *none* is used to balance *few* we sometimes get such curiosities as the following about drug smugglers: *None, or very few, was able to escape detection at the gates.* Clearly *were* is required. *The whole edition, none of which were for sale,* is correct and natural; *none was* would be likewise correct but unnatural.

Untouched by these comments is a *none,* inherently singular, that means *no amount, no part: None of the debris has been cleared away / None of the traffic was diverted / None of the fury the workers exhibited a year ago was seen today.*

nor . . . or. See EITHER . . . OR.

not only . . . but also. See BOTH . . . AND; MATCHING PARTS; NEGATIVES, TROUBLE WITH.

not too. See TOO 2.

notoriety. See CONNOTATIONS.

notwithstanding. See CONTRARY.

noun plague. 1. Modern style is sorely afflicted with misplaced emulation of the abstractness of the scientific or technical report. Thought on all sorts of subjects turns into a chain of static words linked by prepositions and by weak verbs. "Weak" here means that these verbs do not denote any single characteristic action but, like forms of *is* and *have,* draw their strength from the accompanying noun: *apply pressure* as against *press / give authorization* rather than *allow / gain access* instead of *enter / take appropriate action* in place of *act / give support* instead of *help / make a commitment* in place of *decide / have a dialogue* instead of *talk /* *achieve momentum* rather than *move.*

Note that these unneeded nouns do more than attract weak verbs and stop forward movement; they also generate extra words. Hence the prolix *on a daily basis* instead of *daily; on an equal basis* instead of *equally;* and the self-repeating *on a fundamental basis* rather than *fundamentally.* (See BASIS, ON THE.) Brisk adverbs are blown aside by these aimless bursts of hot air.

2. Many abstract nouns in English end in *-tion,* and the effect on the ear of stringing several of them together is narcotic. The prose of science may be left to the scientists, who are more concerned with numbers and diagrams than with words. But the prose of journalists, businessmen, scholars, lawyers, and civil servants amounts to a public act and becomes our intellectual environment. It should, if not enchant, at least inform without causing instant weariness and protracted boredom. The science reporter writes: *The prediction of the existence of antiparticles was made by P.A.M. Dirac in 1927 and its confirmation was an important reason for the construction of the Bevatron at Berkeley in 1954* (compare *Dirac predicted in 1927 that antiparticles exist. Once this statement was confirmed, the Bevatron was built*—one noun preceding each verb). Again: *The educational program of the college is a unique approach to the teaching of the liberal arts and sciences. While offering a new level of flexibility for maximum individual student growth, the curriculum welds together the natural sciences, social sciences, and the humanities into a unified whole throughout the entire*

three years. Apart from the obvious surplusage, these *approaches to teaching* and *levels of flexibility for maximum individual student growth* are unanalyzed abstractions that do not acquire meaning simply by being juxtaposed in familiar ways. The one question that must be put to any description, especially that of a college program, is: What goes on? With nothing but abstract nouns in series, clarity and vividness are unattainable.

3. The sociologist offends in the same way: *In the act of forging [,] an ephemeral personal reorganization occurs in response to situational interactors which may be recognized as a special symbolic process conceived to cover aspects of motivation, feeling, emotion, and the choice of adjustment alternatives. The personal differentiae we have set down here are the original broad limits within which a certain class of situations can impinge upon the person with the possibility of emergent forgery.*

Even the novelists highly praised for style succumb to the noun plague. Here are examples culled from two consecutive pages chosen at random from a highly praised novel: *He had washed the floor before his departure* (= leaving) / *I assumed that . . . harm had come to him* (= he had been hurt) / *Now they would suffer the proximity they had always avoided* (= be together as they had never wanted to be) / *On this occasion there was nothing faltering* (= Now) / *Her blue eyes regarded me in innocence* (= looked at me innocently) / *so compelling that I must have stared at her with*

evident amazement (= stared at her, visibly amazed) / *She yawned in a pretense of indifference* (= with pretended).

The words in parentheses are not proposed as improvements—that would be an impertinence—but simply to show how persistently the modern mind makes its objects out of abstract states, and how the repetition of the words denoting those states dulls narrative and description and helps to impoverish experience. We are at present exceedingly fond of the word *dynamic*, but our characteristic style in many genres is persistently static. The only way to set it in motion again is to avoid abstract nouns like the plague.

See also VOGUE WORDS.

nucleus. See SCIENTISM 2.

number-crunching. See VOGUE WORDS.

number, trouble with. No one disputes the convention that subject and verb should agree in number—singular with singular, plural with plural; but no experienced writer would say that assigning number to verbs is always easy. The chief troubles are four: (1) clash between subject and verb; (2) subversion of verb by predicate noun; (3) failure to identify the part of the subject with which the verb is to agree; (4) illogical shift between singular and plural.

1. Disagreement between subject and verb comes all too easily when their customary order is inverted in a question or in a declarative statement.

A question: *And what purpose has all his objections served?* (which says, *All his objections has served what purpose?*). A statement: *Among the passengers was Ms. G. and her daughter Elizabeth* (which says, *Ms. G. and her daughter was among*). Both experienced and neophyte writers do well to mentally test agreement by restoring for a moment the normal order, as is done after these examples.

Sentences that begin with words like *among* and *along with* frequently put ahead of the verb some noun or pronoun that the writer mistakes for the subject: *Among those attending were* (was) *G., former Presidential aide, who, like R., is an Ohioan.* The first verb became plural through being mistakenly matched in number with *those*, which is not the subject, instead of being matched with G., which is.

But using the normal order of subject and verb does not by itself keep the verb from being misnumbered. When serving a compound subject, the verb should always be plural; but an overhasty writer may give it the number of what is only the nearest noun: *A thirty-one-game exhibition schedule and a quick dash north has* (have) *been mapped out for the spring training campaign / It has the light weight and fine balance that makes* (make) *for a controlled swing / The creation of two top posts and the selection of Ms. L. to fill one of them was* (were) *announced / X. said that new home construction and the demand for store space has* (have) *added to the value of the property.*

Another kind of compound subject dispenses with *and* and mixes singular and plural nouns, again tempting the writer to make the verb agree with whichever noun is nearest: *The demands of the work he had chosen, the worry he felt for his wife, was bringing on blank patches when he could not think at all.* Clearly, a plural verb is called for. Even after the grammar is repaired, some readers may find the construction loose, in which case *and* can replace the comma. An even tighter form: *The demands of the work he had chosen, the worry he felt for his wife—these were bringing on,* etc.

And cements not only some compound subjects but also versions of one subject couched in different words. Such linked variations, if they are all in the singular, take a singular verb: *The resolution and relief and end of this impasse is now in sight.* Restatements strung in this way remain singular whether they use *and* or not: *This inhibition of his, this aversion to wearing his heart on his sleeve, this obsessive reluctance to give himself away, is* (not *are*) *traceable in every one of his relationships.* The numerical meaning of a subject, not its numerical sum, controls the number of its verb.

One other construction masquerades all too plausibly as a compound subject. Expressions beginning with words like *accompanied by, in addition to, including, along with, together with, no less than,* and *not to mention* add secondary subjects to the main one but do not make it plural: *The sultry weather, no less than our daily effort to divert the rising stream, leave* (leaves) *us by nightfall dull and quarrelsome.*

The true and singular subject here is *weather*. More than likely the writer misnumbered the verb by supposing that *weather* and *effort* formed a compound subject.

Agreement should also be watched when one is using collective nouns—words singular in form but most often used in a plural sense. Consider: *No jury or investigating committee are able to bring the dead back to life*. We cannot be sure whether the writer confused an alternative (singular) subject (this *or* that) with a genuine plural (this *and* that); or whether he sees each collective noun (*jury, committee*) in the English manner, as a group composed of individuals. In either case, the *are* is wrong in American usage.

The indefinite pronouns *anybody, everybody, somebody, nobody, anyone, everyone, someone,* and *no one* are singular; the roots *-body* and *-one* proclaim the fact. These pronouns take singular verbs. (See also EACH, EVERY; NONE.)

2. A singular subject and a plural predicate noun can subvert the linking (or copulative) verb that connects them; linking verbs include *be, seem, become, appear,* etc. *The only observable fact that made it real were the dead legionnaires / Just about the only thing that had been left untouched were the television and the VCR / The nearest thing to good manners in her incessant phone calls were opening and closing apologies for disturbing you / Another heartening event were the pledges and outright contributions that flooded in.* The only fact were? The nearest thing were? A heartening event were? The

authors have mistaken the predicate nouns for the subjects and let them misnumber the verbs. Except for inversions, this rule holds: the noun that precedes a linking verb is its subject, and the noun that follows the verb belongs to the predicate.

Linking verbs are also vulnerable when they follow *all* or *what*. In sentences like *All was chaos, all* is a singular pronoun meaning *everything* or *the sum of the things*. Thus it takes a singular verb whatever the number of its predicate, as these statements fail to recognize: *All that she heard as she awoke in darkness were* (read *was*) *voices / All you need are* (read *is*) *a cup of molasses, 2 teaspoons of vinegar, ¾ cup of sugar / All that remained to be done were* (read *was*) *the small jobs of touching up and adding refinements.* We can reverse such sentences and write, say, *A cup of molasses, 2 teaspoons of vinegar . . . are all you need,* because we have changed the subject to a compound and so need a plural verb to match it. Note incidentally that *all* can also be plural, as in *All seem to have recovered.*

What is more troublesome than *all.* It can mean *the things that* (plural) or *the thing that* (singular) or something even less concrete; the choice is up to the writer, but he should make his subject and verbs consistent. *What to watch for along the wall are spots of dry earth and no vegetation.* Here the writer makes *what* mean *the things that,* and so employs a plural verb. But he could as well have in mind such abstract singulars as *the condition, the situation,* or, as we often say loosely, *the thing (to watch for)*; if so, he should use *is*. Indeed, some writers are only at ease with a singular meaning for this kind of *what*. They are within their rights but should hold to their preference throughout a sentence that uses two or more verbs. *What appears to be fragments of a fireplace are the only remaining sign of the eighteenth-century farmhouse.* The subject *What* is deemed singular here; hence *appears* is singular too. But *what* also governs the second verb, which should be *is*. Again: *If we are to take from this stalemate clearer thought, what is needed are patience and good humor.* Since *what* is singular and followed by *is*, *are* should be *is* as well.

There is room for variation. Some sentences read more smoothly with a plural *what*: *What appear to be fragments of a fireplace are the only remaining sign*, etc. *What they saw was the white sand cliffs* is correct but is smoother as *What they saw were the . . . cliffs*.

Consistency between subject and verbs is important, but so is the writer's intuitive rather than reasoned satisfaction. Some authors cannot rest easy with an *in*consistency between verb and predicate complement; they do well to find ways around it. Here are hints: *Watch especially for such things by the wall as spots of dry earth with no vegetation* / *Nothing but the dead legionnaires made it real* / *Almost nothing was left untouched but the television and the VCR* / *The pledges and outright contributions that flooded in were also heartening.*

Lastly, *there* before a linking verb

need not be confusing. If the predicate complement is singular, so should the verb be *(There is no hope)*; if the predicate complement is plural, so is the verb *(There are editors and a deadline to consider).*

3. A subject may overflow the single noun that determines the number of the verb, as in this example: *A wild waving of baseball caps and souvenir programs has swept the stands.* However many objects are waved, the singular *waving* is the subject; it alone decrees that the verb be the singular *has swept*. Yet those who write only by ear will be tempted to give the verb the number of the intervening plurals, *caps* and *programs*. That temptation is yielded to in the following: *On islands like the Aleutians and Iceland, the number of species increase* (increases) / *with a show of friendliness and accommodation that were* (was) *altogether persuasive.* The reverse confusion finds a verb that should be plural yoked to an intervening singular: *Even benefactors of long standing like G., a local manufacturer, has* (have) *concluded that plays of more commercial appeal must be mounted.* Perhaps the author thought that she had written *Even such a benefactor . . . as G. has concluded.*

An added subject that corrects or enlarges the number of the first one—*any voting member or members*—calls for a plural verb. But we often see statements that treat such additions as if they had no grammatical standing: *His father waits every morning to see what bill—or bills—arrives in the mail before setting off.* The author probably hopes that the dashes set *or bills* outside the grammatical pattern; but the punctuation makes no structural difference, and we are left with a verb that fits one subject but quarrels with the other. Here the verb *arrives* happens to mean *will arrive* or *may arrive*; hence the trouble can be neatly evaded by writing *what bill—or bills—will arrive*. But if no evasion is possible, what then? The graphic device sometimes used— *If any student or students enter(s) the basement he or she will be punished*— is a victory of algebra over English. Avoid prolixity and improvisation by coolly examining the sense. You will see that a simple plural takes care of the one and the many: *Students entering the basement will be punished.* In general, constructions that drive a singular and a plural in one yoke pose a choice of evils.

4. Life teaches us that one person has one head, and two persons have two. Language follows suit often enough that we need not uncertainly stagger between singular and plural. Subjects that are obvious plurals should dictate the plural for concrete things they possess: *Owners registered for the competition should walk their dog on a leash when outside the enclosure* (dogs on leashes) / *Those who know these meetings do not check their coat but keep it for a fast getaway* (coats . . . keep them) / *Nothing so calms excitable kittens as having their chin rubbed* (chins). *When the water is hot the garfish require a frequent recharge of their oxygen bladder.* Here the author failed to decide between saying *The garfish* (singular and generic) *requires . . . recharge of its oxygen bladder*

and *The garfish* (plural) *require . . . recharge of their oxygen bladders.*

There are three respects in which usage declines to follow the law of heads and persons. First, the noun remains in the singular when what is plurally possessed is universal, abstract, or figurative: *They say that we foresee our death* (universal) *in order to live more fully* / *We have no doubt of the staff's loyalty* (abstract) / *Once before, we failed to heed their cry* (figurative) *for liberty.* Second, the singular works comfortably—but is not mandatory— for phrases that make a single idea out of plural contents: *I don't think two bathrooms is too much for such a large family*; the sense is *the idea* or *proposal* or *plan of two bathrooms.* For sums of money the singular verb is inescapable: *Twenty dollars is not too much.*

The third exception to the rule of agreement provides that, in modern usage, the title of a literary work with a dominant plural in it is singular; no one would now say that *the neglected* Conversations in Ebury Street *are an autobiographical work*, although eighteenth-century usage shows a high incidence of *recently* The Two Gentlemen of Verona *have been performed*, etc. Conversely, an organization whose name features a plural noun usually takes the plural number. It seems natural to say, *The International Ladies Garment Workers are* but *The ILGWU is.* We can in any event ask that an author stick to the singular or plural with which he begins. It is distracting to read: *The agency Young Audiences has good advice to offer as far as the*

Friends of New Music are concerned.

It does no harm to add the reminder that some nouns denoting single objects use a plural verb: *scissors, pants, pliers, bellows, tongs, (reading) glasses,* etc.

For a discussion of the commonest errors in the realm of number, see ONE OF THE, ONE OF THOSE; THIS KIND, THESE KINDS, THOSE KINDS.

nurturing. See VOGUE WORDS.

O

objective(s), noun. See SCIENTISM 1.

oblivious of (to). Those fiercely loyal to the original meaning of this word—*forgetful*, hence the preposition *of*—deplore for good reasons a later meaning but are fighting the overwhelming current of usage. The Oxford Dictionary now gives *forgetful* first, then *unaware, unconscious of*; and Fowler in 1965 said the word had moved "beyond recall from the area of forgetfulness into the wider one of heedlessness." A respected English novelist, uncowed by these portents, wrote fifteen years later: *To be oblivious to something is not to be unaware of it but to be no longer aware of it.* Note that he himself had forgotten that idiom calls for *oblivious of*.

Follett pointed out in the first edition of this book that *oblivious* sits right beside *oblivion*, which means *forgetfulness*; and that *oblivious* not only denotes a fading from memory but also implies a passage of time. *His reckless treatment of enemies, his risk of a fortune, his vindication by the courts, all this he now seemed oblivious of.* To reduce this richness of meaning to a passing inattention seemed to Follett a waste. But now one sees everywhere sentences like *N. proved as oblivious to the traffic signs as to my attempts to calm him / The rebel leaders are oblivious to the alarm they cause in neighboring states / D. is not oblivious to the arguments of the opposition.* This flattened sense of the adjective can still be avoided by all who care to avoid it; they will write *oblivious of* for the low ebb of memory and *unaware* or *heedless of* (on *unconscious*, see CONSCIOUSLY) for momentary absence of mind. Editors worth their salt will know the difference and know that these adjectives take *of*.

See also PREPOSITIONS.

obverse. See CONVERSE, OBVERSE, REVERSE.

obviate. The root meaning—*against the way*—restricts the use of *obviate* to statements that refer to the removal of a difficulty or obstacle. *N. obviated the threat of legal action by changing the character's name and occupation.* The idea of mere removal (*Lemon juice obviates the need for salt*) is too simple to justify employing a word exactly fitted for other use.

octopus. See LATIN AND GREEK PLURALS.

of. See A, AN, THE 5; IN FOR BY, OF; POSSESSIVES.

of a, ruralism. More often spoken than written, the rural *of a* (*that big of a mess*) sometimes creeps into print, not as the affectation of drugstore cowboys but as the expression of simple ignorance. In speech as well as in writing, it often uses the ambiguous TOO (see TOO 2): *It was not too good of a movie / It won't be too long of a drive.* But often the *too* is blameless and the rest is still a mistake: *You're making much too big of a deal out of this / That was too bad of an accident to walk away from.* In print it should be clear at once that *of* is the alien element in all four examples. In the latter two, *much too big a deal* and *too bad an accident* are enough to do the work. Remove the ambiguous *too* and the first two examples straighten out as *It was not a (very) good movie* and *It won't be a (very) long drive.*

The misconstruction may have arisen from confusion with the proper use of *much* and *less* as nouns. In *too much of a good thing,* the noun *much* means *large amount* (or, strictly speaking, *large an amount*). But in *too big of a deal, big* is without question an adjective. *Big deal!* is the cry in the street, never *Big of a deal!* In *less of a crowd, less* is not an adjective but a noun. Conversely, in *bad of an accident, bad* is clearly an adjective, and *of* must get out of the way of the noun.

For other ruralisms, see COUPLE, MISSING OF; GROW, TRANSITIVE; LOOKING, KNOW WITH INFINITIVE.

often. See PRONUNCIATION 1.

okay. Like the hamburger, this ubiquitous word has been quizzed for its origin, damned for its vulgarity, marveled at for its persistence, and exported throughout the world. That it is homegrown American everyone agrees, and no English-speaker needs to have its uses explained. But it has lately become an impediment to speech and a barrier against understanding. Here is an American teacher, recorded verbatim in class: "The Boston Massacre, now—it wasn't a massacre, a riot, not even that—okay? There was this crowd around the customhouse and the British sent soldiers—okay?—to see—a captain along was supposed to tell them—okay? The crowd shouted, 'Lobster!' —you don't see? That was on account the soldiers' red coats—okay? Well, the captain said, 'Don't fire'—okay? but they were scared maybe and fired. They killed five—okay?"

Most people patch their leaking sentences with *uh* and *um,* but these are meaningless sounds that the listener's mind ignores or discounts. The speaker who *okays* his way to completing his thought coerces the hearer to agree or disagree with speech that declines to make sense.

See also LIKE 3; SPEAKING LIKENESS.

ologies. The *logos* of a thing or activity, from which we derive our fast-multiplying *ologies,* is its theory or reasoning—the discourse about it. The first *o* is merely the joint that combines the identifying Latin or Greek with *-logy.* Thus *meteorology* attaches the Latin for atmospheric phenomena to *-logy* to make the theory or science of all the manifestations of weather. (Exceptional words that do not use the o-joint are *genealogy, mineralogy,* and *psychedelic.*) The long roll of ologies tempts the pompous to use them when what is meant is no more than the thing or activity itself, not its theory. Thirty seconds of a news broadcast will not afford you the promised *meteorological wrap-up* but only a weather prediction.

Most flagrant of the *ologies* that swallow their subjects is *technology;* it should mean the theory of our mechanized world, not the machinery itself. Yet such is our yen for abstraction and technical lingo that not only food processors but also plastic spoons become *new kitchen technology.* This inflation of thing into theory has led some writers to use *technics, techniques,* and *techne* (Greek for *art* or *craft*) to properly name the machine civilization itself. These writers' books on the subject, being analytical, then constitute the *technology* of the *techne.*

Technology cannot be saved from windy misuse, but that is no reason to encourage inflation elsewhere. Do not imitate the self-important who write about their *methodology* when all they mean is their *method. (I approve of his purpose, but his methodology is all wrong.)* One might as well say *gastronomic juices* instead of *gastric.* Again, the trends and events we observe around us are not *sociology* or *sociological* but *social.* The mind or temperament of a human being or of a fictional character is only that—mind or temperament—not an abstruse *psychology. Cosmetology* dates from 1855, but *cosmetics* should do for the laity,

with no touching up. As for bodily needs or urges, they are not *biological* but *organic*—or, as above, *bodily.* Note that new *ologies,* if they must be contrived at all, require the full root unless it ends in a vowel, as do *psyche* and *techne.* One must therefore say (if unavoidable) *symbolology,* not *symbology.*

There is warrant in good writers of the nineteenth century for the revival in ours of *ology* and *ologies* as independent nouns, designating, a little ironically, the wondrous new sciences. Thomas Hughes in 1849, and after him J. A. Froude, Kipling, and others, used the singular in ways that suggest it had some currency in speech.

See also POPULARIZED TECHNICALITIES; SCIENTISM 1.

omission. See PRONUNCIATION 3.

on, upon, up on. In American English today, *upon* is reserved for (1) idioms and set phrases (*put upon, come upon, the fit was upon him, once upon a time*); (2) the avoidance of ambiguity, as when only *upon* correctly links subject and indirect object (*the framed picture of his wife on* [upon] *the desk = picture . . . upon the desk*); (3) very occasional effects of emphasis (*telling lie upon lie*), rhythm, or deliberately archaic tone. Elsewhere our habitual speed makes us *bank on, count on, rely on, comment on, depend on, enlarge on, trespass on, verge on, seize on, hit on, land on, recline on, meditate on, work on,* etc.

The diminished *upon* in no way affects the working of *up* as an adverb followed by the preposition *on.* We go *up on* the roof, take them *up on* an offer, catch *up on* our E-mail, etc. This construction being made of two words, *up* is given an intonation very different from that of the *up-* in *upon*.

on the other hand. Can *the other hand* be raised in a sentence if *the one hand* has not already appeared? Many writers seem to think so and, for justification, point to the streak of lawlessness that runs through idiom. Small wonder, for English provides few other phrases on which to pivot, few adversatives to what has gone before, few springboards to give new direction and impetus. *Contrariwise* is lumbering and states too much opposition; *per contra* is foreign and therefore will seem to some readers affected. And yet our elaborate locution dangles when halved and plainly invites the question: *What* other hand? Those who would avoid the heckling will try *So much for* [the preceding subject]; *that aside; but consider (that)*; or the less figurative and less used *on the other side.*

one (= I). This pronoun serves well in designating an unspecified person who stands for all persons, or for all persons in an understood category: *One can thrive in the Arctic on food that violates every low-latitude definition of a balanced diet / One avoids wear and tear by ignoring the delegate's wilder oratorical flights.* (For the sequence *one . . . he*, see ANTECEDENTS 8.) But *one* does not do well as a simple surrogate for the first-person singular. *One was left somewhat at a loss by this unexpected retort / One could not comfortably appeal to one's parents*

for further assistance. The linguist Otto Jespersen collected sentences from Jane Austen in which the identification of *one* with *I* is similarly absolute: *one should (= I should) not like to have Sir Thomas find all the varnish scratched off.* To American ears the use of *one* where only *I* is meant sounds affected. Even when the speaker believes that *one* lends the force of generality to a subjective remark, the hearer is all too likely to think him pompous. A vein of British humor today often substitutes *one* for the simple *I* as a way of satirizing prissiness or self-importance.

See also WE, EDITORIAL.

one another. See EACH, EVERY 2.

one of the, one of those. There are no more innocent-seeming lures to bad grammar than these two everyday phrases, which delude writers, no matter how practiced, into joining a singular verb to a plural subject: *one of the customs that both shapes and expresses the life of a village / one of the few writers in the country who has made a living being funny / B.'s is one of many stores that supplies this service / one of the most important constitutional problems that has confronted the world organization / one of the best things that has happened to British historiography in a long time / one of those phrases that after four or five hundred years of constant use has lost all sense of its original meaning / He is one of those actors who refreshes a role by unease, not by smoothness.*

The writers of these examples are all

of them educated; some are literary artists. None would carelessly mismate a plural subject with a singular verb. But seduced by a certain pattern of words, they blindly commit themselves to *customs that shapes and expresses / writers who has made a living / things that has happened / phrases that . . . has lost*, and so forth. Worse, we can presume that what they wrote passed under the eyes of experienced editors.

The error is easy to fall into, and perhaps not hard to explain. Someone setting down *Dan is one of those people who talks before he thinks* has foremost in mind, not the class of people who speak too soon, but *Dan*, who is only one person. *Dan*, then, seems the subject of the entire sentence, though he is in fact part of a class (*people*) which is the true subject of the verb and therefore governs its number.

Writers must concentrate while revising as well as while writing. To revise is to question clarity, logic, usage, economy, sound, and grammar—including one's best-disguised errors. Change *people who talks* to *people who talk*.

ongoing. Many writers classify this word with such commercial makeshift adjectives as *upscale, downscale, upmarket*, and *downgrade*. It is, in any case, not needed; *continuing, continuous, present*, and *in progress* do very well.

only. Trying too hard to put *only* in front of the word it modifies goes against sentence rhythm, the customary placing of adverbs, and the whole

American and English literary tradition. To be sure, when particular emphasis is desired, *only* should be moved closer to its partner: *Members were allowed only fifteen minutes each to express their predictably rambling views.* Otherwise *only* belongs before the verb: *only allowed*. Those who would say *He died only yesterday* will sound like a bad translation. Those who insist on such placement across the board must lead the way by saying *Only God knows.*

opera. See LATIN AND GREEK PLURALS.

opposite. See CONVERSE.

opus. See LATIN AND GREEK PLURALS.

or. See AND/OR; BETWEEN 3; EITHER . . . OR; MATCHING PARTS.

order of magnitude. See SCIENTISM 2.

orient, orientate. See VERBIAGE.

Orientals. See CHANGING NAMES.

osmosis. See POPULARIZED TECHNICALITIES.

otherwise. Until the late 1800s this word was only an adverb. It meant (as it means today) *differently, in another way, in other circumstances, for the rest, in everything else, if not*. Some examples: *How could he do otherwise?* (= differently) / *Walk softly; otherwise* *they'll hear us* (= in another way) / *She broke a record with the discus but was off her form otherwise* (= in everything else) / *Come in if you're going to; otherwise leave me in peace* (= if not). For centuries, one sense of *wise* was *way*, as when Disraeli writes: *In this wise, affairs had gone on for a month*; thus the well-read considered the adverbial *otherwise* unshakable by time.

But usage in the twentieth century more and more often called on *otherwise* to act as an adjective: *R. is funny, but I wish he were otherwise / for some reason, selfish or otherwise.* If one takes Fowler's view, *I wish he were not* and *selfish or other* suffice. Similarly, the tendency to draft the word as a noun should be resisted: *We can discuss the merits or otherwise.* Why not simply *discuss the merits, if any* or *discuss the merits or demerits?* But a change that advanced on all fronts proved irresistible in the end. Today both the Oxford and several American dictionaries give *otherwise* as adverb, adjective, and noun.

Both Fowler and Follett suspected that *otherwise* had been cut loose from its moorings by a long-lived pun: *Some men are wise and some are otherwise* (adjectival use). Grammar is at any time beside the point of a pun.

ought (not) (to). Some think it British or a mark of refinement to omit the compulsory *to* in *ought not to*; it is neither. *I wonder whether I ought not take an umbrella* is as wrong as *She oughtn't treat you that way.* The parallelism in *We need not and ought not*

accept is false, for it fails to observe the different demands of two linked verbs. Even in the positive, the people who archly ask *Ought I tell him?* would not dream of saying, *Perhaps I ought go* or *You ought pack an extra shirt.* The preposition *to* is required in both negative and positive statements.

out there. See VOGUE WORDS.

outside, preposition. See PREPOSITIONS.

over-. See LAY, LIE; OVERLY.

overall. See FORBIDDEN WORDS 2.

overlie. See LAY, LIE.

overly is twittering and slack compared to the compact prefix *over-*. *Overly cautious* sounds not much less foolish than *illy fated*, whereas *overcautious* and *ill-fated* are at once frugal and downright, and they do not trill. Dictionaries list hundreds of forms combining *over-* with an adjective—*overfed, overexact, overgenerous,* etc.—and anyone can improvise other combinations at will. It may be that writers resort to *overly* from being unsure whether to do the combining with a hyphen. In fact, almost all combinations with *over-* have lost the hyphen with the passing of years. Always at hand, of course, are *excessively* and the plain *too much: He fusses* not *overly* but *too much.*

For some obscure reason *-ly* and *-y* sounds tempt to repetition: *naturally* *not feeling overly hospitable to the ter-rorists.* Avoid the jingle by substituting *overhospitable.* A change to *overfond* avoids the verse rhythm (dactylic) in *Neither was overly fond of Lucille, and both had solemnly promised* . . . The oversubtle who argue that there is a shade of difference between *overly timid* and *overtimid* must be left to converse with those who insist that they see a different shade when *gray* is spelled *grey.*

Akin to *illy* and *overly* is the super-fluous *doubtlessly, doubtless* being both the adjective and the adverb. Likewise, *single-handedly* serves no useful pur-pose, since *single-handed,* as an adjec-tive modifying the subject, does what needs to be done: *Wilson broke up the fight single-handed.* If not a principle, it is at least good tactics to refrain from an adverb with *-ly* whenever there is an equivalent without the suffix.

See also ADVERBS, VEXATIOUS; PROSE, THE SOUND OF.

owing to. See DANGLERS, BENIGN; DUE TO.

own, intensive. See UNNECESSARY WORDS 4.

oxymoron. Greek and Latin authors liked to join contradictory terms in or-der to sharpen an effect; students who translate from the classics learn not to be startled by expressions that have to be rendered "immensely little," "over-bearingly modest," and so forth. The classifying rhetoricians called this device an *oxymoron,* which means pointed foolishness. English uses many such locutions for vivid emphasis: *deafening silence, crushing polite-ness, unrelenting kindness, distinguished plainness, conspicuous absence,* etc. An *oxymoron* is above all deliberate in its self-contradiction. By contrast, *a pretty ugly dog* is a hapless collision that writers must try to avoid; *pretty* is employed to mean *somewhat,* but a careless pairing calls up its literal meaning.

Being deliberate, an *oxymoron* is no mere *contradiction in terms,* the phrase that should replace it in these exam-ples: *Cheap titanium is an oxymoron / H. thought social science an oxymoron / "Efficient government" strikes voters as an oxymoron / This novel is partly the ultimate oxymoron, a Kierkegaardian comedy / The assumption is so far off the mark that the term "medical sci-ence" is practically an oxymoron /* A headline: WHERE A FAMILY VACATION IS NOT AN OXYMORON. Like too many other words which writers misuse for impressive effect, *oxymoron* is both ex-act and irreplaceable. Should we ig-nore its real meaning, we may lose its very idea.

See also DILEMMA.

P

pacify. See EUPHEMISMS.

package. See METAPHOR 4.

panicking. See CATALOGUE, CATA-LOGUED.

parallelism. See MATCHING PARTS.

parameter. See POPULARIZED TECH-NICALITIES.

paranoid. See POPULARIZED TECH-NICALITIES.

parentheses, brackets. 1. The curved marks known as *parens* among printers and editors are named after what they embrace: a parenthesis is a thought set abruptly inside another to which it applies but may not be attached by grammar.

The intrusion may be slight, as when we put numbers inside of prose: *He made three points:* (1) . . . , (2) . . . , (3). . . . Or again: *The price is three hundred* (300) *dollars.* But more often the insertion is of words. It may be an explanatory phrase: *He gave away large sums of money* (his mother's) *with selfless abandon.* Or it may be a whole clause: *We must not forget that Spencer and many others wrote on evolution be-fore Darwin* (it was Spencer, not Dar-win, who coined the phrase "Survival of the Fittest"), *and consequently we must not keep on . . . saying that the theory of evolution broke upon the world in 1859.*

Many writers think parentheses interrupt more gently than dashes, producing a murmur instead of a full-voiced assertion. Certainly parentheses keep better order in a sentence where several interruptions occur. Dashes show only breaks, but parentheses act as twin ushers: the first twin bends in one way to signal a beginning and the second bends in the other to show an ending (see DASH, THE).

The relation of parentheses to other punctuation is simple. Any period, question mark, exclamation point, comma, colon, semicolon, or dash belonging to the parenthetical matter goes inside the parentheses. Those belonging to the whole sentence go outside. Parentheses enclosing skeptical question marks or ironic exclamation points will disfigure a text and show the writer's inexperience; if the writer has a question or a complaint, let him state it in words, in or out of parentheses. This warning does not extend to the scrupulous question mark that identifies a date as uncertain: *The rec-*

ord of this family line extends back to one Anthon Larson (1707?–1750).

2. Brackets are the square form of the mark of parenthesis and are used for only one purpose in ordinary writing: to enclose any word or words that the writer has added to someone else's text. Thus an author quoting from another may want to clarify something (say, a pronoun) left indefinite in the original: *He [Timothy] sent word to the Senate that his father was ill and could not appear.* One may also insert [*sic*] in italics to note that the foregoing word or phrase is reproduced truly; the device calls attention to misspelling or to ill-chosen words or to matter that the reader should carefully notice.

Parentheses and brackets are used in other ways in the publications of certain professions; such ways must be learned by specialists but not imported to ordinary prose.

See also SET PHRASES 2.

parenting. See Appendix, p. 343.

parliament. See PRONUNCIATION 1.

part, in; whole, as a. Separately, these two idioms are not only blameless but useful. *She was invited to speak, in part because she couldn't be dull if she tried / In part, it was my doing / One's impression of the crowd as a whole was of people with nowhere else to go / The Administration as a whole seems energetic, eager, and sophomoric. In part* is interchangeable with *partly,* hence helpful when euphony wants no more *y*-endings. (See PROSE, THE SOUND OF.) But *in whole* is no id-

iom, and it cannot change places with *wholly*; nobody says *I am in whole against it.* This does not stop *in whole* from being forced into harness with *in part* to make *in whole or in part,* a parallelism nobody needs. Still, legal documents and their imitations have assured this construction a long life: *no councilman or other officer, employee, or person whose compensation or salary is payable in whole or in part from the city treasury / Provided further that restitution in whole or in part is not contingent . . .* Writers who recoil from LEGALISMS where they have no place write *wholly or partly* or the reverse.

See also MATCHING PARTS; SET PHRASES.

partake. See PREPOSITIONS.

partner. See EUPHEMISMS.

pass away, pass on, pass over. See EUPHEMISMS.

passed (past) muster. See SPELLING.

passive voice. See VOICE.

past tense. See MYSTERIOUS PASTS.

people. See PERSONS.

per. For uses like *twelve dollars per hour, wind from the west at eight miles per hour,* etc., see A, AN, THE 7. In general, the user must decide where *per* is a necessary evil, where it is an unnecessary one, and where it is no evil at all. It is not an evil in the set Latin phrases *per diem, per annum, per cap-*

ita, which, if used, should be kept intact. If we convert them into *per day*, *per person*, or *per head*, the Latin preposition has become an unnecessary evil and should be replaced with the English indefinite article: *seven hours a day, four times a year, ten bushels a head*. *Per* is a necessary evil in a few such contexts as *overtime averaging forty hours a month per worker*, where *a month a worker* would stammer.

The use of *per* in business jargon — *as per your letter of the 4th* or *as per your fax of yesterday*—is uneducated and always unnecessary. Use English for what you are saying or doing.

per contra. See ON THE OTHER HAND.

percentage. See POPULARIZED TECHNICALITIES.

performing arts. See TRANSITIVE, INTRANSITIVE.

period, the. Anyone who knows a sentence when he sees one knows that the period goes at the end, provided the sentence is not a question or an exclamation. The signs for these, be it noted, incorporate the period with their own distinguishing features.

A period goes before a closing quotation mark, but its meaning is still an ending. It should not be confused with the *dot* in computerese, which is but one of the clustered scraps of language that haphazardly form a command. Computers have little to do with the conventions of English, as supermarket lingo attests; *mac che* does not abbreviate *macaroni and cheese* but breaks off at the end of a shelf label.

The punctuating of abbreviations, whether initials or calculated shortenings of terms, is muddled. Well-known institutions like *NATO* and the *AFL–CIO* have long since closed ranks between their letters, and no one can doubt that this is the way in which initials are headed. Yet *U.S.A.*, *Ph.D.*, and *M.A.* have kept their periods. As for conventional shortenings of single words—and against the example of the blind machine—the writer should consult the dictionary abbreviation and apply the period as prescribed.

See also INITIALESE; QUESTION MARKS, EXCLAMATION POINTS; QUOTATION MARKS.

permafrost. This mongrel scientific word suggests a commercial invention for keeping oneself or one's groceries cool. But *permafrost* in fact denotes that layer of the earth's crust which in arctic or subarctic regions is permanently frozen. Small wonder that we think the word belongs to trade; look at the trade name *Permalloy*, in which *perm* is *permeable* clipped. Similarly, the trouble with *permafrost* and others of its kind is that the sense-bearing root is incomplete. The Latin root *man* (from *maneo, manere*) contains the idea of *stay*, just as it is *mea* that contains the idea of *flow*. The *per* being only an intensive in *permanent* and meaning *through* in *permeate*, *per* or *perma* lacks the core meaning. Obviously, *permanfrost* was impossible in English, but there are always native words to work with. Just as physics recognizes the *steady state*, so it was possible in geophysics to speak of *steady frost*—hardly longer than *permafrost*, English throughout, and intelligible at sight.

perquisite. See MALAPROPS.

personal flotation device. See EUPHEMISMS.

personal(ly). 1. Do you know what to take and what to leave in obeying the sign that says, *Please take your personal belongings?* Is the man who tells you his *personal opinion* really distinguishing his from a different view held by a group he belongs to? Blame the spirit of the age or the writers of ads or both for turning *personal* into a nervous habit. Most readers ignore the word where it has no meaning, but those new to English ask, with reason: *Personal* as opposed to what?

I had no personal choice in the matter / Let us create your own personal hairstyle / Have you any personal health problems? / As between the green and the blue, do you have a personal preference? / Preserve a personal record of your vacation. To none of these sentences does the adjective bring a jot of meaning. Moreover, an *impersonal preference* is as hard to imagine as *impersonal health.*

What is by definition personal needs only the qualifiers *your, my, our*, etc., if any at all. The death of a friend is a *loss* or *a great loss* but not a *personal loss;* and a wish is a wish, a hope a hope, and so forth. Prudence tells you to keep your checks separate from those of the company you work for; but your checks are *your* checks, not, as the bank insists, your *personal checks.* Similarly, you pay *personal income tax* only if it must be distinguished from a corporate tax. Commerce coined the word *personalize* to pretend that objects were inseparable from the self. But what a machine has *personalized* —a monogrammed pen, embossed notepaper—is not, by an imprint, made *personal*, only traceable. Neither your checks nor your tax nor your stationery has to do with your *person*, which is to say your *being*, your *body* and *self.*

What, then, shall we make of references to your *personal life*—does the self have some other kind? At this point, one sees that *personal* is being substituted for *private*, to avoid the suggestion of secrecy or withdrawal from the group. So interchangeable have the words become that a journalist writes of a millionaire whose house has a *private screening room* but only a *personal bathroom.* What a man describes as his *personal opinion* may depart from the view held by his company, church, or political party, or from his own publicly stated opinion; but it is then a *private opinion*, to which he is thoroughly entitled. You may say that the book you carry is from your *private library* and imply nothing more sinister than a book not belonging to the public library.

Personal appearance has been an ambiguous phrase since the movies introduced a doubt as to what one was about to see in a theater—a celluloid phantasm or a flesh-and-blood creature. To *appear in person* clearly denotes the second possibility. In its other meaning, *personal appearance* has the sense of dress and bodily grooming, not good looks or their opposite. *Personal remarks* are comments about your face, figure, or character that others should weigh before offering. Other SET PHRASES such as *personal friend* and *personal attack* are justified only in a context that offers or implies clear contrasts—e.g., *business friend* as against *personal friend*; *political attack* as against *personal attack*.

2. Nowadays both *personal* and *personally* are also used to ingratiate: *Consider this your personal invitation / These wines have been personally selected with you in mind* (selected personally, or with you personally in mind?). The phrase *personal computer* may have helped to sell many machines, but it only denotes a computer one person can control and lift.

Personally is often stuck in as a mere intensive, even where none is needed: *Mr. W. and Mr. B. were irritated at the awarding of the Pulitzer Prize to the paper and not to them personally* (omit *personally*) / *His love for the movies eventually led him to buy RKO Pictures, making him the only individual who ever personally owned a movie studio* (omit *personally*) / *Each copy has been personally autographed and numbered by the author* (has been autographed . . . by the author himself, or omit *personally*) / *I personally didn't hear anything* (I myself). As intensives, the pronouns formed on *-self* (*herself, themselves*) are less distracting than *personally*, for they make no bones

about merely restating a subject or object for emphasis; *personally* looks as if it were adding something of its own, though it isn't.

Personally can, with economy, show someone's relation to a state of affairs or an action. It can mean *as an individual person*: *He accomplished more personally than his whole crew of aides and advisers / Fed up with working through committees and inert city agencies, she wrote personally to the mayor / None of the candidates for the office were personally magnetic.* And it can mean *in person*: *You must show up personally to answer the summons / The district attorney had always said that he would personally try the first capital-punishment case under his jurisdiction.*

persons. 1. A magazine that calls itself *People* yet chiefly reports on the few who are known to the many ignores the difference between *people* and *persons*. When we say *persons* we are thinking of *ones*, individuals with identities; whereas when we say *people* we should have in mind a very large group, an indefinite and anonymous mass, *anonymous* meaning *of unknown name*. Resting its full weight on its misunderstanding, the magazine in question relies on the names of its subjects being well known.

Everyone sees at once the rough quantitative difference between the phrases *the American people* and *the persons riding in the blue Ford*. The first stands for hundreds of millions, the second for any number up to, say, five. Not that a clear numerical division regulates the use of these terms.

Theodore M. Bernstein offers good advice: "A general guide is to use *people* for large uncounted groups and *persons* for an exact or small number." (Examples: *A spokesman for the ambulance service said that 206 persons had been injured / To several hundred people sitting on blankets and camp stools, the sixteen-year-old musician could do no wrong.*) Even so, idiom has firmly established *No two people think alike* and *the people at the next table.* Such idioms should not be violated —but neither should *persons* be neglected.

Each of us is a *person* to himself or herself and to a small number of others. Yet all of us know that we take part in multitudes of many kinds. Even in an age that rewards the conspicuous, only a few in the world population are publicly acknowledged as *persons*—the few whose personalities, gifts, or circumstances are suited to public projection. A retired President of the United States becomes one of the *people* again, while probably remaining one of those *persons* whose counsels are listened to by his party. Informal and hasty writing leans toward *people* for all occasions, as does the American Heritage Dictionary: "The distinction is now so widely ignored in general writing that it seems pedantic to insist on it." This is as much as to say that if a thing might be lost it had better be.

2. This willingness to devalue an important word may acknowledge the relative infrequency with which persons resist conforming to a mold and manage to be themselves—to be oneself being the only known way to be anybody

in particular. If, as many believe, the English cherish individuals and individuality more than Americans do, we find here a clue to the difference in the British treatment of the collective noun as a plural—*The committee are of the opinion, The government have committed themselves,* and so on, the stress falling on the persons composing the group. Americans tend to say *The staff for the most part supports her, The team is dissatisfied,* the noun conceived of as a single entity.

It may be noted, by the way, that the form *The jury is divided, The committee is agreed* is self-contradictory, since what is being spoken of is the clash or the meeting of individual opinions. *The committee are agreed* is better logic, as reporters concede when they say, *The jury are rumored to be nine for conviction and three for acquittal.* Even that fictive person, the chartered corporation, is made up of persons—a hydra whose heads do not necessarily think alike. But at present, American idiom makes the collective singular.

The difference between *people* and *persons* is roughly parallel to that between the word *folk* and the colloquial word *folks.* The *folk* generates its folklore and folk songs and folk epics and, nameless and faceless, expresses itself in these en masse; but a reporter out to record "what folks are thinking about" goes down the block interviewing this one and that one to quote each as *persons* representing *people.*

persuade. See CONVINCE, PERSUADE.

pervade. See TRANSITIVE, INTRANSITIVE.

picknicked. See CATALOGUE, CATA-
LOGUED.

pinpoint. See LINKING 3.

pivot around. See CENTER AROUND.

place in, put in(to). See INTO, IN
TO 2.

plausible. This civilized adjective
means *seemingly truthful, apparently
reasonable, satisfactory enough*—skeptical reckonings all. The word strikes a
delicate balance between stating belief
and reserving judgment. To say that
someone *showed plausible regret, had
a plausible excuse, seemed a plausible
friend* is not a wholehearted statement.
  Lexicons offer *specious* as a synonym, but that term lacks the tentative
edge. It means *attractive but not genuine; fair on the outside, false within.*
Specious has made up its mind, but
plausible waits to see. Being unique, it
is at the mercy of those who employ it
as just one more word for *believable,
trustworthy, reliable, quite all right.*
Such misusage could, in time, wear
away its distinguishing feature and
leave us without the one word that expresses a common—and often wise—
state of mind.
  See also ALLUDE; DILEMMA.

playing the race card. See VOGUE
WORDS.

pleasantries. See CONNOTATIONS.

pleased. See CONNOTATIONS.

pled. See MYSTERIOUS PASTS.

plenitude. See CONNOTATIONS.

polar opposites, polarity, polarized.
See POPULARIZED TECHNICALITIES.

popular. The well-known meaning
is: *acceptable to the people as a whole
or welcomed by them;* without the idea
of multitude, that meaning collapses.
*Such a procedure will not be popular
with me / It was a favorite of John Wes-
ley, with whom Eliza Haywood's row-
dyism would hardly have been popular /
Her mania for privacy was not popular
with her mother and father.* Those who
tie the adjective to one or a few persons are usually trying for comic effect
but only achieve the facetious. The apt
words are *welcome, tolerated, acceptable, congenial,* and their idiomatic
PREPOSITIONS.

popularized technicalities. The title of this entry explains itself. In our
time what is technical and professional
is in high repute; what comes from the
amateur is regarded as amateurish.
Consequently many words and phrases
have been borrowed from the sciences,
the techniques, and the professions to
adorn and lend impressiveness to ordinary prose. The use of these technicalities, which is ever increasing, has
naturally not been controlled by the
experts; the transfer has been amateurishness itself, and reflection shows that
a good many of the terms simply replace plain words long in use. A full
list of the borrowings is beyond the
scope of this book; but enumerating a
few, with comments, may encourage
speakers and writers to prefer simplicity.

allergy: a pathological sensitivity to certain foods or materials that do not harm the healthy. One would have to experience great discomfort in the presence of a person most other people liked to warrant describing one's feelings as ALLERGIC.

AMBIVALENT: see the word.

begging the question: not to be used when one has the feeling that the other's argument is simply unfair or off the point. It means only: using as an argument some disguised form of the proposition in question; e.g., if the issue is the immorality of cannibalism, the argument *How can it be moral to kill people in order to eat them?* begs the question. A few illiterate speakers misuse the idiom for *ask* or *raise the question*, as in *The story begs the question: What if animals could talk.*

behaviors: a useful plural in the social sciences, which define and enumerate actions. The plural is favored now by untrained persons who pretend to observe the playground, the family reunion, and your dinner plate with scientific detachment and completeness. You see singular *behavior*, but they see All.

catalyst, catalytic agent: part of the true meaning is that the agent, while it aids in furthering the chemical reaction, remains unchanged in the process. So the term will scarcely do for an active participant; one person's vandalism is not the *catalyst* of a riot but the event that sets it off.

category: a long and inaccurate word for *class* or *group*.

closure: at present a VOGUE WORD from the jargon of Gestalt psychology and parliamentary procedure; in the former, it means the completing in the mind of some sequence or situation; in the latter (also as *cloture*), a ruling that debate shall cease and a vote be taken on the matter at hand. In everyday English, things *finish, end, close, are completed.*

comity: from international law, where it means the courtesy traditionally expected of nations in their dealings with one another; not the *company* of nations.

continuum: a whole without parts—rarely applicable to workaday experience.

critical mass: in nuclear physics the smallest amount of fissionable material in a reactor, bomb, etc., able to sustain a chain reaction. Mistakenly thought to refer to a cumulatively large amount.

culture: a word defined many ways in the social sciences but generally embracing the customs, language, costume, arts, sciences, technology, and other attainments of a civilization. Hence to speak of *consumer culture, the culture of advertising, movie culture, the culture of the CIA, our political culture, California beach culture,* and the like is windy pretension. What is usually meant is only the thing itself (*buying and selling, advertising*) or *interest in* (*movies*) or *the ways* or *habits* or *style* or *practices* or *way of life of* (the CIA), or simply *life,* as in *beach life.*

cusp: the "entrance" of a "house" in astrology; either of the "horns" of an eclipsed planet or of the crescent moon; a meeting point in geometry; a projecting point in the tracery of

Gothic architecture; a protuberance on the crown of a tooth. A *cusp* is not, in short, an *edge*, as those who shun dictionaries believe.

dichotomy: a pedantic way of saying *division into two* or simply *division*.

DILEMMA: *di* = twice or double; therefore not the perplexity of choosing among three or four scarves, films, or anything else. The sense of forced option is also part of the meaning.

DYSFUNCTIONAL: see the word.

empathy: a word from psychology and aesthetics meaning *feeling inside* the object of contemplation; hence not a synonym for *sympathy*, which is *feeling with*.

entropy: does not mean disaster or the end of the world; the term relates only to the nonconvertibility of a part of energy into mechanical work: once the steam has vaporized, it turns no wheels. But it is true that increased entropy means less order in the universe—hence the loose use here decried.

ergonomic: in physics an erg is a unit of work or energy; *ergonomics* is the study of human efficiency in work. The adjective refers to such studies and is not honorific, yet it appears all the same in advertisements for office chairs and toothbrushes.

exponential: mathematics JARGON for a rate of change proportional to size. Both the rate and the magnitude of such change are usually beyond imagining. JOURNALESE likes to describe things as *increasing exponentially*, but concurrent figures nearly always belie the description.

extrapolate: carry a pattern or quantity established by data beyond the point where the data stop. In common speech, a piece of pedantry for *project* (verb), *speculate, surmise, guess*.

fixation: silly in *I'd say you have a fixation on Mediterranean tenors*; worse in *her fixation on finding the perfect apartment*. It refers to an exclusive concentration of immature love, as of a child for a parent, with a resulting lack of emotional development.

FORMAT: see the word.

idiosyncrasy: not a peculiarity but the sum of a person's peculiarities.

infrastructure: the subordinate parts of a military undertaking: airfields, missile silos, naval bases, etc., and by extension public roads, bridges, water systems, etc. In any other use a COVERING WORD. Say instead *staff, offices, telephones, computers, kitchen counter, septic tank*—whatever common things you mean.

lifestyle: a footloose term. Coined in psychology to denote a human subject's irreducible character, it wandered here and there in the social sciences to settle in JOURNALESE, where it denotes one's preference in furniture, clothing, and cuisine. Given its history, the word has no reliable meaning. Meanwhile, *style* means manner or fashion, and *life* means the sum of its parts, as in *the physician's life* or *Sally and Norman's life*.

neurotic, psychotic: difficult to use accurately outside a given system of psychiatry. As synonyms for *unhappy, troubled, deranged, crazy*, or *I can't stand him*, the words are pretentious.

of the essence (*time is*, etc.): does not

mean merely important or even essential; it means that the fulfillment of a promise or contract on the specified day is as important as any other provision. Hence not a substitute for *we must get busy.*

osmosis: the slow penetration of a membrane by a liquid when the concentration of some dissolved substance is not equal on both sides. Rather than speak in Greek, use good English words: *My mother was a singer, and I soaked up music from her / learned music by her example / came by singing naturally,* etc.

parameter: in mathematics, a quantity that varies with the conditions under which it occurs. Often illiterately used for *perimeter,* which means the outer boundary of a surface or other geometrical figure. *The parameters of our task* does not mean the limits of the job. *Para* = beside or subsidiary to. *Peri* = around.

paranoid: given to disabling delusions of grandeur, of persecution, etc. Not a synonym for *suspicious, mistrustful, envious, jumpy, stuck on herself.*

percentage: = hundredths; that is, a measure expressed in hundredths of some quantity; hence not to be used merely for *advantage, profit,* etc. Note that *percentage points* is not the same as percentage. Consult a textbook on statistics.

polar opposites, polarity, polarized: why not say *opposites, enemies, division, two factions, marital discord;* i.e., what the *polarization* boils down to.

pragmatism: see PRAGMATIC.

proactive: (1) In the branch of psychology called learning theory this describes a mental effect from an earlier situation which comes into play in a later one. (2) In police work it describes a settled practice of acting before trouble starts; opposed to a *reactive* policy, which favors acting afterward. Used by business people and social agencies, it has come to mean no more than being in favor of (*pro-*) action; resolved not to be inert.

REACTION: by definition automatic, unconscious, uncontrolled. Hence what one thinks about a book or a film is better described as a *response,* unless one reacts to it as a finger does to a flame.

replicate: used in several sciences, always with a sense of exactly repeating, imitating, or reproducing, this VOGUE WORD replaces with Latin the common words *match, resemble, look like, mimic.*

role model: a social-science coinage for one whose performance of a function or functions is imitated by someone else; the single word *model* has for centuries given this meaning for those who feel no itch to sound professorial.

status quo: first used in international law, this implies a return to a previous state, the original phrase bearing the two additional Latin words *ante bellum* (= before the war). At the utmost stretch *status quo* can mean *things as they are* or *as things are now.* Use these when confusion threatens.

synchronicity: not just a Greekish word for *simultaneity* or *happening at the same time* but a technical term invented by the psychologist C. G. Jung to denote events related in time and meaning but having no causal connection. The relation and the lack are of equal importance.

synergy: borrowed from medicine, where it means the action of bodily organs or of remedies which in combination produce an effect different from their separate effects. Mistakenly thought by many to be heightened *energy* resulting from joining forces. A conference *seeking a new kind of synergy between education and entertainment* will end up as neither. The plural, *synergies*, is an absurd VOGUE WORD in business; the Greek root *syn* already denotes joint or plural.

values: borrowed from painting, where it means relative tones of color. As a synonym for *moral principles, political and social beliefs, ethics, code, rules of conduct*, it is worn out and virtually meaningless.

vital statistics: these have to do with births and deaths in a given jurisdiction, not with body measurements or batting averages. See also SCIENTISM.

portly. See EUPHEMISMS.

portmanteau words. See GERMANISMS; TELESCOPINGS.

position. See JARGON.

positive, negative. See SCIENTISM 1.

possessives. 1. False. 2. Obligatory. 3. Neglected. 4. Shared. 5. Paired.

1. False. An American magazine started it as a device designed to save space and to attract attention; now every newspaper thinks it normal and right to speak of *Florida's governor, Broadway's Joe Jones, the town's high school, Columbia's French Department*, and *the nation's capital*. These possessives in the *'s* form, however popular, are false. The error in writing them is to assume that *Florida's governor* means the same thing as *the governor of Florida*. At that rate *the Book of Revelation* would be the same as *Revelation's Book* and *a list of names* could become *names' list*. The *of* in such phrases does not denote possession; it begins a prepositional phrase that specifies the noun it follows. Hence *The Cat in the Hat*, according to the prepositional phrase, is the particular cat that is wearing the hat. *A ruler of men* is similarly defining—marking this ruler off from *a ruler of the ski slope, the ruler of the universe* —and not the same as *a men's ruler. Loss of breath* and *piece of candy* are likewise particular and irreversible; *breath's loss* and *candy's piece* are nonsense. We must stick to the ancestral rule which, with a few exceptions, reserves possessives with *'s* for true ownership, by a person.

Usage is so clear on this point that it differentiates between the defining phrase used, say, in the title of a painting, *The Death of Nelson*, and the event "owned" by Nelson—*Nelson's death* on October 21, 1805. But the use of the possessive where possession is impossible spreads through American writing. *The figure is obtained by mul-*

tiplying the number of school-age children from low-income families by half of the per-pupil public-school expenditures in the district's state. The state cannot belong to the district, but neither can this sentence be fixed by replacing *'s* with *of* and inverting the nouns: *expenditures in the state of the district.* One must give up stinginess and spend a few words to save good sense: *expenditures in the state in which the district lies.* Similarly: *the governor of Florida* is now Ms. J.; *Joe Jones, now acting on Broadway*; *the town high school* is full to overflowing; *the French department at Columbia University*; and *Washington, D.C., the capital of the nation* or *the national capital.*

The point is not pedantic. The apt use of the defining *of* may make a serious difference in what a statement implies. To write that a woman not yet tried has been indicted *for murdering her grandmother* is a libelous statement; it is not libelous to write that she has been indicted *for the murder of her grandmother.* The latter phrase refers only to a crime that has been established; it does not refer to the criminal. But the former statement implies that the accused and the criminal are one. Similarly, to say, as one historian has done, that *Voltaire was the Enlightenment's pope* conveys the false impression that the Enlightenment was a corporate person led by a pope; whereas the idea behind the phrase is a metaphor or analogy—Voltaire was to the Enlightenment as the Pope is to the Catholic Church. That remoteness calls for the construction *pope of the Enlightenment.*

2. Obligatory. Now take the headline TRUCKERS ACCUSE CLIENT OF ZU-BER. On first reading, the thought does not occur that Zuber is a proper name. The mind gropes for a meaning parallel to A. *accuses* B. *of arson,* and the absurdity of this leads at last to the right conclusion that Mr. Zuber's client is being accused. The misdirection occurs because the needed possessive has not been supplied. The headline should read TRUCKERS ACCUSE CLIENT OF ZUBER'S; that is, *one of Zuber's clients.* The neglect of this simple possessive leaves us with puzzles like *a book of Morrison, a letter of Lincoln, a canvas of Lucien Freud,* although no one would ever say *a fan of him* or *a friend of me.* All these require changing to the possessive *'s* (with *his* for *him* and *mine* for *me* in the last pair), or else the replacement of the preposition, as in *a book by Morrison, a letter from Lincoln.* Such precision allows us to separate *a portrait of Warhol* (= his likeness) from *a portrait of Warhol's* (= a painting by him).

3. Neglected. Giving thought to simple possession—what belongs to whom—can not only tighten the structure but also clear the meaning. Consider: *The dislike of a peaceable man for violent action had been communicated,* etc. To the attentive reader the opening phrase remains ambiguous until the rest of the words sink in. *A peaceable man's dislike* would preclude from the start the possibility that the sentence might end up as *The dislike of a peaceable man is always embarrassing,* or something of the sort.

4. Shared. Rodgers and Hart wrote musicals; Laurel and Hardy made

films; Gilbert and Sullivan wrote ope-
rettas. Ordinary fairness suggests that
in all such collaborations we recognize
joint possession of the achievement by
using the *'s* form for both partners'
names. But usage prefers ease over fairness by treating the names of joint pos-
sessors as one, placing the possessive *'s*
after only the final name: *Gilbert and
Sullivan's* Pirates of Penzance; *Laurel
and Hardy's* Way Out West; *Ed and
Marcia's new apartment; Mia, Sandy,
and Sam's former office.* When two or
more persons possess comparable
things but not jointly, each is accounted a separate possessor: *Thoreau's
and Emerson's style; Picasso's and
Leonardo's drawing.*

5. Paired possessives need not produce the oddity of *Your and my children seem to like each other. Your* and
my are movable adjectives, and the
first, unnaturally separated from the
noun, can be shifted: *your children and
mine.* If for any reason this straddle
does not suit and the writer must return to the paired form, the tryout has
at least shown that *yours and my* is
flatly wrong, saying as it does *yours
children.*

See also APOSTROPHE, THE.

potential. See FORBIDDEN WORDS 2;
SCIENTISM 1.

**practical, impractical; practicable,
impracticable.** The person or plan
that is *practical* is in accord with actual
conditions; a *practical person* with a
practical plan takes *practical action,*
paying heed to things as they are. Such
a person's plan is thus *practicable*: capable of being carried out. But no per-

son or thing can be *practicable,* and
not all *practicable* (= doable) plans are
practical.

The negative of *practicable* is *impracticable,* and American usage has
recently changed the negative prefix of
practical from *un-* to *im-,* thus making
the negatives match. The meanings of
the negatives follow exactly the distinction between their positives: *impractical* applies to persons, things, and
ideas, and *impracticable* to ideas but
never to things or persons.

See DANGEROUS PAIRS; PRAG-
MATIC(AL).

pragmatic(al), pragmatism. The
use commonly made of *pragmatic* is to
suggest (1) hardheaded practicality
brooking no nonsense or (2) crude action, scornful of theory and of finer
feelings. We often hear the inexact
word *realistic* for the former meaning,
and we might use for the latter *anti-
philosophical* and, possibly, *unethical.*
The older *pragmatical,* as used by
Swift and Addison, meant *officious* or
opinionated. All this leaves the modern
use not only ambiguous but also false
to an important idea. Pragmatism is a
philosophical theory of truth; its tie to
practicality in the business or political
sense is no closer than that of a dozen
other theories. It is therefore misleading to use the term loosely and according to one's mood of liking or disdain.

Thus an editorial that greets a Supreme Court appointment welcomes
the incumbent's *activism, enthusiasm,
and pragmatism*—these are qualities,
etc. Again, from a single column by a
political analyst: *The aim is to produce
a more pragmatic and flexible posture*

toward China / *this highly desirable pragmatism* / *It is desirable to be pragmatic.* Since in their casual uses *pragmatic* and *pragmatism* fail to denote any intellectual position, but only confer praise or blame on erroneous grounds, we should give the words a rest until the position is better known.

pre-. See LOGIC.

precipitate, precipitous. See ENDINGS 1.

precision bombing. See EUPHEMISMS.

pre-emptive strike. See EUPHEMISMS.

pre-owned. See EUPHEMISMS.

prepositions. There is little logic and less system in the matings of English prepositions with verbs, adjectives, and nouns. The apparent clues provided by prefixes cannot be taken as infallible guides; *compare to* and *compare with* are not interchangeable any more than *agree to* and *agree with*. (See COMPARE, COMPARED.) Nor can convenience or half-baked theory substitute a single preposition for the several or none that idiom long ago assigned to particular words. Some broadcasters have lately taken to employing *against* with any verb or noun that implies an adversary relation. Thus we hear *He will appeal against the verdict* (no preposition needed) / *They launched an attack against the insurgents* (on the insurgents) / *a boy-* *cott against Japanese software* (of . . . software) / *not meant as a criticism against day care* (of day care) / *The peasants are fighting against the tax* (no preposition needed). In *The wall was meant to protect against kidnappers* and *She will defend against charges* the verbs *protect* and *defend* are transitive, requiring objects as well as idiomatic prepositions: *protect* the children *from kidnappers* / *defend* herself *from charges*. (See TRANSITIVE, INTRANSITIVE.)

A mastery of all the combinations is rare, but their study cannot fail to refine meaning and to tighten LINKING. A full list would take many pages; the combinations that follow here are those that seem most often bungled:

acquiesce: always *in* (see ACQUIESCE).

affinity: *with* (sometimes *to*; see AFFINITY).

agree: *to* = give assent; *with* = concur in opinion.

aim (verb): *at* with a verb in *-ing*.

analogy: *with*; *analogous to*.

angry: *with* or *at*, the second suggesting confrontation.

approximate (verb): no preposition, but the noun *approximation* takes *to*.

apropos: always *of*.

ask: *of* someone; *for* something.

behalf: *on behalf of* = as somebody's representative; *in behalf of* = in his or her interest.

belong: *to* with indirect object—e.g., a health club; *with* = to be classified among.

blink: with *at* = flutter the eyelids; with no preposition = overlook on purpose.

capable: of.

capacity: *to* with a verb; *of* with a measure.

commiserate: *with*; now only intransitive.

compare: *to* means *liken*; *with* means *place in comparison* (see COMPARE).

concur, concurrence: *in* an opinion, *with* other persons.

conform: *to* a rule; but *in conformity with* the rule.

connect: *to* (a wire or a pipe); *with* (a person, group, or idea).

consist: see CONSIST (IN) (OF).

continue: no preposition.

control: *of*, not *over*.

correspond: *to* means *match*; *with* means *exchange messages*.

crave: no preposition (but a craving *for* sweets).

dabbling: *in* (but dabbing *at*).

differ: *from* means *be unlike*; *with* means *disagree with*.

different: *from* is preferred; *to* is British; *than* is suspect. See DIFFERENT(LY) THAN.

difficult: *to*; but difficulty *of* or *in*.

divergent: *from*.

encroach: *on*.

equally: *with*, never *as* (see EQUALLY 1).

excerpt: *from*.

forbid: *to* after indirect object *you, her*, etc.

infringe: no preposition (though a few writers who watch their language have adopted the unnecessary *on* or *upon*, which they misappropriate from *impinge*).

inside (as preposition): no preposition for literal meaning; *inside of* with expressions of time is colloquial for *within*.

issue (as passive verb): no preposition; never *with* (*The troops were issued boots*).

knack: *of*, not *for*.

lavish: *on*, not *to* (*He lavished a great deal of attention to detail* is wrongly influenced by *attention to*).

market: *in the market* = as a buyer; *on the market* = offered for sale.

meet: no preposition before persons met for the first time; otherwise *met with the boss for an hour*; and *with* before abstractions: *meet with rebuffs, difficulties, delays*.

mistake (verb): *for*, not *as*.

name (verb): no preposition: never *named as editor-in-chief* or *to be captain*.

necessity: *of* or *for* (*need* with verb, *to*).

oblivious: always *of* (see OBLIVIOUS).

ought: always *to* (see OUGHT).

outside (as preposition): no preposition when physical meaning is intended: *outside of* is colloquial for *except, other than*.

partake: *of*.

participate: *in*.

practice (noun): *of*.

prevent: always *from* after a person named as object.

privilege (noun): *of* (but one is privileged *to*).

prohibit: always *from* after an indirect object.

promote: with title, no preposition (*promoted captain*); with office, *to* (*promoted to a captaincy*).

recommend: no preposition when followed by the substance of the recommendation—*He recommended that I leave at once*; use *to* with in-

direct object—*I recommend him to
the President* (see RECOMMEND).

reference: *to* = a pointing toward: *on* =
books or articles about.

report (noun): *of* and *on* are used interchangeably, though there is a
shade of difference in that a long
study tends to be a *report on*,
whereas three breathless words can
be the *report of* a disaster.

separate: *from*, never *out*.

subject(-ed): *to* (with the adjective
means *liable to*; with the verb =
underwent—e.g., *punishment*).

sympathy: *with* means *sharing another's feelings*; *for* means *having pity or
compassion for another*.

tamper: always *with*.

temerity: *to*, not *of*.

tend: no preposition when meaning is
give care to, but see also DANGEROUS
PAIRS.

tinker: *with* is American usage; *at* is
British.

view: *with* a view *to*; *with* the view *of*.

visit: no preposition. (*Visit with* is colloquial for *chat with*.)

wait: *for* has literal meaning; *on* means
to serve; *upon* means to pay a formal
call.

write: always *to* when direct object is
absent.

With and *by* are often interchangeable after a verb in the passive. The
implication of a human agent is
stronger in *by*: a man is *surrounded by
his enemies*; *surrounded with books*. As
a result, the verb recovers something
of its energy when *by* follows it. In
the sentences above, the enemies are
actively surrounding their victim,
whereas the books are just standing
around on shelves.

Note further that the more common
the verb (*take, get, hold, put*, etc.) the
more easily it joins itself to a variety of
prepositions; but each time the meaning differs, and sometimes a coupling
acceptable on the surface proves wrong
on analysis; e.g., *Mr. J. said that because of the article he will take his design from the approaching award
competition.* One may *take candy from
a baby* or *comfort from a friend's sympathy*, but in the sentence above *take
from* should be *take out of* or *withdraw
from*, since the competition is not a
thing or person.

In joining two verbs that act on the
same object it is important that the required preposition accompany each, as
in *to make use of, and account for,
every penny.* This particular construction is heavy and inelegant, and suggestions are made in PROSE, THE
SOUND OF 4 for getting around it. But
it is a superstition to believe that when
one of the verbs takes no preposition
its meaning is skewed by the following
verb that does. *To employ and account
for every penny* is correct and easy, the
for after *account* having no effect whatever on *employ*. Obviously, in such
pairings, the verb without the preposition must come first.

See also AROUND; CONSIST (IN) (OF);
IN for BY, OF 3; REDOLENT WITH; SUF-
FICIENTLY; THAT, CONJUNCTION 1; TO,
MISSING; WITH; WITH, MISSING; WITH-
OUT.

prerequisite. See MALAPROPS.

prestigious. Carlyle called *prestige*
"a bad newspaper word." But since in
our time it names a quality ardently

sought, we must keep it. But we need not have had *prestigious*, which fifty years ago still described juggling, sleight-of-hand, or cheating, as in *prestidigitation*. Even though it has by now escaped its past, the word does not always mean what is wanted. *The company looked for a year for this prestigious address* says that the address has *prestige*. But *prestige* is an absolute word, like *excellence*; just as we do not say, *Their playing was full of excellence*, we ought to balk at *Stunner Drive is full of prestige* or *is prestigeful* or *is prestigious*. Moreover, the word fills no need, what with *renowned, illustrious, reputable, famous, excellent, notable, respectable, admirable, enviable, praiseworthy*, etc., ready at hand.

prevent. See PREPOSITIONS; TRANSITIVE, INTRANSITIVE.

preventive, preventative. See UNNECESSARY WORDS 1.

previously owned. See EUPHEMISMS.

primal, primary. See ENDINGS 1.

prior to. Too often written interchangeably with the sturdy *before*, this phrase is losing a unique shade of meaning that *before* does not have. From its origin in the law, *prior to* carries the idea of necessary precedence: *The application to the company must be executed and filed prior to the expiration of the policy.* By extension, the philosophical statement *Concepts are logically prior to the existence of particulars* implies an idea of necessity

which would not be felt in a rewording such as *Concepts come before*, etc. It is because of this additional idea (and the starchiness of *prior to*) that the growing neglect of *before* should be reversed: *She twisted her ankle prior to getting home* sounds as if some important point of time were being established in court. And *She eats her muffin prior to her fruit and cereal* sounds less like description than like compliance with a judge's decree.

pristine. This is not a poetical word for *clean*. The natural stand-ins for *clean* include *pure, unsoiled, unsullied, sanitary, cleansed, immaculate*. *Pristine* is not so simple; it denotes an original, untouched, and primitive state. An infant at birth might be called *pristine* but hardly *immaculate*. A *pristine innocence* amounts to utter inexperience. Macbeth comes to wish that Scotland might be returned to *pristine health* — a former or original condition. The painter Gauguin sought a *pristine*, unspoiled locale, not one cleansed by efficient plumbing.

Pleasant nouns like *innocence* and *health*, when paired with *pristine*, lend to it their own pleasant connotation of purity. More confusing, this borrowed sense and the established meaning *primeval* meet in the meaning *untouched*. But *pristine* has a cluster of meanings and should, in its richness, be saved from those who only know that it "sounds like" *clean* (with which, of course, it rhymes). Thus the historian Prescott in *The Conquest of Mexico*: "What, then, must have been the emotions of the Spaniards, when, after working their toilsome way into the upper air, the cloudy tabernacle parted before their eyes, and they beheld these fair scenes in all their pristine magnificence and beauty! It was like the spectacle which greeted the eyes of Moses from the summit of Pisgah, and, in the warm glow of their feelings, they cried out, 'It is the promised land!' " The Spaniards were not agog at cleanliness. See also CONNOTATIONS.

privilege, noun. See PREPOSITIONS.

proactive. See POPULARIZED TECHNICALITIES.

process(es), verb and noun. See CONTACT 2; COVERING WORDS; SCIENTISM 1.

product. See COVERING WORDS.

Professor, title. See TITLES AND PROPER NAMES 3.

prohibit. See PREPOSITIONS.

promote. See PREPOSITIONS.

pronunciation. 1. For convenience one may distinguish several kinds of common mispronunciations: (a) newfangled, (b) illogical, (c) inattentive, (d) overnice, (e) eccentric.

a. The newfangled are born and grow up in the teeth of the prevailing habit. Sometimes an old word is taken up by people who have never heard it spoken. *Surveillance* came from French but is fully naturalized and pronounced *sur-vai´-lence.* The back-formation *surveil,* a JARGON verb, is

spoken as *survail* (though *spy on* or *watch* will do for most purposes). *Comptroller* is an old and now affected variant of the title *controller* and pronounced just like it, not like *Compton* in California. For some speakers the negative prefix *il-* (= not) is not emphatic enough; hence *illegal* becomes the muffled scream *eel-legal,* and *illicit* comes out as *eel-licit.* The poised *illicit* begins with *ill.* Traditionally, *parl(i)ament* does not sound its *i,* and the careful speaker says *sism* for *schism; ark* in *archetype; zellous,* not *zeelous,* for *zealous; aigyou,* not *aig,* for *ague;* and *long-lyved* for *long-lived,* whereas *livelong* is *liv-long.*

b. Illogical pronunciations include *zoo-ology* for *zo-ology.* The word would need three *o*'s at the beginning to permit the *zoo* effect. (See also OLOGIES.) Note too that *height* ends with a *t,* not the *th* which thousands put on it. *Luxury* has no hard *g* before the *x,* nor do *exhibition, execute, excerpt,* or *exigent* begin with *eggs.* The comprehensive sins of *omission* and *commission* are often distorted for the sake of audible parallelism; they should be spoken together just as they would be separately —*oh-mission* and *comm-ission.* (See also COUNCIL, COUNSEL, CONSUL.) Remember, too, that the double *l* in COLLEAGUE prevents it from sounding like *co-league.* And a *memento,* being a reminder, neither rhymes with *pimiento* nor begins like *momentum;* it begins with *mem* as in *memory.*

c. The inattentive read very little and so misspeak. One advantage of knowing how to spell is that the eye can guide the tongue and prevent, for

PRONUNCIATION 1 • 239

example, *simular* for *similar*, *nukular* for *nuclear*, *salutory* for *salutary*, *vunerable* for *vulnerable*, and *esculator* for *escalator*. Fashions in mispronunciation spread with astonishing speed. A linguist will search out their history but may not mention that *eck cetera* and *asterick* and *ax* do no favors for the speaker who means *et cetera, asterisk,* and *ask.* Never in the history of broadcasting have so many amplified speakers mussed up their consonants as do so now, transmitting *produck, subjick,* and *districk* in place of *product, subject,* and *district.* No closer to *district* is *dishtrict* or its fashionable fellows *shtreet, shtricken, shtructure, shtrict,* and *shtrike.* All begin with *st*; *sht* is a strike at their structure. Those who urge us to *inneract* on the *Innernet* drop the *t* in *inter-,* the prefix that carries more than half the meaning. Conversely, a superfluous *i* must be dropped from *heinous, grievous,* and *mischievous*; all end in plain *ous.* Pronounce the three *haynus,* not *heenious* or *heenus; greevous,* not *greevious; mischivus,* not *mischeevious.* Say lightly the *e* in *mathematics,* but say no *e* at all after *ath* in *athletics.* The sleep-inducing drugs are *barbiturates,* not *barbituates,* despite the convenient jingle with *habituates.* Finally, the word *pronunciation* itself gives no warrant for *pronounciation.*

d. Chief among the overnice pronunciations is the sounding of the *t* in *often.* It should be seen and not heard. The same is true of the *th* in *clothes,* which is properly *clo'es*; the first *g* in *suggest(ion),* which is *sud-jest(ion)*; and the first *t* in *chestnut.* As for the re-

placement of the common *sh* sound by a clear *s* in *issue* and *tissue,* it can only be called *preshous*; so too the broadcaster's shunning of *sh* in *appreciate* and *negotiation* for the dainty and wrong *appresiate* and *negosiation. Extraordinary* sounds no *a-o* in the middle, only an *o*; but *eleemosynary* requires the paired *e*'s separately sounded (*el-ee-i-mos´-inary*). And to make things hard after condemning overniceness, the opposite advice must be given about paired words that tend to overlap: say *pine needles,* not *pie-needles,* and *health center,* not *helcenter.*

e. By definition, eccentric ways of pronouncing words do not reveal a pattern; but probably everyone retains from early days one or two homemade deviations from usage. Thus, cultivated speakers have been heard to say *laxadaisical* for *lack-, cut-and-dry* for *cut-and-dried,* and the sneeze-like *eshew* for *es-chew´.* Some dictionaries offer pronunciations as eccentric as any homegrown: both *absorb* and *absurd* derive from Latin and French, their *s* pronounced *ess*; American lexicographers offer the alternative pronunciations *ab-zorb´* and *ab-zurd´,* the eccentric *s* borrowed for no clear reason from German. Almost everyone mispronounces *execrable,* which does not sound right when correct: *ek´-si-kra-bal.* Prefer *a-bom´-in-able.*

In English the accent is recessive, going as far toward the beginning of the word as tongue and breath can manage. Thus *hospitable, exquisite, despicable,* and *secretive* are accented like *ádmirable, cónfident,* and *théater.*

In the first three words on this list, the pattern happily prevents the accenting of *spit, quiz,* and *spic*. And speaking of accents, the word *research*, both noun and verb, is generally accented on the second syllable by those who do the work.

2. Little advice can be given about the pronunciation of foreign words and phrases, because the capacities of speakers for approximating unfamiliar sounds vary widely. Those who feel self-conscious about shaping such sounds should reduce their employment of foreign phrases to a minimum. But within that minimum which ordinary usage requires, it is best to Anglicize the pronunciation up to the point where it does not render the words unrecognizable. It would, for example, be hopeless for many to try to say *apropos* or *Schadenfreude* with their respective uvular *r*'s; but equally foolish to say *ayproposs* and *shaydenfroody*. Many words lend themselves easily to Americanization. Thus *foyer* is now part of the real-estate agent's vocabulary, and to give it a French pronunciation would be both silly and misleading: in French the word does not mean an abbreviated vestibule but the *home* as an abstract entity.

The same applies to proper names. It is difficult at best to make one's lips and tongue and uvula shift gears in the middle of a sentence, and one moreover runs the risk of not being understood at all if one slips in a foreign name with the value of its vowels and consonants unexpectedly different from the rest of the discourse. Say *Flaubert* or *Tetrazzini* in conversation as the French and the Italians would say those names and the first will sound like a murmur and the second like an affectation. All that duty requires is to avoid *Flauburt* with the *t* sounded and *Teetrazinny* without the *ts* sound of the double *z*. To sum up: Give the nearest equivalent, with English sounds and without straining. Our ancestors had a better notion than our pedantic pretense at accuracy when they decided on *Paris* and *Lyons* and *Venice* and *Berlin* in place of *Paree* and *Leeon(g)* and *Venetsia* and *Bayrleen*.

So much for Western Europe and its nomenclature. When we move eastward, all common sense departs; for the transliteration of Eastern languages is evidently difficult, and it has been correspondingly arbitrary. Just as translation is often considered finer if foreign idioms are given word for word in English, so transliteration is a hodgepodge of direct visual counterparts and true-sounded equivalents. Our cosmopolitan ambitions might for now come to rest in a homely hope: that American broadcasters who speak of *Europe* will, with practice, abandon *Yerp* for *Yeurop* and *Yerpeen* for *Yeuropean*.

See also RECREATE, RE-CREATE; SPELLING; X.

proper names. See TITLES AND PROPER NAMES.

prose, the sound of. 1. Most writing is probably never read aloud. But prose that cannot be heard with pleasure is probably badly written. Euphony is not

the highest virtue but a basic requirement of good writing, and the reason
is simple. All readers but the tone-deaf,
when they read silently, hear each
phrase with the inner ear, and they are
just as disturbed by clashing sounds as
if they were reading aloud or listening.
This effect is independent of the
tempo at which their silent reading is
done. So defiant of time are some departments of the mind that we can
read at jet-plane speed and hear the
words as if reading at a crawl. Those
who can read musical notation and
inwardly hear the music know the
analogous but opposite effect. They
cannot, at sight, read at a performing
tempo if it is rapid; but they can hear
at such a tempo while reading at uniformly moderate speed. The writer
who fills page after page with ugly dis-
sonances and thinks them not worth
the bother of repairing because no one
will test him by voice fails to understand reading. Dull readers may not
mind, but better readers will follow
him with pain and inward protest as
the price of their interest in what he
has to say; that interest failing, they will
abandon his words with relief.

2. Of the disturbers of euphony
the two most common are, on the
one hand, unintended assonance and
rhyme, and on the other, rhythmic
staggers comparable to tripping or trying to descend another step after
reaching the bottom of the stairs. Of
course calculated echo has a place in
prose and can achieve telling effects.
The intentional echoing of sounds
lends force to *Man proposes, but God
disposes* and to the tag about inspira-

tion and perspiration in the working
of genius. Echo also gives emphasis
to *We cannot dedicate—we cannot
consecrate—we cannot hallow this
ground / Retaliation is, after all, one
kind of compensation / a society that
seems to us at once despicable and improvable.* Rhyme may be the first rhetorical effect that children respond to,
and this link to the childish enforces
great care on speakers and writers who
make use of rhyme when addressing
adults. For rhyming can trivialize serious matters and, worse, draw the
reader's attention away from sense and
toward mere sound.

A botch when mishandled, echoing
is amateurish when accidental. Writers
too careless, too hurried, or too lazy to
keep their lines free of unplanned repetitions of *-tion, -ation, -ing, -ly, -ty,
-pose, -press,* and so on, neglect their
duty. But such repetitions are easier to
find than to escape, even in respectable writing: *An instinct quite distinct
from thought / the things that he was
formerly determined to reform / I would
never have made any such to-do over
something that my own dignity admon-
ished me to do / Giving us all the facts
as they did was a great factor in preventing panic / The commission has
taken the position that / I think he
would deserve very considerable consideration from the labor movement / no
immediate official reaction to the action
made known this afternoon / Both compositions reflect a concern with the expressive resources of limited forces /
asserted a concerted campaign of vili-
fication had been conducted against
him / to roar like a wounded lion at the*

slightest slight / We wait on tables in exchange for remission of tuition.

The words *say, way, day, (today), may,* and *play* (with its compounds) must be watched with particular care, tending as they do to introduce rhymes within adjacent phrases or sentences. Adverbs in *-ly* and nouns ending in *-ty* jingle frivolously when close together. *The irony of receiving flagrantly inequitable treatment in a society that boasts of its democratic heritage has been a main source of black humor from slavery . . . to Richard Pryor's quip about the contemporary legal system.* These repetitions of *y* are themselves echoed by the *ee* sound in *receiving, treatment,* and *legal.*

The sound of prose is likewise affected by accidentally irregular rhythms. Here again the placing of adverbs is a subject for caution and a test of skill. A parenthesis in an unnatural position or with insufficient grammatical moorings can be even more disruptive, as in *chapters describing the past and present of that great gouge cut by the now-invisible (from the rim) Colorado River.* This is to compound an adjective in English as German freely does: *now-invisible-from-the-rim* is of the same order as Freytag's *the on-the-other-side-of-the-river-lying mountains.* A like affront to the ear is felt in the following: *Yet things have drifted so far without—until very recently—the needed sense of moral leadership at the highest levels . . . that . . .* (See GERMANISMS.)

Long elements placed within the parts of a compound verb will produce similarly bad effects: *Ireland had—as*

Thomas Davis had long ago feared, and Æ repeatedly warned—been made safe for commerce.* The interpolation in dashes might well have begun the sentence. One of the anomalies of English is that whereas a single adverb should, if possible, go after the auxiliary of a compound verb, an adverbial clause cannot go there without great awkwardness. *It is difficult to understand how Fish, with his intimate knowledge of the widespread corruption that existed under Grant, could have, as he did in 1880, supported Grant's attempt to obtain a third term.* Besides stopping the stream of thought by a parenthetical clause, the syntax suggests the impossible form *did supported.* Note that the ungainliness of this sentence is a by-product of VERBIAGE. No more is said than *How could Fish, familiar with the widespread corruption under Grant, support him in 1880 for a third term?*

A hiatus in rhythm will invariably occur when for variety the writer of fiction resorts to the modish trick of interpolating elaborate modifying elements between his subject and a verb of saying: *"Nothing," W., who could not forget the day S. took him out on the green, said.* The gasp for breath is even worse when virtually inseparable words are kept apart by long explanatory clauses, as in *the Immigration Quarantine Station on the other side where they had the six Germans who had given up off of an injured merchant vessel interned.* The passage can be made readable by the simple adjustment *where they were keeping interned the six Germans . . .*

But note how equally defiant of the

reading voice is the following sentence by a cultivated novelist once praised for style: *Modestly, he could be seen asking himself, waiting anxiously to hear, what standards of conduct that G. (abashment said so) privately thought the highest possible would proceed to find on these artful, extralegal, and, as G. himself saw them, if not definitely dishonest, perhaps dishonorable goings-on.* Unnatural parentheses in an un-natural position, subordinations out of place, and coy approaches to fairly simple meanings—all pretend to the intricate structure of a Ciceronian pe-riod; the reader is confronted with the task of parsing which used to bedevil the student decoding second-year Latin.

3. Less common than accidental echoes or tripped-up rhythms but just as distracting is unintended meter. We think of rhythm in prose as easy to come by and rhythm in verse as need-ing skill; but there are times when those who would not attempt poetry find their prose falling into lines of blank verse. The pattern of such un-welcome regularity is generally iambic, the meter that English words favor. *Such freedom as is not enjoyed by any other people in the world* contains eight iambic feet. *Though small, it was a brilliant work—the horses modeled lightly* contains six. Occasional sen-tences of this kind are native to En-glish, but trouble starts when the pattern is unbroken or will not relent. A sample of awful perfection in dac-tylic meter: *spending much of his time in a mountain cabin on the pine-clad slope of a rugged range near a brawling*

stream. Once the writer's ear wakes up to this lyric outburst, he will thin the adjectives, clearly too profuse. But when such a dogtrot takes charge for paragraphs at a time, the writer must give up until his mind has regained its independence.

4. Among hardships to the ear should be listed two constructions not wrong in form but always hectic in rhythm. The first is the familiar pairing of two meanings requiring two differ-ent prepositions: *A long knowledge of, and deep fellowship with, those who are our brethren in Christ.* This arrange-ment of bumps is not required by the thoughts expressed. Separate the two ideas and all is well: *A long knowledge of those who are our brethren in Christ and a deep fellowship with them.* Some writers think they achieve profundity or analytic power by the double-duty formula and inflict it every few para-graphs: *It is appropriate for us to feel a sense of pride in and to offer congratu-lations to the many hardworking men and women who / that the only hope for our schools lies in close cooperation with and participation by the parents,* etc., etc.

Akin to this two-headed form is *as much as, if not more than,* which in-tends to estimate things difficult to measure. Often this tiresome device is further weakened by the omission of the second *as: The competition for these resources by government and in-dustry is increasing as fast [as] or faster than the colleges' need for them.* One would think that *as fast . . . than* might give the writer pause, but even after *as* is restored the sentence continues to

244 • PROSE, THE SOUND OF 5

stammer. Sometimes a writer tries to sidestep the trouble he foresees, only to plunge into worse: *The responsibility rests as much if not more heavily on state and local governments.* (See also AS 3.)

5. Yet another construction that afflicts both ear and logic is the one in which an article in the title of a piece of writing follows a possessive (or duplicates an article): *Shakespeare's* The Tempest *is playing /* Poe's *"The Raven" / his* A Child's Garden of Verses / *the picaresque* The Adventures of Augie March *by Saul Bellow.* Such locutions do not occur to anybody except when citing a title and would never be spoken in conversation. No one dreams of saying *his the hat* or *her the computer* or *Murphy's the law.* It is an implicit property of the possessive that it swallows and contains whatever article would be in order if the possessive were not there. *Murphy's law* is the inevitable way of saying *the law of Murphy's,* and *his hat* the way of saying *the hat of his.* But when a title is involved, the natural resistance to such silly locutions runs straight into an imaginary rule that titles must be repeated precisely as they are. This fanciful commandment (in fact, simple pedantry) overcomes the resistance and we read: *His* The Morning Watch, *which was published to acclaim / The allusion is to Williams's introduction to his* The Figure of Beatrice / *In her* The Origins of Totalitarianism, *Hannah Arendt has written* . . .

The modern prevalence of this error—which leads some copy editors to insert articles sensibly omitted by authors—shows how widely reading matter has come to be thought of as sense without sound, as something for the eye to glance at, with the ear in complete abeyance. It has never been true that in prose a title has to be cited as it is found on a title page. It must indeed be so cited in bibliographies and in bibliographic footnotes, which obey the canons of the library catalogue; but in prose—not just print but *prose*—all that is required is that the work be clearly identified and that the mention be introduced smoothly enough to be readable. Since the definite or indefinite article of a title is ignored in determining the alphabetic order, its inclusion is no help to identification and does nothing whatever for the user of reference books. In any normal sentence *Mark Twain's* Tom Sawyer *manuscript* is quite as competent a reference as *Mark Twain's* The Adventures of Tom Sawyer *manuscript,* besides being stylistically decent. In the nineteenth and the early twentieth century, rhetorics taught by express rule that the articles in the titles of books must be omitted when a possessive precedes. The prescribed forms were: *Shakespeare's* Tempest / *her* Mill on the Floss, and so on. These forms are still called for.

A secondary point is that a good half or more of the possessives that introduce titles are needless and should be omitted simply because they perform no function. As often as not, context settles the authorship without the trouble of including a possessive. *In his* The Lost World of the Kalahari *Colonel van der Post has written* is exactly as clear without the *his*. Why should an encyclopedia article about an author keep pointing out that his works are his, as an article on Yeats, for example, persistently does? (*Yeats's "The Countess Cathleen," His prose A Vision,* etc.) These possessives add nothing but static. And works that are household words do not need identifying by author anyway. *Hamlet* is as unmistakable as *Shakespeare's* Hamlet (else, why not *Shakespeare's* The Tragedie of Hamlet, Prince of Denmark?). It is a pure waste of space to mention the author of *Paradise Lost* unless the work meant is *not* Milton's. Of course, obscure works or works the titles of which might be subtly altered in meaning by the omission of *A* or *The* may occasionally require being named in full, even when a possessive precedes. In such cases, interpose a noun: *Philip Macdonald's novel* The Rasp *unfolds/ J. M. Keynes's study* The Economic Consequences of the Peace *suggested.* Far from being fussy or redundant, these insertions make the sentences exact and euphonious both.

Newspapers and magazines that have the definite article in their titles firmly insist on retaining it, capital T and all, whenever they mention themselves, regardless of what they may do about the names of other publications. Some persons respond to this insistence by writing such forms as *the editors of* The New York Times, as the *Times* itself would do, instead of the more usual form *the editors of the* New York Times. But what happens when the name of the publication or of a regular department is approached by

way of a possessive, as in *Frank Rich's* New York Times *column of August* 17 or *Your* "Talk of the Town" *piece on X will doubtless be widely reprinted?* And what happens when the title is approached by way of the indefinite article, as in A New York Times *reporter has ascertained* or A New York Times *correspondent in London sees indications that?* The same commandment that insists on *Hawthorne's* The Marble Faun, *Wharton's* The House of Mirth, etc., if it were to be consistently obeyed, would equally insist on *Frank Rich's* The New York Times *column* and *Your* "The Talk of the Town" *piece* and A The New York Times *reporter has ascertained.* The only way to push unnaturalness further would be to follow a possessive with a possessive; and that combination can be found in Mencken's Supplement I: *Thus, when Percival Pollard published his* "Their Day in Court" . . . (See A, AN, THE 4.)

See also SENTENCE, THE.

proselyte is the noun which means a *convert*; the verb meaning *to try to convert* is *proselytize*.

prove, proved, proven. See MYSTERIOUS PASTS.

proverbial. See LEGEND(ARY).

provide. See TRANSITIVE, INTRANSITIVE.

provided, providing. *Provided* serves as a conjunction introducing terms and conditions. *Providing* is a participle. This gives us: (1) *You will be* *treated with courtesy and apparent trust, provided that (= only if) you arrive alone and on foot* and (2) *The slope was gentle and unvaried, providing (= and it provided, afforded) a view of each member of the slowly advancing herd.*

See also DANGLERS, BENIGN.

psychology. See OLOGIES.

punctuation. See APOSTROPHE, THE; COLON, THE; COMMA, THE; DASH, THE; ELLIPSIS; HYPHEN, THE; PARENTHESES, BRACKETS; PERIOD, THE; QUESTION MARKS, EXCLAMATION POINTS; QUOTATION MARKS; SEMICOLON, THE; SLASH, THE.

purge. A favorite device of modern governments is called by a metaphor that newspaper usage routinely puts the wrong way around. The physical body is purged of its poison or peccant humors. The body politic is purged of its supposedly harmful citizens. It follows that Minister J. and General M. are not themselves purged; it is the ministry or the assembly they belonged to which is now proclaimed the healthier for their removal. Accordingly, we should say—though there is scant chance we will—*General M., who was removed by the January purge / Minister J., the Maurefluvian purgee of the so-called Kid Glove Coup.*

pushing [the edge of] the envelope. See VOGUE WORDS.

put down, verb. See EUPHEMISMS.

put in(to), place in. See INTO, IN TO 2.

put to it. See HARD PUT.

put to sleep. See EUPHEMISMS.

Q

qualification. This word has two meanings that are subtly opposed and thus make it a trap. *Qualification* means (1) reservation, restriction, exception *(The committee backs your proposals without qualification)*, and (2) ability, competence, preparation *(The youthful commander was ignorant, impetuous, and lacking all qualification)*. If the context does not make clear which meaning is intended, the writer will baffle his readers, as when a reviewer calls a novelist one of the greatest living writers of English *without any qualification whatsoever*. The point intended is not that the novelist, great as he is called, lacks ability but that the reviewer has no reservations in making the claim of greatness.

quantum. See SCIENTISM 2.

question marks, exclamation points. Spanish puts at the beginning of a question or exclamation its appropriate mark, upside down, warning the reader to adjust his mind or his voice to the kind of thing about to be said. English confines the mark, printed right side up, to the end of the passage. Coming thus late, the signal must be fastened firmly to the words whose tone it tells; when quotation marks fig-

ure within an exclamation or question, the signal is easily misplaced and given sway over the wrong words.

In the following, the question mark is easily locked in, for the quotation and the question are one: *Then he asked, "What now?"* But when a quotation occurs within a quotation, the marks for both can confuse the proper placing of the question mark, which must at all times stand by the words it governs: *"I asked you, 'What now?' "* Notice that the entire sentence becomes the question in: *Did I mention that I heard in my sleep the words "What now? what now?"?* When (say, in dialogue) the sentence is both a quotation and a question and contains another question, the question mark must, as it does just above, come after the sentence but within its closing quotation marks: *"Do you mind if I fail to see any special significance in all this 'What now'?"*

Question marks do not belong in indirect questions—those that are reported, not quoted, within another statement: *I thought I'd better ask her what she was doing / Father R. could not refrain from asking which church had refused them.* Another identifying trait of the indirect question is that it does not reverse its subject and verb.

Everything said above about the placement of question marks applies to exclamation points; indeed, a surprising likeness between exclamations and questions can trouble the writer. *Never!* and *Wow!* are exclamations and signaled accordingly, but so are several common expressions whose grammar is that of the question, e.g., *How many times have I told you!* and *Is that so!* The former expresses impatience and the latter a challenge, and neither wishes an answer. Hence, the exclamation points. Among other apparent questions, *Are you kidding?* exclaims in surprise, and *Can I help it?* is only a wail in self-defense. Yet neither strikes the eye and ear as being right without a question mark. For we speak both groups of words as questions though, again, with no wish for an answer.

Some grammarians would have all emphatic rhetorical questions take an exclamation point. Others insist on a question mark for any utterance that reverses the subject and verb. Neither rule holds today, when normal intonation decides which mark should be written. Not that Americans ought to follow the English into what strikes the American ear as unwritable archness: *"I suppose you're going to lunch?"* / *"I gather there is nothing to be done?"*

See also QUOTATION MARKS.

quotation. See QUOTE, UNQUOTE 3, 4.

quotation marks. Quotations set down by Americans wear two pairs of these, one at the beginning, one at the end. A quotation within a quotation dons single quotation marks, and a quotation within *that* calls for double ones again. In most American prose, a period or a comma coming at the end of a quoted sentence is put inside the closing quotation marks. A period: *"I must ask you to listen carefully."* A comma: *"I would do it if I were you,"* he said. This arrangement rarely changes when short quotations fall at the end of a sentence: *The guard demanded to know what he meant by "only a little while."* Nor does it vary when quotation marks proliferate: *"I said to him, 'You can't talk about John Huston movies if you haven't seen what he made out of Joyce's "The Dead." ' "* (For the placing of other punctuation in or outside quotation marks, see QUESTION MARKS, EXCLAMATION POINTS.)

Long quotations may be written as blocks of words set off from the text, all the lines indented on one side or both sides. (Publishers' style books often suggest the number of lines that qualify as a long quotation.) Block quotations do not begin and end with quotation marks but within the block follow the patterns set forth above.

Style manuals differ, but in general the titles of short stories, essays, musical compositions, and other works not normally published as books are enclosed in quotation marks, unlike book titles, which are italicized. At least one style book recommends italicizing titles of movies and television programs. Questions and statements not part of dialogue stand without quotation marks: *I wondered, What can she mean? / He said to himself, Go easy.* See also QUOTE, UNQUOTE.

quote, unquote. 1. The substitution of *quote* for *quotation* is more and more seen in casual writing (*a quote taken out of context / an inaccurate quote*), and there it should stay. No one looks forward to sequels like *The cite is Smith's / The refer is not clear / I didn't catch the allude.*

2. Many public speakers adopt the broadcaster's practice of using the words *quote* and *unquote* in place of visual quotation marks. In this usage, *quote* is a shortening of *I quote,* whereas *unquote* is obsolete jargon from the time of cables and telegrams. *Unquote* being no word, some speakers take pains to say *end quote* instead. This is not an improvement, for it seems to make *quote* a full-fledged noun (see 1).

3. This matter of spoken quotation can lead to fussiness that a little forethought could avoid. Consider first that the words you wish to set off may not merit special attention: *He said he would return—quote—in a matter of days—unquote;* this is pedantic precision with language everyone uses. Second, there are quite a few speakable idioms that signal exact quotation: *She spoke as follows* or *the following / R. employs what he calls* or *what he terms* or *what he refers to as / The result was, in her words,* etc. Third, when reading a long quotation, you need not say *quote* after you have said, *General B. made the following statement.* And when the end is reached, a perceptible pause and a change of pitch will do the business of *unquote.* So will the simple *end of quotation.* Some speakers have taken to signaling opening and closing quotation marks by raising and crooking two fingers of each hand; this miming of scholarly conscience costs a good deal in poise.

4. Apropos of *quotation,* bear in mind that speakers and writers make statements, not quotations—unless they repeat someone else's statement. *Your views remind me of the great quotation from Mark Twain: "Nothing so needs reforming as other people's habits."* Mark Twain was not quoting but stating; the speaker is quoting Mark Twain.

R

rack, wrack. The first is several words, differently derived, and the second is at least two words. The puzzle is their spelling. *Rack and ruin* can also be *wrack and ruin; cloud rack* is also *cloud wrack*; and there are other overlappings. Small wonder that some writers hang a *w* on every *rack* for insurance; if they did not, some mistaken copy editor might. Yet simplification is possible: any sort of framework, including the historical instrument of torture, is a *rack*, not a *wrack*; and *wrack* contains the core meaning of *wreckage*. This differentiation—all etymological hair-splitting aside—modern usage approves.

It follows that *w* is gratuitous, is in fact a mistake, in words that refer literally or figuratively to some kind of framework, or to twisting and straining, or to the kind of mental stress described as *on the rack*. *Clothes rack, hat rack, towel rack* are clearly right. Clearly wrong are the following: *the film made from M.'s wracking novel of love without hope / The machine was wracked with more tremors and seizures / the fog-bound, storm-wracked Gulf of St. Lawrence / No job search was ever more nerve-wracking / to see these pain-wracked bodies.* The expression *rack up* (= score, achieve, be credited with) probably derives from the abacus framework used in scoring pool.

All this leaves very little play in modern usage for *wrack* except as a noun, literal or figurative, for ruination, wreckage, refuse. In *Othello* Shakespeare writes: "A noble ship of Venice / Hath seen a grievous wrack." A playwright today might well use *wreck* but could use either.

range applies to colors in a rainbow, degrees of volume and pitch in sound, a set of points along a straight line—any series of like things that characterize or make up a whole (a *range of mountains*) or else the whole that the series adds up to (*her astonishing range of achievements*). To say, *The speech was an attempt to cover the entire range of his Presidency* is nonsense, for a Presidency is neither a series of like things nor their sum. The writer was probably thinking of time: *the entire length, the entire course, the entire duration.*

See also DIFFERENT, VARIOUS.

rankle. See TRANSITIVE, INTRANSITIVE.

rather. See HAD RATHER, WOULD RATHER, WOULD SOONER; UNDERSTATEMENT.

re-, prefix. See RE-CREATE, RECREATE.

re-create, recreate, etc. Americans do not hyphenate the prefix *re-* (anew, again) in the huge class of words represented by *reread, redistribute, reprint, retype, refigure.* But the hyphen is indispensable in a small group of words that without it run the risk of presenting the wrong meaning. Only the hyphen can distinguish *re-create* (create anew) from *recreate* (divert, amuse); or *re-form* (change the shape of) from *reform* (correct, improve); or *re-treat* (reprocess) from *retreat* (withdraw, fall back); or *re-pose* (put again) from *repose* (rest).

Of this group one of the commonest members is *re-create,* a ubiquitous word in book reviewing and a frequent one in historiography. Hyphenating it is especially important because the companion word is pronounced and syllabified differently. Nevertheless, in American periodicals *recreate* seems to appear without its hyphen as often as with it. *The utter confusion of the regime's final days is memorably recreated / The author recreates the great Alaskan gold rush / If only I could recreate for you the abject grief in that bedroom.* The omission of the hyphen can make for an annoying ambiguity: *For such a recreation few readers can fail to be grateful.*
See also HYPHEN, THE.

re-education. See EUPHEMISMS.

(re-)evaluation. See FORBIDDEN WORDS 2.

re-identification. Except in documents likely to be brought before a court, the re-identification of persons by repeating the name in parentheses is awkward and should be avoided. Example: *The bass player warned the lead singer that if tempos did not pick up he (the bass player) would go somewhere else.* Pronouns were invented for the purpose this practice labors at, and they must be handled so as to accomplish the work, even though the handling may prove difficult because of the lack of gender in English nouns. Consider: *He told his brother that he could send him through a college of his choosing if he were to give up his interest in their restaurant.* No distribution of *Joe* and *Frank* and their possessives — *he* (Frank), *his* (Joe's)—can save this example. Only rewriting will do: *Joe told his brother Frank that if he gave up his interest in the restaurant they owned Frank would receive as payment a college education in the school of his choice.*
See also ANTECEDENTS; THAT, WHICH, RELATIVE.

reaction. Writers do well to avoid *reaction* as a dull-witted makeshift for *response, opinion, thought, impression, answer, comment, feeling. What was your reaction to such-and-such* is the hoary cliché for the clearer and shorter *What did you think of it?* A publisher sent a novel about prizefighting to a retired prizefighter known for his urbanity. "My reaction," he replied, with politeness and candor, "was not propitious," thereby giving the impression that his vocabulary was not quite up to his jab. (See DICTION.)

Reaction in this sense is a figure of speech derived from science—first from Newtonian physics, then from chemistry, and finally from physical psychology. In physical science a reaction is an effect produced in matter or motion by another motion or piece of matter. But the chief characteristic of a good figure of speech is that it makes a meaning clearer by making it more graphic than it would be if literally stated. The trouble with this particular figure is that it makes the meaning graphically absurd. Ask someone, *What do you think of the Dodgers' victory?* and you invite a thought in answer. Ask, *What is your reaction to the Dodgers' victory?* and what you invite should be something like the motion of the leg when the knee is tapped.

Those who live by clichés can always find ways of making them worse. Consider: *Network officials were reluctant to react to this seeming threat from one of its hugely profitable stars.* A reluctance to react is a patent impossibility, reaction being what follows willy-nilly by the operation of natural law.

The case against *reaction* does not apply to this same word when it means the advocacy of a return to some earlier political or social state. *Reactionaries* and *the forces of reaction* we have always with us.

See also POPULARIZED TECHNICALITIES.

readership. What are UNNECESSARY WORDS in ordinary writing may begin as the JARGON of a trade. To those who publish periodicals and who advertise, *readership* means a group of readers they can examine for distinguishing traits such as income, interests, appliances owned, etc. *Circulation* is thought of as abstract and numerical. But *readership* too is abstract, and for the nation at large those who read something ought to be *readers*. It saves one syllable to say, *You're talking down to your readers,* instead of *to your readership.* And the concrete word discourages the frequent *Their readership are . . .*

reading (as in *reading from left to right*). See DANGLERS, BENIGN.

real, intensive. See UNNECESSARY WORDS 4.

realistic. See FORBIDDEN WORDS 2.

really. See VERY, MUCH, REALLY.

reason . . . because. 1. The point is simply made: *because* means *for the reason that.* Therefore *The reason is because* means *The reason is for the reason that.* Still, the habit of composing sentences that say both *reason* and *because* dies hard: *The reason for nominating him is because* (that) *he can bring along the whole North Side* / *My reason for raising the question is because* (that; the promise you made of) *you promised quick action* / *The reason for their protest is not because* (that) *the service was cut back but because* (that) *they got no rebate* (much better: *They protested not because the service was cut back but because . . .*) / *The reason* *for this letter is not because of dissatisfaction with your product* (omit *because of*) / *A psychiatrist suggested that the reason Hamlet could not kill his uncle was because he himself had wanted to kill his father* (omit *the reason* and *was*). Substituting *that* for *because* will generally restore grammar, but it may bring in wordiness. In that event, rewrite in such a way that *reason* equates with another noun: *My reason is . . . the promise you made . . .* / *The reason that he knocked was the light showing under the door.*

2. *Why* can be similarly redundant with *because*: *Why they finally broke up was because of his devotion to that ridiculous dog* (omit *Why* and *was*). Bear also in mind that *because* is a conjunction and cannot act like a noun. *Just because you pay the check doesn't mean that you can plan the whole evening* yields the sequence *because . . . doesn't mean.* Change *Just because* to *that* or start again: *You can't plan the whole evening just because,* etc. Nor can the conjunctive *because* act as the subject of *inclines* here: *Because he went no farther, but instead directed his 1501 expedition to the Labrador coast . . . inclines us to group him with Columbus in the westward search.* Change *Because he* to *That he*; if *because* is kept, change *inclines us* to *we are inclined.*

recognizing. See DANGLERS, BENIGN.

recommend never takes a direct object followed by an infinitive but always an indirect object followed by a *that* clause. *He recommended to his students that they should read all of Gibbon,* not *He recommended his students to read all of Gibbon.* The only way this teacher *recommends his students* is as objects of his concern during their search for employment. He then *recommends* them *to* an employer *for* a job; he may at times recommend the job *to* the student; or, as was said, recommend *to* the student that he or she take a particular job. Bear in mind also the logical relation of the parties. The guest does not say, *I was recommended to this motel,* but *This motel was recommended to me.* (See PREPOSITIONS; TRANSITIVE, INTRANSITIVE.)

record, verb. See TRANSITIVE, INTRANSITIVE.

redolent with is unidiomatic; *redolent* takes *of.* We no more say *redolent with* than we say *smells with.* Those who write *the whole house is redolent with the clean tang of spruce* may be half thinking of *reek,* which takes either *with* or *of,* though usually *of.*

See also PREPOSITIONS.

reference, verb. To say *G. in his book on Nixon referenced the President's table manners* means that G. provided a formal reference note on the subject. This specialized usage has lately been borrowed as a remarkably pompous way of saying that someone *mentioned* or *referred to* something or looked it up: *He referenced* (mentioned) *her speech last week as an example of her poor preparation* / *As for your hunches about D., I'll reference* (refer you to) *the final score of our game against the Pistons / Total snowfall was eight to twelve inches, depending on which source you reference* (look up, consult).

See also PREPOSITIONS; POPULARIZED TECHNICALITIES.

reform, re-form. See RE-CREATE, RECREATE.

regard (as). See AS 2.

regarding. See DANGLERS, BENIGN.

remainder. See BALANCE.

repeat. An act that is repeated must occur at least twice. This seems a simple requirement, but writers of *repeat* often blur the facts. Of a choral performance we read that *every repetition has been received with tumultuous enthusiasm.* The statement fails to report on the first performance, telling us only of those that came after. Of course the writer meant *Every performance has been received,* etc. When something is repeated twice it occurs three times and so on up. *"No, no, no!" she protested, and at the third repetition . . .* But *no* is repeated only twice.

What to make of the following direction, in which clarity is all important? *Indicated dosage may be repeated every three hours but not more than three times in one day, unless prescribed by your physician.* If the indicated dosage may be repeated three times in one day, it may be taken four times. But we are so easy with the imprecise use

of *repeat* that most of us would probably construe the direction as a warning against more than three doses in all; that is, two repetitions. In short, *repeat* has become risky to the point where accurate communication calls either for a total avoidance of the verb or for a precautionary translation: *may be taken not more than three times in one day;* or else: *may be repeated three times (four doses in all).*

One more repetition: if something happens twenty times, it is repeated nineteen times. Only thus can something repeated once occur twice.

replace. See TRANSITIVE, INTRANSITIVE.

replicate. See POPULARIZED TECHNICALITIES.

report, noun. See PREPOSITIONS.

reportedly. Journalists use this adverb less often than they once did, but from the dictionaries we do not learn why it is used at all. *Forty-one passengers and five crew members reportedly died in the crash.* How does anyone reportedly die? And what a way of saying *are reported to have died!* Such convictions are extremely rare, and *reportedly there had been only four previous ones since the law was passed* (only four previous ones had been reported) / *However, the owners of one franchise reportedly set up a scholarship at a cooking school* (are said to have set up) / *The reportedly severe epidemic broke out about two weeks ago in the south-*

western part of the state (the epidemic, said to be severe, broke out).

Most adverbs made by adding *-ly* to past participles sound awkward and often defy sense—*acknowledgedly, despisedly, discouragedly*, etc. The test of rightness for an adverb made from an adjective is that it fits the formula: *in [x] manner*. Thus *wisely = in a wise manner; clumsily = in a clumsy manner*. But *reportedly* becomes *in a reported manner*. Idiom has sanctioned *allegedly* and *supposedly* for more than a century; it may have been their example that promoted *reportedly*. But its predecessors themselves should be used with judgment. *The cast resented her for being supposedly indifferent* does not qualify the adjective as cleanly as does *resented her supposed indifference*.

See also ALLEGE; HOPEFULLY; UNNECESSARY WORDS.

represent. Representation occurs when one or more stand for many, a part stands for the whole, or a token stands for a fulfillment. Only in a mood of irony do things represent themselves: *Senator J. represents only himself*. At all other times things or persons *are* themselves. But because *is* and *are* seem weak, the urge is great to use *represent* in place of *are* or *compose* or *constitute. The twenty-eight seniors who graduated on time represented 35 percent of the entering class* (constituted) / *A flurry of eager phone calls represented her best efforts to resume cordial relations* (were her best efforts) / *Almost 3,000,000 people in and around Paris, representing three out of five per-* sons, had never seen a live performance of any kind (omit *representing* or substitute *amounting to*). The absurdity of 3,000,000 people representing three is evident.

repulsion. See MALAPROPS.

research. See FORBIDDEN WORDS 2.

residue. See BALANCE.

resource person. The pastime of holding conferences as an imitation of work has led to the creation of several new and needless terms. A *resource person*, be it said for the benefit of the fortunate stay-at-homes, is an able man or woman who can be relied on for a few sensible words at the right time. The phrase, besides being an offense to all other members of the group, is formed on the deplorable principle of linking ideas by lumping nouns without a clear joint between them. Everyone knows what a *resourceful person* is, and how he or she differs from a *person possessing great resources*. The new phrase wants to turn the resourceful person into a sort of caddy of fresh thoughts. One suspects that the organizers are vaguely thinking of *recourse person*—someone to turn to in need— an equally foolish phrase.

A second character in the cast of conference members is the *discussant* —needed, it seems, to ensure that some discussion, instead of benumbed silence, greets the speakers' papers. The obvious *discusser* was probably rejected because of *cusser* (= curser), but *commentator*, though not elegant, was available. New creations in -*ant* have a bastard look and sound, because that ending leans toward passive or intransitive meanings. A *consultant* is one who may be consulted (passive); a *disputant* (rare in the singular) is one who does not so much dispute as belong to a disputing group (intransitive). Sometimes, of course, -*ant* merely marks a distinction. Thus an *informant* is one who gives information but who is not an *informer*, i.e., a paid spy or a stool pigeon for the police. *Discussant* is on all counts an unfortunate birth.

Most recently added to this company of players is the *facilitator*. Though the elements of his role have not quite jelled, it seems that his duty is to draw out those who will not talk at all. Time will tell whether the *facilitator* takes the place and strikingly opposite function of the once indispensable *moderator*. In the meantime, certain schools have taken to calling their teachers *facilitators*, the implication being that they should not give but only elicit information.

For one more name bred by innovation out of conference, see *conferee* under -EE, -ER.

resources. See FISCAL.

respective(ly). These words are pointless whenever they are not given the task of clarifying a member-to-member correspondence between one series and another. Jane, Susan, and Ann can be married to Tom, Dick, and Harry respectively; W., P., and T. can be elected respectively magistrate, town clerk, and auditor. The word

need not be used in sentences where no such correspondence exists, only one series being enumerated. *Three of them are married and live in California, Connecticut, and Washington respectively.* The excess baggage of *respectively* may be due here to the worry that without it someone will infer that all three live in all three states. No one will. An encyclopedia article about Hieronymus Bosch tells us: *Two versions of* The Adoration of the Magi *are in Princeton University and the Metropolitan Museum of Art respectively.* The *respectively* is futile unless we are told which version is where, for no one will suppose that both versions are in both institutions. An author can afford to take for granted what every reader will take for granted.

The ultimate affectation of *respective* occurs when it not only fails to match one series with another but also fails to mention any series at all: *Each will spend six months or more meeting American counterparts and observing conditions in his respective field.* In a context so firmly singular, *in his own field* is the utmost that the traffic will bear.

rest. See BALANCE.

retreat, re-treat. See RE-CREATE, RECREATE.

Reverend, title. See TITLES AND PROPER NAMES 3.

reverse. See CONVERSE, OBVERSE, REVERSE.

revulsion. See MALAPROPS.

rhyme. See PROSE, THE SOUND OF 2.

rhythm. See PROSE, THE SOUND OF 2, 3.

right, in his or her own. Since Americans are not born to titles as are English peers, this phrase finds little legitimate work in American English. We attain standing, or so we like to think, by talent and effort, not by right. But the phrase, instead of decently loitering, turns up as a windy substitute for *himself, herself,* and *also.* Consider: *F.'s production of the García Lorca play will run for the rest of the summer. Her husband, a producer in his own right* (himself a producer) / *Their eldest son, a football star, graduated third in his class. Another son, a football player in his own right* (also a football player) / *When Anna Gloria drew ecstatic reviews playing Beatrice, ambitious Elena, as skillful an actress in her own right* (no less skillful an actress herself).

The standings we do claim by right are few. One may speak of a husband as *an American in his own right,* not by dint of marriage to a citizen; and *an*

heir in his own right, through birth, not through bequest.

See also JARGON; SAKE, FOR ITS OWN.

role model. See POPULARIZED TECHNICALITIES.

rubber meets the road. By dint of shrewd design and mechanical repetition, an advertiser's slogan, like a politician's, may haunt the public mind long after its subject is forgotten. So cleverly coined are some slogans that they find new life as common figures of speech. The catchphrase *where the rubber meets the road* pictured for the public the full weight and high speed of a car brought to bear on one brand of tire. The phrase soon stood by itself as an image of converging forces. Lately, speakers of weak imagination have taken to saying *where the rubber hits the road,* evoking an image of cars falling or bouncing. Perhaps *hit the ground running* (a phrase well past its prime) confuses them.

See also CAKE; COULD CARE LESS; CRACKS; FORT; LAY WASTE; SEA CHANGE; SET PHRASES; STONE.

ruralisms. See COUPLE, MISSING OF; GROW, TRANSITIVE; LOOKING, KNOW WITH INFINITIVE.

S

sacrilegious. See SPELLING.

saga. See LEGEND(ARY).

sake, for its own. Those impressive persons who say that they listen to music—or attend to any art—*for its own sake* convey three points: they are not hunting for a story or for correspondences to life outside the work; they are not indulging their emotions in a sentimental way; and they are nobler than others in doing proper honor to art. But a little reflection shows that *its* in *for its own sake* cannot refer to music, which, not being a person, cannot have a sake. The phrase does not parallel *I sent the money for his wife's sake.*

But if music has neither needs nor wishes that we can fulfill, what is the meaning of cultivating it *for its own sake?* One listens for one's own sake. But one may do so, not in the indulgence of reverie, but in more or less accordance with the exacting demands of the medium. So understood, *for its own sake* takes on meaning. But the phrase should not deceive the common listener into thinking it bespeaks a clear connection to the essence of the art.

Phrases like *for goodness' sake* and *for clarity's sake* are not affected by this caution. They mean *in the cause of goodness, of clarity,* which roughly correspond to the interests of a person.

same. When *same* joins two clauses, should it be followed by *as* or by *that?* The answer: either will do. *We hoped for the same welcome that we had found on our first visit / To the driver's alarm, the directions the child gave were not the same as those the man in the town had given.* In choosing between the little words, some writers distinguish the wish to compare (*as*) from the wish to define (*that*).

Another point: even in business English, *same* is not used as a pronoun unless one is joking. Avoid *We have your order for the electric spoon and are shipping same immediately.*

See also SUCH.

sanction. The verb and the noun *sanction* have played tag with each other until they have acquired almost opposite meanings, an oddity that often puzzles newcomers to the literature of international politics. To *sanction* a move or course of action is to authorize or permit it. To apply *sanctions* (economic or other) is to take coercive measures against a person or nation. Thus *to sanction* is to say, "Go ahead"; to carry out *sanctions* is to say, "You mustn't."

The history of this mix-up is not worth retracing. What deserves attention is a new derived meaning that increases the confusion. It comes from sociology and occurs in discussions of the law, whose punishments it correctly interprets as *sanctions*. But then, by using the verb in its participial form, and speaking of the *sanctioning system*, it fuses the two opposed meanings in one doubly ambiguous modifier. It is ambiguous in meaning and in grammatical function: *We expressly disclaim the view that sanctioning problems are "strictly legal questions"* / *Any competent observer of what happens in a courtroom or in any other sanctioning situation* / *The field of sanction law as we understand it is the entire process of sanctioning.* And as headings: SANCTIONING MEASURES AND THE SHARING OF WEALTH / THE IMPACT OF SANCTIONING UPON POWER. In reading these and other examples that might be adduced, the mind has to judge by trial and error whether permission or punishment is intended, for in ordinary speech *sanctioning measures* does not mean *punitive measures.* Let us hope that it never will. As for *sanction law*, it seems a redundancy beyond the license generously granted to sociology.

sanguinary, sanguine. One of Walt Whitman's biographers remarks: *By New Year's 1857 even the sanguinary Whitman could hardly have avoided realizing the seriousness of his failures.* The writer never dreamed that he was

calling Whitman either bloodstained or bloodthirsty; his intention was to say that Whitman had a hopeful, confident disposition. That is, he was *sanguine.*

See also ALTERNATE, ALTERNATIVE; FELICITOUS, FORTUITOUS; DANGEROUS PAIRS; MALAPROPS.

scarcely . . . than. See HARDLY (SCARCELY) . . . THAN.

scarify. See MALAPROPS.

scenario. See VOGUE WORDS.

schism. See PRONUNCIATION 1.

scientism. 1. The deserved admiration attaching to science and technology makes the layman want to partake of their glory by adopting their trappings. The result is all around us in many forms, from the design of household objects to the hybrid vocabularies of commerce and the professions. To be trusted, everything must wear the technical look and sound the scientific note. The frame of mind that produces these imitations, crude or subtle, is properly called *scientism.*

Scientism harms language. It answers neither practical need nor exact thought but is by its nature affected; and nothing so corrupts language in an advanced culture as affectation. Some of the foolish results of pretending to the technical are found in this book under other headings, notably DYSFUNCTIONAL; POPULARIZED TECHNICALITIES; COVERING WORDS; -IZE; NOUN PLAGUE; TELESCOPINGS; GERMANISMS;

and INITIALESE. Here the general tendency will be described and more examples offered.

At its most flagrant, scientism simply borrows a word from technology or science and puts it to commonplace use, there working it to death. Who hears any meaning now in the mechanistic *focus? The group will focus on the schedule of the January summit / The mayor's statement focused on recent charges of police misbehavior / The trustees say that those changes were part of a plan to reduce the university's size, refocus its mission, and . . . / Law enforcement authorities have focused on tackling the drug-supply problems at the source / Most of their programs have focused on benefiting families with children / men's growing focus on physique and self-improvement . . . / too obsessive a focus on the bottom line . . .* Many journalists prefer this exhausted figure of speech to the simple exactness of *plan, think about, talk about, change, revise, draw up, concentrate on, consider, study, discuss,* etc. (See META-PHOR.) Editors should note that a *growing* or *obsessive focus* is unimaginable—and that in the fourth and fifth examples *focused on* merely takes up space; *have tackled* and *have benefited* would do. (See UNNECESSARY WORDS 2.)

Other users imply that fiddling with a lens or a button is identical with thinking. *Would you like to sharpen the focus of your career objectives?* The writer is selling a service and may intend to be vague, but his vagueness goes badly with the technical term *sharp focus.* Worse, we commonly think of a device focusing on an object but not of something being *focused on* by an *objective.*

To these criticisms, writers might answer that it is unfair to hold them to the strict meanings called for in engineering or science. But why then write in technical words? Why not say in the first place, *Are you sure that you know what you want to work at and what jobs are best for your purposes?* But no, the air must vibrate with the click and hum of scientism—with *objectives* and *processes, potential* and *focus* and *factor*—until few people easily think in such science-free terms as *goal, work, purpose, know, ideas,* and *choose.*

But thinking is obviously not what scientism wishes to promote. It wants to simplify everything down to mechanistic action, one action to a subject. The fashionable suffix *-driven,* from computer lingo, lets an airport executive simplify grandly: *Our competition with the Denver terminal is fare-driven.* A stock analyst, equally sweeping, discerns *a liquidity-driven market.* And a city planner turns sense inside out by speaking of *automobile-driven Los Angeles.* From here it is but a short step to making believe that persons too are devices run by one type of fuel: *Lyndon Johnson was ambition-driven from the first / A praise-driven junior employee will only make trouble later on.* Presumably, reductive thinkers will always be with us, but scientism adds a tin-plate luster to their notions. (For predecessors of *-driven,* see *-minded* and *-oriented* under LINKING 3.)

Interface, stolen early from computer jargon and used for *meet* or *talk,* soon became an office joke through incessant use. Likewise on the way out is *input*—anything from a nod to a thick report. But *access*, already ambiguous in computerese, struggles to remain a pseudo-technical replacement for words as distinct as *nearness, permission,* and *knowledge of*; as a verb, *access* renders vague and pretentious every kind of *getting* and *taking*. Meanwhile, *capability* and *capacity* give a mechanistic rumble to even the simplest ideas (*reading capability* only means *can read*). Such words conceal the workaday truths about what people think and do. Hear a congressman: *I personally would be supportive of the capacity for that to occur.* What *capacity*, where? These kidnapped technical words encourage belief in imaginary entities and measurements: ad men discourse expensively on your *comfort level* and *the ah-hah factor*. (See LEVEL.) Even the everyday use of *positive* and *negative* to mean *good* and *bad, right* and *wrong, beneficial* and *hurtful* implies a ghostly gauge.

2. Scientism, often reductive in its effects, has but one aim: to impress. It disdains particulars and speaks in the general, the big abstraction that sounds inclusive and sweeps aside petty distinctions. Parlor psychologists talk of *acting out*, thereby "explaining" both a nursery tantrum and a multiple murder. The clinical *frustrated* is widely favored over words that say what we feel: *disappointed, impatient, jealous, puzzled, bored, teased, annoyed,* etc.

Scientism mars what should be clear with the aid of instruments that should not be dulled—words like CONTINUUM, *entropy, quantum, correlation,* EMPA-THY, *potential, nucleus, maximize,* DYSFUNCTIONAL, INFRASTRUCTURE, *process, fusion, mode, coordinates,* IMPACT, *component, critical,* CRITICAL MASS, *median, end product, side effect,* PARAMETER, *order of magnitude*. Some of these terms, to be sure, do no harm to prose except when they are used to suggest the solemnity of science. One naturally speaks of a book review as a *critical article* or asks for *critical comments* on a proposal; but the writer who, with some vague notion of *critical mass*, remarks that *such was the size and fury of the crowd that it threatened to go critical* (he means *to explode*) misleads his readers about the very word he is proud of.

The temptation to sound scientific hovers over office and classroom alike. Once students went to college to learn; now they go to *further their educational objectives* (much like the clients offered career advice above), and it is these objectives they are asked to INDICATE on their applications. Meanwhile, the faculties tell us that their own reports REPRESENT *the distillation of a series of discussions* and that they are *contemplating the stimulation of international interest* in their *uniquely articulated experimental programs*.

3. This fake engineering of simple things inevitably leads to coining new words for what is not in fact new. Scientism thus has much in common with advertising, where names of products differentiate makers at least as often as they distinguish unique commodities. Science works the other way: only to the demonstrably new will it assign the new label. *The name "Quadri-Science" signifies the four*

great areas to which the corporation devotes its resources: earth sciences, oceanography, atmospherics, space research. For *devotes its resources,* which suggests a charitable foundation, read: *will provide consultants and perform research.*

Quadri-Science recalls Winston Churchill's wartime neologism *triphibious*—as distinguished from *amphibious*—for which Churchill was rightly reproached. His *phi* is a broken-off piece of *amphi,* meaning *both*; *three-way* would have served better. But Churchill's temporary lapse brings up yet another bad habit. Science has traditionally forged its new words from Greek and Latin roots; it was able to do so intelligently because its practitioners knew the rudiments of these languages. Now commerce picks up the roots, or parts of the roots, without knowing what they mean and tacks them on to others or to English words indiscriminately. Thus we have the meaningless *-tron* (half of *electron,* the whole of which means *amber*) attached to *magni-, puri-, cavi-* (from *cavity*), *trini-, laundro-, reserva-,* and so forth. (See -ATHON, -THON.) It is sad that in christening discoveries and new products more effort has not been made to combine native words, as did the English physician who found the *knee jerk* (American: *patellar reflex*) and the English mechanic who made the *loud-hailer* (American: *megaphone*). One shudders to think of the words we would be using had it been left to our age to name *table, chair, luggage, house, father,* and *mother.*

4. Scientism also mimicks the scientific practice of writing in clusters of unarticulated words, as though English prose were arranged like the names of chemical compounds. The style can be expected in ads that wish to impress us with supposedly learned lingo. In the cluster *advanced German silicon cartridge technology,* is the silicon German or is the technology? We are not meant to care, only to goggle. In *a unique four-column distillation and three-step filtration process,* is the distillation part of the filtration process or a process unto itself? The fault becomes an embarrassment when one of the world's great libraries announces a lecturer who is *on the core faculty of the low-residency graduate writing program at B. College. Core* is no common adjective met every day, and *low-residency* is an improvisation which may apply to *graduate* or, then again, to *program.* Syntax aside, what do these curious modifiers *mean*? The writer of the brochure has lifted strings of words from an ill-written résumé and put them down without change or thought. Similarly, the English department of a great university publicizes its *Third Annual Victorian Studies Group Graduate Student Conference.* What seems to be meant, once we sort the adjectives from the nouns, is a *conference of graduate students in Victorian studies.* Prepositions articulate a sentence by showing the relations of words to each other. (See ARTICULATION; PREPOSITIONS.)

5. The scientific aim is ultimately that of the classifier and enumerator. Scientism imitates this sober outlook as best it can through the name or number affixed to a denoting word, as in botany or chemistry: *Operation Des-*

ert *Storm, World War II, Mark IV, age twenty, phase three, zone 5.* The same influence helps to explain the almost universal preference for *initial* over *first*—the *initial phase* instead of *the first step*—*initial* being a very old term in mathematics. It likewise makes adjectives out of every noun that acquires even a slightly technical sense: *societal, dialogal, interdisciplinary* (see ENDINGS 2), *interpersonal, group dynamical,* and dozens of others. We already misuse the adjectives ending in *-ological* (see OLOGIES), and the conviction grows that the best way to express our thought is to write *backers of the rose as the national floral symbol* for *backers of the rose as the national flower.* The same itch makes us say *Only 5 percent of the company trucks were mobile* instead of *were moving* or *were able to move.* And the urge to classify leads to tortured ways of saying simple things: *For passenger convenience* (as distinguished from what other kind?) *this bus is restroom-equipped.* The universe of buses becomes divided into *restroom-equipped* and *non-restroom equipped,* and ours belongs to the superior species.

The spirit of scientism will not die out from horror at seeing its effect on our language and thought. But it can be repudiated without much loss or strain if one always tries to say what one knows, wants, or remembers, instead of resorting to abstraction. Praising a renowned choreographer and teacher of dance, one of her pupils said, *She gave us a foundation to move in any direction we liked.* Setting aside the slipped grammar, one detects in the remark the highest compliment to a teacher, were it less technically worded: *She taught us how to dance and let us make our own styles.* It is in the two words *foundation* and *direction* that we can see the subtle symptoms of our trouble and can begin to cure it.

sea change. In JOURNALESE this bit of Shakespeare's lyricism has become a waterlogged cliché for any change that is rapid or large. *There has been a sea change in our whole political AGENDA since last year / The old ideals of movie machismo underwent a violent sea change.* No one in fact knows what a *sea change* looks like, for Shakespeare, in *The Tempest* (Act II, sc. 2), speaks only of decaying parts of a drowned man which *suffer a sea-change* into coral, pearls, "things rich and strange"; nothing is said of changes rapid or large.

See also CAKE; COULD CARE LESS; CRACKS; FORT; LAY WASTE; METAPHOR; SET PHRASES; STONE.

secondly. See FIRST OF ALL.

semicolon, the. 1. The COLON unites clauses or phrases that complement each other like close friends. But the semicolon links what might be called associates: two or more clauses or phrases gathered like partners to explore an interest in common. *I gave up trying to reach them with reason; self-pity was all they knew and respected / I do not wish to comment on the work; if it does not speak for itself, it is a failure / He cared nothing for money; he cared only for power / This sycamore is* *old; its lower bark is always dusty from years of floodwaters lapping up its trunk / One can never really explain a man, or track talent to its lair; and all attempts to do so are works of the imagination / Theirs are diversions which do not refresh; their minds will stiffen at forty; they will all think alike.* The semicolon tells its function by its form: part period and part comma, it signifies a short halt, a pause longer than the comma makes. It is made for connecting related thoughts that a period, the most emphatic break of all, would force too far apart.

The following passage shows, in its commas, semicolons, and periods, the gradation of pauses that punctuation conveys: *Once you discover your subject, it is no longer yours; you belong to it; you are lost. Your subject sits, walks, and lies down beside you, muttering about itself. It is there when you wake, it dictates a note about itself, it cannot stop talking at breakfast. Afterward it says with impatience: "Where was I?"* In this author's invention, the semicolons build piece by piece a premise; then comes a period, a definite break. The next two sentences illustrate ownership in action—both using commas, the shortest possible pauses, to build momentum. (For a discussion of linking clauses with commas, see SENTENCE, THE 1[f].) Once again, the period calls a decisive halt, after which the clinching statement arrives.

The timing of pauses in prose is a mark of style when they exactly serve what is said. Writing is itself a way of finding out what one means and how to fit the pieces together with links and

stops. Some British writers abuse the semicolon by making it a hook for an afterthought: *No one spoke out in objection to his treatment of the miners; but his son had fallen ill.* Americans who have just taken up the semicolon often succumb to the fancy that *all* their thoughts are joined by a secret logic for which they now have the right notation.

When using semicolons to link independent clauses, you may or may not want to add the standard connectives: *however, moreover, therefore, furthermore, nevertheless, whereupon, indeed, because, hence, whence,* and *whereas.* Examples without connectives: *They had started with provisions for three years; they had been in the field sixteen months / But it could be endured for one night; tomorrow they would be on their way / But truth is complex; we see it not whole but in bits and pieces; half-truth makes its contribution.* Examples with connectives: *She could sustain a conversation on court, theater, and social gossip more entertainingly than most; hence those who met her only at large gatherings thought her disappointingly superficial and frivolous / She replied that she would be happy to pay her share with no strings attached; whereupon he looked blank, agreed, and left.*

2. The semicolon not only joins clauses but briskly puts loose or unruly sentences in order. Use it wherever an introductory explanation founders in a floating *that* or *that is* which has no direction (see COMMA 10): *Dignity is the important thing, says Ms. M., that, and a real desire for an education*

(semicolon at the short halt after *Ms. M.*) / *This was only another term for prudence, which could be interpreted in an Epicurean sense, that is, enjoy life but act in such a way as to prolong the enjoyment* (semicolon or dash before *that is*).

The mark does yeoman service in preventing the appearance of parallelism where none is intended. *He agreed with Victor Hugo that Germany would become a republic in time, and that she had power to invade other countries . . .* At this point the reader is sure that the second *that* clause is parallel with the first and states a second point of agreement with Hugo. But the sentence continues: *was of little interest, since she would herself be invaded in her turn.* To forestall misreading, put a semicolon after *time.* True, the sentence remains faulty, for it does not show whether Hugo's agreement extends to the second clause or stops with the first. Only the author can settle that point.

The semicolon cannot stay clear of the tiresome question whether to include a comma before the last member in the series *a, b, c, . . . and n.* This old dispute is explored at length under COMMA, THE 1, where the advice is strong: include it. Note here that in a list of units which themselves contain commas and conjunctions, only the semicolon can distinguish between the units: *He is survived by his wife, G.; a brother, E., of Omaha, Neb.; a daughter, C., of Spokane, Wash.; two sons, M. of Bethlehem, Pa., and O. of Allendale, N.J.; and a stepson, H., of Carbondale, Ill.* Some newspapers change from semicolons to commas when such a list ends in simpler units: *six grandchildren, and two great-grandsons.* The change seems fussy. Those who follow through with semicolons should heed the advice for commas in a series: include the one before the final *and.*

senior citizen. See EUPHEMISMS.

sense of. See UNNECESSARY WORDS 2.

sentence, the. 1. With subject and verb. 2. Fragments.

1. The old schoolroom formula defines the sentence as a complete thought expressed in at least one subject and one verb. Sir Ernest Gowers collected ten other definitions from standard sources. But one could collect twice as many such specifications and do writers no service if abstractions did not yield practical guidance for dealing with wayward sentences. Some precepts are offered below.

a. A sentence should clearly name what it is about. It follows that the first precept is to set down an unmistakable subject. This may seem an obvious point, but one need only examine sentences in print to see how often their framers are eager to mask what is on their minds. Here is the opening sentence of an article from a great newspaper: *He kept to a dichotomous, back-and-forth regimen, and it was the same way with his Arab friends.* What is this statement about? We gather that somewhere, at some time, a male did something in a way characterized both by division into two and by alternation; next (and even more obscure), what he did or his manner of doing it somehow resembled the doing or manner of his Arab friends. Note also the technicalese: *dividedness* is rendered by *dichotomous*, derived from Greek and used in biology, astronomy, and logic; *regimen* is a medical term for a routine imposed by a physician (see POPULARIZED TECHNICALITIES). In the article following this jumble no physician appears, much less an astronomer. A reader with unusual patience will discover, instead, that the subject is a Yemenite immigrant killed by mistake in a Brooklyn shooting; the man had worked in a local delicatessen and often returned to his native country on visits. Four sentences later one learns that such visiting was the *it* and the *way* that were somehow *with* the subject's friends (see WITH 1). The writer might object that *it was the same way with* is idiomatic and thus exempt from grammar. But the writer has already done the following: deprived the pronoun *He* of a required earlier antecedent; stitched with hyphens the adverbial phrase *back and forth* to make it pass for an adjective; and dragged in two technical words that in his usage mean nothing. (He seems to have meant that the man *led a divided life*.) The ramshackle construction prevents the sentence from conveying any thought to the reader.

Inspecting obscurity is tedious, but it here makes the point that pretentious words and arty suspense are two of the vices that keep prose from speaking clearly. Should all dramatic effects be left out of news reporting? No indeed, but they must allow the facts to register promptly and plainly. The reader values the press not for teasing and tricks but for giving the sense of the news.

b. The second precept: writing prose requires that the writer bear steadily in mind the reader's convenience and absolute right to stop reading. Placing a pronoun before its antecedent is a slight that may turn into a blunder. Judge whether the author has respected the reader's rights in the following: *The preparations for the Queen's marriage were going forward, and the Emperor was turning over in his mind the desirability, since he could not have her put to death, of removing the heiress to the throne from her country before the son's arrival.* The Emperor is Charles V of Spain, and the Queen is Mary I of England. Charles is not ruling out the killing of Mary but the killing of *her* and *the heiress to the throne*, who are one and the same person: the Queen-to-be, Elizabeth. The son is Philip, later Philip II of Spain, who is arriving to be wed to Mary. By giving names to these persons before giving them pronouns the writer would not have snubbed and probably lost the reader. The function of a pronoun is to avoid repetition, not to pose a riddle. Other secretive sentences follow with repairs offered in parentheses. *An aerial camera was fastened to its nose, four or five big tin cans equipped with white parachutes and firecrackers were loaded into its cabin, and the red-and-white twin-engined aircraft raced down the uneven, short runway, took off, and roared low toward the north* (The red-and-white twin-engined aircraft, with an aerial camera . . . and four or five big tin cans . . . raced . . .) / *during the early summer when, after reaching its low point, business activity turned around abruptly and headed upward* (when business activity, reaching . . . turned). These sentences might become good ones through simple recasting; or they might entail the reworking of other sentences fore or aft. (See ANTECEDENTS.)

c. A coherent sentence stays with one subject until the writer has said what there is to be said about it, omitting all matters whose connection with it is not crystal-clear. This sentence buckles under five distinct subjects: *G.'s public career has been rough-and-tumble, but observers of the city schools, which have suffered their third budget cut in as many years, do not believe that increased overcrowding and scarcity of funds can be reversed by a new appointee at all soon.* The first subject, *G.'s career,* is elbowed aside by a second, *observers,* and a third, *which,* and a fourth and fifth, *overcrowding* and *scarcity.* The reader is whirled off in five directions by a writer who has, for the moment, forgotten what she started out talking about. At least two sentences ask to be written instead: *G. is well accustomed to the public rough-and-tumble, but not even she can soon reverse the problems of the city schools, observers say. School budgets have been cut every year for the last three years, and overcrowding has worsened.* In this version, two sentences are four words shorter than one.

Sentences in obituaries and eulogies often join facts that have nothing to do with each other: *Mr. R., who was born in St. Paul, Minn., entered television production after six years of teaching preschool children / Ms. H., a longtime resident of Greenwich Village, is survived by a son, D., of Concord, Mass.* From here it is but a short step to *A leading authority on poisons, she married four times but leaves no survivors.*

d. A sentence lacking unity of form or voice will achieve no momentum. *One could stand in front of Willard's Hotel and sooner or later nearly every soldier in the Union Army would pass by.* Unity of form can be given to this sentence by holding on to its first subject's point of view: *Standing in front of Willard's Hotel, one would sooner or later see every soldier . . . pass by.* Note next the jarring change from active to passive voice: *B. rushed to Hastings but was told that he could not go farther south.* Allow the active subject to rule, and it moves the sentence at a steady speed: *B. rushed to Hastings, where he learned that he could not go farther south.* Avoid the same lurch in the other direction, from passive to active: *The papers had been blown from the desk, and the wind was pasting them to the wall.* Rewrite: *The papers were being blown from the desk by the wind and pasted to the wall.*

e. No one should be forced to reread a sentence because its parts have been misarranged. A travel magazine states: *Expensive and somewhat snotty, golf tourists still fall all over themselves to play at Royal Troon, no doubt because of its long history.* Rewrite: *Golf tourists* still fall . . . to play at the expensive and somewhat snotty Royal Troon. A film-festival program reads: *Four young men . . . chart their futures with varying degrees of uneasiness while their formidable girlfriends move ahead with considerably more confidence.* This implies that the young men use their uneasiness as a guide to advancement; the sentence should have begun *Feeling varying degrees of uneasiness, four young men.* From a government statement to the press: *The agency has not the slightest intention of backing down from the course it believes to be right because of popular opposition.* The agency does not feel justified by opposition but rather intends to defy it; begin *Despite popular opposition, the agency.* All of the following misarranged sentences must be read twice to coax out their meaning: *Few listened as he spoke his piece patiently and without fidgeting in their chairs / Distinguished his career may have been, though some would say merely fortunate in his dispraise / How she managed to learn every one of the fifteen songs I'd like to know myself.* (See also LINKING.)

f. One kind of sentence profits by joining two or more independent clauses with no more than a comma. Such a sentence should probably have but a single subject, carried forward by a pronoun or else repeated, and the clauses that follow the first should add force to the single idea: *Life is the higher call, life we must follow / Lawrence needs to be gossiped about, he was that kind of man and writer / With each lie his mood improved, he*

felt exhilarated and full of power / *Conventions may be cruel, they may be unsuitable, they may even be grossly superstitious or obscene.* Julius Caesar's well-known dispatch *Veni, vidi, vici,* usually rendered *I came, I saw, I conquered,* is more than a series of related and compact statements. It elegantly condenses some such statement as *I not only came but also saw, and I not only saw but also conquered.* Only extreme fussiness would check the mounting force of Caesar's clauses by stopping them with periods or semicolons.

But Caesar's sentence and those which are like it in English do not contradict the schoolteacher's ban against what is termed the comma fault or comma splice: the casual use of the comma to join clauses so independent as to show barely a nodding acquaintance. *She wrote the song in 1990, it wasn't recorded until 1996* exemplifies this mistake. Its second clause neither gives nor takes force by adjoining the first, and the subject of the first surrenders to the subject of the second. The comma in this mismatch should be replaced by a period.

Those who have trouble distinguishing the comma fault from the lawful comma link had better avoid the latter and stick to semicolons, conjunctions, and sentences stopped by periods.

2. Among definitions of the sentence, Sir Ernest Gowers includes one from the Oxford Dictionary: "such portion of a composition or utterance as extends from one full stop to another," a *full stop* being a period, a question mark, or an exclamation

point. The Oxford definition takes in even the briefest imperatives (*Stop! / Relax / Come here / Forget it*), the shortest interrogatives (*Who? / Can we? / What's next?*), and the one-word exclamations (*No! / Ouch! / Wow!*). It also includes what are usually referred to as sentence fragments: groups of words that lack a subject, a verb, or both. The construction means to imitate casual speech and is often called the particular vice of the young. But such fragments are found in Tacitus and Dickens, and have for generations been used in the prose of advertisers. Some kinds of journalism now use them, as do several kinds of fiction. A sportswriter: *It's hard for him to think the Yankees would just let him drift away. But he's working for the wrong owner. Always has been.* An advertisement for medical insurance: *And more important, people can recover in a somewhat more comfortable environment. Like home, for instance. With family.*

Sentence fragments are neither so easy to use nor so charming to read as some writers think. Writing is both public and private, the writer serving as host or performer to one or one million, none of whom he can see, much less compel to keep reading. Nor will his tone of voice or facial expression be of the slightest help to the words he chooses to print. Only the words emerge, and by them alone is he judged. By using sentence fragments in imitation of speech, he means to heighten his intimacy with the reader. But even as he succeeds at that effort, he encourages closer inspection and subtler judgments.

Here are some sentence fragments and the judgments they can invite. From a novel: *Now Marco conceived the idea of giving his father pleasure, or comfort. A kiss, perhaps, on the temple? A few restorative pats on the shoulder? / Here came Richard. Umbrella, bow tie, portly biography wedged into the armpit, cigarette;* this is lifelike indirect quotation and brisk, straightforward description. Two examples from a journalist: *I like dirt bikes and off-road vehicles and all the rest but sometimes I like comfort. Like it a lot /* [A car tested earlier] *did better than 20 miles per gallon. The new engine gets a little less. Price of power, I suppose;* both passages decline into a curious tone of smugness. From an advertisement for a watch: *Bold easy-to-read numerals shout out loud and clear. Luminous hands and markers light up in the dark. Engineered to provide Swiss quartz precision accuracy at all times. Water-resistant to 330 feet. With a clean-cut date calendar;* this is the prose of someone writing to fit a cramping layout; hence *Swiss quartz precision accuracy* leads the reader to wonder whether *quartz* and *precision* are meant to be adjectives and what *Swiss* modifies; *resistant to 330 feet* is ambiguous. From a lumber company ad: *Well, I'm proud to tell* [children] *that at my company . . . we're growing 50 million seedlings a year. And then planting those seedlings on millions of acres of land. I think it makes the kids feel good to know that we care. That we're doing our part. And that we're going to make sure there will always be plenty of trees. For them. And for their kids, too.* This is bathos; the fragments lend a ham actor's emphasis to commonplace sentiment.

From an ad for men's shoes: *To succeed, no matter what the odds, is what separates you from the rest of the pack. Life is something you have mastered. In style. Because that's the only way you move. Always. And that's a powerful state. For if not for men like you, every winning shot would be hopelessly out of reach.* Since the act of writing is private, it allows us, sentence by sentence, to test the coherence of our thoughts. Snip sentences into phrases or single words and you lose the mental links that should have joined the fragments; what remains may be gibberish to the reader.

See also LINKING; PROSE, THE SOUND OF.

separate, verb. See PREPOSITIONS.

sequence of tenses. 1. In English as in other modern European languages, the relation between one time and another is usually told by the tense—present, past, or future—whose name marks it out for the purpose. This does not mean that all idioms use tenses logically; nor does it mean that ordering tenses logically is easy.

No ordering is needed when the adjoining clauses of a passage speak of times that do not differ. Take two such clauses in the past tense: *The two girls knew that they were hated because they stole for a living.* All of these events—stealing, being hated, knowing it—occur at the same time in the past. Change *stole* from the simple past tense to the past perfect tense, *had stolen,* and the meaning changes: the girls

were, in the past, objects of hatred for stealing done at an even earlier time. The past perfect conveys a past now finished, completed, "perfected" because unchangeable.

The statement of a present reality can take the present tense even when the statement is introduced by a reference to the past, in the past tense: *He said yesterday that evidence exists that will exonerate all three people.* Here the time of the saying (yesterday = past) does not affect the time when evidence exists (now and for an indefinite time = present).

The present may also, in the midst of a past-tense recital, tell a permanent truth: *His taunts fell on them like a rain of stones, and because scorn wounds as mere anger does not, they turned in a fury.* But this so-called eternal present (*scorn wounds,* etc.) can make ambiguous an adjoining clause if the tense of that clause is not carefully chosen. For example: *For the first ten minutes we kept the children busy and hardly aware of the storm. Being with us makes them quiet. But Mary stirred something wild in them just by her presence.* The eternal present of the second sentence leaks into the third, raising two possible meanings: (1) Mary's presence always has this effect and (2) it had this effect only on this occasion. Rewrite as *Mary had stirred* and the meaning is, as the author intended, the latter one.

2. Even when it strictly confines itself to past occurrences, narrative does not invariably use the past tense. The tense called the historical present may break in for vividness: *Indignant that the paper had said nothing, he wrote* an unsigned letter to the editor telling what he had seen. *Three days came and went, and not a word on the subject appeared. On the third night sleep eludes him.* Much favored as this variation is, skilled writers know that frequent seesawing between past and present will disturb the steady flow.

The infinitive likewise lives harmoniously with the past tense if the writer pays attention to what happened when. *She was the first woman to be elected to the House* is a perfect statement. But *He would have liked to have learned to drive* is written with verbs in parallel and puzzles common sense. Does he still wish he had learned? Then *He would like to have learned,* etc. (would like in the present [to have] learned in the past). Is his regret a thing of the past? *He would have liked to learn.*

3. The past is also the essence of the tenses called the present perfect (= complete, "perfected" now) and future perfect (= will be complete). These use one or more of the auxiliary verbs: forms of *be* and of *have, do, will, would,* and *may.* Keeping these auxiliaries in mind, one must make consistent the form of the past tense that applies to events taking place at about the same time. Here the writer fails to do so: *Surely the faucets must have leaked once in a while, or the refrigerator went out of order, or the drains stopped up, so that the handyman would be called over from the village.* Starting at the present perfect *must have leaked,* the reader expects the tense to be maintained through the list of probable mishaps, and he "hears" the false parallel [*must have*] *went.*

Much the commonest misuse of auxiliaries occurs with *may,* which far too often steals the place of *might. It was occupied by a Mr. Schneider, who had been particularly annoyed because the detectives seemed to think that they may find some papers that Brown left behind.* Clearly *may find* intrudes the present tense in a sentence that has used the past (*It was*), the past perfect (*who had been*), and the implied past perfect (*detectives* [*had*] *seemed*). The finding of papers is something that has not occurred, a matter of speculation (*seemed to think*), and so both require the subjunctive *might find* to parallel *might be.* Again: *If the family could have traveled, they may have found what they were looking for.* Here the first verb, *could have traveled,* is a past, stating an action that did not occur— and ruling out the use of present-tense *may* in the second verb; the past subjunctive *might* is called for. Yet again: *Had I been informed of the very real risks of permanent handicaps in babies of this small size, I may* (might) *have changed many of the medical decisions I approved then.* As before, the sentence begins in the past with a condition contrary to fact (*Had I been informed*); thinking of her possible choices in that same past time, the speaker does not mean to say what she *may* have done—she knows what she did and did not do—only what she *might* have done had the conditions been different. Notice the absurd uncertainty that *may* imparts to the following sentences: *Four of the eight persons killed may have escaped if the sprinkler system had worked / If the de-*

ceased had found counseling and legal advice he may be alive today / *Arthur here is the offspring of one amorous night that may have been avoided.* It takes no unusual grasp of cause and effect to see why each of these statements makes sense only with *might.*

4. The auxiliaries must be chosen with care if the tense and the mood of the verbs they modify are to be clear. But unmodified verbs are licensed by idiom to use the present tense to convey a future meaning. To say *If you go, I go* is the same as to say *If you will go, I will go.* In fact, one may mix the two forms without changing the future sense of either: *If you go* (present = future), *I will go* (literal future).

5. Note in conclusion a common error with the perfect *would have.* People say *I'd* as the contraction for both *I had* and *I would;* hence the colloquial statement *If I'd hit him, I'd have killed him,* in which the first *I'd* means *I had* (past tense) and the second means *I would* (future tense). Thus it is wrong to write or say *If I would have hit him I would have killed him.* No *would haves* of this kind follow each other.

See also SINCE 4; SUBJUNCTIVE.

set phrases. 1. Uses. 2. Inviolability.

1. Uses. For more than half a century conventional opinion has taught that clichés should be indiscriminately condemned. But in fact a great many set phrases are indispensable both for easy conversation and for effective writing. Such phrases offer brevity, clarity, and unobtrusiveness to those parts of a sentence that require no more. To try, for example, to explain in fresh language the ideas conveyed by *wear and tear* is to affect originality where none is wanted and to draw attention to what should stay neutral and vague.

2. Inviolability. The attempt to liven up clichés by inserting modifiers is a mistake: the phrase thus distended is neither original, unobtrusive, nor brief, and may not even be immediately clear, as in *They have been reticent to a tactical fault.* Again, what purpose beyond a distracting facetiousness is served by inflating the common phrase into *steady wear and accidental tear?* These are precisely the ideas embodied in *wear and tear* by itself. To speak of *Robert Redford, Paul Newman, and a roomful of lesser-known lights* does not enhance the figure of speech *lesser lights;* instead, it shows that the writer does not understand it. *At its best* is not improved or made vivid by the advertiser's *at its tastiest best* or by the ironist's *We saw him at his unexpected best.* The writer who thinks in ready-made images does not look inventive by adding redundant filler, as in *like a dog wagging an obviously gratified tail* or *The status, he announced, was to be strictly quo.*

Too often archness, bad enough in the open, winks coyly from parentheses. *At his (very good) best* and *does not mince (many) words* and *a (dubious) quid for a (nonexistent) quo* each distract twice over: how do the parentheses change the meaning of the words they enclose, and why use a set phrase at all if it does not say what you mean?

See also CAKE; CRACKS; FORT; HARD PUT; LAY WASTE; RUBBER; SPIRIT OF ADVENTURE; STONE.

sex, gender. Like many short words, *sex* is made to do a great deal of work. As a noun, its principal meanings are: (a) the classification of organisms according to their reproductive organs and functions (*The sexes were sorted at birth, the girls taken to live with the women, the boys with the men / She seemed to think women the sex which bears children and men the sex which bears watching*); (b) sexual intercourse (*Whenever she came to town they would meet for sex / We were not quiet after sex but silly, almost euphoric*); (c) the genitalia (*His sex he covered with the sofa cushion / Up came her skirt and there was her sex. What was I to suppose?*). The third usage is called slang by the Oxford Dictionary but is indispensable to journalism and fiction not at ease with FORBIDDEN WORDS. Then too, *sex* is a verb in science and commerce, and means *to determine the sex* of an organism.

Note that all of the meanings above have to do with biology. Some scholars in the latter part of the twentieth century, persuaded that men and women were dissimilar—or similar—in ways other than the biological, looked for a word to denote a distinction according to the rights and functions assigned by tradition; that noun would be a social category corresponding to *sex* in the first sense given above. The word chosen was *gender*, which had hitherto denoted (and still denotes) the grammatical classifying of words in some languages as being masculine, feminine, or neuter.

As often happens, the new academic usage has leaked into ordinary speech and writing. As happens less often, it has there proved of use in clarifying certain spare and ambiguous statements: *What determined promotion at our place wasn't skill but sex.* Does this mean that workers had to engage in sexual acts in order to be promoted, or that one sex was favored over the other? If the latter, *gender* might well replace *sex.* But *gender,* too, can be ambiguous. Consider: *L. came now to think him obsessed with her sex.* Here *sex* could refer to women in general, to L.'s femaleness in particular, or to her sexual parts. The context tells us to rule out the third interpretation, and to do so we may want to substitute *gender* for *sex*—whereupon we will find *gender* no great improvement on the shorter word. *Obsessed with her gender* could still mean *with women* as a group or *with her femaleness* in particular. The modern reader will need a clearer statement if the right point is to be made.

One more example shows *gender* in a somewhat different use: *T. failed to notice when sex relations colored a dispute between two longtime employees.* Here *sex relations* irresistibly brings to mind *sexual relations,* physical intimacy. But the author may have meant instead that the two employees differed in part over their assumptions about women and men. If that is in fact the meaning, the better phrase would be *gender assumptions.* But best of all would be a sentence that spoke of one worker *lording it over* the other or some such concrete description of what went on.

Notice that *gender* in the preceding

usage becomes an adjective; this may be the form it most often takes in its new academic employment. Lest phrases like *sex studies* and *sex language* evoke the biological, scholars in social science and even in the arts talk of *gender studies, gender roles, gender identity, gender language,* and *gender models,* often with the strict consistency that technical language calls for.

But specialists are using these abstract phrases as parts of theories that are largely unknown to the general reader. By contrast, good writing selects words that are particular, idiomatic, and clear on their face. No one seriously doubts what is meant by the Ogden Nash couplet *The turtle lives 'twixt plated decks / Which practically conceal its sex.* Nor do sly double meanings trip us up in *She's the ornament of her sex* (Dickens) / *For spirits when they please can either sex assume, or both* (Milton) / *The right of citizens of the United States to vote shall not be denied or abridged . . . on account of sex* (the Constitution of the United States).

Sex is an overtaxed word and should yield to *gender* when real ambiguity threatens. But the short word has served for five centuries, and modern readers generally know how it works.

shall (should), will (would), auxiliaries. In 1966, in the first edition of this book, Follett explored an intricate set of considerations that governed *shall* and *will* in British usage and, to a degree, in written American. Today many of these old refinements have ceased to affect our choice between auxiliaries; for most users both *will* and *shall* simply express the future tense. And of the two, *will* has undoubtedly become the more often used. A long-time American coolness toward *shall* has by now spread overseas; one British commentator writes that it is "broadly true that *shall* and *should* are slowly retreating in the standard language as used in England."

But *shall* and *should* remain well entrenched in certain American uses. *Shall* is still widely paired with the first-person singular and plural: *I shall get there late / We shall not be able to make it.* And *shall* speaks in all three persons in certain SET PHRASES (*We shall see what we shall see / You shall pay for this! / This too shall pass*) and when a tone of certainty or determination is wanted: "*We Shall Overcome*" / *You shall not be forgotten / They shall not go unanswered.* *Will* would not be wrong in any of these seven examples, but it would to varying degrees alter their tone. In particular, the song "We Shall Overcome" would lose elevation and force with *will;* so strong is *shall* that it suggests an inevitable future. American usage finds power in *shall* in declarative clauses, yet vaguely fears, for this very reason, that *shall* sounds undemocratic.

Shall takes a relaxed tone in questions, but in these it pairs with the first person only: *Shall we begin? / Shall I get it for you? / Shall we think it over? / How shall I recognize you?* But more and more often this *shall* is traded for *should,* which joins with all three persons and implies advisability or asks for a decision: *Shall (should) we risk it? /*

Shall (should) I call you tomorrow? / Shall (should) they consult you next time? Should also implies advisability in statements: *You should mention my name / I should have kept my mouth shut / We should give it a try.* Should also states likelihood (*N. should be here any minute / It shouldn't take long / This shouldn't hurt*) and states obligation: *He should be ashamed of himself / R. should have notified me beforehand / They should bring some identification.* (One can use the somewhat more forceful *ought to* in this kind of statement.) To turn an obligation into a command or requirement, use *shall* or *will* interchangeably: *Contestants shall (will) present their entrance pass.*

Lastly, *should* is the mark of the conditional: *If he should come around here, I'll call you immediately.* The indicative more casually serves the same construction: *If he comes around here, I'll call you*, etc. All told, *shall* and *should* still find much to do in American usage.

Even so, *will* and *would*, as noted, do more and more work in conveying futurity. *Will* pairs with all three persons in asking for information (*Will* [or *shall*; see previous paragraph] *I be in the way? / Will you be able to hear them? / When will he be finished? / How will the rest of us find you?*) and pairs with the second person in making simple requests: *Will you wait in the car? / Will you please quiet down?* In requests, *would* often replaces *will* (*Would you come in?*), as does *won't*, a contraction of an early form of *will not*.

Another *would*, which needs vocal emphasis, ruefully speaks of obstinate or predictable actions: *The lights were out, but you would barge in / The audience was leaving, but she would go on clapping.* This *would* has a corresponding *will*: *You will get excited over nothing / I plan carefully, but I will put things off when the time comes.*

Futurity aside, *would* also expresses, in all three persons, regular occurrences or characteristic actions: *We would sit enthralled every year, as if this story had never been told / Ah, the money. You of all people would think of the money! / He would do anything to make us like him.* Taking the speaker's viewpoint, *would* voices the wish that something were true: *Would that you had stayed an hour longer and seen the effect of your flippant remark / And that isn't all. Would that it were!* An older usage makes the first-person subject explicit: *I would that neither of them had ever set foot in this house.*

For centuries *will* and *would* by themselves expressed willing or wishing (Judges 1:14: "And Caleb said unto her, What wilt thou?" / *Troilus and Cressida*, Act V, sc. 5: "Hector! Where's Hector? I will none but Hector"). That function survives today in one form of courteous usage: *Will you come in?* means, literally, *Is it your wish to come in?* A courteous intention is likewise implied when *would* is used to moderate first-person verbs that express an opinion or preference: *I would say that the damage has been done / We wouldn't want you to go to any trouble / I would hope so / We would prefer that the party be put off.* To some American tastes, this subdued way of speaking is overhesitant or too deferential. But those uneasy with it may unknowingly use its barely detectable form in certain contractions: *I'd say that the damage has been done / We'd prefer that the party be put off.* *Would* lurks in *I'd* and *we'd*, just as *will* is contracted for *I'll* and *we'll.*

Contractions have long made life simpler for those who would rather not choose among *shall* and *will* and *should* and *would.* But many writers avoid contractions except for casual purposes (E-mail, letters, memos, etc.) and, when they spell things out, find *should* and *would* competing for a place in verbs. How to choose between them? Remembering that *shall* can exert a force that *will* cannot, we can organize the other pair accordingly: *would* for thought or preference that is easygoing and *should* for the same when stated emphatically. With practice, the ear will discern the difference. For example: the statement *I would like to explain our position* seems to wait for a warrant to go ahead. By contrast, *I should like to explain our position* intends to do what it says right now. Again: gentle or offhand agreement courteously says, *I would think so.* By contrast, nothing could sound more decisive than *I should think not.*

But even in first-person statements, American usage shies from *should* when it thinks that *would* can do just as well. One doubts that *would* takes force or anything else from the following: *I should (would) imagine that he thinks the same about you / I should (would) like to see more volunteers / I admit the point and should (would) even want to insist on it.* Those favor-

ing the downright style might omit both *should* and *would* in the last example, where *even* adds the emphasis. Those who stand by *should* for forceful statement do well to see that the context makes clear the meaning they intend; Americans frequently read or hear *ought to* when *should* is said. *I should have answered the phone immediately* can be read as avowing the strongest intention or only acknowledging humdrum duty. And the commonplace *I wouldn't say that,* emended by *shouldn't,* can be read as *I ought not to.*

shocked. See COVERING WORDS.

should. See SHALL (SHOULD), WILL (WOULD).

showed, shown. See MYSTERIOUS PASTS.

sic. Latin for *thus, in this manner.* See PARENTHESES, BRACKETS 2.

side effect. See SCIENTISM 2.

significant. See VOGUE WORDS.

significant other. See EUPHEMISMS.

simplistic. See ABSOLUTE WORDS.

since. 1. Causal conjunction. 2. Adverb. 3. Subordinating conjunction. 4. Implied lesson for use of temporal *yet.*

1. Causal conjunction. A groundless but long-lived notion says that *since* refers only to time and therefore cannot

be used as a causal conjunction. By this view it is an error to write: *Since you cannot keep quiet, you cannot expect to be confided in / Since you're dying for a vacation, why don't you borrow the money?* But there is no reason at all to avoid this usage, which goes back beyond Chaucer to Anglo-Saxon: the succession *sith-than, sithence, sins, since* meant literally *after that* and soon generated the figurative meaning of *given that* = because.

2. Adverb. Nor should it be doubted that *since*, when not a conjunction, serves respectably as an adverb interchangeable with *ago. How long ago was it? Oh, many years since / We expected delivery some time since.*

3. Subordinating conjunction. The right use of *since* as a subordinating conjunction depends on the tenses near it being correctly formed to show what has happened *since* the occurrence spoken of: *We have not seen Max since the money disappeared.* Two actions are spoken of here: not-seeing and disappearing. The earliest and completed action is *disappeared* in the past tense; the action *have not seen Max* occurs nearer to the moment of speaking and is not yet completed—Max may still turn up—and thus takes its place on the time line in the present-perfect tense. If you rewrite the main clause using the past tense (*We did not see Max since the money disappeared*), *since* will mark no division in time, there being none in the grammar. Everything—the we, the not-seeing, and the disappearing—floats in a vague, general past. The same is true of a simpler sentence: *Since A. was a child, the neighborhood changed.* Both *was* and *changed* are in the past tense, and thus seem to occur at the same indefinite past time. Change the wording to *Since A. was* (past tense) *a child, the neighborhood has changed* (present perfect); immediately A.'s being a child moves back in time, and the neighborhood's changing takes place *since.*

4. Implied lesson for use of temporal *yet.* The adverb *yet* in the sense of *until now* likewise unrolls a strip of time up to the spot where the speaker stands, and the verbs along its course mark by their tenses particular times in relation to the future that *yet* implies: *I hadn't looked at the photographs, and I told her so and said that we couldn't discuss them yet.* Here *hadn't looked* is the oldest action and takes the past perfect; nearer in time to the speaker are *told, said,* and *couldn't discuss,* and they take the simple past. *Yet* implies a change to come, on the order of *but we would.*

See also SEQUENCE OF TENSES.

single-handed(ly). See OVERLY.

skill(s). Until the educationists laid their hands on it, *skill* was a generic term that fused the meanings of intelligence and adroitness. A diplomat showed *skill* in negotiations; *diplomatic skill* was required for their success. The adjectives *skilled* and *skillful* retain the qualitative idea that has been battered out of the false plural *skills.*

The aim of the plural is not precision but pomp and advertising. When a course in writing is labeled *commu-nications skills*, it is not because of new complication in the teaching of rules, forms, and discipline useful in writing. The new phrase means instead to convey a scientific abstractness, a hitherto-unknown theoretical savvy, and to boast of the obvious fact that the student of writing learns more than one rule or technique. The plural now inflates an almost unlimited list of learn-able subjects: *computer skills, cooking skills, home repair skills, investment skills, library skills* for which the plain *computer lessons, learning to cook*, and *library use* are deemed insufficiently grand. As the glossier catalogues show, the next step up in pretension is *such-and-such arts*.

See also COVERING WORDS; EDUCA-TIONESE; SCIENTISM.

slash, the. Printers call the slash a *virgule*, and for centuries its life was blameless. Today graphic designers and curators of art exhibitions believe that the mark lends alluring mystery when used between two words or phrases in a title. But then the relationship between such words seems mysterious to the users. The slash has thus become the mark of lazy thought and of having things both ways. The exhibition title *Painting in Poetry/ Poetry in Painting: Wallace Stevens and Modern Art* implies that the poet referred in his work to paintings and, in turn, that some painters used the poet's words; the reader is to view these facts as somehow identical or— who can tell?—as different. But relationships too vague or complicated for

ready statement are normally expressed with a modest *and*, as the curators acknowledge with their subtitle: *Wallace Stevens and Modern Art*.

The woolliness of AND/OR always envelops the slash when it enters ordinary print; if *and/or* means anything, it means, unhelpfully, *and or or*. A movie thriller about enemies who assume each other's faces lost the colloquial title *Face-Off* in favor of the arty and confusing *Face/Off*. Does it mean *Face or Off? Face and Off?* When *bed and breakfast* becomes *bed/breakfast* or *a singer and dancer* becomes *a singer/ dancer*, what exactly is presented? Nobody would wish his bed to be his breakfast, yet no one could doubt that the *singer and dancer* were one to begin with. If space is short, he or she might be called *a singer-dancer* on the model of a *secretary-treasurer*. Conclusion: devices that catch the eye do not necessarily inform the mind.

The slash has been used since the Middle Ages to separate lines of verse when they are not printed in the conventional way on successive lines. It also occurs in abbreviations, such as *ac/c* for *account*, or to mean *a* or *per* in designating rates; e.g., *50 miles/hour, an acceleration of 16 ft/sec/sec*.

In works of reference (such as this book) the slash is sometimes used to simplify reading by marking off examples more sharply than periods can do when the sentences or phrases are not consecutive in meaning.

slightly. See UNDERSTATEMENT.

so, do so, done so. See VOICE 2.

so that. This conjunctive phrase should lead to a descriptive clause or a clause denoting result or intention: *Arrange the pieces so that they slightly overlap* / *So teach us to number our days that we may apply our hearts unto wisdom.* (The first could be written *So arrange the pieces that,* the second *Teach us . . . so that.*) In both examples the phrase means *in such a way that* such-and-such happens or is made so-and-so. But the phrase is unidiomatic and can be ambiguous when it means *to the amount that* and introduces a measurement of quantity or degree, as after *enough* or *sufficiently: The ice is still thin enough so that the beast's powerful head can make a hole from beneath.* It is not the intention of the ice to be thin for the beast's benefit— *so that* he can push his head through. Recast: *thin enough for his head to make; thin enough to let his head make.* In *the crops were sufficiently large so that we could buy local vegetables,* the crops act on no purpose involving us. Recast: *sufficiently large for us to buy.*

For *sufficiently . . . that* see THAT, CONJUNCTION 1. See also ADEQUATE.

societal. See ENDINGS 2; SCIENTISM 5.

sociological. See OLOGIES.

somewhat. See UNDERSTATEMENT.

sooner. See HAD RATHER, WOULD RATHER, WOULD SOONER.

spark, verb. See FORBIDDEN WORDS 2.

speak to. See ADDRESS, SPEAK TO.

speaking. See DANGLERS, BENIGN.

speaking likeness. Consider the number of English speakers who cannot bear to complete a sentence. They resort instead to lines of imagined dialogue, the more banal the better. *I took one look at him, and I'm, like, what am I doing here?* / *She worked on the exam really hard, but all the time she's, like, we never had this in class* / *The whole staff worked till midnight last night, but now they're, like, what do you want from me?* This is not slang, for although it follows a fad, it is not inventive. It is self-disabled speech, apparently afraid to finish what it has started. The form depends on *like,* which here has no meaning but only signals short-circuited grammar and dissolving intention.

See also LIKE 3; OKAY; VERY, MUCH, REALLY.

special. See VOGUE WORDS.

spelling. It is not yet four hundred years since spelling began to be made uniform by convention, and already people are restless under the convenience of it. On the pretext that English spelling is difficult and at times highly irregular, they want to change it radically, whether by using the present alphabet in some more representative way, or by devising a new alphabet of thirty, forty, or more letters.

Now, spelling reform is possible; it has taken place within the memory of living man, even though the many proponents of reform have rarely agreed about their recommendations. But a revolution in spelling can be faced with equanimity only by someone for whom the accumulation of knowledge has no vivid reality. For in a single school generation everything in our libraries, public and private, would, under a new system, become as unreadable to the vast majority as Cretan Linear B. And to suppose that "everything worthwhile" would shortly be transliterated and republished in the new alphabet or scheme is to know nothing about publishing or economics.

The gain, moreover, would soon prove illusory. The object of the revolution in spelling would be to make spelling easy by making it conform exactly to pronunciation. This sounds sensible until one asks: Whose pronunciation? The slightest variation from the norm (however defined) would lead to one of two results—different spellings of the same word or a single spelling which for many people would be arbitrary since it would no longer conform to their pronunciation. A Southerner may string *bob wahr* on a pasture fence, a New Englander use *bahb'd wiyah*, a Midwesterner use *barrb wirre*—and this is to give but the barest differences of three extremes within which dozens of different vowels, dentals, and *r*'s can be detected by the trained ear. The more an expanded alphabet distinguishes among the many possible vowel and consonantal

sounds, the further apart spellings will spread and the harder reading and writing will become. Or else the present disparity between a set spelling and a variable pronunciation will return, much aggravated.

Those who can see difficulties before they are on top of them are nonetheless willing to consider and adopt modest changes in our present spellings—e.g., the reduction of unneeded double consonants, and the like. But to carry out such changes is delicate work and of limited scope. Above all, the general outline of the word as spelled must remain what it was in Shakespeare and Bacon and Locke and Addison and Swift, or we are throwing out known good things for a dubious exchange. It is only conventional spelling, "false" to the eye, that keeps such a word as *raft* common to English and to American, despite the marked difference between the sounds *rahft* and *raaft*. And there is plain nuisance to be apprehended from misspelling, whether systematic and reformist or casual and coy. Even the uneducated *alright* is harmful as affecting *all*. The spellings we have are far from perfect but their irregularity has been much exaggerated, and the attainment of perfection is not so easy as the impatient destroyers think. No system of spelling, it can be safely affirmed, is going to be so simple and obvious as to teach itself, be learned in childhood without pain, and leave no uncertainties to middle age and beyond.

While tenable reforms are being devised, some few spelling difficulties and distinctions may be profitably listed here. For the example of *blond* and *blonde*, see FRENCH WORDS AND PHRASES. Note that *aneurysm*, the billowing out of a blood vessel, is no sort of *-ism*, but requires *y*. Remember the *s*'s in con*sens*us (= sense) and super*sede* (= *sed*entary) and the *u* in GLAMOUR—not an English spelling—which is dropped in *glamorous*. For *likable, salable*, etc., see -ABLE, -IBLE 2. And apropos of *e*, the way to avoid misspelling *sacrilegious* is to recall *sacrilege* instead of *religious*, with which the word has no connection. If it is necessary to write *desiccated*, think of the dried flowers in the hortus siccus—one *s* and two *c*'s. For *rack* and *wrack*, see RACK, WRACK. *Accommodate* has two of each of the consonants typists are in doubt about, and so has *embarrassed*; but *harass* has only one *r*.

Words in *-able* and *-ible* have to be learned one by one. Because of *responsibility*, most people spell *responsible* correctly with *i*; but they fall into *irresistAble* and *permissAble* because the nouns are rare. Similarly, the *correspondent* group with *e* and the *ascendant, confidant* group with *a* (there is also *confident* with *e*) must be memorized—or at least those words in each group that give one particular trouble. The doubling of final consonants or the failure to double them is often harmless. Everybody acknowledges the right of *traveller* to be *traveler* and vice versa. But *combatting* and *benefitted* each have by common consent one *t* too many.

Those who care about etymology will spell *autarky* when they mean economic or other self-sufficiency. *Autarchy* designates absolute rule by one person. Again, the phrase *passed master* should be so spelled when it refers to one who has become a master by passing the test—of the guild or of public opinion; for one writes that he has *passed*—not *past*—the examination. Hence *past master* is ambiguous unless one clearly means the former master of a Masonic lodge or incumbent of some other mastership that the person referred to no longer holds. The same relationship obtains between *passed muster* and [a] *past muster*. A different distinction is made with *e* in *therefor, therefore*. The first means *for the purpose just mentioned: He lacks the ambition and the ability therefor*. The second is the far commoner transitional word meaning *in consequence, accordingly: Man is mortal, therefore anxious*.

For the young who are learning to spell, the great trick is to close eye and mind to the incessant misspellings forced upon everybody by the advertiser. How natural that the school child, who reads predigested books of narrow vocabulary, should succumb to misspellings (mostly wrong vowels), when the television and the signboard, the newspaper and the magazine show him *Froot Loops, Eesyfit, Acuvue, Thick'n Fudgy, Wisk, Corn Chex, Tastee, Seequence, Fantastik, Lite*, and thousands of other pseudo-phonetic renderings of ordinary words, all carefully wrong in order to qualify as trademarks.

See also CATALOG, CATALOGED; PRONUNCIATION 2.

spilled, spilt. See MYSTERIOUS PASTS.

spirit of adventure, the. Many blunders encountered in print are the result of a single sally into the unknown, not to be repeated and perhaps never noticed by any critical user of the language. Charity should no doubt be shown to solitary lapses, but the restraining thought occurs that there is no telling when the venturesome flight will not inspire others. And when it does, everybody is brought face to face, sooner or later, with the misused *abrasive*, COHORT, DISINTERESTED, PRISTINE, and the rest.

The originators of possible disasters are to be found in all walks of life, just like geniuses. One of them is inspired to say *the make-ready* for *the preparation*; another speaks of his *upcoming play*—i.e., from the depths instead of from wherever it would come if it were merely *forthcoming*. From a college dean comes the sentence *Mr. F.'s inauguration was a happy and impressive event with abundant* good augury *for the future of the college.* The head of a foundation, addressing a committee of consultants, says he will *leave them to* coagulate *their thoughts.* A law reporter told newspaper readers that *lawyers, jurists, and heads of law schools* dominated *the list.* Diversity *was given by the presence of Lady J., who is,* etc. A State Department official confides: *I can say* in a distilled form *that the cease-fire will lead in time to release of the captives.* A novelist hoping to write an original sex scene describes his hero as *taking her almost attritively.* The

music critic, not to be outdone, advises *Don't miss this* exuberant program. And the amiable executive suggests that names be exchanged around the table *so that everybody can* earmark *everybody else.* All these locutions illustrate that spirit of adventure (or novelty hunting) which lacks judgment, sows confusion, and may cause permanent harm to the language.

split infinitive. The superstition that deplores the split infinitive dates from the nineteenth century. But the practice—putting words, most often an adverb, between *to* and the verb—has gone on since the thirteenth. To modern ears, the infinitive economically cuts out the stately *that* clause in sentences like *They have agreed that they will start on Thursday.* The sentence sheds weight and gains speed in becoming *They have agreed to start,* etc.

Of the split construction, Bernard Shaw wrote: "Every good literary craftsman splits his infinitives when the sense demands it." The sense of *She offered promptly to send over the money* is that the offer came promptly. If the writer means to say that the sending was prompt, he should move the adverb: *She offered to promptly send over the money.* The meaning is saved and, quite incidentally, the infinitive is split. The meaning will be likewise saved by putting *promptly* after *money*.

Some adverbs that double as adjectives will only sit still when wedged within a split infinitive: *They have no desire to hinder further efforts to rescue the children.* Notice that, looked at one way, *further* is an adverb modifying *hinder*; the sentence speaks of hindering that has gone on in the past. Looked at another way, *further* is an adjective modifying *efforts*, and the statement speaks of future hindering only. As it happens, the writer meant the latter sense and so should split the infinitive: *desire to further hinder*. Had he meant the former sense, he would have done well to change *further* to *future*.

stance. See CONNOTATIONS.

status quo. See POPULARIZED TECHNICALITIES; SET PHRASES 2.

stone, carved in. Being democratic, we wish to accommodate others, hence the reassuring statement, always negative, that a particular rule, decision, or practice *is not carved in stone*; i.e., it can be changed. In the positive, the image comes quickly to mind: laborious carving in the nearly indestructible stone. But those who misstate the negative seem never to imagine the positive. They say that something or other is *not written in* or *not cast in stone*. In the positive, the first is unlikely and the second impossible; thus the reassurance is feeble.

See also CAKE; COULD CARE LESS; CRACKS; FORT; LAY WASTE; RUBBER; SEA CHANGE; SET PHRASES.

stout. See EUPHEMISMS.

strived, strove, striven. See MYSTERIOUS PASTS.

stroll, stroller. See TRANSITIVE, INTRANSITIVE.

structuring. See JARGON.

style, type as appositives. 1. The use of these words in apposition with the name of a person or a thing is bad syntax. Even in speech *a champagne-style drink, an Elvis-type look* are felt to be either slovenly or comical—slovenly because the locution comes raw from the wholesaler's showroom (*a snakeskin-type plastic, Brentwood-style window treatment*), comical because there is some faint humor in sounding like a sales pitch.

2. Good usage has long preferred *like* in loose comparisons: *childlike, statesmanlike, lifelike*. Such established formations propose simple likeness, which the reader can judge, and do not appeal to categories—styles and types—trumped up on the spur of the moment. When the comparing word is not established but resorted to for a temporary purpose (*December-like, sheep-like, trance-like*), it should have a hyphen. Hyphenate also a word (*doll-like, troll-like*) that will look strange if printed as one piece.

subject. See PRONUNCIATION 1.

subject(ed). See PREPOSITIONS.

subjunctive. Except in a very few forms, the subjunctive mood is retreating from English speech and, more slowly, from written prose. The purposes it once served, of expressing doubt, contingency, or matters contrary to fact, are now quite often taken care of by verbs in the indicative, with nearby words and phrases to clarify the state of things. The Authorized Version of the Bible is full of subjunctives: *if it die, lest he forget, except ye be converted and become as little children.* But today it puzzles the ear when an editorial asks a question like *By what Constitutional right may we refuse such ads, if the group, as recent events suggest, be peaceful and law-abiding?* The *if the group . . . be peaceful* is archaic. The normal mood is the indicative *is*, the lack of full certainty being sufficiently expressed by *if* and the preceding *as . . . events suggest.* The indicative likewise serves for many suppositions, contingencies, and the like: *If I am stupid to go into this venture, you'd better say so.* No one today would think of saying *If I be.*

But this concession to simplicity does not yet carry over to statements — or rather hypotheses—contrary to fact. The dividing line between educated and uneducated speech is as clear about this usage as it is about *ain't*. One does hear *If he was to move to Seattle*, but educated speakers say *If he were.* And no one needs to be taught the formula for giving advice: *If I were you.*

Educated writers and speakers likewise insist on the subjunctive in subordinate clauses after verbs of saying, thinking, hoping, wishing, demanding, imagining, and so on: clauses that set forth what is not—or not yet—accomplished or true. Perhaps no one is tempted to say *I wish that he lives here*, but one runs into carelessly written

novels that say, *His grandmother gave him the house on condition that he lives here*, which is the same fault hardly concealed. Again—and this example will explain the retention of the subjunctive—one reads in a volume of musicians' letters in translation: *Mme Viardot suggests that she plays both Cassandra and Dido.* If she suggests that she *plays* both, she must be doing so right now. The forms *she suggests that she play both* and *on condition that he live here* not only present the distinction but correspond to the expanded forms *suggests that she should play both / on condition that he should live here.* Again, *It was vital to their case that not one but both drugs were present* is correct if it is a statement of fact; it must read *be present* if, as the context shows, the supposition is false or in doubt.

As for the rest of the surviving forms mentioned above, they are so usual that they cause no one any trouble. *Be that as it may; God forbid; far be it from me; come October we're leaving; I move that the minutes be accepted* have the force of idioms, and no one not a grammarian need even know where the subjunctive lurks or why. See also HAD RATHER; SEQUENCE OF TENSES 3.

such. 1. Pronoun. 2. *Such as, such that.*

1. Pronoun. *Such* is not a personal pronoun and so cannot replace *it, they,* or *them.* One or the other of these genuine pronouns belongs in the following sentences: *He declared that he had never had to depend for his safety on bodyguards and had no intention of*

having recourse to such / Men and women wrote poems for centuries before the computer; I fail to see how the use of such will make poetry better.

2. *Such as, such that.* Such as is close in meaning to *like* and is often interchangeable with it. The shade of difference between them is that *such as* leads the mind to imagine an indefinite group of objects: *great discoveries such as penicillin, the DNA molecule* . . . Comparisons using *like* suggest a closer resemblance among the things compared: *direct satisfactions of sense, like food and drink.* It is owing to this extremely slight distinction that purists object to *a writer like Shakespeare, a leader like Lincoln,* and similar phrases. No writer, say these critics, *is* like Shakespeare, but in this they are wrong; writers are alike in many ways and the context usually makes clear what the comparison is driving at. *Such as Shakespeare* may sound less impertinent, but if Shakespeare were wholly incomparable, *such as* would be open to the same objection as *like.*

When *such* acts as an adjective and closely precedes the noun, it must be followed by *as,* not *which* or *that. As* then introduces the defining clause. *The play was such nonsense, from start to finish, as we have not seen for years / We are such stuff as dreams are made on / It was such a battle as the local Republicans never had a taste for.*

The right use of *such that* is rigidly controlled by idiom: *such* must be an adjective followed by a defining clause signaled by *that,* as in *The terms of the contract were such* (or *Such were the terms) that no self-respecting actor could accept them.*

See also THAT, CONJUNCTION 1; for *as such,* see AS 8.

sufficiently. This adverb, like ADEQUATE, has a way of subverting idiom. It should be followed by an infinitive or *for* with a noun: *sufficiently tired to sit quietly / sufficiently light for use by beginners.* But it goes against idiom to follow *sufficiently* with SO THAT, as in *The hoofs of the young are sufficiently strong so that they can walk everywhere* (sufficiently strong to allow; sufficiently strong for them to). Those who dislike the chewy sound of *sufficiently* can try *enough,* as in *light enough for use / strong enough to allow.*

suffixes. See -ABLE, -IBLE; -EE, -ER; ENDINGS; -ING; -ION, -NESS, -MENT; -IZE; -LY; PROSE, THE SOUND OF 2; TRANSITIVE, INTRANSITIVE.

suggestion. See PRONUNCIATION 1.

superlatives, abuse of. See JOURNALESE.

supplement, verb. See AUGMENT.

supplement, supplementation, nouns. See VERBIAGE.

supplemental, supplementary. See ENDINGS 1.

surveil, surveillance. See PRONUNCIATION 1.

suspect 1. Adjective. 2. Verb.

1. Adjective. A great many innocent persons stand self-accused by saying they are *suspect* when they mean *suspicious*. A *suspect* person or thing is regarded with suspicion or distrust: *His account of his whereabouts that morning is suspect from start to finish / A promise by this commissioner to consult with local people always seems suspect / The entire water supply will be suspect until the tests are completed.* In these statements an *account*, a *promise*, and a *supply* are each *suspect*. But to say, *I'm suspect of the tax-incentive proposal*, both defies usage and turns the finger of suspicion 180 degrees. A *suspect* person or thing is the object of suspicion by others.

Persons harboring a suspicion are *suspicious*. It follows that one cannot be *seen carrying a suitcase in a suspicious manner*. (See TRANSITIVE, INTRANSITIVE.)

2. Verb. Only certain subjects qualify as objects of suspicion. *Arms are suspected of having been smuggled to the island by helicopter*. Arms are neither guilty nor innocent, and become even less so when treated in the passive voice: a subject cannot be suspected of something done to it. Nor should we say that *P. is suspected of having been murdered*. Find his last visitor and suspect him or her. The right form for this kind of statement will use the active voice with the acting agent as subject: *Detective R. suspects that P. was murdered*. If the agent cannot be named, the impersonal and passive will serve: *It is suspected that arms have been smuggled / that P. was murdered*.

See also VOICE.

suspicious. See SUSPECT 1; TRANSITIVE, INTRANSITIVE.

swimsuit. See -ING 1.

sympathy. See *empathy* under POPULARIZED TECHNICALITIES; PREPOSITIONS.

synchronicity. See POPULARIZED TECHNICALITIES.

synergy. See POPULARIZED TECHNICALITIES.

T

tacit. See IMPLICIT, EXPLICIT.

taking (account of, into account). See DANGLERS, BENIGN.

tamper. See PREPOSITIONS.

target, verb. See FORBIDDEN WORDS 2.

technics. See OLOGIES.

technology. See OLOGIES; SCIENTISM.

telescopings. Using an old term denoting a piece of luggage, Lewis Carroll called them *portmanteau words:* one could pack several meanings into a single container as one packs belongings for a trip. The author's purpose in "Jabberwocky" and other parts of *Through the Looking Glass* was comic. When James Joyce went back to the device in *Ulysses*, the purpose was the serious one of expressing related or divergent ideas simultaneously. Between *Alice* and *Ulysses*, the inventors of trademarks had made the practice familiar by their coinages. Today *Band-Aid, MasterCard,* and *Touchtone* are among the most readable of these compounds, whose aim is in part to be attractively playful, as in Lewis Carroll, and in part to suggest a fusion of powers, as in James Joyce.

Telescopings lost their charm for writers, but remain the marketers' preoccupation. Each new appliance, service, or patent medicine must have its virtues recorded in a hybrid name to show "dual," "all-purpose," or "innovative" uses, real or imaginary: *transistors, transponders,* and *selectrics* worked in new ways; but from the road a *TraveLodge* can hardly be told from the old *motel* (= *mot*or ho*tel*). Many of the newer companies and brand names glue together bits of Latin and Greek instead of borrowing known English words or their signifying parts. Only the creators know what *SynCronamics, Systacom,* and *Omnitek* are trying to say. Such toy language may be groping its way back to *Kodak,* which had the great merit of not pretending to meaning and of borrowing nothing to distort.

Magazines now tease their readers with *advertorials,* ads masquerading as editorial matter; the editors presumably know that the hanging *-orial* gives no intimation of journalism; it means only *of, pertaining to,* or *characteristic of,* as in *equatorial.*

This strip-mining of language ignores its continuity and its units of meaning. *Edu-* is no root, and the television coinage *edutainment* is baby talk, as are *infomercial* and *infotainment*. *Info* shows a mastery of slang but no awareness that the work to be done can only be accomplished by the root form.

Journalism coined the inaccurate *palimony* when it wrote about a claim for alimony in the breakup of an unmarried couple—not pals but lovers. It gave us also *workaholic* and *shopaholic*, whose frail link with sense could have been the root *-cohol*, which is absent in both. Nor is the business of government, education, and the law free from the desire to record multiple meanings by agglutinating words and parts of words into awkward but briefly catchy designations. This desire is quasi-scientific in its search for COVERING WORDS.

If compounds must be made, they will have a better claim to respect if they (1) clearly articulate the paired meanings, (2) denote a distinct and real thing, and (3) can be pronounced without distorting the constituent sounds. By this test *Hovercraft, flashback,* and *scofflaw* are excellent. But the British term *Chunnel* (the English Channel tunnel) derives an ugly sound by blending two words into pulp. And the American *sitcom* chops a meaningless phrase (*situation* fails to define a kind of *comedy*) into nursery babble.

See also SPIRIT OF ADVENTURE, THE.

temerity. See PREPOSITIONS.

tend, attend. See DANGEROUS PAIRS.

tense. See SEQUENCE OF TENSES.

testament, testimony, testimonial. See MALAPROPS.

than. See HARDLY (SCARCELY) . . . THAN.

than whom, than which. See WHO(M), WHO(M)EVER 4.

thankfully. See TRANSITIVE, INTRANSITIVE.

thanks to. See DUE TO.

that, conjunction. 1. Mishandling of *that*. 2. *That* omitted.

1. Mishandling of *that*. Surely the most frequent subordinating conjunction in the language, *that* introduces nearly all indirect discourse and follows the many verbs of saying and thinking. No word so much in demand is secure against mishandling. The commonest fumbles with this one are four: (a) absentminded duplication, (b) use after verbs of saying to introduce constructions that cannot be idiomatically joined to *that*, (c) use after words that idiomatically require other sequels than *that*, and (d) substituting *such that*, which has only one good use, for the much more useful *such as*.

a. In a longish sentence containing indirect discourse, it is natural to follow the verb of saying with a *that*; but on resuming the main line of the sentence after the intervening of other ideas, it is a blunder to slip in a second *that* without noticing that its function is already performed: *We are asked to*

*believe that when more than twenty lo-
cally elected delegates from the border communities met to list their problems — overlapping police jurisdictions,
conflicting inspection routines, and differing court policies—that this procedure brought out no facts which the
commission need take account of.* The
second *that* is only the first one repeated. Which shall we omit? If the
first, *when* will seem to the reader to
modify *asked* or *believe*, a mistake that
will blur the meaning of the clause
that follows. If we omit the second, *this
procedure* will seem to refer back to
routines and *policies*, an ambiguity the
writer's choice of *procedure* invites in
any case. Indeed, it was probably after
sensing that the reader needed help
that the writer added the redundant
that. Considerateness would be better
shown by a reconstruction that requires no such emergency aid after
long suspense: *After more than twenty
. . . met to list . . . should we be asked
to believe that this meeting brought
out . . . ?*

b. An imperative or a direct question
would never be introduced by *that* if
it was isolated and stripped of qualifiers. No one would write, *He told them
that why should such things be permitted* or *He demanded that let the
suggestion be publicly debated.* Yet
when just these constructions are
approached through an intervening
clause, we often find them heralded by
a *that* which has nowhere to go. *The
electorate seems to be saying that if the
Republican politicians cannot govern
themselves, why should they be allowed
to govern the state?* (seems to be asking

why, if the Republican politicians cannot govern themselves, they should be
allowed to govern the state) / *I can only
tell you that since you have believed in
the possibility of so many tragic and romantic villains having existed, why can
you not believe in the reality of P.?* (I
can only ask you why, since you have
believed . . . you cannot believe?) / *She
rounded on the council and told them
that if they wanted to convert Catholics
to Protestantism, let them do it by the
example of their lives* (they should
do it by) / *There is a growing feeling among environmentalists that if a
long, cold winter will end this bitter
controversy—let it come* (it should be
welcomed). (See also SPEAKING LIKE-
NESS.)

c. It is difficult to explain why *hopeful* can be followed by *that* whereas *optimistic* requires *about* or *as to*; the
reason is perhaps that *optimism* began
as a doctrine, not a feeling. But there
is no doubt about the idiomatic requirement. *Optimistic* and *pessimistic*
are samples of adjectives unfit to govern *that*; yet they are continually being
asked to do so, not least because politicians and broadcasters by nature prefer four syllables to any lesser number.
*They nevertheless are optimistic that
eventually they will be able to* (hope
that; are hopeful that; are optimistic
about being; confident of being) /
*Many are optimistic that an acceptable
substitute can be provided* (Many hope
that; trust that; are optimistic about the
provision of).

Idiom allows us to be *sure that* but
not to be *firm that*: *A studio executive
was firm that no changes smacking of*

censorship would be made (said firmly that). Similarly, we cannot be *definite that* nor *suspicious that*, nor need we be: *Senator G. was definite that she will not run again next year* (said definitely) / *Are you suspicious that he's not telling the truth?* (Do you suspect that). (See also SUSPECT 1.)

The word *sufficient(ly)* is likewise not to be coupled with *that*; it takes *to* or *for*. *The insurance companies may feel that their financial support of the candidates is sufficient that they can* (for them to) *dictate medical policy in this matter* / *He seems to think that he has impressed me sufficiently with his admiration that he can ask* (to ask) *for any favor.* The adjective and adverb *enough* could replace *sufficient* and *sufficiently* in these examples and be just as mismated with *that*. (See also SUCH; SUFFICIENTLY.)

Like these adjectives and adverbs, some colloquial expressions offer themselves as eager for *that* but must be denied. To *have one's fingers crossed* (in the sense of hoping for luck) is a case in point: *Network executives have their fingers crossed that the show will capture good ratings* (crossed hoping that; in the hope that). In general, speakers so favor *that* as a universal joint that they maim SET PHRASES: *Don't hold your breath that he'll repay the money* (waiting for him to) / *I do not intend to lose any sleep that H. will come back* (over the chance that) / *The speech was a shot across the bow that the nomination should not be entered* (across the bow, warning that the nomination).

d. The only construction in which

such *that* properly appears is one that denotes result: *His campaign was such that it won him more respect than votes* / *Turgenev's disappointment was such that for a month he did no writing.* Everywhere else in modern usage, *such as* rules. *You tell us only such news that* (as) *suits your purpose* / *We will leave only such forces that* (as) *may be necessary to keep the peace* / *packing only such food that may* (as can) *be readily eaten with a spoon or with the fingers.* (See also SO THAT.)

2. *That* omitted. Many writers, hoping to reduce the number of *th* sounds in a sentence or to avoid repeated *that*'s, look for chances to omit *that* as a conjunction coupling a clause to its verb. Two considerations govern the omission: (a) the sentence will remain clearly articulated only if it is short and simple; (b) the verbs with which the omission is least likely to do harm are those of saying, denying, thinking, feeling, hoping, fearing, etc. Conversely, those of answering, retorting, rejoining, complaining, and a handful of others will rarely work well if *that* is omitted. Here are a few successful sentences: *He thought she had already gone, and he was in a fury* / *The consul hoped the case would not come before him again* / *We felt we had been taken advantage of* / *Because he feared she was dead, he ran.* With the wrong verb or the wrong kind of complication, if only in rhythm, the need for *that* makes itself felt, as in the following: *He answered no one was able to describe the gunman* / *They could all certainly remember nothing had seemed to depress her.* Note how the omission

makes for false linking: *answered no one; remember nothing.* More bad examples: *If you sifted through all those words, they came down to this: he complained he was underpaid / Aristotle thinks (contrary to what others think he thinks) the ideal will stem from the natural in regular progression / Yet why should one among a group of so many refuse to acknowledge her behavior had seemed perfectly normal?* This misleading will occur every time a noun clause is the direct object of the verb and begins with a noun that makes its own sense with the verb—e.g., *He denies the allegation was based on fact* must be rewritten *denies that the allegation,* etc.

that, which, relative. 1. The alert reader will notice that quite a few excellent authors decline to use *that* and *which* in precisely the ways that late-twentieth-century grammar books recommend. Fowler in 1926 urged as a rule of thumb that the relative pronoun which introduces a restrictive clause should be *that* and the pronoun introducing a nonrestrictive clause should be *which.* The preceding sentence violates the rule while showing one reason for doing so: to avoid a cascade of *that*'s. Why set down *that the relative pronoun that introduces* if changing a *that* to a *which* can, with no ill effects, head off repetition? Note that *which* can replace only the relative *that* in *that introduces*; it has nothing to do with the conjunctive *that* of *states that.*

But what is a restrictive relative clause? It is one that gives a limiting, defining, particularizing description of the antecedent: *They uncovered the scandal that ended the mayor's political career* (= that particular scandal and not another). Nonrestrictive clauses—those where *which* occupies the place of *that*—add a comment about the subject, not a defining mark: *the curiosity of children, which has to be served / the suburban mind, which dwells on itself / a mania for storytelling, which had pretty well taken him over / the facts, which did not match up.* (For more on the difference between restrictive and nonrestrictive clauses, see COMMA, THE 3.)

Fowler summed up his prescription on the subject this way: "If writers would agree to regard *that* as the [restrictive] relative pronoun, and *which* as the [nonrestrictive], there would be much gain both in lucidity and in ease." By and large, American writers have so agreed, but not all at once and not without steadfast resisters (who join most writers in England today). Some writers hear a weakness or slackness in *that,* and some think *which* gives desirable emphasis to important restrictive clauses, as in *It was a noteworthy performance which did not find the arena packed.* The trouble with many such sentences is that only the absence of a comma distinguishes between two possible meanings. Here the writer probably means that the arena was packed for almost every performance (i.e., her *which* clause is restrictive); yet she could just as well be making no general point but only mentioning one performance both worthy of note and sparsely attended (i.e., the *which* clause taken as nonrestrictive). The difference in substance is left to depend on the presence or absence of the least of the punctuation marks, the comma, which is easily lost on its way to the printed page. The comma should not bear a burden that one of two words could take from it.

2. The well-read are accustomed to the use of either relative in the classics of the English language. Until about 1900 it was standard practice to interchange the two words and often to enclose restrictive clauses with commas, just as we now enclose nonrestrictive ones. In the King James Bible, Matthew 22:21 is translated as *Render therefore unto Caesar the things which are Caesar's; and unto God the things that are God's.* Dryden writes: *All, that can bring my country good, is welcome.* Given historical practice so free and easy, there is much to be said for systematically using *that* and *which* along Fowler's lines for the sake of greater precision.

3. But having said this, one must point out some useful departures from system. We have already seen that too rigid employment of *that* can lead to dull repetition when the relative pronoun and the conjunction come hand in hand: *We believe that that machine that we built will work.* Style apart, the desire for clarity should lead the conscientious writer to repair a sentence as bad as this one: *It is understood by government agencies that award grants that applications must not cite as referees members of the panels by which the case is to be judged.* No grammatical system designed for use should

prevent the first *that* from being changed to *which.*

Then too, *which* is the unavoidable word for restrictive clauses in which the relative pronoun follows a preposition. This last sentence illustrates the fact. And if one chooses not to write the perfectly good *We taught him the skill that he owed his promotion to,* then *the skill to which he owed his promotion* is the only way out.

Into every writer's life there comes the inevitable *that which.* You cannot write *The best soporific is that that experience recommends: hard work.* Although the second *that* is restrictive, it must be changed to *which* no matter what.

Repetitive *that*'s loom again in parallel clauses tied to a common antecedent. Consider: *The training that we got in the Army, and that we could have got nowhere else, stood us in good stead in civilian life / The courage that let him withstand repeated provocation, and that kept him going ahead, paid off in the end.* There are several ways to give an easier gait to such sentences as these. In the first, note that the second clause can be taken as either restrictive or nonrestrictive without any difference in meaning. Try: *Our Army training, which we could have got nowhere else;* or *The training that we could have got nowhere but in the Army.* The second sentence is improved even more simply: *The courage that let him withstand repeated provocation and kept him going ahead* or *The courage that, despite repeated provocation, kept him going ahead.* Thus the question of pairing *that*'s or *which*'s

THAT, WHO • 295

does not arise, and wordiness departs.

But what of the writer who wants, for emphatic effect, the insistent rhythm of parallel clauses? He can be assured that repeated *that*'s are in every way better than the switch from the second *that* to *which* or *who*. (See THAT, WHO.) He should act on the principle that equal elements ought to be kept rhetorically similar. *No village that has felt such destruction, and that can rise again, will lack for friends among the nations* may not be a sentence you cherish. But it avoids the awkward overcorrection of *No village that has felt such destruction, and which can rise again . . .*

that, who, relative. As is shown under THAT, WHICH, RELATIVE, there is a fairly strong historical tendency to use *that* as the characteristic pronoun of the restrictive or defining clause, and many writers conform to it by consistently beginning such clauses with *that*, thus distinguishing them from nonrestrictive relative clauses beginning with *which*. But a great many of these same writers do not feel comfortable with *that* as the signal of the restrictive clause about persons, for which they retain the *who* of the nonrestrictives. Kipling, for example, seems not to mind whatever appearance of inconsistency there may be in shifting from *The Light That Failed* to *The Man Who Would Be King* and *The Man Who Was*. As a matter of fact, the dislike of *that* applied to persons is not to be written off as a mere caprice. It is a usage that unquestionably leads into more frequent and

more extreme awkwardness than we can charge to the same *that* applied to things. Any writer or editor has to wriggle through a variety of such snarls as *fully persuaded that children that undergo the handicap of teachers that have only a perfunctory grasp of these fundamentals are to be pitied;* and it will not take many of them to persuade him that the substitution of *who* has its advantages.

Historically there is not much ground for objecting to *that* as a personal relative pronoun. *He that hath clean hands / the world, and they that dwell therein / He that is most knowing hath a capacity to become happy / They that on glorious ancestors enlarge / vile man that mourns / thou that listenest to sighs of orphans / I am he that walks / children that belonged to a man I didn't even know / An optimist is a guy that has never had much experience.* Such a scattering, which happens to reach from the King James translation of the Old Testament to Whitman, Mark Twain, and Don Marquis, could be extended to prove that the relative *that* refers to persons quite as naturally as to things, and quite as naturally as *who* refers to persons. Perhaps only habit will help one choose between *He that hesitates is lost* and *He who hesitates*. It often happens that *that* is obligatory and *who* impossible; for example, in Marlowe's line *Who ever loved that loved not at first sight?* it would be distracting to pile a relative *who* on the opening interrogative *Who*. We are, then, free to use *that* instead of *who* for a sign of the restrictive clause about persons, exactly as many elect to use it instead of *which* in a restrictive clause about things—and for similar reasons. Consider, for example, the ease with which we can remove the blight from *a couple who like(s?) music* by making it *a couple that likes music*.

Yet it is fair to say that the advantages of using *that* for *who* in personal restrictive clauses are not so clear and consistent as those of using *that* for *which* in impersonal ones. For writers who altogether reject *that* in restrictives and stick to *which* for all impersonal uses, there is of course no problem: they will also stick to *who* as a matter of course. But the writer who makes a general policy of the restrictive *that* for *which* will encounter more snags and drawbacks in the use of *that* for *who*—more causes of awkwardness, more occasions for making exceptions. The recommended practice, then, is (1) use *that* as an auxiliary sign of the impersonal restrictive clause except on those occasions when difficulty or ungainliness results; and (2) shift freely between *that* and *who* in personal restrictive clauses, according to which produces the greater ease and naturalness in the sentence. To these precepts a third might be added: (3) do not force yourself to use *that* in personal restrictive clauses if you think it an artificial way of referring to persons. A writer, after all, does not owe it to anyone to swallow his aversions. Style is, among other things, a product of what we avoid as well as of what we do; and there are writers to whom the use of *that* for *who* is not warranted in prose by examples from poets or the Bible.

To their ears *that* carries a thing-like connotation. In titles they feel that the excess of *th* sounds calls for relief by the euphonic insertion of *w*: just as television had *That Was the Week That Was*, because *which* would have made it a tongue-twister, so we have *The Man Who Was Thursday* and *The Man Who Died*, because *that* would bring on a lisp. To all such analysts of prose and of their own sensations, one can only pay respect while reminding oneself of Henry James's dictum that there is nothing in the world that anyone is obliged to like.

the. See A, AN, THE 4 and 5.

then. See ABOVE.

thinking, noun. See VOGUE WORDS.

this. See ANTECEDENTS 9.

this kind, these kinds, those kinds. A foreigner learning English would find these pairs no more difficult to master than *this key, these keys, those keys*. Quite soon, the learner would rattle off sentences like *I love this kind of movie* and *Do you sell these kinds of books?* By contrast, it never occurs to many native speakers to join singular *this* to singular *kind* (or *sort* or *type* or *style*). Many natives write: *These sort of paintings are little dramas / The neighborhood does not want these kind of shops / Cheating, lying, stealing—with these type of scandals dogging college campuses, integrity seems out of style / Today we'll talk about food and drink and those sort of gustatory pleasures /*

They decided not to run these kind of articles / *It isn't the implied promise of instant riches that I worry about; nobody believes those kind of promises.* What will the foreign learner make of *these sort, these kind, those sort, those kind, these type,* etc.? *These* and *those,* two plural demonstratives, are trying to modify the singulars *kind, sort,* and *type.*

The American Heritage Book of English Usage points out that it finds this hapless construction "in the works of British writers from Pope to Churchill." Nonetheless, the error in logic and grammar is an error, early and late, whoever commits it. No one writes *these army* or *these crowd,* though both nouns imply a group.

At first glance, the blunder appears as easy to repair as to commit. To rectify the grammar of *The neighborhood does not want these kind of shops,* make number consistent: change *kind* to *kinds,* thus telling how the neighborhood feels about more than one sort of shop. But watch out: the original context states that what is disliked are pornography shops. The singular *kind* was correct to begin with, and the sentence should read *this* (or *that*) *kind of shop.* Again: *Today we'll talk about food and drink and those sort of gustatory pleasures.* It takes only a moment to correct the grammar to *this sort* or *that sort* and to change *pleasures* to *pleasure.* But notice the sense. Once food and drink are specified, what gustatory pleasure is left to be implied by *this sort?*

The fact is that many statements using *kind, sort, style,* or *type* or their plu-rals have nothing to say about classes or groups of things; their real subject is only the thing or things they specifically name. Consider: *For what he did, he got power, possessions, status; those sorts of things were important to him.* Either *sorts of* or *sorts of things* is mere VERBIAGE. Try *those things were* or *those were* or add a comma and *which were.*

-thon. See -ATHON, -THON.

though. See ALTHOUGH.

thrift shop. See EUPHEMISMS.

thrived, throve, thriven. See MYSTERIOUS PASTS.

thrust. See METAPHOR 4.

time factor. See JARGON.

tinker, verb. See PREPOSITIONS.

-tion. See NOUN PLAGUE 2.

titles of books, movies, etc. See QUOTATION MARKS.

titles and proper names. 1. *Mr.,* etc. 2. *Née.* 3. Professional titles. 4. Nicknames and women's surnames. 5. When to use *de.*

1. *Mr.,* etc. Democratic ideas discourage Americans from thinking of *Mr., Mrs.,* and *Ms.* as the titles they are; hence we mix up titles with names: *I went to the house expecting to meet a woman named Mrs. Herbert. She proved to be a man named Dr.*

Harvey. Nobody's *name* is *Mrs.* or *Dr.* anything; one's name is acquired years before one's title. One should introduce oneself with *My name is Arthur Sherman* or *I am Mr. Sherman.*

The title *Ms.* was invented to resemble *Mr.* in not divulging the marital status of the bearer, which should, for public purposes, make no difference. Many women prefer to be called *Ms.*, but many others continue to call themselves *Miss* or *Mrs. Ms.* is used with both Christian and surname (*Ms. Elizabeth Jones*) or with the surname alone (*Ms. Jones*) regardless of whether a woman has kept her name or taken her husband's. But *Ms.* serves no purpose if used to refer to a woman by her husband's full name, as in *Mr. and Ms. Richard Jones.*

2. *Née.* The term *née*, meaning *born*, points out a woman's maiden name: *Mrs. Smith, née Jones.* Reason tells us that *Mrs. Jean Smith* was not *born Jean Jones* but *Jones* only; she was tagged with a first name later.

3. Professional titles. The use of the titles traditionally assigned to the professions varies greatly nowadays. In particular *Reverend* is battered by those who forget its adjectival meaning: *deserving reverence.* The respected man or woman so described must be called by the definite article *the* and a first name or initials (or a title, such as *Mr.*, *Dr.*, etc.) along with the surname: *the Reverend Daniel Blake* and *the Reverend Dr. Blake*, but not *the Reverend Blake.* It is not Blake or some Blake or other who is *reverend* but this particular Daniel Blake or Mr. Blake.

We address a physician as *Doctor* with no hesitation, but the title *Professor*, with or without a surname, enjoys no such settled usage. Its uneasy status may be traceable to its having been borrowed in the late nineteenth century by patent-medicine salesmen and bordello piano players. We may well call a full professor by his rank: *Professor Brown.* But no power on earth should persuade us to hail *Assistant Professor Stone* or *Adjunct Professor Martinez.* Today modes of address for academics appear to be matters of local custom, differing from region to region and even from department to department. There is much to be said for an older practice sidestepped rank by using *Mr.*, *Ms.*, etc., for all and sundry.

4. Nicknames and women's surnames. Democracy recommends informality, which we confuse with familiarity. *Informal* means *unceremonious*, but *familiar* derives from the Latin for *family* and implies both intimate knowledge and long-standing ties. When politicians call themselves by their nicknames, they invite us to feel familiarity. When journalists indiscriminately refer to politicians by nicknames, they invite us to infer long-standing ties which may prevent the detachment that good reporting requires.

Biographers too must consider how names will strike the reader. Should the writer of a life refer to his subject on paper by first or last name? Many use the first name throughout to induce in the reader the sense that both he and the author stand in a familiar relation to the subject; such writers run the risk of seeming too close to the person they have chosen to judge. Other biographers use the last name only, in the hope that it will guarantee their critical distance. Still others achieve subtle literary effects by moving back and forth between names, depending on the nature of the passage at hand.

In an earlier time, it was thought impolite for biographers of women to refer to their subjects by last names alone. A female subject was either *Emily* or the formal (and awkward) *Emily Dickinson*. Today biographies of, for example, Mary McCarthy, Gloria Steinem, and Simone de Beauvoir treat of *McCarthy, Steinem,* and *Beauvoir.* Journalists follow suit in referring to women in news stories.

5. When to use *de.* The French author named above brings us to the question of when, in writing French names, to use *de* and when to omit it. The full name gives no trouble—*de* is an indispensable part: *Alexis de Tocqueville, Alfred de Vigny.* The same is true if a title is used: *Comte de Gobineau.* But what of the last name when taken by itself? The answer may seem complicated, but in practice it is soon mastered.

To begin with, *de* is always used when it is attached: *Robert Delattre* when halved is invariably *Delattre.* All names whose *de* is separate fall into three classes: names of one syllable, names of more than one syllable, names of more than one syllable that begin with a vowel. Most names of one syllable must always have *de* before them: *De Thou, De Mun.* All longer names, unless they begin with a vowel,

must drop the *de: Maupassant* (not *de*) *wrote innumerable short stories / Vigny's poems are austere / Gobineau died in 1882.* But names longer than one syllable that begin with a vowel break the rule for long names and require *D': D'Argenson, D'Artagnan.*

To remember this rule of three, think of an example of each: *de Gaulle, Tocqueville,* and *D'Artagnan.* A further comfort: all the foregoing applies exclusively to *de. Du* and *des* are invariably used with the last name, short or long, voweled or not: *Des Moines, Du Guesclin.*

to, missing. Like *as,* the word *to* can perform only one grammatical task at a time. (See AS 2.) The writer of the following left out a *to: It was Rousseau, however, whom Madame de Staël singled out to acknowledge her intellectual debt.* The *to* that is present as the sign of the infinitive cannot at the same time say what must be said: the acknowledgment of debt is *to* Rousseau. Read, then: *singled out to acknowledge her . . . debt to.* Those who mistakenly shrink from ending a sentence with a preposition often revise such a statement by inserting the additional *to* before *whom.* The device would work here had the sentence been *It was Rousseau, however,* (to) *whom Madame de Staël chose to acknowledge.* But with *whom* set up as the object of *singled out* no such adjustment is possible—a reminder that the dogma about terminal prepositions is contradicted by the plain fact that they are unavoidable.

See also PREPOSITIONS.

together with. See AS 11.

too. 1. Meaning *also*. 2. Illogical uses.

1. Meaning *also*. Native speakers of American English so batter *too* that newcomers to the language often wonder what we are saying. Even used logically in its meaning as *also, in addition to, along with,* the little word can be ambiguous. Sometimes misplacement of *too* does the mischief, sometimes the choice of the word instead of one of its substitutes. The question to be asked of each sentence is: What is being added to what? *Japan was willing to donate supplies too* could mean *supplies in addition* to something else or that Japan *along with* some other nation was willing. To say the latter, put *too* after *Japan*. To say the former, put *donate supplies in addition* (*to* something).

2. Illogical uses. The idioms *none too* and *only too*, though fallen from the commonest use, remain crystal-clear in meaning. *He was none too pleased with the suggestion* = He was not pleased with, etc. *He was only too pleased to be asked to leave* = He was very much pleased indeed, etc., a note of irony attaching to his pleasure. But careless writers and many more careless speakers have converted *none too* to *not too*, producing a plague of ambiguity. After each of the following statements come a pair of equally possible interpretations: *I am not too worried about their objections* (a) I am not sunk in worry; (b) I care very little / *I don't have too much on my mind* (a) I don't have so much on my mind that

nothing else matters; (b) I have very little on my mind / *She is not too hopeful of the outcome* (a) She is not ridiculously hopeful; (b) she has little hope. Using *none too* instead of *not too* would restrict each example to only one meaning: *care very little, little on my mind, have little hope.* But it is also true that in these examples and in those that follow, omitting *too* has the same clarifying effect: We do not see [too] *much difference between the storekeepers' claims and those of the homeowners / Accusations from a man in that condition should not be taken* [too] *seriously.* Without *too*, all is well.

These tips for repairing the ambiguous *too* assume that the writer, editor, or teacher knows what a statement is intended to mean. But imagine the reader who, as a stranger, faces sentences like these: *As a collection of first poems it cannot be praised too much / This fabric is not too good for the purpose.* Are the poems bad or good? Is the fabric unsuitable or of just the right quality?

tool, metaphorical. COVERING WORDS impart flatness and grayness to the statements in which they are used. Few such words are grayer than the metaphorical *tool*, much favored in EDUCATIONESE: We utilize our urban setting as a tool / D.'s stories serve as a tool for bringing children's fears and dreams to light / Experience is a tool with which children grow to know their environment. So much for the surprise and variousness of actual cities, the originality and power of D.'s stories, and experience itself, which is no sort of tool but is life. Calling a city a *tool* would be patently absurd to the least imaginative child.

The incessant use of METAPHOR assumes that speaking and writing in figurative language can have no drawbacks. But to believe this, one would first have to doubt that language has power at all. No one who has watched small children mastering words can doubt that language, at the very least, strongly affects its user. Adults who habitually call the most disparate things by a noun denoting an implement of work should train themselves to call a spade a spade.

tool, verb. See CONTACT.

tortuous, torturous. See DANGEROUS PAIRS.

total, totally, modifiers. This adjective and adverb carry, as Fowler points out, "a latent sense . . . of things being added up." (See also MAJORITY, MINORITY.) *Total box-office receipts* means the sum of admission prices; *total hours worked* means just what it says.

In another use, the adjective implies not things added up but things *complete, absolute, utter, entire. Total war* is war that draws on all of a nation's resources; *total abstinence* is complete avoidance, usually of alcohol; *total recall* remembers everything noticed in the past. These are SET PHRASES.

But when *total* is made to modify nouns denoting a concrete unity or similarly single abstraction, the effect is silly. *The total executive* unintentionally evokes its opposite: the boss with pieces missing. Advertisements boasting of *total quality* propose what cannot be imagined: infinite satisfaction. Choosy as the adjective is, the adverb is made even more so by the persistent sense of "things being added up"; the mind infers an inventory. *The guerrillas were totally* (= all of them) *routed* gives no trouble; but *I was totally disgusted* brings you to mind in your constituent parts. This last is a slang use, the idiomatic words being *wholly, absolutely, completely, utterly, entirely.*

transitive, intransitive. Most frequently used in describing verbs, these terms can also mark what is implicit in several sorts of words: the source, the direction, or the place of an action. Heedless writers or speakers ignore this implication both in using verbs and in choosing adjectives and nouns. In one familiar example, we have the two adjectives *nauseous* and *nauseated,* whose endings show that the first describes the substance that causes the condition named in the second (*-ous = characterized by*; *-ated = acted upon by*). To call oneself *nauseous* is not to complain of illness but to boast of unpleasant powers.

Among verbs, *prevent* is an active (in our sense, *transitive*) word if ever there was one, just as *avoid* is by contrast *intransitive.* Yet a national bank instructs its depositors in the filling out of a form: *Avoid numbers touching one another.* These are not numbers to keep away from but to *prevent* from colliding as one writes them. And a business consultant is quoted as saying, *Giving advice* [to clients] *is a way to avoid me from giving unsolicited advice to my friends.* Her own action may *prevent* her *from* doing something else; it cannot *avoid* her *from* anything.

The coining of the noun *babysitter* has led to but one of several unfortunate colloquial verbs pertaining to infants. In *babysitter*, *sit* is intransitive, an action located in the sitter. But the statements *I babysit* and *I used to sit their Jennifer* may bring to mind the very transitive *sitting a horse* or a *saddle.* Along the same lines, the noun *stroller*, for an infant carriage, has led to the all-too-transitive usage *I was strolling the baby.* Idiom approves *strolling the boardwalk* and *strolling the fields* but draws a line thereafter.

The broadcaster who says, *The discovery culminates a four-year study to identify the gene,* has the matter backwards. The study itself *culminates* (= reaches its peak) *in the discovery,* which need not go anywhere. Often the dropping of the idiomatically paired preposition (in this case *in*) will send a verb in the wrong direction. A book review says of an author that he is *a life-loving anarchist more imbued in the whimsical tradition of Abbie Hoffman than the stern politics of Eugene Debs.* Neither reviewer nor editor heeded the fact that *imbued* means *dyed, stained,* or *pervaded,* all of which take *with.* One cannot *pervade* someone *in* something; the process goes in the opposite direction.

Provide has similar long-standing rights. A news story tells of a researcher looking into claims of outlandish abduction: *Several of his subjects provided R. accounts of being snatched out of* *their beds and whisked into outer space.* And an obituary for a writer states that his chronic illness *provided him a metaphor that runs through much of his subsequent work.* We can say that *Israel provided Mr. P. as an advisor* or that *Alice provided her son for the clean-up.* But no one *provided*—that is, gave over—the researcher R. and the ailing writer. Going in the other direction, the researcher's subjects and the writer's illness *provided* each man *with* something. Again: a letter states that *Commissioner Smith is attributed as writing,* etc. But he is not. A. *attributes* a statement to B.—it is a transitive act; B. cannot be *attributed as* doing anything. Similarly, *rankle* is intransitive, and no one's *remarks rankled the speaker*; they *rankled* (= festered) *in* the speaker.

Inexact writers ignore the practice of centuries in trying to turn a word from transitive to intransitive for no other purpose than to achieve a comfortable vagueness. Business and popular psychology make such an attempt with the verb *commit*, and journalists further the damage. *Why does R. think Congress and the Administration will commit to showing this kind of favoritism toward the cities? / B. is lucky to have found a man who could commit to marriage and a family. Many women face a barrage of men twenty-eight to forty who can't seem to commit to more than three dates in a row. / I felt that if we couldn't commit to living with each other for the long haul, how could we take on a dog?* The question is: *commit what* to cities, to marriage, to dates, to others, to a dog? The answer might be oneself, time, thought, money—and the answer is surely important. (No one would think of saying, *The son cannot seem to devote.*) Writers who lament non-committers but cannot say what is at stake will have made no point.

As if in response to these half-baked commitments, Americans like to declare that they are giving their all as if it were cash: *We are completely invested in the children / Our staff is invested in caring / I can't depend on someone who is so invested in the moment / Professor G. is invested in one idea.* Leave investments to brokers. (See VOGUE WORDS.)

Often, as in *nauseous-nauseated,* correlative ideas have bred paired words. To use them interchangeably is to destroy good work done. *An excellent compensatable compass* (compensating) / *All is not roses for the permissive child* (permissively reared child). Sometimes one form of a word is used so incessantly that its meaning is forgotten: *It is called the Foundation for Aging Research.* Whiskey but not research is improved by aging; try *Foundation for the Study of Aging.* By similar dinning we get *the performing arts,* which do not perform, *the creative arts,* which create nothing, *creative playthings, creative closets,* and the rest. Before adding *creative* and *performing* the careful writer will ask what arts—properly so-called—they exclude or include and whether that affects the point at hand.

The writer who embraces words for just their good looks learns their inclinations too late. Consider *A corpora-*

tion is the one place left where a man can accrue a considerable amount of power (power can *accrue* to a man; the man cannot *accrue;* he must *acquire*) / *I am constantly reminded to serve you with all the knowledge and ability I possess* (this advertiser can *remind* himself, can be *mindful,* or simply *remember;* unless nagged by someone, he is not *constantly reminded*). Again: *These were some of the foreign lands hied to during his travels* (he *hied himself to,* if so arch a verb must be used at all) / *Our speaker will envisage you the future of this great institution* (one can only *envisage* for oneself; *will describe to you*). Other examples that show the extent of the damage being done: *The lack of plumbing will not deter its being leased* (a circumstance *deters* a person from doing something; the verb wanted is *keep it from* or *prevent*) / *The new office will enable a closer liaison between the company and its public;* a device *enables* someone to perform a task; shun *empower* (see VOGUE WORDS) and write *make possible.*

Invented words, lacking a history, have no established direction. The auto industry invented *downsized* in the 1970s to describe the smaller American cars it was building. The term sounded technical and avoided adjectives like *small* and *shrunken,* which seemed downright belittling. Soon businesses of every kind adopted the coinage to describe a firm reduced in size by the firing of employees. Then the direction of the word was reversed: those discharged were themselves called *downsized* (the connotations: *reduced, diminished*), the switch avoiding such old, plain words as *fired, laid off, dismissed, let go.* (See EUPHEMISM.)

Coiners of technical and scientific terms often think they are achieving compression when they adapt a common word to a new use in disregard of what is here called its direction. Scientific practice leads to saying a *signed graph* for one bearing plus and minus signs and *lawful behavior* for a change governed by a scientific law. These extensions of meaning are neither necessary nor good. It is just as easy and does less harm to logic to say a *sign graph* and a *change the law of which is understood.* If *sign graph* sounds like *sine graph*, expend two more syllables: *plus-and-minus graph.*

Small improvement can be hoped for in the ragtag lingo of computers, which for now seems set; but some of its terms are worse than misleading. *Replace* in common use may mean either *substitute* or *put it back where you found it.* In computer jargon it means *obliterate old material in favor of new.* Then too, the basic apparatus of a computer program is termed, with masterly misdirection, its *environment;* thus what is inside a box is called by the word for what surrounds it. Predictably, *environment* has begun to float free of its logical moorings and to bring contamination to ordinary prose: *S. grew up believing that his father's setbacks stemmed from bad luck alone; in such an environment all of life seemed mysterious* (this conviction made all of life seem mysterious) / *All these years she had eaten what she liked, and the diet environment imposed by the doctors drove her wild* (omit en-

vironment) / *T. is said to be responsible for the environment of trust and security instilled in the minds of middle managers* (for the trust and security now felt by middle managers). In these examples, an effect is produced by a cause whose action and direction defy understanding. *Environment* has joined the COVERING WORDS.

Such ham-handed tinkering with language has influenced the writing of instruction booklets, once a high calling. Look up the procedures for using an electronic typewriter and you find that *the paper will then insert.* In no sense does the paper insert, and you yourself had better insert it. Farther on, grandiloquent transitives state that *the light illuminates* and *the light extinguishes.* In fact and intransitively, it only *goes on* and *goes off.*

Another technician's need inspired the use of *cladding* to denote the *clothing* of a metal with another substance — as if *clad* were not a past participle, which makes *cladding = clotheding.* Now *cladding* has invaded the house: the carpenter will *clad* your walls for insulation from heat and cold.

Such heedless wrenching of words leaves some adverbs, not pointing in the wrong direction, but pointing in no direction at all. *Thankfully, the governor vetoed the bill* (this is meant to say, *We are thankful that*, etc.; see HOPEFULLY) / *incredibly, the results will have to be gone over* (in context this may mean either *Hard as it is to believe* or *Because they are hard to believe*) / *Reportedly, both were unavailable for comment* (It is reported that or Reporters were told that; see REPORTEDLY).

See also ACCOUNT FOR; DIVEST; GROW, TRANSITIVE; -EE, -ER; INCULCATE; PURGE; REPRESENT; UN-, IN-, NON-.

transpire is the old, rather pompous word for what we now call *leak out*. Accordingly, it is not a synonym for *happen, occur, take place*. The sense of disclosure is clear in *It transpired that his brother had cheated him*. But *What transpired at the meeting is not known* states a flat impossibility: if anything *transpired*, the very word says that it is known. A reporter ties his thought in a knot with *Since little transpires that does not leak out, the Vatican is somewhat embarrassed*. Use *leak* or *happen*, whichever suits the case, and leave the flowery *transpire* alone.

trigger as a verb was foredoomed to be a VOGUE WORD the moment it was borrowed to signify the fission device that sets off a fusion bomb. By now it has eclipsed such varied terms as *set off, induce, occasion, precipitate, touch off, produce, be preceded by, initiate, incite, lead to, bring about, bring on*, and the plainspeaking *cause*. *What made that handclasp dramatic was the chain of events it triggered off* / *The sight of her standing there triggered a quick, unreasoning anger* / *lest a false move, as in a Grade B Western, trigger bloodshed* / *What triggered the long-dormant memory was the sight of a tearful child banging on a door*. In this way, diverse actions are all made to sound the same.

JOURNALESE likes short, dramatic verbs with hard consonants, which is doubtless why *ignite* rivals *trigger* as the word that most quickly short-circuits the rich vocabulary of precedence and causation. *Ignite* means *set fire to* or *begin to burn*; thus *igniting a race for governor* cannot be imagined.

triumvirate. The suppressed longing for Latin is shown in curious ways. COHORT is perverted by writers whose understanding stops at its first syllable. *Triumvirate* is similarly misapplied by those who grasp only the prefix *tri-*. *Harvard, Yale, and Princeton—this triumvirate ruled the ambitions of parents like ours, who imagined that learning depended on good name brands*. Dictionaries give support to the extension of *triumvirate* from its basic meaning of government by three men to administration by three parties or powers. But if the word is to survive as more than a pedantic substitute for *three, trio, triad*, and *trinity*, the parties or powers must be represented by individuals: *Radios all over Europe strained to hear word of Churchill, Roosevelt, and Stalin, the triumvirate on whom deliverance waited*. The writer means that deliverance waited on armies personified by three heads of state. The more one thinks about the applicability of this Latin coinage, the less useful it seems to English.

See also OXYMORON.

try and. Not suited to the highest reaches of eloquence, *try and* is nevertheless a sturdy idiom that need not be avoided or changed to *try to*. There is in fact a shade of difference between the two locutions. *Try to* is unmistakably purposive. Nobody is likely to say, *I'm going to try and walk from Maine to New Mexico; I will try to* comes naturally. But the very casualness of logic in *try and* is useful for occasions when no definite time or effort of will is implied. *He knows we want one; he'll try and pick one up.*

The English form is an old imitation of the Latin rhetorical figure called *hendiadys*, which means two for one. *The program is up and running* and *I'm good and mad* or *good and ready* are other examples.

type. See STYLE.

U

un-, in-, non-. Bottles, tanks, and trucks containing certain liquids, notably gas and oil, are apt to display the word *flammable*. This term came into being when it was found that more and more people mistook the word *inflammable* to mean *not capable of burning* instead of its opposite. The mistaken were reasoning by analogy from the many words beginning with *in-* in which the prefix means *not*; they were forgetting the smaller group in which it either means *in* or serves as an intensive or locating particle: *indrawn, ingrown, infect, inspire, incarcerate, insure*, as well as *intensive* itself and, of course, *inflammable* in its now less frequent use.

The change to *flammable*, if it averts accidents, is justified. But note that the shortening of the word has not touched *inflammatory* or *inflamed*. Speeches that incite to violence are still described by the former, as living tissue that is red and swollen is by the latter. Perhaps too the figurative use of *inflammable* (= easily aroused) will remain unaffected by the practical change and biographers can continue to speak of an *inflammable* temperament, rather than a *flammable* one.

The use of negative prefixes in general can puzzle speakers and writers who fail to pay attention to the usages that prevail in this realm of anarchy and strict rule. The only competent guides are a dictionary and wide reading. Still, a few hints can be given.

1. One group of words can take either *in-* or *un-* with no change of meaning and no unfortunate sound: *inalterable* and *unalterable, inconsolable* and *unconsolable, indisputable* and *undisputable*, etc.

2. Two other groups divide between them the *in-* and *un-* words that never vary: *incoherent, inescapable, indelible, indistinguishable, intolerant*, etc. / *unmentionable, uncontrollable, undiscovered, unusual, unacceptable, unenforceable*, etc.

3. Some words take *un-* in one of their forms (usually that based on the verb) and *in-* in the other (usually the adjective form): *undecided* but *indecisive, undivided* but *indivisible, undefended* but *indefensible, unsupported* but *insupportable, unvarying* but *invariable, unstable* but *instability, undifferentiated* but *indifferent, uncertainty* but *incertitude*.

4. Words occasionally but not often used in the negative take *un-*: *Despite their promise, they left the equipment unrepaired / He seemed pleasant enough by nature, but he was obviously*

undomesticated / *At that point the stream became unnavigable.*

5. Some words that take both *un-* and *in-* undergo a slight shift in meaning—or at least in connotation—when the form is changed. Americans are likely to say that an assertion or an argument is *inadmissible* and that a rowdy is *unadmissible*; that a course of action was *inadvisable* but that a man in a pitch of anger was *unadvisable*. The difference usually shows *un-* to be literal and *in-* figurative.

The difficulty of threading one's way through this maze tempts the cautious to simply avoid it by taking refuge in *non-*. This path is made still more attractive by the increasing desire to classify everything into two groups (see SCIENTISM 3); e.g., *fiction* and *nonfiction, alcoholic* and *nonalcoholic, age-determined unemployment* and *non-age-determined unemployment*. This tendency should be deplored, both because of the ugly, unarticulated compounds that it produces (see GERMANISMS) and because the twofold division with *non-* may suggest a strictness not always true to the facts. Moreover, the *non-* forms are often unnecessary, either because established *in-* or *un-* forms exist or because the contrast would be better made between a positive and a negative word. There is no need to say, *Weapons can be classed as defensive and nondefensive*, when the pair *defensive* and *offensive* is available.

Usage has set a positive meaning for certain words that bear negative tags. *Invaluable* is the best known of these; it means *highly valuable*, as does *price-less*. If one wants to say *without value*, one must say *valueless* or *worthless*; and for the literal sense of *lacking a price* one must say *unpriced*, because *without price* has also come to connote high value.

These results of idiom and rhetoric should warn a writer or speaker against believing that negatives are always what they seem and can therefore be coined or turned into their opposites by the adding or dropping of a prefix or suffix. The fact is that numerous words diverge in meaning from their ostensible opposites. Thus *shamed* is not the direct opposite of *shameless*, which refers to some flouting of morality or convention. The obvious example of *canny* (= shrewd) and *uncanny* (= ghostly, mysterious) should serve as a reminder of divergence in negatives.

Two other words that cause confusion or paradox deserve mention—*unloose* and *unbend*. The meaning of *loose* as a verb is clear in Shakespeare's image *many arrows, loosed several ways*; yet writers and speakers show a strong desire to intensify that meaning by saying *unloose*. It is as if *he loosed the dog* creates confusion with *lost*, or at any rate seems incomplete without an additional syllable. The urge to commit this mistake can perhaps be satisfied by saying *set loose*.

Unbend also lives in self-contradiction, but is beyond help. Figuratively, it conveys a stiff manner relaxing under the influence of civility, kindness, alcohol, or some other emollient. Logically one ought to write: *After a drink or two he bent*. But we say and will

continue to say *he unbent*. The confusion is made worse by the equally established use of *unbending*; a person of *unbending* courage or honesty is obviously one whose virtues will remain stiff and strong against pressure, fear, or temptation. So we are left with the linguistic curiosity of *unbend*, which means *soften, relax, become flexible*; and *unbending*, which means *stiff, braced*, and *inflexible*.
See also NEGATIVES, TROUBLE WITH.

unbend. See UN-, IN-, NON- 5.

uncanny. See UN-, IN-, NON- 5.

under-. See LAY, LIE.

underclass. See EUPHEMISMS.

underdeveloped   (undeveloped) countries. See EUPHEMISMS.

underprivileged. See EUPHEMISMS.

understatement. Like exaggeration, understatement must be used sparingly or it loses its ironic force and becomes an annoyance. Nor is it attained by merely coupling strong words with contrary adverbs: *faintly, slightly, rather, somewhat*. It takes more than such costume jewelry as *faintly appalled, slightly distraught, somewhat bizarre*, or *rather demented* to achieve ironic wit, even if that were proved more desirable than sincerity and good sense. Examples of what to avoid: *Her bringing up his name in the wrong conversations would prove, in the end, more than somewhat fatal to the secret* / Lis-

tening *to a story of failure by each in turn, he must have been rather enraged* / *Can you see how, coming from R., such a show of self-righteousness left me faintly nauseated?* To be sure, one can feel *faintly nauseated*—hence can logically say so—but the phrase runs the risk of seeming yet another two-step in pretentious understatement.
See also TOO 2.

undue, unduly. It is the occasional sport of these two little words to imply what is either perfectly obvious or should not be implied at all. You may, for example, instruct an employee to *avoid delay*. But if you tell him to *avoid undue delay*, you are telling him nothing he did not know before as a general proposition: what is *undue* should be avoided. Again: a police force that excused itself by saying that *we did not coerce the accused unduly* made a poor case, unless it thought coercion allowable in small amounts.
Similar illogicalities haunt other words beginning with *un-*. A treasurer's report does not reassure when it boasts of *a reduction in unnecessary expense*. See also UN-, IN-, NON-.

uninclined. see DISINTERESTED.

uninterested(ness). See DISINTERESTED.

unique. See ABSOLUTE WORDS.

unless and until. In common usage this LEGALISM, like AND/OR and WHEN AND IF, says no more with two heads than each head says by itself. If *the doc-*

tor will not lift a finger unless the account is fully paid, he will be likewise adamant *until* the account is paid. Nor does the full phrase gain point when *and* is changed to *or*. What needs changing is the wish on the part of ordinary citizens to sound like lawyers. Those who find the urge overwhelming will soon be writing *unless and/or until*.

unlike. See DANGLERS 3; LIKE 2.

unloose, verb. See UN-, IN-, NON- 5.

unnecessary words. First among words we could do without might be popular pedantries, like *parameter* and *synchronicity*, which displace common words so as to dazzle more than inform. The particular badness of such words receives a full discussion under POPULARIZED TECHNICALITIES. Here we consider: (1) needless variants, (2) filler, (3) adverbial dressing gowns, (4) dud intensives.

1. A number of words in modern English rarely serve useful ends, and some do no work at all. *Utilize* is of the first kind. The occasions when *use* will not do what is required are exceedingly rare; they show something being turned to a purpose it does not normally serve: *To clean the shivering cat's fur, they utilized corn meal.* But those who write *utilize* to imply abnormal use may find that the nuance goes unnoticed by readers accustomed to seeing the long word employed where mere *use* is meant. In short, the mishandlers of *utilize* have all but destroyed the nuance that makes it useful.

Preventative never was useful, it being no more than an antique misreading of *preventive*. Because the impostor is centuries old, some dictionaries give it as a variant; no writer need give it a thought.

Similar variants we could dispense with are *author* as a verb, *differential* (for *difference*), *disassociate* (for *dissociate*), *disassemble* (for *take apart*), *correlative* as a noun (see CORRELATE), *crafted* as an adjective (for *made, built,* or *designed*), and OVERLY.

2. Some otherwise good words are better off absent from a phrase or sentence where they only take up space. Such words as *sense of, factor, field, area,* NATURE, CHARACTER, *issues,* and *conditions* are most often filler. *I felt a sense of disappointment when the hour ended* means only *I felt disappointed when,* etc. And *He considered that the time factor was all-important* means nothing more than *He thought time all-important. Things of that nature* are only *such things,* as are *things of that character. A study in the field* (or *area*) *of economics* is probably nothing more than *a study in economics.* Those who urge that a candidate *discuss unemployment issues* want no more than to hear the candidate talk about unemployment. The weather bureau windily warns of *wind conditions; wind* will do. For the popular and empty use of *culture,* see POPULARIZED TECHNICALITIES.

3. One could make a long list of what Ernest Gowers aptly named "adverbial dressing gowns." These occur

in official prose, academic, corporate, and governmental, and follow the pattern of cliché in coming always with certain verbs: *seriously consider, thoroughly satisfy, uniformly lack, closely scrutinize, completely exhaust, deeply resent, satisfactorily complete,* and so on. The removal of the dressing gown discloses not nakedness but strength. And this goes for the couples made up of adjective and noun, whether the exact parallel (e.g., *serious consideration*) or the separate pairing (e.g., *avowed purpose, painful necessity,* and the worn-out *long, hard look*).

4. Note too that in most sentences the intensives *all, own, whole, very,* and *real* fail to intensify, and can be left out: *She swore she would have her own say whatever the lawyer's objections* (omit *own*) / *They expected to be bored by the speaker; instead they found her very stimulating and witty* (omit *very*) / *It was not a modest ambition— no singer's is—to want to be known throughout the whole world* (omit *whole*) / *Keeping three children occupied was a real test of his patience and stamina* (omit *real*) / *How much do two bad teachers matter in the achievements of the whole school?* (omit *whole*) / *The management refused to admit that it was a real mistake* (omit *real*).

The imported British intensive *all that* (sometimes shortened to *that*) is as illogical as it is tiresome. In *We weren't all that pleased with his work* and *She wasn't that happy,* the demonstrative *that* refers to nothing. Omit the affectation and write, *We weren't pleased* and *She wasn't happy,* etc.

See also FORBIDDEN WORDS 2; LIKE 3; LITERALLY; PERSONAL(LY); VERBIAGE; VERY, MUCH, REALLY; VOGUE WORDS.

unpractical. See PRACTICAL.

unquote. See QUOTE, UNQUOTE.

unthinkable is one word that cannot be sensibly taken as meaning what it says. The very fact of calling an idea unthinkable is an implicit assertion that someone has thought it. "*It is unthinkable,*" said the senator, "*that the Southern Republicans would offend Baptist voters by backing down.*" The senator could not have said this unless he had thought about the possibility he describes as *unthinkable.* What we mean by the word is of course *preposterous, impractical, not worth considering,* or *wholly repellent.* But even a square circle is thinkable; it is merely unattainable in actuality. Whatever can be named can be thought.

until. See UP TILL.

up till, up until, up to. The wish is very strong in American English to give more and more emphasis by gathering prepositions and other linking terms in little clusters around main words. First we *check,* then we *check up* (or *out* or *into*), and finally we *check up on* someone's progress or state of health. The practice is wasteful but harmless, except when the words so joined contain a hidden overlap or duplication, as in the phrases before us. *Till* means *as far as* a certain point in time or space; that is, *up to* that point.

Therefore *up till* actually says *up up to*, as does *up until*, whose skipping rhythm may be a further disadvantage.

upcoming. See SPIRIT OF ADVENTURE.

upon. See ON, UPON, UP ON.

upscale. See ONGOING.

usage, use. The noun *use* in the singular can be interchangeable with *usage* in the sense that a word aptly spoken is in either good use or good usage. But substituting *usage* for *use* when the meaning is usefulness, wear, or employment shows the speaker's dubious liking for unnecessary syllables. Phrases like *a graph of subway usage* and *a course in computer usage* are stately to no purpose.

utilize. See UNNECESSARY WORDS 1.

V

values. See POPULARIZED TECHNI-CALITIES.

various. See DIFFERENT, VARIOUS.

venue. Those who think the language of the legal profession useful in everyday English must not have thought long or well about the law. Legal JARGON is, quite properly, abstract, general, and distant. How then explain its present lure for those who should be fluent and precise?

Venue denotes the place of a trial (any place, any trial), as in the phrase *change of venue*. It could not be more abstract. But writers in the course of a year in one newspaper alone used it to stand for a theater, a kitchen, a tennis court, a community hall, an office, a rural district, a neighborhood, a meadow, Broadway, and the city of Belfast; the contexts mentioned no legal proceedings: *Anyone can bring a show here so long as they find a venue / spends the day cooking in clients' kitchens—a venue she says she vastly prefers to a restaurant kitchen / a [tennis] match at Flushing Meadow, a venue that could be mistaken, Mr. B. writes, "for a coal-fired hydroelectric facility" / In a neighborhood with few venues to serve its civic groups / Pro-spective clients [of fortune-tellers] should be wary; there is no venue for complaining about a lame prediction / As the show is cast and rehearsed and tried out at bucolic tourist venues in Oxfordshire / Men and women of the better classes could tour, for a fee, the dance halls, saloons, opium dens, and red-light venues of the city / Though there are paddle-ball courts all around the city—and high-caliber play can be found at venues like North Meadow in Central Park / Julie Andrews's return after more than thirty years' absence to the venue that made her / You may guess that Belfast is a swell venue for the action-adventure novel.*

In each of these examples, a COV-ERING WORD from law deprives a particular place of feature and interest.

A special case: The best print journalists call the sites of events in the Olympic Games by their simple, right names: *stadium, park, pool, track, court,* etc. Referring to groups of these, they say, quite properly, *sites.* By contrast, many broadcasters speak legalese in talking about the *yachting venue* instead of the *marina,* the *boxing venue* instead of the *ring,* the *swimming venue* instead of the *pool.*

For other legalisms, see also AD-DRESS, SPEAK TO; AND/OR; AS 5; IF AND

WHEN; PRIOR TO; RIGHT, IN HIS (HER) OWN; UNLESS AND UNTIL; VOGUE WORDS; WHEN AND IF.

verbal means *associated with words*; it does not specify whether the words are spoken or written. Thus no thoughtful person uses the phrase *verbal agreement* to mean an accord that is not written down. The right phrase is *oral agreement—oral* meaning *by* [word of] *mouth.*

verbiage. 1. The idea of excess or waste is inseparable from this term; it denotes words that ought not to be present, like weeds in a garden. *Verbiage* is an offensive label, whether apt or not, and no synonym for *speech, words,* or *wording.* When a sports broadcaster means to make a long story short but says that he will use *economy of verbiage,* he commits himself to a contradiction in terms: his phrase promises a shortage of excess, or not too much too-muchness. It follows that *You make the policy and I'll provide the verbiage* itself uses verbiage; what the speaker means by the second clause is *I'll write it up,* but what he says amounts to *I'll wrap the policy in a cloud of words that obscure it.*

The quite different term *wordage* denotes the number of words in a piece of writing. (See also CONNOTATIONS.)

2. As to what constitutes verbiage, opinions may differ about particular instances. But it is safe to say that in ordinary prose some verbiage is probably present. The classic excuse is that the writer of the topical book, the article, the memo lacked the time to make it shorter. Conciseness takes not only skill but patience, qualities no one learns in a week. In particular, young or inexperienced writers need encouragement to be succinct. Their first promptings to write have perhaps come from a love of words, and this love often takes the form of a belief that the more words *and syllables* they can use, the better. Only with practice does the amateur learn to express his love of words by making fewer of them count for more.

Getting rid of superfluous words has an advantage commonly overlooked: the automatic suppression of the half-baked ideas that flourish in diffuse writing but are starved out by economy. There is nothing like terseness for protecting the writer against himself—except silence. Anyone who will struggle to reduce one hundred words to fifty without losing meaning will see looseness, inconsistency, and aberration vanish.

To test this by example, take a passage from a book about life within the Arctic Circle—a book crammed with information about human and animal behavior, weather, travel, scenery, and other phenomena of the high latitudes; a book that has everything one could ask for except good, tight writing. Here is a representative paragraph about one of the ways of catching seals:

> Another way of luring the seal—although not so profitable as the first—is to fool him while he is under the water. Two men walk behind each other, keeping step with one another, so that the seal down below hears them. To the seal it sounds as if only one man were walking. When they reach the blowhole, the location of

which must be known first, the first man continues on, while the other takes a stand by the hole without moving at all. The seal thinks that the man has passed by without noticing the blowhole, and after a while he confidently comes to the hole, only to find out too late that he has been fooled.

Notice the defects. First is the illogicality of *Two men walk behind each other*—A. walks behind B., B. behind A. Next the clumsiness of calling the pair *each other* and *one another* in the same sentence. Notice also the chance echoes of *another* repeated, of *first* repeated, of *seal* occurring four times. Why write *continues on*, and mention *luring the seal*, since that is the subject of the whole section from which this passage comes? Why point out that the seal is under the water? *Blowhole* is enough, and it is obvious that the two men could not approach it if its location were not known. Further waste occurs in having the seal listen twice to their footsteps (*hears them; it sounds as if*). And a good reader will not care what the author thinks a seal thinks about what the hunter thinks. The writer talks as if to feeble minds. By the right kind of effort he could have said his say in a paragraph as short as this:

> Another, less profitable way is this: Two men approach a blowhole, keeping step, so that the seal hears them as one. The leader walks on past the blowhole; the harpooner stops by it, motionless. Soon the deluded seal confidently comes to the hole and is caught.

Protracted suspense has doubtless been lost in reducing 119 words to 46, but such an exercise in compression shows how much bad writing and bad thinking disappear in the boiling down: there is no longer room for them.

Verbiage and loose thought are at once the cause and the result of JARGON. In our foolish attempts to ennoble the commonplace, jargon lengthens the expression of every idea. Instead of *talking things over*, we *engage in a positive dialogue*; instead of *asking her why*, we *inquire as to her perception of her motivation*; instead of *clearing the air*, we *facilitate the mutual expression of underlying roadblock issues*. We do not *play* or *have fun* but *participate in recreational activities*. We do not *hunger* or *thirst* but *experience nutritional deficiency* or *significant dehydration*.

The very words themselves expand with the hot air put forth. The verb *orient* (for *set right*) has become *orientate*; *difference*, *differential* and *differentiation*; *delimit*, *delimitate*; *supplement*, *supplementation*; and so on through the vast realm of our earnest vocabulary for public use. Verbiage is the rule, clear prose the exception. Since readers everywhere complain of the length and dullness of what is put before their eyes, they are obliged, when they write in their turn, to reduce as much as they can the world output of verbiage.

verbs. See MYSTERIOUS PASTS; SEQUENCE OF TENSES; SUBJUNCTIVE; TRANSITIVE, INTRANSITIVE; VOICE; WHAT IS "UNDERSTOOD"?

very, much, really. Inexperienced writers are routinely warned to avoid the intensive *very*. Overworked for countless years, it has so lost force that it can perversely weaken the adjective or adverb its user hopes to make stronger. Those who respect its condition and its need of rest learn to call on it rarely—and then for an emphasis little more than polite.

Very might regain some strength if more writers were taught that it goes with ordinary adjectives (*tall, sorry, lazy*) but not with adjectives formed on verbs (*disappointed, delighted, neglected*); careful writers use *much* with these. *Much* modifies an action undergone (*I've been much entertained and much instructed by her stories*). *Very* modifies adjectives implying no action but only a quality (*A. is very obtuse; his manners are very inept*). Again: *much annoyed* but *very lazy; much engrossed* but *very stupid; much applauded* but *very drunk*. The combined *very much* is only an intensified *much* and goes where *much* goes.

But today in edited print *very concerned, very delighted, very disappointed* are common. Yet the blurring does not go both ways: no one is called *much stupid* or *much drunk*. The confusion of *much* and *very* may have to do with a general weakening of the adverbial sense, a feebleness marked by the rise of *really* as another all-purpose intensive. Flimsy though it is, *really* now tries to underscore adjective and verbal adjective alike: *really rich, really bad, really disappointed, really frustrated*; when pronounced *rilly* it is as thin in sound as in sense. Some who helplessly use it for all occasions have never learned that adverbs are expressive devices which increase and invigorate meaning. The educated who lazily lean on *really* ignore a God's plenty of lively words.

See also LIKE 3; LITERALLY; PERSONAL(LY); SPEAKING LIKENESS; UNNECESSARY WORDS 4.

vested interest(s). See VOGUE WORDS.

viable. See METAPHOR 3; VOGUE WORDS.

view, noun. See PREPOSITIONS.

view (as). See AS 2.

viewing. See DANGLERS, BENIGN.

virgule, the. See SLASH, THE.

vis-à-vis. See FRENCH WORDS AND PHRASES.

visit, verb. See PREPOSITIONS.

visitation. See CONNOTATIONS.

vital statistics. See POPULARIZED TECHNICALITIES.

vogue words. Public figures no less than poets strike off phrases that fit a mood or an occasion, and the words, for a time, supply less inventive minds with ready-made wit or force. But quite soon, through excessive repetition, not only the charm but also the point of the phrase wears off. The shopworn image fails to square with the facts at hand; meaning leaks away, yet the empty syllables patter on. *Window of opportunity* never summoned a clear idea from the two nouns it joined, but its sound was pleasant, and it looked original; it became a public nuisance when it shouldered aside every *chance, inning, turn, occasion, opening,* and *timely moment.* The figurative *level playing field* has likewise become, as language, flat as can be. By no means all *risks* in life are *calculated,* though from public speech one might think so. A novelist's *catch-22,* an insidious rule binding fictional naval fliers, has eclipsed *swindle, hoax, fraud, imposture, fast shuffle, gimmick,* and *shell game,* and by its incessant use become mere noise. Those who say they are figuratively *sending a message* already suggest its triteness.

Most ready-made images decay as part of the natural order. But many are today kept alive, not for their color, wit, or visual fitness, but because the gift of vivid coinage seems for now to have left us. Americans rightly admire *eating high on the hog, stuffed shirt,* and *to Hell in a handcart;* but who can imagine the look of *pushing [the edge of] the envelope, playing the race card,* and *down the tubes*—what *tubes?* We all know that litmus paper turns red in acid. But how little that suggests the *questions, standards, benchmarks, dictates, principles, queries, challenges, feelers,* and *loaded questions* that politicians describe as the *litmus test. Number-crunching,* another Washington favorite, amused by its sound for a very short time, as baby talk does. *Bottom line* turns us all into bookkeepers. The mock-adverb *for starters,* so far

from being jaunty, is old-fashioned British slang.

Melodrama and sentimentality are sun and soil to vogue words. The once ominous *out there (There is poverty out there)* no longer evokes vistas, daunting or bright, but serves as filler when the writing or speaking mind dozes. The adjective *special* persists, with its tone of confident coyness implying merits or attractions unstated *(Of all the counselors in the camp, Elizabeth was special to me / Chinese restaurants come and go, but S. remains special to its patrons).* The intention of this empty honorific is to produce a mood without saying anything concrete. The suffix *-bashing (corporation-bashing / mother-bashing)* now makes melodrama of a slighting remark, whereas the sentimental *nurturing* no longer pertains to feeding or to anything clear.

Among other single words whose vogue is dusty, the careful will note *creative* (for doing or thinking anything), *viable* (for any form of possibility), *significant* (for *large, important, representative, new;* it means no more than *signifying*), *empower* (it means *to give authority by force of law*), *hands-on* (for *paying attention*), *define, defining, re-define* (for *summing up, standing for, exemplifying, forming, illustrating, changing, revamping*), *issue* (for *subject, problem, question,* or as a COVERING WORD or UNNECESSARY WORD), *scenario* (for *plan, speculation, what might be, imagining*), AGENDA, IMPACT, *in-depth* (when *deep* might be seen as untrue or grandiloquent), *initial* (for *first*), DIALOGUE (for *conversation, negotiation, interview, we talked,* or as a verb), *massive* (as an omnibus sign of magnitude or importance), ADDRESS (verb, for *discuss, remedy, change, state, resolve, handle, deal with, treat, take on, mention, acknowledge*, etc.), *legacy* (anything traceable to the past), *focus* (see SCIENTISM 1), *delicious* (for things other than food), *fault* (as a verb), *commit* (without an object; see TRANSITIVE, INTRANSITIVE), *credible, credibility* (for *trustworthy, believable, honest*, PLAUSIBLE, *presentable, reasonable, he looks as if he might do it*), *thinking* (my, your, hers; why not *thought, idea, brainstorm?*), *decisionmaking* (in one word and where *deciding* has prior claim), DEVELOP, *frustrated*, and *shocked* (see COVERING WORDS).

Finally, the conscious user of words has an obligation to keep alive in their established meanings the words that politics may suddenly restrict to one emotionally charged sense. In Europe after the Second World War it was impossible for a time to refer to a *collaborator* in an enterprise: the word had become a term of abuse applied to persons who had assisted the Nazi occupation forces. Now in the United States *discrimination* is in danger of meaning only invidious choice according to race, sex, or other condition. *Segregate* and *integrate* are likewise constricted, as are words and phrases such as *integrity* (which means *wholeness*), CONTROVERSIAL, *interest groups* (we all have interests to guard), *vested interests* (another phrase for *interest groups*), and *rhetoric* (misused to mean only empty words). Topical use has pinched or misapplied these words out of all recognition. But words are too valuable to be tied down in this way; their particular import must be continually restored by proper use in clear contexts.

See also CONTACT; DYSFUNCTIONAL; EDUCATIONESE; FORBIDDEN WORDS 2; ICON; JARGON; LEGALESE; METAPHOR 3; PLAUSIBLE; POPULARIZED TECHNICALITIES; SCIENTISM; VENUE.

voice. 1. *Voice*, active or passive, is a linguistic option that doubles our expressive resources: it allows us to choose between saying that M. did such-and-such and that such-and-such was done by M. *The Niagara Falls Suspension Bridge was designed and built by the elder Roebling* says in the passive voice what is said in the active by *The elder Roebling designed and built the . . . Bridge.* There is not the slightest difference in substance between the two statements, but the difference in effect is large. The first presupposes a context about the bridge or about suspension bridges; it would be a poor sentence in a paragraph about the Roeblings. The second directs attention to the elder Roebling and would not work well in a passage whose subject was bridges. In short, voice is an expedient for throwing the weight of the sentence where the writer wants it. Although a property of verbs, voice in fact determines subjects. *Voltaire's novel was drawn on by Hellman for the plot of the musical* Candide *in the 1950s* (passive) is a sentence about Voltaire's novel. Reverse the subject and object, and Lillian Hellman is the center of attention: *Hellman drew on Voltaire's novel for the plot of . . .* Candide, etc. (active).

2. Books on style urge the active voice for the writing of narrative and plain exposition; the active tells who did what. To be sure, scientific English departs from the active when strict considerations of accuracy require it to do so. Military English does the same for reasons of secrecy, as does bureaucratic English out of an instinct for group self-defense, best shown in the classic statement *Mistakes were made.* Still, most writers today who are not bound by lodge rules seem to honor the virtues of the active voice and to use it. They get into trouble with voice, not through lack of enlightenment, but because of an inability to see that the passive cannot be treated as if it were active.

To avoid this trouble, hold to the precept that no one can *do* an action previously stated in the passive. Consider a writer on airline safety: *Mr. G. noted that the ATR–42 had a "tendency" to roll or tilt in icy weather that "has never been duplicated in testing." And so he set out to do just that.* The phrase *do . . . that* prompts the question: Do what? The strange answer is *do be duplicated,* a collision of active and passive. Again: *This rug may be sent to a laundry. If you do so, ask to have it hung up to dry. Do so* can refer to an act that you perform, but not to an act that is performed by you. Beginning as it does, the example can be coherent only if the second sentence begins with *If you send it*—a restatement of the first sentence in the active voice to conform with the active verb in *ask to have it hung up.* Conversely, restate the second sentence in the passive: *If sent, it should be hung up.* The

collision can be averted entirely with *If you send this rug to the laundry, ask . . .*

Here are a group of examples with parenthetical suggestions showing how to restore agreement. *These berries can even be gathered under the snow in winter, which the inhabitants of southwest Greenland actually do* (as they actually are by) / *It is doubtful that it could be said as well or as meaningfully as Rand has done* (as Rand has said it; see MEANINGFUL) / *If a plan had to be altered, delayed, or abandoned to fit a political necessity, he was quick to do so* (quick to alter, delay, or abandon it) / *The degree of recovery from the economic trough is shown wherever it is possible to do so* (possible to show it) / *agreeing that severe pressure must now be put upon the Queen and admitting that no one but Burleigh could do it* (could apply it) / *And staff meetings will be held regularly three times a week unless wars or politics prevent his doing so* (prevent his holding them; or, perhaps better: *And he will hold staff meetings . . . unless wars or politics prevent his doing so*) / *More time has got to be given to the household chores, but I fail to see why it's up to me to do so* (to give it).

Disregard of agreement in voice is not confined to the lower or higher journalism. The preface of an excellent dictionary announces that *the reader is given the necessary additional connotative information, even if it means devoting a good deal of space to doing so* (to it).

3. Since alternating active and passive voices confuses the point of view, it often leaves part of the sentence dan-

gling (see DANGLERS). Notice that *By calling the volunteer office at St. Anne's Hospice, duties can be specifically described* asks no one to call. Rewrite: *If you call . . . can be described.* Writers of recipes often mix voices along with ingredients: *By using both brown and green lentils an interesting varicolored look can be achieved.* The agentless participle could be avoided by beginning *By the use of;* but one may keep the participle by using the sequel *you can achieve.* Failure to consider the agent leads to curious imperatives addressed to the cook: *Turn into a preheated earthenware dish.*

The double passive—usually a passive verb followed by a passive infinitive—often makes for awkward changes in point of view. Consider: *New members of the planning committee would not be permitted to be appointed if they had served within the previous five years;* permission is denied to the prospective members instead of to those who appoint them. Rewrite: *Appointing new members of the planning committee would not be permitted,* etc. Straightening out such zigzag constructions is not always easy: *By these swift measures the likely consequences were attempted to be averted.* This is obvious nonsense, pretending as it does that *consequences* can be the subject of *were attempted.* What is needed is a reconstruction with a new subject naming the person or persons who did the attempting. In sorting out the confusions that arise from mishandling voice, the question to ask is always: Who is doing what?

W

wait. See PREPOSITIONS.

we, editorial. *We* can stand for the consensus of an editorial board or the collective identity of a periodical or organization. A related *we* signifies any understood collectivity, from a committee of two to the entire human race. In certain books *we* means you, the reader, and I, the author, conceived as joined by a common interest.

But *we* is still sometimes used, especially in scholarship, where it clearly means a single person who should step forth as *I*. True enough, the vertical pronoun, routinely repeated, can turn tiresome; but no one any longer believes the old reproof that *I* is self-important. Indeed, the uncalled-for *we* strikes many readers as downright pompous, pretending, as it does, to speak for a body of opinion. The same trap of self-inflation awaits the unwary user of the first-person ONE.

The authorial *we* is suitable in a collaborative work, but not at every point. A book by two authors records: *We have had a coat of unborn musk-ox calf that lasted for three or more years.* The coat was not owned in common, and this wrong impression could have been avoided had the facts been stated impersonally: *A coat . . . has been known to last three or more years.*

Annoying self-presentations include the memorandum or signed newspaper feature in which the author pointlessly lurks as *this writer, this* (or *your*) *correspondent, the interviewer, the present writer,* or, by becoming part of the woodwork, *this desk, this office, this department, this column. This writer* risks ambiguity whenever a writer other than the *I* has just been mentioned; yet the phrase is bound to occur at that very point if a contrast is to be made between two views. Resort to *the present writer* is inadvisedly metaphorical: the writer is absent. Resolve then to take the great leap and say *I*. Everyone now understands that a mask is more conspicuous than a face.

wear and tear. See SET PHRASES 2.

weave, weaved, wove. See MYSTERIOUS PASTS.

wed, wedded. See MYSTERIOUS PASTS.

what, singular or plural. See NUMBER, TROUBLE WITH 2.

what is "understood"? Writing is the art of saying part of what we mean and of implying clearly what else we mean without saying it. The well-placed pronoun is only one device by which we make such an implication. Indeed, we rarely consider the blessings of pronouns until we reckon the cost of not having them in a sentence like this: *Members of the House of Representatives, if they did not have the privilege of extending their remarks, would be cut off from a principal means of communicating with their constituents.* But for pronouns, this statement would have to read: *Members of the House of Representatives, if members of the House of Representatives did not have the privilege of extending the remarks of members of the House of Representatives,* etc.

Other devices that effect economies include the many words and phrases of reference: *thus,* SUCH, *so, hence, thence, accordingly,* RESPECTIVELY, *likewise, same, former, latter, vice versa,* all the demonstratives (*this, that,* etc.), transitional phrases and words (*even so, on the contrary,* etc.), and hundreds of other locutions that point backward or forward (or both ways) to related matter. Then too, our commonest nouns can serve in context the purpose of pronouns; when we say that the problem is insoluble, this truth self-evident, that theory unsound, or his proposal foolish, we are using *problem, truth, theory,* or *proposal* to stand for some idea already expressed. We avoid its repetition by using the noun, exactly as if we had said *it.* What with all the pronouns, all the nouns used like them, and all the reference words, the management of language becomes a subtle and intricate adjustment of names and pointers in sequence; it resembles not so much the building of a wall with uniform bricks as the weaving of a patterned fabric on a loom.

Granted the stupendous miracle that language exists—by all odds the greatest fact in human history—we must view with particular wonder this freedom of substitution whereby a few words take the place of many and what is left unsaid is no less present through its delegates. Yet even this magical power is eclipsed by another, namely the force of words that are present without delegation at all—words in a speaking vacuum. That vacuum is called an ellipsis. *The earth belongs to the living, not to the dead / Priests are no more necessary to religion than politicians to patriotism / I will come in and sup with him, and he with me / It is easier for a man to be loyal to his club than to his planet / Render therefore to all their dues; tribute to whom tribute is due; custom to whom custom; fear to whom fear; honor to whom honor.* The twenty-four words of the last example become thirty-five if you fill in those that are invisibly at work; indeed, all the ellipses occur in eighteen words, which alone do the work of twenty-nine while achieving as well an incalculable gain in force. We hardly notice such examples in context; yet they recall Carlyle's observation that writers ought to be paid by the quantity they do not write. To the trained writer it is second nature to go through his copy striking out every syllable he can do without. Those who skip this stage may know the A and the B of writing, but they have yet to arrive at its C.

In using this privilege of omission it is all-important that the words left out in the writing will infallibly be the words supplied in the reading. Should the gaps suggest the wrong words—words that miss our meaning or contradict it or say it askew—we are thrown on the dubious mercy of unknown readers who have better things to do than to correct what cannot be seen.

Mismanaged elliptical sentences are often only technically flawed, not downright misleading. That is why as readers we can without complaint supply an *a* or an *an* in front of a noun when all we can borrow from the previous noun is the wrong article. Writers ought to say *an awkward and a stupid man* but often say *an awkward and stupid man*, hoping that the absence of the correct form in the second instance lends force or bluntness to the passage. Whether it does so or not, supplying the *a* is no big job for the reader.

But thin ice awaits the writer who likes the speed afforded by implying repetition of a verb regardless of its number. Many writers on usage approve this shortcut and see nothing wrong in *His black shirt is buttoned at the neck, his black pants gathered at the waist and ankles.* In this they are surely mistaken. It makes no sense to assume, on the one hand, that all readers supply the bracketed words in *It is easier for a man to be loyal to his club than* [it is for him to be loyal] *to his planet*—but to assume, on the other hand, that readers do not "hear" *his black pants* [is] *gathered at the waist.*

Again: the reader remembers eleven words in the example beginning *Render therefore to all their dues;* the same reader cannot help remembering the misnumbered verbs implied in these examples: *Mr. E.'s eclecticism is refreshing, his research rigorous, and his portraits sometimes stimulating* / The Notebooks of Malte Laurids Brigge *is misnamed, for the language is far too polished, the episodes too artfully arranged* / *The play appears smaller now, its characters more crudely drawn, its schematic elements more blatant* / *His broad forehead was lined and his eyes wide with distress and bewilderment* / *The board of trustees waited until graduation was over and the students safely out of sight.*

In ellipses longer than these, we may piece out the sense, but not without feeling that we are doing the writer's job for him. *No true insect eaters could exist in the Arctic, and certainly could not rear a brood* is clear but not English; the writer has said that no true insect eaters could not rear a brood. We rewrite in our minds: *No true insect eaters could exist in the Arctic or could rear a brood there.* But if the reader is expected to rewrite, what is the writer there for? Notice that this example fails through mismanaging negative expressions, something all too easy to do. For general guidance on slippery negatives, see NEGATIVES, TROUBLE WITH.

What is all too well "understood" in the group of examples that follow may look like the work of writers not fully awake. But each writer was probably trying for force or concision or speed, and thus lost the self-skepticism that ensures our saying—or implying—just what we mean: *The time ought never to come—we hope it won't—when movies cannot be watched on a screen of proper size in a theater* (we hope it never will; the author has implied *we hope it won't never*) / *The question had no answer, nor will it have until the voters see the results of this bill* (nor will it have one; the author has implied *nor will it have no answer*) / *Military vessels have and do navigate the bumpy waters of Pillsbury Sound* (the writer has set down *vessels have navigate*, though *vessels navigate* or *continue to navigate* would say all that is meant) / *The family was confident that it could ride out this crisis as it had the previous two* (had ridden out or had weathered the previous two; the author implies *had ride*, though the clashing constructions are not cheek by jowl). Notice that some misjudged ellipses must be dropped altogether for clarity and order. To permit the device, the opening words must be given a form which the words to be understood will readily match; it follows that ellipses can rarely be hit upon in mid-sentence. When an ellipsis fails, it is worth the extra syllables to write *had ridden out* unless the writer thinks of other expedients.

As was shown above, an illogical verb form, stated or implied, calls attention to itself. But it becomes doubly conspicuous when word order is inverted for emphasis: *She was chosen to shake things up, and shake things up she has.* This is emphatic but not correct, for the parts it supplies make *has*

shake things up. The grammatical *shaken things up she has* is available, but it is also ungainly and unemphatic; for emphasis the author wants an exact echo. A good solution is *shake things up she did*, or *does*, or (if the action continues) *did and does*.

The forms of *do* also act as substitutes for a verb or verbs previously stated, as in *They asked if I wished to enter, and I said that I did* (I did = I wished to enter) / *Come to the airport and see her off, but if you do, come early* (you do = you come . . . and see her off). But if *do* is to properly replace another verb, that verb must be in the active voice, as it is not here: *A. was never addressed as "Professor," and when I phoned I didn't do so.* (For more on *do* mismatched with the passive voice, see VOICE 2.) Nor will *do* substitute for forms of *be* and *have*: *He is true to his principles when something can be gained by doing so* (being so) / *The play has something to say and does so with honest competency* (and says it).

Sometimes a misjudged ellipsis makes a hash of meaning: *Their efforts are not limited to feeding AIDS patients but helping all who suffer from physical disabilities.* The writer does not mean that efforts are limited to *helping* or that they are not: he means the reverse of *limit*, as in *but extend to* or *include helping*. An even more baffling sentence: *The July increase in production of the steel industry was secured with about 2,000 fewer workers than in the preceding month.* This states that the July increase also took place in June; for what the construction invites us to supply is *2,000 fewer workers than* it was secured with in the preceding month. The writer doubtless wanted us to supply 2,000 fewer workers than there were in the preceding month.

Wrong verbs or wrong forms of verbs are not the only botches the hasty or preoccupied writer leaves behind in ellipses: In both his completed term and the one that was not, the commissioner proved his skill in reducing crime. Unwrapping the ellipses, we see that we are meant to supply completed after not, but the fit feels wrong. Small wonder, for completed has been set up as an adjective and now we ask it to do the work of a verb: was not completed. Prose writers ask for trouble when they require one word to perform two tasks in a single sentence. Keeping completed as an adjective, we can rewrite: In both his completed term and the uncompleted one. To use the same word as a verb, we can say, In both the term that was completed and the one that was not.

The more intricate the construction, the easier it is not to notice that one word is doing two jobs: There is no point in talking to those who never have and never will read the book to its end. The read to be supplied after never have is the past participle, pronounced red; but the word we can see spelled out is the future tense, pronounced reed.

When asked to cover an ellipsis, the little words so, SUCH, and thus can do disproportionate damage if not handled with care: The residents wanted to have the streets cleaned and kept so. So works as an adjective here, standing for clean—which is not in the sentence

and so has no right to a stand-in. Let cleaned do its work as a verb; put an adjective where an adjective belongs: have the streets cleaned and kept clean. For an important group of useful ellipses, see WHICH AND (BUT) WHICH.

whatever, whoever, etc., interrogative. The suffix -ever is intensive. It gives force to the pronouns whatever and whoever (Do whatever you think best / Give the package to whoever is on duty); to the adjectives whatever and whichever (Tell whatever fib you prefer / Use whichever wrench you have); to the adverbs wherever and whenever (He goes wherever I go and does the talking whenever I can't); and to however in one of its senses. If we were to assign a meaning to -ever, it might be among all the possibilities, as in Do what [among all the possibilities] you think best.

This far, American and British usage fully agree. But American written English has lately broken with British practice by employing these solid compound words as interrogatives: Whoever invited you? / Wherever did you find that? By contrast, the strict British way of setting down questions uses the two-word form what ever, who ever, and so on down the list. Fowler tersely explained in 1926 that ever when put beside what, who, etc., is a mere colloquialism, comparable to Who [on earth] invited you? He saw it as adding force but no meaning to the words that were doing the work, hence not to be joined to them indivisibly.

Some American authorities, noting the local drift away from this view, construe *ever* as an adverb and fear that the change brings with it a problem of grammar. But the change is simply idiomatic and entails no serious confusion, except in one instance: *how ever* as an interrogative still needs two words, as in *How ever did you find us?* or *How did you ever find us?* Without the break, the mind can too readily take the solid form, *however*, in the conjunctive sense of *but*. It is true that when used in that meaning and at the head of a sentence, *however* must be followed by a comma. But the hasty reader is all too likely to mistake *However can I make it up to you?* as saying, in effect, *Nevertheless, can I make it up to you?* Hence: *How ever can I* or *How can I ever*, etc.

when and if. An exact parallel to *and/or*, this piece of legal JARGON when used by the laity says the same thing twice. Suppose that you make up your mind to *throw the phone out the window if it rings once more*; you resolve at the same moment to commit the act *when* it rings once more. Conversely, when you promise a friend to *make suggestions when she needs them*, you promise that you will do so *if* she needs them. The attraction of the wordy phrase may be that it sounds both tentative and firm: it suggests that nothing will be done unnecessarily but action will be taken at the proper time. But that can be emphatically said without sounding like an overwritten lease. *Believe me, when she needs suggestions I will make them / I swear I'll throw the phone . . . if*, etc.

See also AND/OR; IF AND WHEN; LEGALISMS; UNLESS AND UNTIL.

whereas. See WHILE.

wherever. See WHATEVER, WHOEVER 1.

whether. See AS 11; DOUBT.

which, relative. See THAT, WHICH, RELATIVE; THAT, WHO, RELATIVE.

which . . . and (but) which; who . . . and (but) who. According to an old superstition frozen into a rule, *and which* or *but which* may not begin a clause unless an earlier *which* has referred to the same antecedent. By that standard these sentences would be judged faulty: (a) *The job, ideal for someone of her training and talent, and which had gone begging for months, went to you instead;* (b) *We lack any record of the accident, in frigid darkness, deep in a field, and which only farmers and wakeful mice may have heard;* (c) *It was a gathering of surly tempers, used to exploding, but which were not yet too riled to see reason.* In fact all three examples are clear and correct, though not all will suit every writer's stylistic preference. What makes each correct is the proper balance of elements equal in status. The sentences contain two clauses of equal weight—though the first clause makes use of ellipsis: (a) *[which was] ideal . . . and which had gone begging;* (b) *[which was* or *which took place] in frigid darkness . . . and which only farmers;* (c) *[which were] used to . . .*

but which were not yet. In each sentence what is left out but implied is the *which* (with its verb) that parallels the *which* (with its verb) to come. This construction is balanced on the conjunction as on a fulcrum: let *and* or *but* coordinate two equivalent clauses, whether both are fully written out or not, and the grammar is blameless.

Those unsatisfied with the style of our three examples must exercise care in changing them. Put the missing *which was* into (a) and the later *which* will echo distractingly; delete the *and*, and the *which* will grab *talent* as its antecedent; recast the sentence by leaving out nothing and the syntax becomes a loose-jointed ramble: *was ideal for someone of her training and talent and had gone begging for months but went to you.* The best change (it is none too good) might delete *and which* and thus read: *The job, ideal for someone of her . . . talent, had gone begging for months before it went to you instead.* The same threat of paired *which*'s or a wrong antecedent hangs over (b); to rewrite, move *which* forward and give it a verb that will command the first two descriptive phrases: *We lack any record of the accident, which took place in frigid darkness, deep in a field, where only farmers and wakeful mice may have heard it.* To rewrite (c), again move *which* forward so that it governs two expressions instead of one: *which were used to exploding but not yet too riled to see reason.*

The same logic, cautions, and hints apply to *who . . . and who; whom . . . and whom;* and *who(m) . . . but who(m).*

while. Glib writers steal this conjunction from its primary meaning, *during the time that,* and bend it to the work of *and, whereas, although,* and the semicolon without connective. The result is muddle or nonsense. *Fifty-nine of the 84 female victims were pedestrians, while the 316 male victims included only 56 pedestrians. Sixteen of the women were drivers, while nine were passengers.* The first *while* plainly means *whereas* (= by contrast), and the second, meaning nothing, can be omitted (sixteen were drivers; nine were passengers). *He said this last storm had taken the shingles, while* (and) *the wandering creek had long ago leached the foundation* / *recalled that while* (although) *born left-handed, he had learned to bat right-handed* / *The terms of the grant promise a sum with which to begin renovation, while* (whereas), *later on, the agency will be reimbursed for expenses.* Note that in the last three specimens the facts linked with *while* belong to times expressly stated to be different. To write that something happened today *while* something else happened ten years ago is to work hard at achieving contradiction.

Ideally, the conjunction *while* should be restricted to the linking of simultaneous occurrences in a situation where simultaneity has point. *Then it is the brave man chooses, while the coward stands aside.* Writers lose nothing by declining to use *while* in any other way; by just such a small refusal, they resist a general watering down of solid meanings.

A borderline use occurs in *While*

over a hundred calls have been made, the list has not been exhausted. This *while* is a concessive that means (like too many *while's*) *although;* its claim to grudging acceptance is that it entails no temporal clash between facts.

See also ALTHOUGH, THOUGH.

who, relative. See THAT, WHICH, RELATIVE; THAT, WHO, RELATIVE.

who(m), who(m)ever. The objective form of the pronoun *who* has a hard time asserting its hereditary rights. On one side, it suffers at the hands of those who will put in the *m* where it does not belong, out of fear of being thought uneducated; on the other, it is belabored by free-spirited grammarians who find it bookish and to be avoided. Between those afraid of sounding ignorant and those afraid of sounding superior, *who(m)* causes increasing and needless discomfort in its users.

1. The first kind of fear can be seen in locutions like *I know perfectly well whom you are,* in which the speaker sees *whom* as the object of *know,* though in fact *who* is the subject of *are.* The lapse can be seen in writing put forth under the best auspices: [He] *asked them, saying, Whom say the people that I am?* (Luke 9:18) / *Ahead of them on the Nonesuch Road they descried Lord Grey de Hilton, whom Essex declared was his enemy.* Note that the second statement, rearranged, would say *Essex declared him was his enemy.* We can avoid this trap by imagining the subject and verb of the second clause as being placed between commas: *who, Essex declared, was his*

enemy. Clearly *who* is a subject, and *was* is its verb, the commas remaining imaginary.

In another construction, which closely resembles the one just examined, the objective *whom* is in fact required: *The woman whom I took to be his wife turned out to be his daughter / The character whom he seems to admire most is the one I care least about.* In both examples the pronoun is paired with an infinitive, which, like any verb, may or may not take an object. Here too a purely mental recasting will clarify the sentence. Turn the part of the statement that contains the infinitive into a simple declarative form and an easier pronoun leaps to mind, its form not in doubt. In the first sentence, *whom I took to be* becomes *I took her to be,* the *her* confirming that the objective form is correct. Again: *whom he seems to admire* becomes in the mind *he seems to admire her* or *him,* the objective pronouns showing that the real sentence wants the objective *whom.* The same test works for the doubly daunting *Our hope was to find out who they thought we were and whom* (not *who*) *we were thought to endanger.* Think: *we were we* (not *us*) and *thought to endanger them* or *him* or *her*—not *they* or *he* or *she.*

2. The other kind of fear, that of the educated who want to conceal their grammatical assets, prompts statements like this in a work of history: *N. departed eight days later in humiliation as the man who, more than anyone else, the President had repudiated.* Freewheeling grammarians would approve this *who,* undeterred by the fact that it

makes the reader look for a clause whose subject it is—a fruitless search. These grammarians favor this *who* for echoing the way we speak, especially in questions: *Who are you thinking of?* / *Who's kidding who?* But we also say to each other, *To whom should I send this?* and *With whom did you stay?* and our store of tag lines holds few better known than *for whom the bell tolls* and *To whom it may concern.* In short, we have not thrown out *whom* but continue to use it unevenly: not always putting it where grammar expects it when we speak, but doing our best when writing to put objects where objects belong, as we do with *us* and *them*, *him* and *her* and *me.*

3. It is time to ignore and forget the archaic construction *than whom*, as in *than whom there is no one prettier* and *than whom no one enjoys more respect.* It only appears nowadays as a wistful form of wit. Educated writers know that *than* is comparative (*taller than I*) and cannot take the objective case.

4. *Who(m)ever*, meaning *anyone who(m)*, works exactly the same way as *who(m)* and goes wrong for the same reasons. When either is the subject of a clause that specifies or defines it (*He will punish whoever gets in his way*), the pronoun does its subjective job and declines to be an object, whether of verb or preposition. The following is wrong: *Willy meant to maintain the truce and would clamp down with all his might on whomever disturbed it.* Willy would not clamp down on B. or M. indiscriminately, only on specified culprits: *whoever disturbed the truce.* See also WHATEVER, WHOEVER.

whole, intensive. See UNNECESSARY WORDS 4.

whole, as a. See PART, IN.

-wide, suffix. See -WISE, -WIDE.

will. See SHALL (SHOULD), WILL (WOULD).

window of opportunity. See VOGUE WORDS.

-wise, -wide, suffixes. 1. There is at first sight no reason why -*wise*, interchangeable with -*ways* in many combinations (*crosswise* or -*ways*, *endwise* or -*ways*, *slantwise* or -*ways*, etc.), may not be appended to any given noun — call the noun X—to make an adverb meaning *after the fashion of X, like an X, in the manner of X*, as in *crabwise, clockwise*, etc. The Oxford Dictionary quotes from Melville and Thoreau: *Ahab . . . took Stubb's long spade . . . and striking it into the lower part of the half-suspended mass, placed its other end crutch-wise under one arm* / *Waiting at evening on the hilltops for the sky to fall, that I might catch something, though I never caught much, and that, manna-wise, would dissolve again in the sun.*

But the privilege of judiciously changing single nouns becomes a cause of havoc when taken as a license to manhandle all nouns at whim. The habit of doing so has grown on present-day writers and speakers, especially those in business and entertainment, where language is rarely heard at its best. Handlers of large sums of money seem to doubt that they are making full use of their rights over English unless they pepper their analyses with *profitwise, marketwise, audiencewise, competitionwise, percentagewise,* and so on. What was handy as a device has been made ugly as a mannerism, and it should be outlawed from good usage. What is reprehensible about the vogue is its surrender to inarticulate English; that is, the use of words in juxtaposition with no clear joint, conventional or explicit. The effect of briskness does not redeem the pollution of sense. The head of a great corporation tells a gathering of employees: *How we do netwise is in your hands.* One suspects that he first wrote or dictated *Whether we make a profit or not is up to you* and then translated it into the company JARGON.

Until the fad abates, a sensible writer will resort to such coinages with *-wise* only to make fun of them, as S. J. Perelman does when he speaks of *what was going on, prose-wise, from 1930 to 1958.* Ruskin sounded the satirical note even earlier: *Just because it is deep* [his respect for Dickens's genius], *I have not the least mind to express it dinnerwise* (1867).

2. The syllable *-wide* has no more right than *-wise* to go piggyback on whatever noun walks by. *Worldwide* and *nationwide* are established in usage through frequency of need, and the second avoids the implication of government sponsorship, as in *national holiday, national health plan.* But *region-wide, area-wide,* and the like merely parrot the form where plain words do the job better: *across the region, throughout our area.*

See also STYLE, TYPE.

with. 1. Omnibus use. 2. Missing.

1. Omnibus use. The preposition *with* is clear and tight enough when it introduces the agent of an effect: we sweep with a broom, write with a computer, reach the high shelves with a stepladder. The word causes no trouble in showing, as well, simple accompaniment: we hike with a friend, drink tea with lemon, speak with (or without) eloquence, face the future with hope. A third foolproof meaning is *at the time of: With the arrival of these reinforcements the whole battle picture changed / With the hiring of a drummer the band was complete / His prophecy was upset in 1914 with the publication of the Tenth Edition.* If definite causation is meant, it should be stated: no simple *with* will do: *The arrival of the reinforcements changed the whole battle picture.* No less reliable is the *with* that signifies reciprocity: *Don't you want to talk it over with me?* or opposition: *fight with, argue with,* and numerous other verbs to which idiom always ties *with.* This last use shows the original force of the word, which is found in *withstand, withhold,* and, curiously, in the draft animal's *withers,* the part that strains against a load.

But lucidity flies out the window when *with* is used ad lib to attach some fact or circumstance whose relation to the rest of the sentence *with* by itself cannot make clear. *With the shortage of food on the shelves, it will be increas-*

ingly difficult for the defenders to hold the village. Here a causal relation is meant, but the sentence fails to state it; when we reverse the order of parts, the weakness of *with* is exposed: *It will be increasingly difficult for the defenders to hold the village with the shortage of food on the shelves.* If we rewrite, the intended meaning comes out clear: *The shortage of food on the shelves will make it difficult . . .*

No standard repair will suit the varied occasions on which *with* is a feeble link; each sentence must be searched for exact meaning. *At other times (as with the Normans), the victors adopt the language of those whom they have subdued.* Why *with?* Nothing here uses, accompanies, or is associated with the Normans, much less happens at the same time as they appear. The meaning: *the victors, like the Normans, adopt.* Again: *It seems probable that these notes were for the Vietnam screenplay, and so with many others* (and that many others were as well) / *The most detailed reminiscence of Whitman's personality and habits during his editorship of the* Eagle *comes again, as with the "Aurora" period, from a young printer who worked on the paper* (reminiscence . . . comes again, as it did for the "Aurora" period, from a young printer) / *In the movie, food is a metaphor for life, a sweet, sour, salty, bitter experience that, as with food, is sometimes in balance, sometimes not* (a sweet . . . bitter experience that, like food, is sometimes, etc.) See AS 9.

So tempting is *with* as a wild card to fill out a sentence that two more examples are not superfluous: *Their em-ployers, the Florida orange growers, made handsome profits because the freeze put oranges in short supply and the frostbitten fruit could be marketed as "fair" frozen orange juice at a high price per can. So too with other fruit and vegetable crops.* Obviously other fruit and vegetable crops were not marketed as frozen orange juice. *Other fruit and vegetable crops were likewise profitably salvaged* or *were similarly turned into profit.* In *The theater was completely filled, with many people standing hopefully outside* we have a flat contradiction—filled with people outside. The simplest solution is divorce: *The theater was completely filled; many stood outside still hoping to get in.* Writers who exploit the evasive *with* avoid clear thought about what they mean and how to say it. But the effort of communication must be theirs, not the reader's. (See also LINKING; PREPOSITIONS.)

2. Missing. Like *as* and *to* (see AS 2 and TO, MISSING), *with* is handy and short but does only one job at a time. In a complicated sentence, the mere presence of a *with* does not ensure that all parts requiring the word are served: *As with other occupations, journalism, with all of the charges of censorship and corporate control that critics burden it, suffers most from old habits of thought.* Here the writer uses *with* twice but needs it yet again after *burden it.* Too ready a distaste for repetition has made a grammatical botch. All this withery can be sidestepped by taking thought and then recasting: *As is true of other occupations, journalism, which is burdened with charges of cen-*

sorship and corporate control, in fact suffers most, etc.

withdrawal. See EUPHEMISMS.

without. Unlike WITH, this preposition generally does not tempt to omission or false linking. Because it is negative, it is not so handy a catchall. Yet, when abused, it is likely to produce even more disconcerting results than *with.* Especially when it begins a sentence and is followed by what is variously called a gerund, a verbal noun, or a verbal, it has to be watched lest it merely spin its wheels in an imitation of work. *Without wishing to be obstinate, it is difficult to see the relevance in such an analysis* cannot be cured until the wishing is ascribed to whoever does it—I, one, we, anyone. (See DANGLERS.)

Worse confusion greets us in a university statement about the need of free funds: *Without in any way detracting from the desire of some to support specific activities, unrestricted gifts permit a college to make maximum use of its ready funds.* No one supposes that unrestricted gifts can detract from anyone's desire to make restricted ones. It is the speaker himself who does not wish to detract, and he has been drawn into this fog by a wish for self-effacement. What he should say is: *I mean no disparagement of the desire to support specific activities when I remind you that unrestricted gifts,* etc.

worthwhile. It is not worthwhile to use *worthwhile* unless you split it up first to see whether the *while* portion fits the context. Time, in other words, must be involved in the thing labeled *worthwhile.* This is why we say *worthwhile activities,* such as sports, hobbies, reading, etc. But a sandwich cannot be worthwhile, or a pair of shoes, or a suggestion. It is better and simpler to say *worth eating, worth buying, worth making,* and leave *worthwhile* a little distinctiveness among terms of praise.

would. See SHALL (SHOULD), WILL (WOULD).

would rather, would sooner. See HAD RATHER, WOULD RATHER, WOULD SOONER.

wrack. See RACK.

write. See PREPOSITIONS.

X
―

X. The transformation of the normal sound of *x* into *egs*, as in *exaggerate, exult,* etc., occurs only when *x* falls after *e* and before a vowel (and not always then; *lexicon=lecks*). The altered sound should not be heard after any other vowel. *Luxurious, uxorious, oxygen* should not begin with *lug, ug,* and *og,* but rather with *luks, uks,* and *oks.* See PRONUNCIATION 1.

Y
―

yet. See SINCE, YET 3.

Z

zeal, zealot, zealous. The first denotes great ardor in pursuit of an end, the second a person animated by that ardor, the third the character of the person or of the pursuit. But the writer may well have a feeling that one or two or all three connote excess. Consult several dictionaries and you play a kind of shell game in which the sense of excess lurks first under this form, then under that. In fact there is no agreement; hence *excess of zeal* and the cumbersome *overly zealous* (for *overzealous*) to denote too-muchness. Some writers avoid this group of words altogether, adding qualifiers to such words as *passion, ardor, devotion* in order to convey disapproval. *Zealot* has several synonyms with bad reputations built in: *fanatic, crank,* etc.

See also OVERLY; for pronunciation of *zealous,* see PRONUNCIATION 1.

zoology. See PRONUNCIATION 1.

APPENDIX:
ON USAGE, PEDANTRY, GRAMMAR,
AND THE ORDERLY MIND

Despite the modern desire to be easy and casual, Americans from time to time give thought to the language they use—to grammar, vocabulary, and gobbledygook. And as on other issues they divide into two parties. The larger, which includes everybody from the so-called plain man to the professional writer, takes it for granted that there is a right way to use words and construct sentences, and there are many wrong ways. The right way is believed to be clearer, simpler, more logical, and hence more likely to prevent error and confusion. Good writing is easier to read; it offers a pleasant combination of sound and sense.

Against this majority view is the doctrine of an aggressive minority, who make up for their small number by their great learning and their place of authority in the world of scholarship. They are the professional linguists who deny that there is such a thing as correctness. The language, they say, is what anybody and everybody speaks. Hence there must be no interference with what they regard as a product of nature; they denounce all attempts at guiding choice; their governing principle is epitomized in the title of a speech by a distinguished member of the profession: "Can Native Speakers of a Language Make Mistakes?" (A. W. Read, *Abstract for the Linguistic Society of America Meeting,* Dec. 28–29, 1964).

Within the profession of linguist there are of course warring factions, but on this conception of language as a natural growth with which it is wrong to tamper they are at one. In their arguments one finds appeals to democratic feelings of social equality (all words and forms are equally good) and individual freedom (anyone may do what he likes with his own speech). These assumptions further suggest that the desire for rightness, the very idea of better or worse in speech, is a hangover from aristocratic and oppressive times. To the linguists, change is the only ruler to be obeyed. They equate it with life and accuse their critics of being clock reversers, enemies of freedom, menaces to "life."

Somewhat inconsistently, the linguists produce dictionaries in which they tell us that a word or an expression is standard, substandard, colloquial, archaic, slang, or vulgar. How do they know? They know by listening to the words people use and by noticing—in conversations, newspapers, and books—how and by whom these words are used. Usage, then, is still real and various, even though the authorities refuse to point openly to a set of words and forms as being preferable to others. "Standard" gets around the difficulty of saying "best" or "right."

To the majority, usage also exists about fine points—ingrained connotations, distinctions between close synonyms, suggestions of tone, applicability to concrete or figurative situations, indications of time or purpose or action; in short, the many hints and echoes that words carry within them and that a good speaker or writer brings out as if he were playing on a keyboard. Skill in expression consists in nothing else than steadily choosing the fittest among all possible words, idioms, and constructions. These differ in the qualities that usage has bestowed upon them; and the qualities, in turn, are known by the speaker or writer because he has attended to words and forms as they occur normally, in the company of other words spoken or written.

This choosing among words is done by every user of the language, and not exclusively by professional speakers and writers. A truck driver does not talk to a policeman as he does to his fiancée or to his pals, and we change our verbal as well as our facial expressions when we pass from a wedding to a funeral. In personal relations this adjustment is called tact. In the attempt to make the best use of words, the same mental work is performed. Yet no writer or speaker switches from one complete language or usage to another when he adapts his words to a situation or to the expectation of his audience. All the usages, standard and other, can be drawn on and mixed. It is this bewildering abundance, coupled with the insidious strength of bad examples, that makes most people speak and write carelessly and clumsily, even while they respect clarity and good usage.

Hence, in the task of "communicating," to which everybody these days is strenuously invited, we have to think not only of rules but also of the infinite requirements of tact. Readers even more than hearers respond to what is well put, whether or not they perceive what makes it so. Actually, language is made logical and clear by observing the norms of grammar and syntax; and it is made precise, vivid, and easy ("readable") by respecting the demands of idiom, connotation, tone, rhythm, and the other more fugitive virtues.

Accordingly, a book on usage such as this seeks to serve two related purposes. By analyzing structural errors and ambiguities it reminds writers and speakers of grammatical norms that are frequently flouted; and by discussing words and idioms it demonstrates ways of distinguishing false coin from true and of getting to the point by the quickest route. In neither department can it be complete; it does not pretend to be a grammar book, nor does it profess to discuss every failure of judgment or subtlety in the use of words. It concentrates on the prevailing faults of current speech and prose. And the most useful service it can render is to make its readers think for themselves on these matters. To become sensibly self-conscious about words is more important than to memorize and act on this or that suggestion without thought. For, once again, tact is the overriding concern, and a locution deplorable in the wrong place may yield the needed effect when put in the right place, as Shaw demonstrated when he wittily used *contact* as a verb: *Etonian toffs and Polytechnic cads should contact each other only in street fights, the organization of which might be regarded as a legitimate part of their physical exercise.*

But, it will be asked, is tact not an individual gift, therefore highly variable in its choices? And if that is so, what guidance can a manual offer, other than that of its author's prejudices—mere impressionism? The more such a writer makes a point of his preferences, the more he will be likely to produce a system of purism and pedantry. Would it not be better to find out statistically what the people of this generation actually say and write when they are being careful but not too careful? And since this is what certain dictionaries do, why not go straight to a good dictionary?

The first and obvious reply is that a dictionary does not necessarily give reasons even when it gives examples of varying usage in one or two brief quotations. Often, what makes a word preferable is its relation to others in a passage. The narrow context of a dictionary sentence gives too few clues to the force and versatility of a particular word. Definitions must be supplemented with discussion. This discussion draws its authority from the principle that good usage is what the people who think and care about words believe good usage to be. They have—and their critical reading and listening verifies—the impression that *dearth* means *scarcity*, that *concept* is pedantic, that J. writes like a purist with a taste for the archaic, and that such-and-such expressions are slang or vulgarisms, or again that they may be allowable in loose colloquial speech but would jar or mislead on other occasions. The fact that those who attend to language disagree on many points does not alter the nature and force of good usage, any more than the diverse judgments of critics about fine art or of courts about the law alter the nature and force of art and of law.

In opinions on usage, it is cogency and reasoning, not numbers, that give weight to the decisions arrived at, just as in judicial opinions. And since there is no police power to enforce good usage, no one suffers, except perhaps in skill, by ignoring it.

Consider the book dealer who in his catalogue of rare works describes one as adorned with *photographs of amorous Hindu sculpture.* The reader familiar with usage understands what is meant, but knows that *amorous* is the wrong word. The writer should have used *erotic; amorous* can only be used of persons and, by extension, of words or scenes in which actual persons are involved. Recourse to a dictionary will not help, for the definitions generally assemble rather than separate synonyms. Only the reading of literature will tell the uninformed what that distinction is.

Some may object that if the book dealer's wording was readily understood, the distinction is silly and he who makes it is a prig. Why raise a fuss over *any* expression that is intelligible? The answer is that a language has chosen ways of putting things and rejects others equally clear. *We does* is intelligible but not English; and in the pair of adjectives before us a second substitution clinches the point: if *amorous* is just as good as *erotic,* we should be able to say *loving* as readily as *amorous.* But what would the least sophisticated of readers think if he were told of a book with *photographs of loving Hindu sculpture?*

So much for the positive effect of usage and misusage. Negative discrimination is nowadays even more important for anyone who dislikes pedantry and who wants to avoid falling into it. The temptation to that fall is very great, for science and scholarship dominate the intellectual world and confer prestige on whoever imitates their literal mind and abstract tongue. The worst enemy of modern languages is the universal desire to show off in this pretentious way. Thus a secretary sends a fax to inform you that the VENUE of the meeting has been changed. What she and her employer mean is the *place* of the meeting, but she feels no discomfort in writing the pompous word, for her conversations and her reading are peppered with pedantries. Her friends talk about their children's BEHAVIORS in the *schoolyard* CULTURE (or ENVIRONMENT) as perhaps being a result of wrong *parenting*. The ads tell her to buy a cosmetic that contains *a unique enzymatic-release system,* and when a television show is not forthcoming she is told by a voice from the set that the trouble is *temporary program impairment.*

It is a commonplace that the professions tend to develop jargon, but it is less often recognized that the modern professions seem to wish their jargons to be pedantic, as the older jargons of sailors, farmers, and thieves were not. Today, a person who would like to make his neighborhood pleasanter to walk in is told by a planning agency that *we'll need to retool our street-level environments . . . For example, we could cut crossing-the-street distances with extra sidewalk area, add amenities, and spruce up deteriorating* INFRASTRUCTURE. And a man who worries about losing his job in the future reads this advice from a counselor: *The increase in white-collar terminations has required that economic security replace job security as a goal . . . Family financial planning must now reflect periods of unemployment as natural catalysts in career development . . .* [Money must be] *available, if needed, for a self-management transition between severance and payroll.*

In both extracts the pretentious words string together half-realized metaphors, a mode of thought that now characterizes educated and uneducated alike and shows them to be—at least in words—pedants who only half-think. The danger to the language, therefore, does not come from those unhappily sunk in ignorance and vulgarity; it comes from the entire range of the population, which is sunk in the swamp of jargon, and which complains of it without knowing how to extricate itself. To begin, it must hear itself talk: *We need more cutting-edge thinking, Try to de-emphasize that particular focus, You've failed to penetrate their motivation, Let's highlight the bottom line.*

Any revulsion from jargon should ideally take the speaker back to direct colloquial speech, but human recoil is extremist, and the effort to avoid error often lands the self-improver in what is known as purism. The difference between purity and purism is as hard to define as that between modesty and prudery, but in either domain the foolish excess is easily distinguished. Purism is another form of the pedantic. It singles out in the language of science and scholarship what is literal and minute, as pedantry does the abstract and long-winded. Purism haggles over trifles and refuses to know when errors and confusions no longer matter. We all understand what a *spiral staircase* is; the purist reminds us that a spiral lies flat in one plane, so that our staircase is properly a *helix*. But even if each of us has his one or two pet pedantries, collectively we shall not go down the helical staircase. We shall continue to *drink a cup of coffee* and assuredly not a *cupful*; we shall speak of *captions below the pictures*, though *caption* by a confused etymology suggests *head*; we shall speak of being *buttonholed* by a bore and not *buttonheld*, from the supposedly correct *buttonhold*; and we shall certainly *cross the bridge* (but not till we come to it), instead of agonizing over the truth that it is the river that is crossed and not the bridge.

In these and dozens of other instances, the reason for avoiding the pure or pedantic truth of the matter is that it no longer serves (or never did serve) an expressive purpose. Conversely, the reason for urging the thoughtful to retain the strict sense of CONNIVE and DISINTERESTED is that a creeping abuse threatens to rob us of an expressive instrument. The confusion between two words or two senses may be an old one repeatedly cleared up, as in *perspicuous* and *perspicacious*—words that no one is obliged to use, but that everyone who does should keep straight, like *dearth* and *wealth*; or confusion may come from ignorant innovation, as when *viable* suddenly replaces *possible* at every turn. It is worth noting that when a distinction is commonplace, even though of trivial effect, the advocates of laxity do not overlook it. The young foreigner who apologizes for the fact that the chocolates he has brought as a gift are *molten* is told with a smile that that is not English: the right word is *melted*. Similarly, we are bound to say *awestruck* and *grief-stricken*. If we are to be bound when it makes as little difference as this, we should be able to comply with good grace when it makes much more.

For it often happens, as in *disinterested*, that the meaning now being threatened by confusion was arrived at by a distinction not originally felt. When it was at last made, it presumably answered a need, and in all probability that need still exists. Almost always, the move toward a distinction, the positive work of mind on language, is a gain. The negative change, away from distinct ideas, is generally the result of heedlessness or ignorance, and hence a loss.

It follows that the appeal to the catchphrase "change means life" needs reconsideration. Change means death too, and in our own bodies we take steps to arrest or reverse certain changes by medicine, inoculation, surgery, and other strong measures. We choose what we want to preserve and what we want to slough off. In fact, analogies from life and evolution are poor ways of thinking about language. Change is inevitable in language as in other institutions—a truth known and accepted long before modern linguistics—but change is only a name for changes in the plural; that is, change affects the manifold elements of language unevenly and unpredictably. A language does not move as a solid mass like a glacier. In English, a very large number of forms and words have not changed for six hundred years—which is why with a little help an English speaker can read Chaucer at sight. And throughout much of this period the persistence of a standard has prevented some equally persistent deviations from becoming good usage: SCARCELY . . . THAN has been written for nearly two centuries without becoming acceptable; *hand me them pliers* has been said over and over again without breaking down the distinction between the adjective and the pronoun form.

There is, in short, more to the history of language than the restless agitation of molecules of speech, out of which the best of all possible worlds of language must emerge. Conscious purpose and reason have interfered with "nature," and the result has been embodied in the written tradition. Present-day linguistic theory writes off the written, saying it is not language at all; only speech is language. If this were so, the materials of linguistic science would go back only as far as the invention of the phonograph: everything before then would be irrelevant, and the boasted evolution itself would be irrecoverable for lack of records. Babel, moreover, would long ago have overtaken us, for the rate of change in spoken sounds is very rapid, and only the written language—indeed, only a fixed conventional spelling—now enables us to understand Shakespeare and to share (as we say) the English language with him.

It is useless to speculate about the motives of scholars whose zeal for enshrining the slip of the tongue makes them despise the richest source of fact about their subject. But it is important at the end of the twentieth century to reassert the worth of the alphabet. The spoken language is not independent of the written. One need only listen to colloquial talk to discover how much the mother tongue owes to the conscious work that writers have always felt entitled to perform upon it. No scientific pretensions can remove that right. It would be a curious state of affairs if only those who seldom think about the words they use, who read little, and who "cannot be bothered" with distinctions should be the only ones with full powers over vocabulary and syntax.

Even on grounds of free democratic choice the hands-off attitude about language receives no support. If the citizen as taxpayer, parent, teacher, motorist, litigant, reader of poetry, or user of gadgets were delighted with the millions of words he endures annually, there might be some reason for letting everything alone and scrapping freshman English together with manuals of usage. But on the contrary, the articulate public continually complains. The children, we hear, are badly taught and cannot read, spell, or write; employers despair of finding literate clerks and typists; the professions deplore the thickening of jargon which darkens counsel and impedes action; scientists cry out in their journals that their colleagues cannot report their facts intelligibly; and businessmen declare many bright people unemployable for lack of the ability to say what they mean in any medium. This is enough warrant for dozens of remedial measures; many are suggested and followed; but most of them are of the mechanical-miraculous kind which in the end prove futile.

Resisting the tide, then, is not antidemocratic but simple self-preservation against the decay of mind itself. Some wonder what is the good? On this point individual temperament decides. Brave writers resist chiefly by example and sometimes by precept: Rex Stout has one of his characters say, *"Contact" is not a verb under this roof*, and those who read this prelude to hospitality either applaud or pause in surprise. Newspaper and magazine editors, publishers, and certain business firms fight a guerrilla war in the jungle of jargon and pick off—a few at a time, over and over again—some of the worst enemies of logic and usage. It is hard to imagine where we would be without this effort, and it is at least conceivable that if the pressure is kept up it will hasten the increasingly obvious and imperative reform—a resumption in our schools of the teaching of grammar and the reading of books.

In any event, fatalism about language cannot be the philosophy of those who care about language; it is the illogical philosophy of their opponents. Surely the notion that, because usage is ultimately what everybody does to words, nobody can or should do anything about them is self-contradictory. Somebody, by definition, does something; and this something is best done by those with convictions and a stake in the outcome, whether the stake of private pleasure or of professional duty or both does not matter. Resistance always begins with individuals.

Previous generations also had their cant words and pedantries, which were destroyed, not by empty time or by the indifferent, but by the choice of those who were offended or bored. Jonathan Swift, who is damned by the hands-off school for denouncing what seemed to him objectionable in 1710, actually accomplished much of what he hoped for, though he failed once. He disliked fashionable shortenings such as *mob*, from *mobile vulgus*, the fickle crowd. Since *mob* has become part of good usage, it is held proved that Swift was wrong to raise his voice. But we can well imagine that *mob* was offensive when new; it has only gradually become deodorized. The lesson is that when repeated use has worn down the novelty, the word we hear and the associations we sense are not what they were at first. That is why we would still agree with Swift about the other shortenings he reproved and vanquished: *phizz, hipps, poz, rep, incog,* and *plenipo*. One need not suppose that he got rid of them all by himself in order to see that he was right to take his chance and speak out. At any time and about any word, one should exercise the right of free speech that some would abridge. By simply using or rejecting the locution, one casts a vote, repeatable as often as one likes, in favor of one's views. To arrive at these views and achieve consistency among them is much the harder part of the task, and it is this difficulty that brings the thoughtful to discussions of usage.

It is no doubt possible for a writer so to train himself, or so to be trained, that his only merit is freedom from faults. But even the most fanatical believer in the efficacy of hunting down errors will not pretend that we can distinguish at sight the negative from the positive merits of writing. It is a mistake to imply an opposition between the absence of faults and the presence of vitality, as if correct writing had to be dead writing, or as if we had to choose between power and polish. In writing as in morals, negative and positive merits are complementary; resistance to the wrong and the weak is, *ipso facto*, cultivation of the right and the strong.

For example, to eliminate the vice of wordiness is to ensure the virtue of emphasis, which depends more on conciseness than on any other consideration. Wherever we make twenty-five words do the work of fifty, we halve the area in which looseness and disorganization can flourish, and by reducing the span of attention required we increase the force of the thought. To make our words count for as much as possible is surely the simplest as well as the hardest secret of style. Its difficulty consists in the ceaseless pursuit of the thousand ways of rectifying our mistakes, eliminating our inaccuracies, and replacing our falsities—in a word, editing our prose. When we can do this habitually (even though it never becomes easy) we shall find ourselves honoring the faculty that can do more toward this end than a mastery of prescriptive grammar, more than the study of etymology and semantics, more than an observance of idiom and the maxims of rhetoric. And what is this faculty? It is the blessing of an orderly mind.

No mind, to be sure, is completely and consistently orderly. But some minds are incomparably more demanding of order than others, and in consequence some writers lapse into disorder more rarely than others. Still, all writers drowse at places where they should have stayed awake; all writers are guilty of oversights without which they would have been better writers—one reason why some of the cautionary examples in this book are drawn from authors ranging from respectable to illustrious. A great deal of our language is so automatic that even the thoughtful never think about it, and this mere not-thinking is the gate through which solecisms or inferior locutions slip in. Some part, greater or smaller, of every thousand words is inevitably parroted, even by the least parrotlike.

Anyone inclined to doubt this statement can prove it to himself by a simple test. Let him skim through a recent book or magazine at random. Most articles and stories will require the turning of a page in the middle of a sentence. At these moments he will find that he has mentally read the next word—frequently the next several words—without turning the page at all. He will occasionally have guessed wrong, but more often he will be right. Where so much of language falls into automatic and predictable patterns, there will certainly be a good measure of standardized error that the orderly mind has not even noticed. Hundreds of educated persons have written, for example, *center around* or *center about*. They know as well as Euclid that a center is a point that other things can surround, not an area that surrounds other things; their sense of order, if they used it, would tell them that circles find their centers *in* or *on* or *at* a point, and that this fact must control our metaphoric use of *center*. But this reasoning is just what does not come into play.

Order, reasoning, is sidetracked again in the construction that we may call the *one-of-those-who-is* blunder, probably the commonest in speech and print alike, in spite of being one of the most easily detected. *He is one of those who fights back:* the orderly mind sees where the singular statement about the individual ends, where the plural statement about the group or class begins, and such a mind avoids mixing the forms. But to see such matters one has to look. The many who never think of looking have therefore sprinkled millions of lines with *those who fights, prophets who goes unrecognized, children who has never known parental companionship, peaks that wears a perpetual crown of snow,* and so on without end.

This particular mistake will yield to a hint of rhetoric or to a touch of the old-fashioned prescriptive grammar now in disfavor with linguists. But there are thousands of other mistakes that fall outside the grammar book, since grammar deals only with what is amenable to classification and rule. For the irregular error, the unique blunder, a superior sense of order is the sole corrective. Without its discipline, the faults can only be dealt with one at a time, laboriously, after the damage has been done. Perhaps a third to a half of the offenses against usage illustrated in the Lexicon would need no description or analysis if the faculty that makes for order were always alert.

Consider what pitfalls may hide even in the simple device of listing, the very basis of logical organization. Any educated person can surely make a list of items under a heading designed to govern them all. Such an arrangement will be what the track is to the train, the fence to the field, or the straitjacket to the unruly patient: it will be inescapable. But is it? Look at the description that a widely esteemed desk encyclopedia gives of its contents on the jacket of its second edition. The inventory begins with a centered head:

HAS SEPARATE ARTICLES ON:

under which we read:

EVERY proper name in the Bible, with reference to passages where they occur.

EVERY incorporated place in the United States with a population of 1,000 or over, as well as many smaller places of historical interest.

EVERY U.S. President, every Supreme Court Justice since 1908 (plus many earlier ones), all outstanding Senators, Representatives, and Cabinet members.

So far, so good—three entries, in parallel, answering to the verb and noun in their common heading. But now comes the fourth entry:

BASIC articles on major literatures, as well as innumerable biographies and shorter articles.

Where now is the link with the centered head? Forgotten, consigned to limbo, along with the orderly mind. The column runs to four more items, not one of which matches the announcement *Has separate articles on*. What we have articles on in these four is:

EXPANDED articles on music, modern literature, European geography, science, and many other subjects.

MORE economic information and social history in articles throughout the book.

ARTICLES covering thousands of species of plants and animals (and ten pages of illustrations on animals, four pages on plants).

AND countless additions and improvements that put this . . .

ENCYCLOPEDIA in a class by itself.

Of the eight entries under one rubric, only three have a logical connection with it. The grand culmination of senselessness is reached when we bring together the first statement and the last: *Has separate articles on* and *countless additions and improvements*. (As an afterthought one might also ask how, in a reference work, *separate* articles differ from just articles.) The lesson here is simply that where the orderly mind is not continuously in charge—before, during, and after the act of writing—all the signs and gestures of sound organization will not rule out blunder and chaos.

The chief trait of the orderly mind is tenacity, concentration—that undeviating attention which in various sports is enjoined in the precept "Keep your eye on the ball." What we must keep our eye on in prose is the object, idea, or wording that we start with. In any list of items, the heading sets up a promise; if anything below fails to fit, the promise is broken, the thought is derailed. For all who speak or write, the road to effective language is thinking straight.

In ordinary prose the counterpart of an inventory is the simple enumeration of three or more members separated by punctuation (usually commas), with a conjunction (usually *and*, but sometimes *but* or *or*) as the signal of the closing member. This sort of series, one of the commonest of all patterns, can be represented by the formula *a, b, and c* or (when expanded) by *a, b, c, . . . , and n.* Examples: *red, white, and blue / tea, coffee, or milk / woke up, got up, bathed, dressed, breakfasted, and hurried out / Boston at Detroit, Cleveland at Chicago, New York at Minneapolis, Kansas City at Los Angeles, and Baltimore at Washington.* One might think offhand that these series provided about as little opportunity to go wrong as any standard construction in English, but to think so is to underestimate the capacity of language for laying traps and the propensity of writers for stumbling into them. The conjunction *and* is one of the most troublesome words in the vocabulary. Because it is so regularly a signal of the last member, the absentminded writer automatically accepts it as signaling a last member that in fact never turns up. The result is a structure with the look but not the reality of an honest enumeration—a false series in which the last item is a misfit. *The tanker has an over-all length of 736 feet, a beam of 102 feet and she is capable of carrying 16,581,000 gallons of oil.* To have a genuine series of three, you must either link the *length* and *beam* phrases with *and*, or turn the last unit into a matching noun—e.g., *and a capacity of* . . . (See COMMA, THE.)

We saw in the discussion of *one-of-those-who-is* why and how the clash of number between subject and verb should be avoided—though not all compound subjects constitute a plural. The genuine clash occurs in many other constructions, usually when the attention is distracted from the true subject by some intervening word that differs in number, or else by some inversion that causes the subject to follow instead of precede its verb. Consider such a sentence as *Ms. W.'s list of special methods include those developed for the home as well as for the school.* Here *includes*, the singular verb that belongs to *list*, is corrupted into a plural by the intervening *methods*.

The attraction of a properly plural verb to an intervening singular is only a little less frequent than the reverse. *Even devoted friends of the communications industry like Professor W. has (have) finally become con-*

vinced that curbs on that monopoly are necessary. Sometimes a quasi-collective noun that might be construed as a plural provides a sort of escape hatch for the careless: *A combination of lectures and fashion shows are planned to stimulate playgoing in various cities.* The writer might protest that he conceived *combination* as a plural and was not derailed by *lectures and fashion shows;* but it may be doubted whether he would write *combination are* with nothing in between.

It is of course by means of the critical spirit that one learns the unteachable things about writing. One forces oneself to be critical about everything one reads or hears, and this must not exclude what one says or writes. Self-criticism, which begins by being an arduous discipline, ends by becoming second nature. But habit also protects familiar faults. Without a continual scrutiny of his successive drafts, even a good writer will fall into bad writing. Here is an author so intent on what he means that he fails to see what he is actually saying—all the more regrettably since he is dealing with questions of language. Of a particular level of diction he says: *It is so universal that few people in the United States escape its influence entirely, including all but a small portion* (number?) *of schoolteachers.* He is not aware that he has bundled in nearly all the schoolteachers with "the few that escape." His intention was to say the exact opposite; namely, that most people, including most schoolteachers, do not escape.

Order or the lack of it is sometimes hidden well below the surface of the words, and the analysis that would disclose error is not undertaken, because the reader's mind willingly follows the writer's concealed confusion. Thus a storyteller starts off a paragraph with these words: *Some hours later, after an excellent lunch had been swallowed untasted by a silent assembly* . . . The riddle here is: Who could testify to the excellence of the lunch?

The great classics are no better off when they rely on habit or technique without self-inspection. James Fenimore Cooper, who could write superb narrative prose when he resisted his mania for calling every bullet *a leaden messenger* and every eagle *a monarch of the air,* would from time to time produce a sentence that in its perfection of chaos staggers credulity. In *The Pathfinder,* one of his Indians, startled by the smoke of an unexpected campfire, stands on tiptoe watching it: *Then, falling back on his feet, a low exclamation, in the soft tones that form so singular a contrast to its harsher cries in the Indian warrior's voice, was barely au-*

dible. The cry that falls back on the warrior's (or someone's) feet is but one of the troubles here.

The miscellany of common blunders here assembled shows, not that the orderly mind is a rarity, but that its lapses are frequent and easy. No one would contend that the faculty of order by itself will overcome all the difficulties of writing sound prose. It gives the security of the good tactician, but it is not the whole art of war and not even the full arsenal. What it needs as a first supplement is a command of traditional grammar and of some tested rhetorical principles. We must accordingly glance at them forthwith, beginning with what in all the Western languages but English is still officially known as grammar.

As Robert Browning tells us in his "Grammarian's Funeral," the grammarian must die, but the logic and grammatical forms of the beautiful inflected language he has cherished live on. Today the cultural descendant of Jefferson or Mark Twain makes the same assumption about the permanent need of grammar to govern his own much less highly inflected language. By grammar he means primarily syntax—parts-of-speech grammar, subject-verb-and-predicate grammar, the traditional apparatus for analyzing the structure and logic of the sentence. According to that tradition, any good sentence will stand parsing: it can be broken down into subjects and objects and antecedents, cases and parts of speech, modes and tenses. The comprehension of these goes with the comprehension of meaning itself: grammatical relations are the offprint of logical relations. Grammar explains how the elements of language that everybody rearranges so swiftly and easily come together to form meaning.

Any such descendant is likely to suffer shock when he comes upon the discovery that everything he was taught about grammar is now in disrepute among the scholars of language; is, indeed, officially as dead as Browning's grammarian. If someone of inquiring mind turns to the article *Grammar* in an up-to-date encyclopedia, he will learn that grammar no longer deals primarily with syntax. It has become morphology— the science of the formation of words, how they are built out of the smallest bits and pieces of meaning; e.g., the *s* that usually turns a singular common noun into a plural. Since the inquirer's troubles probably have to do with constructions rather than with the makeup of words, he turns to the entry *Syntax.* All it tells him is "See *Grammar.*" Back where he started, he discovers that what he is seeking is a reprehensible doctrine called *prescriptive grammar*—something now outlawed because it is unscientific: it prescribes—that is, recommends—certain uses of English as grammatical and correct, others as ungrammatical and incorrect. This is as bad as to point out correct usage in words and idioms. In true grammar it is wrong to say that anything is right.

By now our inquirer is at a loss. He wanted guidance and has been denied it in the name of science. It dawns on him that modern linguistics regards language as a set of facts and tendencies; it has nothing to impart about the successful ways of composing English or the relative merits of forms and constructions. Grammar has renounced all these concerns as so many value judgments. Yet what the seeker was after was precisely a system of value judgments, such as he can get from any mechanic or builder about the appropriate use or relative strength of materials.

There is of course much to be learned from the so-called objective or purely descriptive grammar, whose foundations were laid by an Englishman, Henry Sweet, the model of Shaw's hero in *Pygmalion* and *My Fair Lady*. Sweet's *New English Grammar* (1891) inspired the Danish scholar Otto Jespersen to perfect the method and produce *A Modern English Grammar on Historical Principles* (7 vols., 1909–31). After these two came a host of laborious analysts and collectors of what are now called speechways. This term puts writing in its place among things artificial and unimportant, and the objectivists deride the grammar book and the schoolmarm who together tried to maintain the norms. Actually, the old grammars were in general quite objective, and it was society rather than the books that enforced correctness.

Thus do cultural ideals change and, in changing, obscure or repress permanent human needs. For the "science" established by the appeal to liberty and the tactics of ridicule during the past century is in effect not about language at all, if language is defined as the art of skillfully conveying intended meanings. Rather, what the linguists have studied is that portion of human behavior which is articulate—a branch of social psychology. Whether the stuff of this new learning is indeed a natural product like cobalt or ambergris is something to be debated elsewhere. What concerns us here is that the other thing also known as language, language as the art of self-expression, language as a material conformable to the rules of creation, remains a subject deserving man's best care.

If, then, we assume that language is not only to be spoken impulsively but can also be used—and well used; and if we believe it possible to make words serve purposes that are more than momentary, we find the linguistic critique of grammar irrelevant and we recover the right to judge between those forms that are awkward and false and those that are delicate and expressive. To help us compare and choose, we must accept judgments of value and adopt suggested remedies—quite as if we were curing an ailment. This enterprise involves reading books about language that do not simply describe, and it means mastering that part of grammar which is the most potent aid to composition; namely, the rules of syntax.

Prose is not necessarily good because it obeys the rules of syntax, but it is fairly certain to be bad if it ignores them. Professional writers have generally felt it a duty to face and solve the difficulties of grammatical agreement, time sequence, and natural linkage, considering this effort not slavery but protection against unreadability and wrong meaning. The perceptions codified in grammar supplement the orderly mind if one has it, and serve as a substitute for it if one has it not. Examine this short, simple sentence from a widely read murder story: *And what purpose has all his objections served?* That is what happens to those who trust the ear alone: *purpose has* is a natural sequence; it sounds right. Unhappily, the question asked is not about *purpose* but about *objections*. The author has actually written: *All his objections has served what purpose?* The orderly mind being at fault, nothing is left but grammar to save it from falling victim to the reversed order characteristic of questions.

Nor does it take a question to bring about such accidents. Any singular that leads into an inverted order of words can do it. Here is an instance the more curious for occurring in a book devoted entirely to the niceties of diction: *From this use has sprung certain quaint verb specimens;* that is, *Certain . . . specimens has sprung . . .* When instinct fails, grammar helps by naming the fault and the remedy: a singular noun ahead of the verb must not blind a writer to his delayed plural subject. This help of course presupposes assent to the principle that verbs had better agree in number with their subjects. Anyone is free to dissent, but the rebels are likely to find that the convenience won by anarchy can become terribly inconvenient. Such opportunism has all the disadvantages of changing signals without consultation or the rules of a game without foreseeing all the consequences.

It is commonly said that English is a language in which a standardized word order performs the functions assigned to endings in inflected languages such as Latin; but English is so free in its order that it is often hard to make sure where the subject is. The discovery calls for an act of grammatical discernment. *Silver and gold have I none / Gone are the days of effortless ease / Peaceful lay the valley / Desperate if not hopeless is such a diplomatic assignment*—such idiomatic inversions contribute to vigor and variety. But in dislocating the normal order they bring next to the verb some noun easily mistaken for its subject. At this point, again, a grammatical rule is a means of rescue and reassurance. As in the *one-of-those-who* construction, analysis (parsing) sets us or keeps us on the track: the subject, antecedent of the relative pronoun *who*, is the plural *those*, which requires a plural verb *are*. The demonstration will of course be Eskimo to one who does not know what a subject is, or a pronoun, or an antecedent. But to the technically equipped the explanation is quicker and simpler than the appeal to logic.

Some, to be sure, insist that errors committed so often by so many must not be called errors. One libertarian quotes a sentence of Shelley's: *I am one of those who am unable to refuse my assent* and asserts that in the United States the singular (more usually *is* than *am*) offends no one but grammarians. This is not true, to begin with—it offends every good writer; and next, the assertion misconceives the role of examples, great names, and majority rule. As Jespersen showed with his 50,000 classified examples, a precedent can be found for practically any construction or locution. At this rate, anything goes and there is no use arguing either for the rules or for unlimited freedom.

But whoever has a meaning to convey finds that in order to say anything briefly and well he must choose among many possibilities. As a thinking being, he cannot help responding to sound and rhythm or favoring logic and smoothness over their opposites—whereby he is once again engaged in generating rules. And to the extent that he can think straight, the rules will come close to those already in the tradition. Let three thousand say *one of those who believes* while only three say *those who believe*; and as long as the three thousand do not also say *we believes, you believes, they believes,* the three thousand will be wrong from the only point of view that is relevant here, the point of view of form. Mere prevalence can sanctify many sorts of popular error—it can, for example, make words eventually mean the opposite of what they originally meant—but it cannot make a singular verb consort with a plural subject for the convenience of a writer who has not taken the trouble to find out what the subject is.

Many of the snags that every writer encounters cannot be recognized without the sort of analysis that underlies grammar. Agreement presents riddles impossible to formulate except in grammatical terms. Punctuation is difficult to discuss (for example, as it relates to restrictive and non-restrictive clauses) without a good grasp of grammatical forms. Like the carpenter or plumber, the writer cannot carry on his own trade without technical terms; he cannot judge or describe his own work or confound his editors without using grammatical categories. Diction itself, the choice of words, cannot easily be discussed apart from grammatical names, for each of several synonyms may allow a construction with which the others would clash. If, for instance, we want to argue whether *commiserate* takes a direct object without a preposition, it is desirable to know what a direct object and a preposition are.

In short, if in taking up speech and writing we throw grammar overboard, we shall find that little will be left that can be generalized about. The language will have become a catalogue of forms and phrases, a confusion of idioms to be individually conquered, a jungle of irregularities; we shall be like the beginning student of Chinese, who must memorize ideograms by the thousand. For despite all its deviations and excrescences, English does have a structure, a logic at its center, a set of principles, a consistency matching that of the orderly mind. Of this structure grammar is the working diagram and teachable plan—reason enough why, to the worker in prose, grammar remains indispensable.

Powerful arguments from utility, then, confirm the value of grammar to those who take language as an art to be practiced rather than as the flora and fauna of linguistic naturalists. The opponents of grammar are quite right to say that it is an artificial analysis made after the fact, and not a statement of natural laws; they are quite wrong to think this condemns it. As much could be urged against the map that saves us from getting lost on land or against the chart that enables us to read our way about the seas. Yet we do not hear these denounced as artificial or gratuitous; the only question ever raised is whether they are reasonably accurate. All systems and diagrams are conventions, all are imperfect, and all that gain currency evidently satisfy the purpose for which they were devised.

To be sure, one hears the further complaint that what we call English grammar was framed by scholars as if English were Latin, a dead language which they knew better than English. The assumption is that an analytical description of one dead language cannot be relevant to another which is living and growing. This indictment no longer corresponds to anything in modern experience. The English grammar inherited by people now living is actually a grammar of the elements common to various modern Indo-European tongues. It applies with slight readjustments to the Romance languages and the Germanic, to the more and the less inflected; and it has long ceased to proffer definitions and distinctions that cannot be grasped without a knowledge of Latin.

The hostility to Latin among linguists and educationists is in fact perverse. Those who speak so harshly against Latin do not show much familiarity with it, whereas few of those who have even a tincture of Latin deny that it throws light on both the structural and the stylistic features of English. The English vocabulary, besides having hundreds of Latin words taken over *literatim*, consists so preponderantly of Romance elements that the reader equipped with some Latin will understand at sight a great many words of which another cannot make head or tail without a dictionary; and of course even a nodding acquaintance with this dead language opens the way to picking up a reading knowledge of French or Italian. Among the classics of English literature a large number are the work of authors who read (and sometimes wrote) Latin like their native tongue. Who more characteristically English than Milton, Dryden, Swift, Dr. Johnson?—yet how full their minds and works of Latin speech and forms of thought. It would be rash to maintain that the connection between their powers and their knowledge was accidental. Certainly one still hears of students to whom the hang of their native English suddenly became clear when they began to learn Latin grammar. For the analytic method of grammar appears all the more clearly in a language where inflections show the function of the word in the sentence, and where meaning is not so immediate as to make the form negligible. If there exists a better pedagogic device than Latin for showing how the Western languages work, it has not yet been found.

Now, if we are to keep grammar because we do not know how to replace the teaching it gives, we would be wise to keep also the best formulations of which it is capable. Afraid of everything traditional, modern theorists have devised several new terminologies (said to be easy) and various systems (supposedly simplified) to take account of the difference between a highly inflected dead language and a less inflected living one. The chief of these revisions affects the treatment of grammatical case in nouns and pronouns—a subject suitable for testing whether the simplification really simplifies.

The American grammarian's new definition restricts the idea of case to change marked by inflection. To the personal and relative pronouns that have three forms—e.g., *he, his, him; they, their, them; who, whose, whom*—the modernist grants the like number of cases, which he calls either subjective, possessive, and objective or (in the old "Latin" way) nominative, genitive, and accusative. The possessive or genitive, whether of pronouns or of nouns, we can ignore in this connection, because it acts not as a noun at all but as an adjective. Since nouns, aside from the possessive, inflect only for the plural (*dogs, matches, counties, monkeys, oxen*), the new definition confines case to a handful of pronouns. The pronouns that have the same form whether they are used as subject or as object (e.g., *you, it*), together with all nouns, are said to be in the common case—the grammarian's way of pronouncing them caseless. His "common" means that the one form serves every possible use—subject, object of verb, indirect object, object of preposition, predicate complement, appositive, vocative, and even interjection. The grammarian is in effect asserting that case, except as it survives vestigially in a few pronouns, has disappeared from English.

Anyone is free to dispose of case in this way; but he should reflect, and we should note, that washing his hands of case makes him poorer, not freer. He remains (or rather, he keeps himself) in the dark about the way sentences hold together and words function. "Common case" describes nothing and analyzes nothing. But grammar is essentially analytic; it names things not for the fun of having a nomenclature but so as to understand the relations of working parts. One can analyze an English sentence without using the word "case"; what matters is to know that a given word is subject or object, and of what it is the one or the other. Assuming that we invoke case at all, as we do for the pronouns that show the case by inflection, we will find it advantageous to learn the broadest possible definition of case, so as to be able to name the relation of any substantive to other words, whether or not that relation is shown by a changed form of the word (*he*, subject; *him*, object). On this view, every noun has case; the case is objective if the noun serves as an object, subjective if it serves as a subject: Boy (subject) meets Girl (object); Girl (subject) meets Boy (object). Since, in spite of all antigrammarians, transitive and intransitive verbs still differ, as do active and passive voice, strong verbs and copulas—all matters involving case—the notion and the name *case* are indispensable for talking about sentences after seeing into their machinery. No garage mechanic would tolerate a doctrine that prevented him from naming the distributor and its role, on the pretext that to do so was arbitrarily to divide a unified electrical system.

The firecracker exploded under the horse's hoofs (intransitive verb) / *He exploded the firecracker under the horse's hoofs* (transitive verb). How can we specify and explain the formal difference here between the two firecrackers whose role as an explosive is unaffected by the form? Quite simply: we say that the first *firecracker* is in the subjective case, the second in the objective case; the first names the agent of the verb; the second suffers the action of the verb, the agent being *He*. If we say that both *firecrackers* are in the common case we brush over a radical difference of function and describe nothing. It may be remarked in passing that in Latin itself nouns may have identical forms in the nominative and in the accusative, in the singular and in the plural, yet no one dreams of lumping them in a common case or parsing them otherwise than according to their function in the sentence.

What counts, of course, is not system or terminology but perceptiveness. For lack of it one may struggle with a vague sense of wrongness in something one has written and be unable to find or correct its cause. For example: *Your neighbors and friends will never mention, and thus may remain unsuspected and uncorrected for years, these traits that rub everyone the wrong way.* Here the word *traits* is compelled to be in two cases at once, as the object of *will never mention* and the subject of *may remain*. Nothing short of a knowledge of grammatical case will tell writer or reader precisely what the trouble is. Likewise, allowing grammar to merge ideas formerly distinct is a bar to understanding. The loss of inflection in English does enable us to treat alike an indirect and a direct object after a transitive verb that takes both. *Please grant the bearer* (= to the bearer) *time to state his mission* / *She threw P.* (= at P.) *a quizzical look* / *He read the gathering* (= to or for the gathering) *some of his unpublished poems.* But the indirect objects here—the objects of omitted prepositions—are called by some modern grammars objective, like the direct objects *time, look,* and *poems.* Anyone with a smattering of Latin cannot help feeling those indirect objects as datives, which illustrates again how the dead language lights up the realities of the living one. The non-Latinist who does not scorn grammar knows that the indirect object implies a preposition. Both Latinist and non-Latinist, without speaking of datives or prepositions, or even needing to reflect that the indirect object almost always precedes the direct one, use that word order instinctively, for it is usually not reversible. Why should not both speakers also share the means of knowing explicitly what they are doing?

The antigrammarians and homogenizers who have little use for case often oppose the inflecting of *who* in the objective case; they prefer *Who were you talking with just now?* to *Whom were you . . . ?* They grant that we have to say *To* (or *With*) *whom were you talking?* but demand the suppression of the *m* when the object precedes the preposition. At the same time, some of them will perversely permit *whom* in one of its fairly frequent misuses: *I got my information from someone whom I believed was in a position to know.* This *whom*, as the subject of *was* (not the object of *believed*), has to be *who*, and the defense of it by *whom*-haters raises the suggestion that what they really hate is not so much any particular locution as the general idea of grammatical punctilio. Jespersen rationalizes this false *whom* as the natural outcome of a rather involved speech instinct; he does not recoil even from such a monstrosity as Disraeli's *individuals whom, if you do not meet, you become restless.* But you can read a thousand pages of Jespersen's own prose without encountering any such aberration.

It is, in fact, one of the striking features of the libertarian position that it preaches an unbuttoned grammar in a prose style that is fashioned with the utmost grammatical rigor. H. L. Mencken's two thousand pages on the vagaries of the American language are written in the fastidious syntax of a precisian. If we go by what the liberators do instead of by what they say, we conclude that they all believe in conventional grammar, practice it against their own preaching, and continue to cultivate the elegance they despise in theory.

Meanwhile, the scientist who investigates words as the natural byproducts of unconscious behavior and the artist who delights in words as miraculous and lovable creations are talking from opposite shores of a pretty wide gulf, and it is small wonder that they do not hear each other very well. To the scientist, choice and taste are prejudice, standards are pedantry, and the distinction between fit and unfit, grammatical and ungrammatical, is reprehensible. The artist, on the contrary, could not live or work without exercising the critical faculty, which at its highest applies taste and at its lowest applies grammar. As for the great majority, in spite of being by turns careless and embarrassed, it is certainly on the side of the artist. The poorly taught, the foreign-born, the ambitious young aiming at the professions, the unassuming toilers at business, each individual for his own good reasons struggles over dimly felt obstacles to make his meaning clear. He or she may seek help in the "Words" column of the monthly magazine or in the headier manual of usage, but all hope to find somewhere the way to better means of self-expression. The professional writer, of course, is concerned not with what is allowable or defensible but rather with what is good enough to need no defense. From the common root of their desires the artist and the user of language for practical ends share an obligation to preserve against confusion and dissipation the powers that over the centuries the mother tongue has acquired. It is a duty to maintain the continuity of speech that makes the thought of our ancestors easily understood, to conquer Babel every day against the illiterate and the heedless, and to resist the pernicious and lulling dogma that in language—contrary to what obtains in all other human affairs—whatever is is right and doing nothing is for the best.

FULL TITLES OF BOOKS CITED IN THE TEXT

AMERICAN HERITAGE DICTIONARY
The American Heritage Dictionary of the English Language, 3rd ed. Boston and New York: Houghton Mifflin Co., 1992.

OXFORD ENGLISH DICTIONARY
The Compact Oxford English Dictionary, 2nd ed., complete text reproduced micrographically. Oxford: The Clarendon Press, 1993.

SHORTER OXFORD ENGLISH DICTIONARY
The Shorter Oxford English Dictionary on Historical Principles, 3rd ed., revised with addenda. Oxford: The Clarendon Press, 1955.

FOWLER
A Dictionary of Modern English Usage, by H. W. Fowler. Oxford: The Clarendon Press, 1926.

GOWERS
A Dictionary of Modern English Usage, by H. W. Fowler. 2nd ed., revised by Sir Ernest Gowers. Oxford: The Clarendon Press, 1965.

JESPERSEN
A Modern English Grammar on Historical Principles, i–vii, 1909–49, by Otto Jespersen. Ed. Niels Haislund, London, Copenhagen: G. Allen & Unwin; Munksgaard, 1965.

RANDOM HOUSE DICTIONARY
The Random House Dictionary of the English Language, 2nd ed. New York: Random House, Inc., 1987.

WEBSTER'S THIRD EDITION

Webster's Third New International Dictionary of the English Language. Springfield: G. & C. Merriam Co., 1976.

WEBSTER'S NEW WORLD DICTIONARY

Webster's New World Dictionary of American English, 3rd college ed. New York: Simon & Schuster, Inc., 1988.

EDITOR'S NOTE

Wilson Follett was born in North Attleborough, Massachusetts, in 1887. He graduated in 1909 from Harvard University and taught English at Texas Agricultural and Mechanical University, Dartmouth College, and Brown University. From the 1920s on, he worked as an editor for Yale University Press, Alfred A. Knopf, and New York University Press. Follett wrote for many magazines, including *The Atlantic Monthly*, *Harper's*, and *The Yale Review*. He also edited a twelve-volume set of the works of Stephen Crane and Crane's *Collected Poems* (1930) and was the author of books on Joseph Conrad, on Zona Gale, and on the modern novel. He began writing *Modern American Usage* in the summer of 1958 and worked on it steadily until his death in January 1963.

Since that time, Jacques Barzun has been a true friend of this book, of Wilson Follett, and of its publisher. Perhaps the simplest words are best to express our gratitude, words that Follett himself might have chosen—thank you.

Printed in the United States
85914LV00013B/52-60/A